The Open University

SOCIAL SCIENCES THIRD LEVEL COURSE

**UNDERSTANDING ECONOMIC BEHAVIOUR:
HOUSEHOLDS, FIRMS AND MARKETS**

MARKETS

**A. TRIGG
S. HIMMELWEIT
N. COSTELLO
G. DAWSON
M. MACKINTOSH
R. SIMONETTI
J. WELLS**

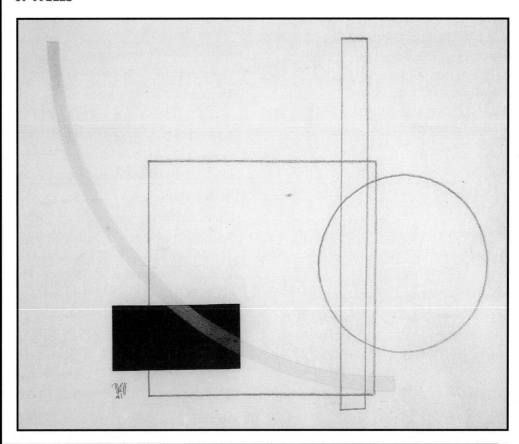

LIST OF CONTRIBUTORS

D319 MARKETS

External Authors

Professor David Gowland, Professor in Division of Economics, School of Business, University of Derby

Dr Robert McNabb, Distinguished Senior Research Fellow in Economics, Cardiff Business School

Professor Robert Sutcliffe, Professor Asociado, Departmento de Economia Aplicada, Universidad del Pais Vaco, Bilbao

Professor Andrew Tylecote, Professor of Economics and Management of Technological Change, Sheffield University, Management School

Dr Keith Whitfield, Senior Research Fellow in Applied Economics, Cardiff Business School

External Assessors

Dr Shaun Hargreaves-Heap, Senior Lecturer in School of Economics and Social Studies, University of East Anglia – D319 Course Assessor

Dr Paul Auerbach, Reader in Economics, School of Economics, Kingston University

Professor Ben Fine, Professor of Economics, School of Oriental and African Studies

Professor Nancy Folbre, Professor of Economics, University of Massachusetts at Amherst

Mr Ben Knight, Senior Lecturer in Economics, University of Warwick

Internal

Betty Atkinson, Course Secretary

Sally Baker, Media Librarian

Penny Bennett, Editor

Vivienne Brown, Senior Lecturer in Economics

David Calderwood, Project Control

George Callaghan, Residential School Consultant

Robert Cookson, Senior Editor

Lene Connolly, Print Buyer

Neil Costello, Senior Lecturer and Staff Tutor in Economics

Graham Dawson, Lecturer in Economics

Michael Dawson, Course Manager

John Dixon, Tutor Consultant

Suzanne Edwards, Research Assistant

Lucy Faulkner, Residential School Consultant

Andrew Fitch, Tutor Consultant

Fran Ford, Course Co-ordinator

Alan Gillie, Lecturer in Economics

Ed Hall, Research Assistant

Caitlin Harvey, Course Manager

Eddie Head, Compositor

Martin Higginson, Lecturer and Staff Tutor in Economics

Susan Himmelweit, Senior Lecturer in Economics and Course Team Chair

Liz Lack, Secretary

Jack Leatham, BBC Producer

Avis Lexton, Course Secretary

Maureen Mackintosh, Professor of Economics

Iris Manzi, Discipline Secretary

Georgina Marsh, Secretary

Anne-Marie McCullum, Course Manager

Christine Meeks, Secretary

Carole Moyle, Secretary

Ray Munns, Graphic Artist

Peter Richardson, Software Designer

Sue Searle, Faculty Clerk

Jane Sheppard, Graphic Designer

Karen Shipp, Software Designer

Roberto Simonetti, Lecturer in Economics

Paul Smith, Media Librarian

Hedley Stone, Tutor Consultant

Grahame Thompson, Senior Lecturer in Economics

Andrew Trigg, Lecturer in Economics and Course Team Chair

Christine Tucker, BBC Production Assistant

Linda Watson-Brown, Tutor Consultant

Julian Wells, Lecturer in Economics

David Whigham, Residential School Consultant

Chris Wooldridge, Editor

Other external contributors

Hardlines, Charlbury, Oxford, Technical Illustrations

Heather Clarke, Cartoonist

Margaret Cronan, Indexer

The Open University

SOCIAL SCIENCES THIRD LEVEL COURSE
**UNDERSTANDING ECONOMIC BEHAVIOUR:
HOUSEHOLDS, FIRMS AND MARKETS**

MARKETS

The Open University, Walton Hall, Milton Keynes, MK7 6AA

First published 1998. Reprinted 2002

Edited, designed and typeset by the Open University

Printed in the United Kingdom by Bath Press, Glasgow

ISBN 0 7492 77319

1.2

This text forms part of an Open University Third Level Course. If you would like a
copy of *Studying with The Open University*, please write to Course Enquiries Data
Service, PO Box 625, Dane Road, Milton Keynes, MK1 1TY. If you have not already
enrolled on the Course and would like to buy this or other Open University
material, please write to Open University Worldwide, The Berrill Building, Walton
Hall, Milton Keynes, MK7 6AA.

17426B/d319b2prelimsi1.2

CONTENTS

Introduction

The standard argument for a market-based economy is that it generates the means of material well-being much more abundantly and reliably than any alternative economic system. In the broad sweep of history, the market-based economies of industrial capitalism have experienced a higher level of material well-being than that achieved by any alternative economic system. The dominance of this view has been demonstrated by the embracing of market capitalism by countries in Eastern Europe, with the collapse of the Soviet bloc in the 1980s, and by the wholesale privatization of state-owned assets, together with the introduction of additional market pressures in markets for health care and education in Western economies.

During the 1990s, however, political debate has also centred on the limits to the market. In Eastern Europe, for example, the early optimism about the benefits of unregulated markets has been tempered by the need to examine closely the institutional structures which may best generate growth and prosperity. It has been argued that Japan and Germany have demonstrated the benefits of government intervention in the market, by successfully co-ordinating the relationship between financial institutions and companies; an argument that Eastern European countries have begun to examine in relation to their own institutional relationships. Deep unease has also been expressed about the inequalities that the market system can generate. While markets do generate increases in material well-being, this can be unevenly distributed if government institutions do not intervene in the market.

In writing *Markets* our objective has been to explore ways in which economic theory can be used to discuss issues which arise in the management of market economies. Key to this exploration is our understanding of the neoclassical approach, which is the dominant school of thought in economics. This is usually, but not always, used to demonstrate the benefits of markets. Markets can be shown to provide efficient allocations of scarce resources in response to the demands of insatiable consumers. This book will show how neoclassical theory is used to model market mechanisms, both in particular markets and in the market economy as a whole.

One of the criticisms of the neoclassical approach is that markets are analysed independently from the social institutions around them. Broadly the same theoretical framework is used to model markets in different types of goods and services, be they financial markets, for example, or markets for health care. This can be argued to be both a strength of the neoclassical approach, since it provides a box of tools for analysing all markets, and a weakness, since neoclassical theory may not take into account the differences in institutional structure between markets. To address this issue, *Markets* will look at the ways in which neoclassical, and other theoretical approaches, are used in the analysis of particular types of markets, with varying institutional structures.

Among these institutional structures are norms concerning the distribution of income and wealth. A market outcome may represent an efficient allocation of resources from the perspective of neoclassical economics but it may also be associated with an unequal distribution of resources which is judged to be inequitable or unjust from the standpoint of the norms current in society. For example, is it fair that the salaries of directors of newly privatized companies are many times more than the salaries of ordinary workers in those companies? *Markets* examines the philosophical foundations, in libertarian and contractarian ethical traditions, of norms concerning the just distribution of resources.

The content of *Markets* is specifically that of microeconomics, which considers the behaviour of individual agents in the economy. This focus on the behaviour of agents in markets locates the book as part of a three-book series, published by the Open University, as the main texts for its third level intermediate microeconomics course D319 *Understanding Economic Behaviour: Households, Firms and Markets*. Whereas the other two books in the series, *Households* and *Firms*, focus mainly on the behaviour of particular types of economic agents; in *Markets* we bring together the behaviour of all agents in the market arena.

Markets opens, in Chapter 1, with a discussion of industrial capitalism and market systems, in which Bob Sutcliffe develops a historical perspective on the rise of industrial capitalism, explaining how closely the capitalist method of production is bound up with the exchange of goods and services in markets. One of our objectives in writing this book has been to make sense of markets as systems, in which the various linkages and feedbacks between different parts of the economy are closely related to the institutional structures which occur. Chapter 1 provides an introduction to the types of institutions which prevail under industrial capitalism.

Chapter 2 introduces some of the key economic theories used in microeconomics to analyse markets. A brief overview of the neoclassical, institutional and Austrian approaches is provided, together with a discussion of what distinguishes each approach. Each theoretical approach is considered later in different parts of the book, with a particularly in-depth analysis of the neoclassical approach provided by Chapter 7. In this chapter Vivienne Brown examines the theory of competitive general equilibrium, which models the interrelationships between the various markets that make up an economy. A discussion is also provided of the main theorems of welfare economics and their relationship to general equilibrium theory.

Several chapters in *Markets* examine the interlinkages among incentives, decisions and market institutions for particular kinds of markets. We have chosen for examination three kinds of markets that are problematic, in that the good or service traded is not quite like an ordinary marketed good. These are labour markets, financial markets and markets in social goods such as health care.

In Chapters 3 and 4 on the labour market, Robert McNabb and Keith Whitfield discuss the central role of the price mechanism – the flexible adjustment of wages – in the neoclassical model of the labour market. This model is contrasted in Chapter 3 with the alternative institutional approach in which the labour market is argued to be segmented between primary and secondary sectors. In Chapter 4 segmentation theory is further developed in the form of a positive feedback model in which increases in wages can, contrary to the predictions of neoclassical theory, lead to a favourable response by firms in terms of their investment decisions. Other issues such as the role of trade unions and skill formation in the labour market are also considered in this chapter.

Chapters 5 and 6 look at financial markets. In Chapter 5 neoclassical and institutional ideas are again interwoven as David Gowland analyses the imperfect nature of financial markets and how market economies have developed a range of financial institutions to deal with these market imperfections. The institutionalist theme of markets in their social context is further developed in Chapter 6, where Andrew Tylecote examines the impact of the whole financial system on innovation by firms. Financial systems dominated by stock markets are compared with those in which banks are more directly involved in corporate decision making, with a view to evaluating how each system can reduce uncertainties which are inherent to the innovation process. In Chapter 8 Maureen Mackintosh considers social markets. The chapter examines the problems of private markets in social goods such as health care, drawing on both neoclassical and institutional analysis. It also investigates the scope for overcoming some of these problems in a market-like framework through clubs and quasi-market mechanisms.

Chapter 8 also picks up the discussion of ethics in *Markets*, which is first introduced in Chapter 2. In markets for care an ethical approach by providers is essential to the effective delivery of care. A further insight into ethical issues is provided by the last chapter of *Markets*, Chapter 9. Here, Graham Dawson develops the theme of the boundaries or limits of market exchange or contracting in the context of the environment. Insights drawn from libertarian and contractarian philosophical traditions are used to analyse the question whether the just distribution of goods is whatever is thrown up by market transactions, or whether justice requires impartiality and hence institutional arrangements to curb the free play of self-interest in market contracting.

Some of the material in *Markets* builds closely upon the chapters of *Households* and *Firms*. Links to these chapters are shown as (*Households,* Chapter number) or (*Firms,* Chapter number). Links are also made to the main text of the Open University's introductory economics course, D216 *Economics and Changing Economies*. This text is available as *Economics and Changing Economies* by Mackintosh *et al.*, 1996, London, International Thompson Press (ISBN 0 412 62846 6). Links to this text are referred to as (*Changing Economies,* Chapter number).

In putting together this book we gratefully acknowledge the help and advice of Shaun Hargreaves-Heap, the D319 course assessor, and the external assessors, Paul Auerbach, Ben Fine, Nancy Folbre and Ben Knight. We are also very grateful for the comments provided by John Clarke and Janette Rutterford. Any mistakes are the responsibility of the editors and authors.

Graham Dawson and Andrew Trigg

CHAPTER 1

INDUSTRIAL CAPITALISM AND MARKET SYSTEMS

by Bob Sutcliffe

1 Capitalism: change and difference

If we reduce the whole history of our planet since its origins to a single year, so that it is now midnight on December 31, then the first humanoids appeared at four o'clock this afternoon, settled agriculture began a couple of minutes ago and the capitalist system has so far lasted about three seconds. But those are three seconds which have shaken the world. Almost all analysts agree on this, however their opinions differ on the nature of the change. Some believe that capitalism will free humanity from all its material problems, while others see the capitalist epoch as the precursor of military, economic or ecological catastrophe.

Decompressing these three dramatic seconds into real time, we can date the beginning of the industrial capitalist epoch to around the end of the eighteenth century. To measure how this new epoch has improved economic welfare, Maddison (1995) estimates that, in the 180 years since 1820, the world's population has increased sixfold while average real income has increased by a factor of 10, from about US$500 to US$5000 (valued at constant 1992 prices). Thus total production of goods and services has increased by a factor of 60. This contrasts with the preceding 320 years, in which the world's population increased by a factor of about 2 and its average income by about 50 per cent, meaning that total production expanded by a factor of about 3. Measured in terms of world production, industrial capitalism has produced a dizzying acceleration in economic development. Previous epochs had their accelerations and slowing down, but there is no convincing evidence of anything remotely like the gigantic unleashing of demographic and productive forces which has occurred during industrial capitalism.

The results of capitalism, however, have been far from homogeneous. Each country, and even the world as a whole, has experienced periods of fast and slow growth, or even decline, during capitalism's two centuries. East Asia between the mid-1970s and the mid-1990s experienced faster economic growth than Western Europe during its industrial revolution; in the same period much of Africa experienced slower economic growth than the industrialized economies during the Great Depression of the 1930s. Capitalism as a system, then, has undergone many changes; and it continues to exhibit major differences.

Out of these bare facts emerge a number of important interrelated questions:

- What is the difference between capitalism and preceding epochs which has made it so much more dynamic, producing rapid long-term growth of both productivity and output?

- What has caused such great fluctuations in the dynamism of the capitalist system in different periods?
- What are the differences between capitalism in different countries which makes some grow much faster than others during the same period?

And what are the relations between the answers to these questions? In other words, what is the relationship between temporal and spatial differences in the nature and functioning of capitalism? Was the reason that Western European capitalism did so badly during the 1930s the same as the reason why Africa did so badly in the 1970s, 1980s and 1990s? And were the determinants of the Industrial Revolution in Western Europe the same as the determinants of the rapid industrialization or economic growth of East Asia after the 1970s? How far can the recent success of East Asia be transposed to other areas of the world?

In this chapter we will look at these issues which bring history and geography, the real worlds of time and space, temporal and spatial change, into economics.

Definition

Temporal and spatial change

Temporal change is change over time; spatial change is change between different areas.

2   The age of industrial capitalism

Thinking of industrial capitalism as a stage in history implies at least one preceding stage which was either pre-capitalist or pre-industrial or both. In fact, at the start of the age of industrial capitalism many aspects of economic life began to change rather suddenly. While neither industry nor capitalism were new, the sudden acceleration of industrial growth coincided with the expansion of capitalist production and property relations. The historical moment of capitalism and that of industry arrived together. What was new and different about them?

2.1   The capitalist method of production

The distinctive feature of the capitalist method of production is that profit-seeking producer institutions (firms) who own the means of production – machinery, tools and raw materials – employ free and independent workers for wages in order to produce goods and services to be sold in the market for money. Workers do not own their own means of production and so they have to take on a job to make a living. These characteristics, in principle, distinguish capitalism from the systems of production and class relations of other periods in history.

Definition

Capitalism

In the capitalist method of production, firms, who own the means of production, employ workers for wages to make a profit by producing goods for sale in the market.

- Under communal, village, clan or family forms of production, workers were not usually employed for money wages nor were their products distributed through the market.
- Under feudalism, producers consumed mostly their own products although marketed products did have a limited role. Although they owned some means of production, peasants also had to give part of what they produced to pay their customary dues to lords and priests.
- Under slavery, workers were not free to leave their employment.
- Under centrally planned economies, the role of the market in the distribution of output has been limited and profit has not generally been the aim of production.

As with any definition, there are grey areas of ambiguity where forms of production and distribution resemble capitalist methods in some ways, but not in others. Examples of grey areas include putting-out systems (such as that used by the Italian knitwear giant Benetton) where workers own their own tools, profit-oriented worker co-operatives, profit-motivated producers who employ unfree (slave and bonded) labour, and socialist economies which make extensive use of profits and the market. Economics, like biology, has to recognize hybrid and transitional species. Capitalist institutions and activities also coexist, in conflict and in synergy, with a large range of other institutions and activities, such as the state and the family. Across time and place, capitalist firms take a variety of forms and the environment in which they exist varies even more.

The exact reason why capitalist forms of organization suddenly became much more extensive and successful from the end of the eighteenth century in Western Europe, and have since spread to most of the globe, is the subject of much debate. Karl Marx attributed it to the coming together of a large quantity of money wealth with the increasing availability of labour detached from the land due to the collapse of feudalism. Capitalism, he argued, divided human beings in a new way. To the landowner, serf and peasant classes, characteristic of many pre-capitalist societies, were added the capitalist class or bourgeoisie, and the working class or proletariat who worked for them. As capitalism extended, so the bourgeoisie and the working class became, in many countries, the dominant classes and a struggle between them became a dominating feature of economic development (Marx and Engels, 1848, reprinted 1973). More orthodox economists tend to attribute the development of capitalist production to the opening up of markets. Others, like David Landes, have stressed the importance of technological change (Landes, 1969). Yet others such as Weber (1930) and Tawney (1942) argued that religious and associated social and ideological changes had a major effect.

A problem with almost all of these explanations is the familiar one of first cause. If many factors are interdependent, which changed first? Did markets change in a way which encouraged the growth of capitalist production or did capitalist producers discover and create new markets? Did new technologies give rise to new opportunities or did the pressure to compete and produce more profit stimulate technological changes? Did new supplies of free labour encourage capitalist production or did capitalist production create new free workers? The answer to such pairs of questions, which history and social science continually throw up, is nearly always 'both'. At certain times in economic history, such as the Industrial Revolution or the Great Depression, a number of interdependent factors change in such a way as to produce virtuous or vicious circles which lead to periods of rapid self-sustaining change.

Even if there is no single factor which causes such cumulative movements, one of the key determinants of the overall movement of the economy must be investment. Capitalist production implies investment. In order to survive, a capitalist firm must constantly replace its capital stock – the means of production – as it deteriorates. (For further discussion on capital stock, see *Changing Economies*, Chapter 25.) But in a competitive market, a capitalist firm which did no more than that would not survive. The more intense the competitive struggle, the more each capitalist will be under pressure to invest in new, more productive plant and equipment which will

Definitions

The two main classes of capitalism

The capitalist class, or *bourgeoisie*, owns the means of production and employs workers to make a profit.

The working class, or *proletariat*, does not own any means of production and has to take employment to make a living.

Definitions

Investment

Gross investment is the process of replenishing and adding to a firm's capital stock: its plant, machinery and raw materials.

Replacement investment replaces the worn out capital stock to keep it at the same level.

Net investment increases the firm's capital stock and is equal to gross minus replacement investment.

reduce costs and increase labour productivity and the efficient use of raw materials. All other things being equal, therefore, higher rates of growth should be found in countries with higher rates of net investment.

A simple picture of this connection between investment and growth can be shown on a scatterplot. Read the technical box if you feel a need to revise your basic knowledge of scatterplots, correlation and regression techniques.

In Figure 1.1 each point represents one country's rate of economic growth per head plotted against that country's average level of gross investment as a share of Gross Domestic Product (GDP) during the years 1981 to 1993. The scatter on Figure 1.1 is so dispersed that it is scarcely possible to see any tendency for fast growth to be associated with higher investment. This diagram is, therefore, a useful lesson in the complexity of economic life. The theoretical argument that higher investment should lead to higher growth is convincing and yet this diagram hardly suggests a relationship. How can we interpret this? At the very least it means that there are many other forces at work in determining the rate of growth than the investment rate alone.

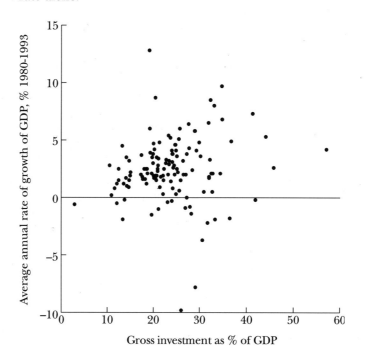

Figure 1.1 **Average annual percentage growth in real GDP per head against gross investment as a percentage of GDP, 132 countries, 1981–1993**

Source: World Bank, *World Data on CD-ROM*, 1995a

Exercise 1.1

Why might the relation between investment and the growth of national income not show up clearly in Figure 1.1? (Hint: why might investment be more effective in producing growth in some countries than in others?)

Scatterplots, correlation and regression

Much of economics, like other sciences both social or physical, is about relationships between different variables. Economics explores connections. It asks: is there a consistent relationship between two or more variables, and if there is, could it be that one of them influences the other? The first of these questions can be explored by looking at data displayed on a scatterplot, a type of graph which displays the connection between two variables. The values of each of the two variables is measured along one of the axes. Each point on the graph represents a related pair of values of the variables. Scatterplots can be plotted over a period of time – a time series – in which case the dots represent the values of the two variables in different years; or they can be plotted over a range of different places – a cross section – in which case the dots represent the values of the two variables in different places. The four examples in this chapter (Figures 1.1, 1.4, 1.5 and 1.8) are all cross-section diagrams.

How do we decide if such an association exists between two variables? If there is an exact relationship between them, so that for any increase in one there is a proportionate increase in the other, then we could represent this as a straight line on the graph. Relationships of this exactitude almost never exist in economics, but we can look at the scatter of points and ask if they suggest an approximate relationship of the kind we are expecting. Do the points cluster roughly around a hypothetical straight line? If so, some association exists in our data. Simple visual inspection of data is a necessary first step in assessing whether two variables appear related, and indicates whether the variables are highly correlated, slightly correlated or not correlated at all, without needing more sophisticated analysis.

To go beyond simple visual inspection of the relationship and see how to find the straight line which best approximates data, we need to use linear regression and correlation analysis. Linear regression is a technique which fits a line through data on a scatterplot (see *Changing Economies,* Chapter 26, Section 2). If we call the two variables x and y such a regression line can be represented by a linear equation of the form:

$$y = a + bx$$

where y is the 'dependent' variable and x is the 'independent' variable.

Here a is the 'intercept', the point at which the line crosses the y or vertical axis; it shows what y would be when x is zero, if all the points actually lie on the regression line; whereas b gives the slope of the regression line and measures the extent to which the y values change with changes in x.

Definition

Scatterplot

A graph in which pairs of variables are graphed, one along each axis, in order to display the connections between them.

Definition

Linear regression

A technique for fitting a line through data on a scatterplot.

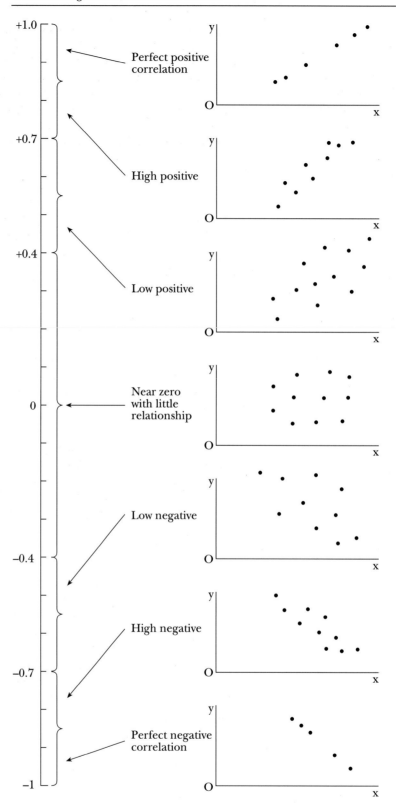

Figure 1.2 **Different correlations between two variables**

Definition

Correlation coefficient

Measures how well a regression line fits the data and the direction of the correlation.

The correlation coefficient, R, can be calculated from the data to give a measure of how well the regression line fits the data and the direction of the association (see Figure 1.2). If $R < 0$, there is a negative correlation and high values of x in the data tend to go with low values of y. If $R > 0$ there is a positive correlation, and high xs go with high ys in the data. The absolute size of R matters too; R lies between 1 and −1. If R is near 1 or −1, there is a near perfect positive or negative correlation. If R is near zero, there is no linear relationship in the data between the two variables.

Therefore, R^2, which is always a positive number between 0 and 1, is used as a measure of the 'goodness of fit' of a regression line, that is, if R^2 is near to 1 the regression line provides a good summary of the variation in x and y; if it is near to 0 it provides a poor summary.

For how to calculate the intercept, slope, correlation coefficient and R^2 of a regression line see *Changing Economies,* Chapter 26, Section 2. *Households,* Chapter 3, introduces multiple regression techniques, which are used to explore relationships between three or more variables.

We use scatterplots and the techniques of correlation and regression to find patterns in the data usually in order to explore an underlying causal relationship; so we talk of x as the 'independent' or 'explanatory' variable and y as the 'dependent' variable which is to be 'explained'. There can, however, be a correlation in the data without a causal relationship and vice versa.

If there appears to be no linear relationship between two variables in a scatterplot, and thus no correlation, it does not necessarily mean that no causal relationship exists. One possibility is that some other variable which we are not observing is responsible for some of the variation and if we correct for that other variable we will see the relationship we were originally expecting. It may be, for instance, that the size of the country is an important influence on the way in which growth and investment rates are related. If we compared separately countries above or below a certain population size, perhaps we would find clearer relationships.

Another reason why we may not see a relationship between two variables even though one exists, is that we are looking for a relationship that is too simple. We are looking for a straight line, a linear relationship, when the relationship that exists may be more complex. For example in both Figures 1.4 and 1.5 a curve might be more appropriate; if so, we would need more complex methods of analysis. Meanwhile, our scatterplots usually provide enough information to tell us whether there is a simple linear relationship between any two variables.

Finally, it is important to remember that even the clearest looking pattern of scatter points indicating high levels of correlation between two variables tells us only that there is a connection in the data between the two variables. It tells us nothing about whether it is reasonable to think that there is a *causal* relationship between the two, which requires a convincing theoretical argument about the possible direction of causation. That cannot be provided by the data alone.

2.2   The development of industry

Definition

Industrial capitalism

An economic system in which capitalist methods of production apply across all employment sectors, and particularly in industry.

Definition

Sectors of the economy

A three-fold division of economic activity into, roughly, agricultural (primary), industrial (secondary) and service (tertiary) sectors.

Shifting our attention from the 'capitalist' to the 'industrial' part of industrial capitalism, what is the significance of seeing the last two hundred years as an industrial age as well as a capitalist one?

Industry, in the sense in which it is used today, was a new word two hundred years ago. A new name seemed to be called for because the activity it came to connote was so different in quality from the previous traditional activity of most of the people – looking for and producing food, clothing, heat and shelter. The division between agriculture and industry seemed to coincide with two different ways of life: the urban and the rural; the new and the traditional.

Economists later used the term 'industry' as part of a tripartite division of economic activity by product into sectors:

1   primary sector: agriculture and fisheries (with raw materials extraction usually added in)

2   secondary sector: manufacturing and other industrial sectors which transform primary products into more complex finished goods (including energy production even though it is not strictly material)

3   tertiary sector: services and forms of activity which do not produce material objects.

From the evidence studied by Kuznets (1966) and later writers it appears that, over the last two hundred years, the major changes in the distribution of labour and output between these three main sectors have been:

- a continuous decline in the share of output and the workforce in the primary (agricultural and extractive) sector

- a rise in the share of the secondary (industrial) sector for countries in the early stages of their modern economic development

- a tendency for the share of the industrial sector to stabilize and then even to decline in the latest stages of economic growth

- a corresponding tendency for the share of the tertiary (service) sector to rise steeply in the most developed countries.

These tendencies can be seen in the series of graphs in Figure 1.3 which show available data on the three-way division of the labour force in six countries during the last two hundred years. In Great Britain, for example, the share of agricultural employment fell dramatically and that of services rose from 1820 to 1992. The changing share of industrial employment can be seen by the widening/narrowing of the intermediate band.

Question

Are the trends in the proportion of employment in the industrial sector, as shown in Figure 1.3, similar in other countries? How can you account for the differences?

Figure 1.3 shows that for all six countries the proportion of the labour force in the agricultural sector fell as that of the industrial sector rose during the early stages of modern economic development, but in all the examples, with the exception of China, this process has subsequently tailed off.

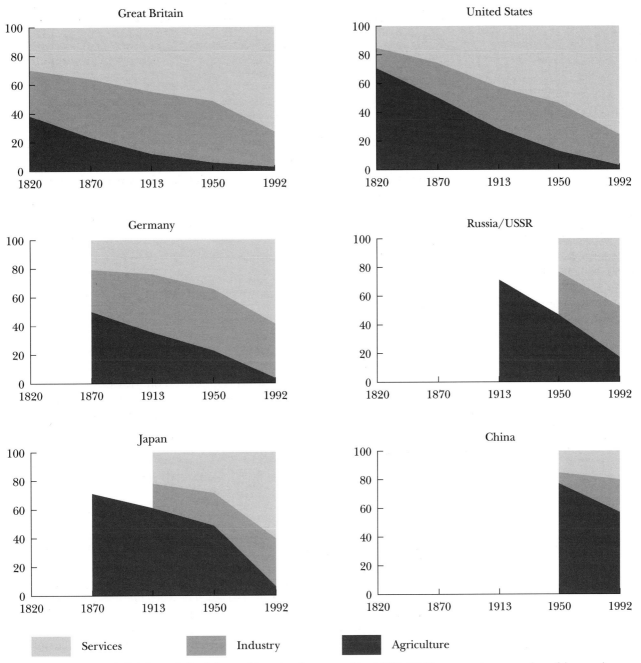

Figure 1.3 **Sectoral division of the labour force in six countries, 1820–1992, percentage employed in services, industry and agriculture**

Source: Maddison, 1995

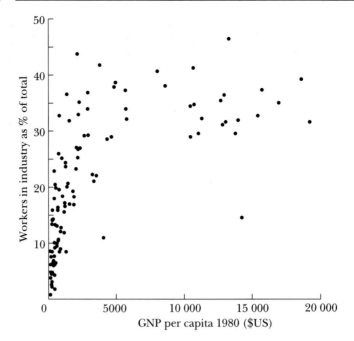

Figure 1.4 **Scatterplot of industrial workers as percentage of total workers against national income per head in 109 countries, 1980**

Source: World Bank, *World Data on CD-ROM,* 1995a

This process of tailing off can be examined by looking at Figure 1.4, a scatterplot in which each point represents one country in 1980. Each country's national income per head is measured on the horizontal axis and its share of the labour force in the industrial sector on the vertical axis. Income per head has been used as an indicator of economic development. Figure 1.4 does not show a purely linear relationship between the two variables. There does, however, seem to be a somewhat more complex pattern in which the proportion of industrial workers is correlated with income up to a certain level of income, although thereafter there is no clear relation between the two variables.

The increasing relative size of the services sector, which in the richest countries accounts for well over half of both output and employment, needs to be explained. Some analysts, especially sociologists such as Daniel Bell (1973) and Alain Touraine (1973), have seen it as representing a transition, which started around 1960 for the most advanced economies, to a new phase known as 'post-industrial' society. They emphasize the effect that the change from industry to services has had on the type of work people do. Far fewer people in such economies now work in factories; they do white collar jobs, generally in smaller-scale units. This changes people's attitude towards their work, their colleagues and their class position.

A second line of argument interprets the observed decline in the relative weight of industry in the richer economies as 'de-industrialization', a very different interpretation from post-industrialism. It suggests a backward rather than a forward movement, and is often regarded as a pathological condition which economic policy should aim to reverse in order to restore and modernize ailing industrial sectors (see Rowthorn and Wells, 1987).

This second approach is often linked to a third: the suggestion that the decline in industrial employment in the richer countries is the other side of the industrialization of some underdeveloped countries, especially the so-called newly industrializing countries (NICs) which are concentrated in East Asia and which we will look at in Section 5. This alleged shift in the location of industrial employment is often called the 'new international division of labour' and is thought to be linked to the practice of multinational corporations looking for new, low cost production sites from which to serve old markets (see Fröbel *et al.*, 1980; Gordon, 1988).

Although these arguments raise interesting questions, I find none of them convince me that capitalism has entered a new stage. Service employment is by no means as different from industrial factory employment as is often supposed. Many service industries have experienced 'massification' (the employment of many workers in one place) and have instituted mass production methods which are as machine-paced and productive as any in industry, for instance in the processing of insurance claims. In addition, a large proportion of services are off-shoots of industry. Some services, for example, involve the maintenance of industrial products, such as car repairs; other services can lead to the development of industrial products as in the music industry; or are activities which have been hived-off by manufacturers including various management services, such as transport, cleaning and catering. The rise of services in the capitalist economy does not imply that its economic rules of operation have changed; a 'post-industrial' society is, in many senses, simply an evolution of industrial capitalism.

'De-industrialization' and the 'new international division of labour' are efforts to characterize a change which is seen as more reversible and temporary than 'post-industrial society'. They refer to real processes but there is little reason to think that they are new. They have occurred before in the history of capitalism as the balance of advantage and power shifts from one set of countries to another. Although some of the traditional industries of Britain and the US have rapidly declined in the last few decades, there is no reason to believe that new industries will not be established there in the future. De-industrialization and re-industrialization are likely to be continuously alternating phenomena in capitalist countries, especially in conditions of growing international competition. By the early 1990s, some economists were already detecting signs that the tendency for industrial jobs to migrate from countries of the north to those of the south was beginning to be reversed (Kaplinsky, 1991). By 1996, Asian multinational companies were investing in Britain as they found that they could pay British factory workers lower wages than they paid in Korea.

De-industrialization and post-industrial society do not seem to me to be convincing reasons to say that the age of industrial capitalism has closed. We have seen that in countries which have undergone modern economic development, the industrial sector has expanded initially, but has then remained relatively constant as a share of output and employment until, in the end, it may fall. The fall in the relative importance of agriculture and the rise of the service sector are more striking and longer-term tendencies than the rise of industry. But the crucial point is not the division of output and employment into sectors: it is the application of capitalist methods of production (mechanization and a disciplined labour process to produce goods and services for the market in pursuit of profit) to all sectors. This is known as 'industrial capitalism' because it was frequently in industry that such a regime was implemented in its most complete fashion. Agricultural and service production have progressively taken on more and more of the characteristics previously associated with industry and factories even though, nowadays, in the developed countries, most of us work not in factories but in offices, shops or classrooms.

3 The institutional framework of capitalism

Definitions

Economic agents

Individuals and institutions who initiate and react to economic events.

Institutions

These include not only organizations like households, firms and states but also the legal framework and the social rules, norms and culturally specific customs within which people act as agents.

Studying the capitalist economic system means studying economic agents. Firms aiming to increase their profits are economic agents; so are workers and consumers. All agents operate in an institutional context. While industrial capitalism has produced its characteristic institutions, they have taken different forms in different parts of the world, and at different times in its history. Nonetheless, capitalism has brought about some fundamental institutional changes which have been more or less universal.

3.1 The nature of work

As capitalist activity grew and replaced previous ways of producing goods, the relationships between people and their work and between different groups of people became transformed. Concepts which we use today to describe our lives would not have been understood by our predecessors. As a generalization, we can list pairs of concepts which have only come to have significance under capitalism.

- *Producers and consumers (and production and consumption):* In nearly all systems before capitalism, households themselves produced the greater part of what they consumed. This remains true in parts of the Third World today. Producers and consumers were, therefore, to a great extent the same people. They did not make separate decisions about what to produce and what to consume. They produced what they needed, plus some extra to fulfil their obligations towards others such as their landlords.

- *Work and leisure:* The idea that 'work' is a separate aspect of life is relatively new. A member of hunter/gatherer society could not say what was their 'work'; it was simply the same as their life. Now when we ask someone what their work is, we mean what kind of job do they have, which industry do they work in, what is their level of responsibility, their job title and so on. This is a very particular notion of 'work'. A mother who spends all her non-sleeping hours looking after children and doing exhausting household work may feel she has to reply 'No' when asked 'Do you work?' because its common meaning is 'Do you have a paid job outside the home?'

- *Home and workplace:* In the industrial capitalist epoch, work has become separated from home not only organizationally but also physically. Most employees go to work and then return home. In earlier epochs, even though a worker would work in the fields for part of the time, a good deal of work would also take place in the home.

- *Employer and worker:* In pre-capitalist economies many hierarchies existed but none specifically over the control of work. Slave owners controlled all aspects of their slaves' lives, not only their work. On the other hand, peasants needed no boss to order them to hurry or produce more; they knew that their survival depended directly on the amount of work they did.

Capitalism, therefore, creates new dichotomies. It has created working life as something physically, socially and conceptually apart, and not completely integrated with life in general. Capitalism has changed where people work, how they relate to others, when they work and how they interpret their work.

3.2   Households and firms under capitalism

The institutions which economists analyse – households, firms and markets – are not timeless and unchanging human institutions which now find themselves playing a part on a capitalist stage. They are institutions which, to a great extent, capitalism has created or transformed and in many cases continues to transform. Households relate to firms, and different firms relate to each other through markets: product markets, labour markets and financial markets.

Under capitalism, households in developed countries (in the western sense of development) have changed a great deal and have tended to become smaller. Among the secular, long-term changes that have been observed over the past century are:

- a reduction in the number of children per couple
- greater instability of couples
- less multi-generational, more nuclear, families
- increased participation of women in paid labour
- the changing role of children, from workers to scholars and consumers.

Changes in households are influenced by, and in their turn influence, changes in firms and markets. For example some markets in the Third World are so unstable and competitive that employers who sell their products in them concentrate hard on minimizing their labour costs by paying extremely low wages and giving little or no security of job tenure to workers. This may make it impossible for such workers to buy or rent a house and support a family. Such jobs are often designed for young people without families or for migrant workers, separated from their families. In other cases, more stable and less competitive markets have allowed employers to stabilize their workforce and pay a family wage to male workers. Here the nature of the market and the firm influence the nature of the household. In recent years in Spain, to give a specific example, households have been profoundly transformed, partly as a result of conditions in the country's labour markets. High levels of unemployment have raised the age of marriage, reversed the trend for people to leave home earlier and reduced the total fertility rate (the average number of children a woman would bear at current fertility rates if she lived to the end of her child-bearing years, see *Households*, Chapter 7, Section 2) to the lowest in the world (along with Hong Kong). Despite old stereotypes about Catholic communities, the two European countries with the lowest fertility rates at the start of the 1990s were Spain and Italy.

Very little reliable international data exist on the size of households either today or historically. The total fertility rate, however, is a figure readily available in demographic statistics and is a variable which is closely related to household size. As an example of a connection between changes in households and changes in firms and markets, we can examine whether GNP and fertility (and so perhaps household size) are related. Figure 1.5 shows the relation between the total fertility rate and the level of GNP per head for 148 countries. In this case there is a clearer pattern than in Figures 1.1 and 1.4 but, as in the case of Figure 1.4, it is not a linear pattern.

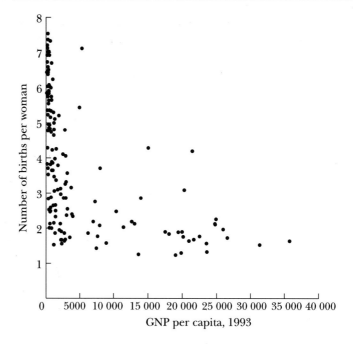

Figure 1.5 **Scatterplot of total fertility rate against GNP per head, 148 countries, 1993**

Source: World Bank, *World Data on CD-ROM*, 1995a

Exercise 1.2

1   What relationship do you see in Figure 1.5 between GNP and total fertility?

2   What reasons are there to expect fertility to decline with increasing GNP per head?

3   Do you expect the currently low fertility rates in a number of European countries to continue?

3.3   Determinants of capitalism – some general theories

Figure 1.5 above suggests that there might be structural links between household forms and economic performance. Finding such a statistical pattern, however, says nothing about causes. To explain such patterns we need a theory of the structural links between varieties of households, firms and markets, and also between these and related institutions and indicators of economic performance such as GNP.

Protestant work ethic

One of the most famous of such theories is that of R.H. Tawney, a Christian, socialist, economist and historian, who believed that the rise of Protestant Christianity was an important determinant of the growth of industrial capitalism in Western Europe (Tawney, 1942). The so-called Protestant ethic of industry (in the old sense of 'hard work') – what Adam Smith called 'parsimony' and saw as leading to high levels of saving and investment as opposed to consumption – depended on a particular structure of families and so of households. Tawney argued that the rational pursuit of economic gain by increasingly isolated individuals was encouraged by the rise of the nuclear family which was, therefore, the appropriate form of capitalist family.

Tawney's conclusions have been strongly contested by recent researchers (Harris, 1987). And even if a particular change in the nature of the family and the household was indeed related to the rise of capitalism in Europe, this does not mean that the same change has been essential to the rise of capitalism elsewhere. Successful industrial capitalist development has coexisted with radically different forms of the family and household. In Japan, for example, a more extended and less nuclear form of the family survived the rise of industrial capitalism.

Japanese capitalism as a special case

The case of Japan is one which has fascinated economists because during the course of capitalism's great post-Second World War boom, Japan's economy has performed much better by almost all criteria than those of other developed capitalist countries. Many economists have noted the peculiarities of Japan's firms, households and markets in comparison with those of the West. Japan's economy is dominated by a small number of huge conglomerates operating in many different industrial sectors and linked to a vast number of small firms which act as subcontractors. Within the large firms especially, a significant number of workers have obtained guaranteed lifetime employment which has been unheard of in the West. The other side of this employment stability has been that wages have been lower than in western countries. And, in addition, even working-class Japanese households save a significant part of their income. The combination of high profit shares and high levels of savings has led to a very high investment regime which has been part of the secret of Japan's success. The other aspect of Japanese firms which often draws comment is the way in which they are more closely involved with their workers' lives, not only in official working hours but outside them as well. Japanese firms have aimed to foster an extra-economic loyalty to the enterprise, a counterpart of which has been relatively weak trade unions, relatively low wages, and a need for Japanese firms to produce for foreign consumer markets rather than domestic ones (Armstrong *et al.*, 1991).

That is one version of the story of Japanese capitalism. But it does not satisfy all observers. Morishima in his book *Why Has Japan Succeeded?* (Morishima, 1982), concludes that an essential part of the story is ideological, more particularly, religious. He believes that Japanese Confucianism, the religion of the majority of the people (though not of the ruling class) has fostered values such as loyalty and discipline. These have produced a particular form of both the family and the firm in Japan which has been favourable to Japan's unique economic success. As with Tawney, the unifying feature of the explanation is based on religious values, although these are different values from the Protestant ones stressed by Tawney.

Regulation theory

'Regulation theory', a marriage of theoretical and institutional economics, provides yet another hypothesis concerning the interconnections between markets, firms and households (Aglietta, 1976). Regulation theory divides the twentieth century roughly into three periods: the periods of Taylorism, Fordism and post-Fordism, defined according to the way firms have tried to exercise control over their workers.

Taylorism derives its name from the management analyst Frederick Winslow Taylor, whose aim was the maximization of workers' productivity by specialization (Braverman, 1974). Although Taylorism increased the productivity of industry, it did not address the lack of demand for its products. The result was the Great Depression of the 1930s, brought on by a shortage of demand.

In the long boom experienced by the developed countries after the Second World War, the problems of demand for products was kept at bay by changing the method of regulation to Fordism. Machine-paced mass production and assembly line operation techniques continued to raise productivity, but the problem of demand was attended to by increasing wages. The model was Henry Ford's motor company which produced automobiles for the masses. Ford's workers were highly controlled and productive but they were also, by the standards of their day, well paid.

Fordism, however, brought about changes not only in firms and markets, but also in households. The working-class household became the centre of mass consumption, as well as a producer of labour and a maintainer of social discipline. New products such as the radio, the television, Henry Ford's and his rivals' motor cars, houses and household electrical equipment, were produced and designed to be consumed by a majority of families. Such consumption was possible as a result of shorter working hours and higher wages for individual workers. This, in turn, brought two further developments: an increase in the number of women in paid work and a reduction in the number of children per family.

This has contributed to what regulationists see as the crisis in Fordism. As the traditional nuclear family declines, the working class provides a less reliable centre of mass consumption. Fordism is consequently being replaced by new 'post-Fordist' forms of control of the labour process, such as 'just-in-time' methods of production. These, however, have proved much more difficult to classify in a general way.

Here there is no space to elaborate and evaluate far-reaching hypotheses such as those discussed above. But these ideas of Tawney, Morishima and the regulation theorists are all examples of theories which take account of the two main themes of this chapter: first, that the micro-institutions of capitalism, such as households, firms and markets, while they are not constant over time or undifferentiated in space, are always interconnected in important ways; second, that economic growth and performance in the aggregate – in national economies or even wider – are closely linked to the way such institutions function together.

4 How capitalism has changed

Capitalism ... is by nature a form or method of economic change and not only never is but never can be stationary ... The fundamental impulse that sets and keeps the capitalist engine in motion comes from the new consumers' goods, the new methods of production or transportation, the new markets, the new forms of industrial organization that capitalist enterprise creates.

(Schumpeter, 1939)

Changes can be of many kinds:

● secular changes tend to occur gradually over long periods and are usually seen as irreversible

● cyclical changes are periodically reversed and have some regularity

● non-cyclical reversible changes.

Economists often agree that changes have taken place in capitalism, but differ strongly about which of these three categories a change exemplifies.

The most easily available evidence that capitalism does not function in the same way in all its epochs is given by macro-economic data about growth rates. Figure 1.6 divides the history of the last 180 years into a number of different periods according to the growth rate of world income per head.

Question

Look carefully at Figure 1.6. Do you think it suggests any of the following?

● rates of growth decrease/increase with time

● variations in growth increase/decrease with time

● there are long cycles of growth

● Asia will become the dominant region in capitalism.

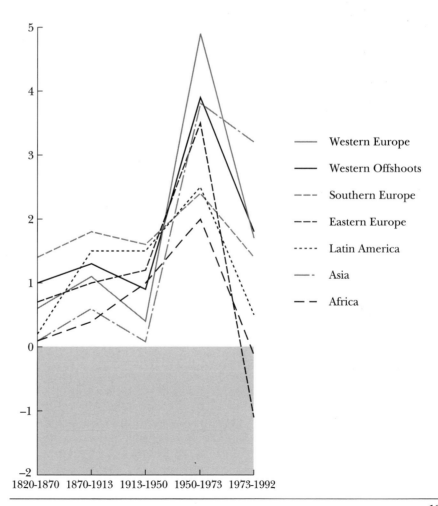

Figure 1.6 **Rates of growth in different regions at different times: average annual percentage growth in real GDP per head**

Source: Maddison, 1995, Table 3-1, p. 60

It is clear that growth rates under capitalism have fluctuated enormously. Growth during the second period (1870–1913) was faster in all areas than in the first (1820–70). It slowed nearly everywhere in the third period (1913–50) and accelerated equally generally in the fourth (1950–1973). The most recent period (1973–1992) is the one with the widest range of different experiences. Although in this period all regions experienced some fall in growth rates, in Eastern Europe and Africa the slowdown was catastrophic, while for Asia the growth rate remained very high. In fact, from the data presented here, we can say that there seems to be some general tendency for the variability in regional growth rates to grow over time. Changes in time and differences in space are both important when looking at what happens to growth rates.

The overall fluctuations shown in Figure 1.6 have been interpreted in many ways. Kondratief in the 1920s developed a theory according to which the world economy developed in rather regular 50-year cycles (see *Changing Economies*, Chapter 25). This was later taken up by Schumpeter (1939) in terms of successive waves of innovations, for example, railways followed by automobiles, and now computers. The theory has been frequently revived, despite the weakness of the evidence for it. While growth has certainly fluctuated between periods, there are probably numerous causes. It seems unwise to rely on a single mechanism, which allows all periods to be interpreted as part of the same theory (Mandel, 1980).

4.1   Changes in the nature of the firm

In the previous section we looked at some theories of long-term change based on observed or hypothesized changes in the institutions of capitalism. The quintessential capitalist institution is, of course, the profit-seeking firm. Data on the size, structure and functions of firms suggest that some long-term secular changes have taken place. In particular, the assets, sales and employment of today's largest firms dwarf those of the largest firms of one hundred or even fifty years ago. Attention is often drawn to the size of firms by comparing the value of their sales to the size of the national product of whole economies. Although this is not comparing like with like (firms' sales are a gross value and so include the value of the product of supplying firms, while the GDP is based on value added) the comparisons are quite striking. So for instance, in 1994, General Motors had total sales of US$150 billion, more than the total GDP of Indonesia, a nation of nearly 200 million people. To put the General Motors figure in historical perspective, it was actually four to five times greater than the GDP of Britain in 1820, when Britain was already considered the workshop of the world (Maddison, 1995, Table C1). By most measures, large firms have been getting larger in this century, although since the 1970s this trend has declined.

This is sometimes taken to mean that the concentration of industries (the proportion of the total market supplied by the largest producers) is also growing, and that capitalism is becoming increasingly monopolistic. Despite the increasing size of large firms, the constant birth of small and medium size firms has been sufficient to ensure that overall industrial concentration (as measured against national markets) has not, in general, grown very much. Recent studies of concentration have confirmed Adelman's (1951) view that '[a]ny tendency either way, if it does exist, must be at the pace of a glacial drift' (quoted in Scherer and Ross, 1990).

In any case, greater concentration does not necessarily mean less competition. A large supplier in the national market can experience its fiercest competition from international competitors. Even though concentration is high, this can disguise the threat of competition from abroad. The opening up of markets, therefore, tends to increase the degree of competition and counteracts monopoly tendencies which may exist. In other words, firms grow but so do markets and so real market concentration may not increase (*Changing Economies*, Chapter 12).

Some accounts stress the increasingly multinational nature of firms rather than their size. The multinationalization of companies is shown by a number of indicators: exports, foreign direct investment and sales, the international integration of productive processes between different branches of the same firm, and the internationalization of management and ownership. By the mid-1990s, firms had become international to very different degrees according to these criteria.

The proportion of firms' output exported rose steadily in nearly all countries from 1950 onwards. For the world as a whole, exported output as a share of total output rose rapidly after 1950 to reach 13.5 per cent in 1992 (Maddison, 1995). Yet this level was by no means unprecedented: it had been even higher in 1913 (Glyn and Sutcliffe, 1992).

After 1950, foreign direct investment also expanded considerably, although more unevenly than foreign trade. By 1993 the total stock of foreign-owned capital had reached US$2.3 trillion, which probably represents about 3 per cent of the world's capital stock. That figure was probably the highest ever; at the previous peak in 1913 it reached about 2.5 per cent of the world's capital stock (Sutcliffe, forthcoming).

A United Nations report identified 40,000 firms world-wide which had direct investments abroad in 250,000 foreign subsidiaries (UNCTAD, 1995). While large firms (especially from small countries) tended to hold more of their assets abroad than smaller ones, the vast majority of multinationals, by this definition, are medium and small-sized firms whose foreign subsidiaries often amount to no more than sales and service centres to assist the marketing of their exports from their country of origin. Nonetheless, it is clear that to become very large by world standards today, firms must invest in many different economies.

Data about internationally integrated production is more difficult to find and is often anecdotal rather than quantitative. An often quoted figure is that about 33 per cent of world trade represents goods transferred between different branches of the same international firm. While it seems high, the rather poor evidence which exists suggests that it has been constant for a rather long time (UNCTAD, 1995). Further, much of it represents trade in raw materials from mining and plantation companies in the raw material producing countries to other branches of the same firm in the processing countries, a form of multinationalization almost as old as industrial capitalism. A number of multinational companies have tried to integrate their production internationally but many of these, such as Ford's first efforts at producing a 'world car', were abandoned and the trend now seems to be against this bold form of internationalization (Ruigrok and van Tulder, 1995).

Jan Kregel has made the useful suggestion that the process of internationalization requires a more discriminating vocabulary to indicate different degrees of international integration. He suggests that the move to global organization by firms may be divided into three prior stages: international, multinational, and transnational. Internationalization involves a large proportion of output exported; multinationalization implies large amounts of foreign direct investment and production in foreign markets; transnationalization implies significant intra-firm integration at the international level and 'in the global firm, primary and semi-manufactured inputs, as well as production and assembly plants, move across country borders just as easily as do the final products' (Kregel, 1992).

Using Kregel's vocabulary, I suggest that the post-Second World War capitalist system has been experiencing strong internationalization, moderate multinationalization, weak and fluctuating transnationalization and very little true globalization.

4.2   The rise of the state

It is sometimes argued that globalization is making the individual nation state powerless and redundant. There are, however, few signs of the demise of the activities of the state and its rise in importance arguably constitutes the biggest change experienced by capitalism in the modern epoch.

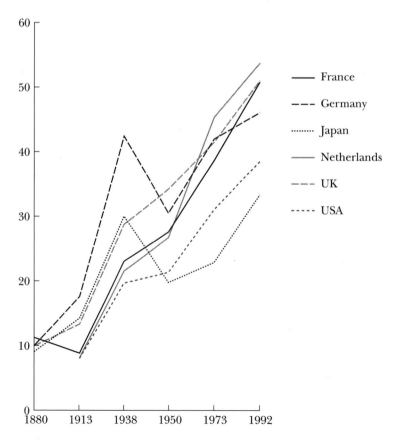

Figure 1.7 **State spending as a percentage of GDP: six developed countries, 1880–1992**

Source: Maddison, 1995

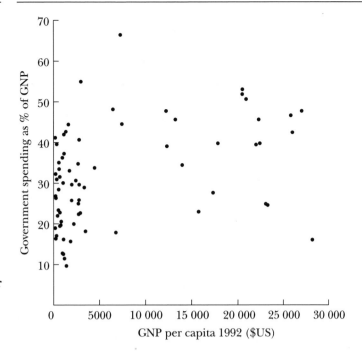

Figure 1.8 **State spending compared with level of GNP per head, 71 countries, 1992**

Source: World Bank, *World Development Report*, 1995b

There are three important ways in which the role of the state in capitalist economies has grown.

1   The state has taken increasing responsibility for general economic conditions by conducting active fiscal and monetary policies and in some cases introducing a form of economic planning.

2   An increasing amount of production has been undertaken in state enterprises (though the privatization wave of the 1980s and 1990s may have reduced this to some extent).

3   The state spends an increasing proportion of the national income.

As you can see from Figure 1.7, in the late nineteenth century in nearly all the developed countries, the state spent about 10 per cent of national income. Most of this spending was on relatively small standing armies, navies and police forces, and on public administration. According to Gough (1979) spending has grown in three particular areas during the last 100 years:

●   the state has employed many more people to provide social services, such as health and education

●   the state has paid more money out in social benefits to people unable for a variety of reasons to get sufficient income from employment

●   since the Second World War, nations have maintained higher levels of peacetime military forces.

Exercise 1.3

1   Looking at Figure 1.7, what trends in the proportion of state expenditure over the past century can you find?

2   Look carefully at Figure 1.8 which shows how the percentage of GDP spent by the state varies with GDP per head. Does this suggest any reason for the trends you found in Figure 1.7?

There is much debate about whether the rise of the state has changed the very nature of the capitalist system, as opposed to merely adjusting the details of the way it works. Are modern welfare state economies still really capitalist market systems or are they something qualitatively different, often called 'mixed economies'?

We could try to answer this question with reference to each of the three already mentioned themes: households, firms and markets.

- *Households:* What difference does the 'mixed economy' make to households? In countries with an advanced welfare state, there are many benefits and services, such as unemployment pay, compulsory education, pensions and free or subsidized health care, that go directly to households.

  The growth of the welfare state has had an influence on many aspects of households' economic behaviour: on the pattern of spending, on strategies for survival, on the number of children the family chooses to produce and so on. Despite the importance of state spending related to the needs of households, it remains true, even in the most advanced welfare states, that the great majority of family income comes from employment or property, a fact which may suggest that the changes caused by the rise of the state have not been so fundamental.

- *Firms:* These have also been affected in many ways by the rise of the activity of the state. In the first place a new form of firm has arisen, the state-owned firm or nationalized industry. State-owned firms in the developed countries as a whole produced between 7 and 9 per cent of GDP at the end of the 1980s, though this percentage is falling. In most countries, public utilities (energy, water, communications and transport) have, at some time in the twentieth century, been publicly owned. For a time at least, the widespread existence of nationalized industry meant that areas of the economy were closed to private investment, that privately-owned firms had to purchase many of their inputs from state enterprises, and that a significant proportion of the labour force worked in publicly-owned firms. Such state-owned firms found themselves shielded from the full force of market pressures by possessing a monopoly and/or having access to state loans. But they were never allowed to operate simply as public services producing according to need, and they always had to pay attention to market criteria. Starting in the 1960s, most governments attempted to make nationalized industries operate more strictly according to profit-making principles and from the late 1970s there has been a strong tendency towards privatization.

  The state has been more important as a customer for such goods as military equipment, pharmaceuticals, medical equipment and educational materials. Many capitalist firms encounter the state as their major, or even exclusive, customer. For these firms the nature of the market in which they operate as sellers may be very different from other firms. Technically these markets often have aspects of monopsony (a single buyer) and the forms of competition between sellers may be very different from those which operate in consumer markets.

- *Markets:* The state affects capitalist market economies not only by producing and consuming but also by regulating. This activity extends from active macro-economic fiscal and monetary policies down to the detailed regulation of the way in which products may be sold in a particular market. Despite the more deregulatory spirit in most capitalist countries since about 1980, the state still regulates almost everywhere more than it did in the nineteenth century. Privatization has created a new need for regulation. Literally millions of state regulations have an effect on the economic activities of households and firms and on the nature and functioning of markets.

Besides these general international tendencies relating to the economic role of the state over time, there are also great spatial differences in the economic role of different contemporary states. Once again we can ask the question about the relationship between these temporal and spatial differences: does the fact that differences exist across countries at a given moment mean simply that they are at different stages along a common trend, or are there *qualitative* differences between different countries? Probably the answer is a little of each. Certain reasons for state intervention and expenditure have applied to most developed capitalist countries, and state expenditure has grown in all of them during the twentieth century. But the differences between them are also very durable and appear to reflect differences in political traditions and social philosophies, as shown by the following examples.

- State welfare spending has been particularly significant in certain parts of Western Europe but not in the US or Japan.
- In the US there is a tradition of state intervention against monopolies; this rarely happens in Europe and Japan.
- Japanese capitalism since World War II has been characterized by a very high level of government intervention by the enormously powerful Ministry of Trade and Industry which has directed investment and developed export markets; there has been no comparable intervention by governments in Western Europe or the US.

If we observe the less developed countries the picture is equally variable, but there has been a general tendency towards higher levels of government economic activity and control in comparison with the developed countries at a similar level of economic development. A comparison of Figures 1.7 and 1.8 shows that all but one country out of the 71 for which comparable data exist now spends more as a share of the GNP than the developed countries of Figure 1.7 spent in 1880. Economic history cannot be seen as a repetition in one country of what happened in another. Space once again cannot be reduced to time.

5 How capitalism differs in time and space

Differences between countries at any one time may be just as great as those between one period and another. To illustrate the extent of this variation, we can look at data from five countries in one particular region of the world, East Asia, and compare them with a West European country, Britain, both today and as Britain was at an earlier stage in its industrial development. There is a good reason for choosing East Asia. Recent economic experience in this region has been so dramatically different from most of the rest of the world that to give a good explanation of what is happening in East Asia is a real challenge for any theory of world development.

Look back at the last two periods of Figure 1.6: 1950–73, the great post-Second World War boom, and 1973–92, often regarded as a prolonged economic crisis. It is striking that the only region not to have suffered a severe reduction in its rate of economic growth between the two periods is Asia. A finer regional division would show that the growth rate of East Asian countries is even higher and better maintained than that for Asia as a whole. Can a comparison with Britain suggest any of the possible causes of this remarkable economic phenomenon?

The annual average growth of GDP per head for the five East Asian countries in the years 1973–1991 ranged between 5.4 per cent and 8.2 per cent. This growth rate is faster than in any of the developed countries over a similar period at any time in the past. The annual growth of GDP per head in Britain during the years of the Industrial Revolution was no more than 1.2 per cent a year. Even the recent development of Japan, which in some ways resembles the growth of the five East Asian countries, did not exceed 4 per cent a year for a similar period (Maddison, 1995). They appear, therefore, to have acquired an economic dynamic which is both historically unprecedented and, to a great extent, independent of changes in economic conditions in the rest of the world.

Fast growth and innovation may be passing from the former leading economies of Europe and North America to East Asia. But we should not imagine that East Asian capitalism is any more homogeneous than was European capitalism in its heyday. Table 1.1 shows that, while the economies of the five East Asian countries are similar in some ways, they are very different in others.

Question

What evidence is there of an East Asian pattern of growth and development? Think of ways in which the East Asian countries described in Table 1.1 are similar to each other and ways in which they differ.

At first sight it is difficult to find a clear East Asian formula, although many commentators have sought to show that the success of these countries confirms their own pre-conceived notions about what is needed. For example, South Korea is used both as an example of the virtues of the market and trade, and of the virtues of state intervention and planning! The matrix below lists some of the similarities and the differences between the East Asian countries detailed in Table 1.1.

Similarities	Differences
High rates of growth of GNP per head	Agriculture/industrial employment percentages.
Fertility rates	Agricultural/industrial output percentages.
Industry/services as per cent of total.	GNP per head
Female participation in the workforce (except China).	Exports as per cent of GNP.
Weak or controlled trade unions.	Foreign capital as per cent of total.

Table 1.1   **Features of East Asian capitalism**

	China	South Korea	Taiwan	Singapore (a)	Hong Kong
Total GNP in 1992 (international US$ bn)	3615	436	239	40 (a)	98 (a)
GNP per head (US$)	3098	10010	11590	14,663 (a)	17,120 (a)
Rate of growth of GNP per head 1973-1992 (%)	8.2	8.2	6.6 (b)	6.1	5.4
Exports as % of GNP (c)	2.3	17.8	34.4	180	130
Foreign owned capital as % of total	—	19.3	18.5	62.9	17.3
Total international assets/liabilities 1988 (US$ bn)	—	24/35	—	44/18	310/270
Form of government	Communist Party	Recent presidential democracy	Formal democracy dominated by single party	Formal democracy dominated by single party	British colony to be transferred to China 1997
Form of capital	Mixed state, private and foreign	Dominated by a few giant conglomerates	—	High presence of foreign capital, much from Asia	Large local banks, firms of many sizes
Government spending as % of GDP	9.2	17.1	16	19.7	9
Position of trade unions	Virtually banned	Small, growing	—	Highly controlled	Highly controlled
Agriculture/ Industry/ Services as % of GNP	19/48/33	7/43/50	4/39/57	0/37/63	0/21/79
Workers in Agriculture/ Industry/ Services as % of total	61/18/21	16/36/48	—	0/35/65	1/35/64
Participation of men/ women aged 15-64 in paid labour(%)	96/80	76/41	—	84/53	86/50
Women in labour force as % of adult labour force	43	34	38	36	37
Productivity (output per hour worked) (1990 $ per hour)	2.79	8.48	11.06	—	—
Education enrolment rate %	55	79	—	68	70
Life expectancy at birth	69	71	—	75	79
Fertility rate (children per woman)	2	1.7	—	1.7	1.2
Hours worked per year (full time worker average)	—	2800	2500	—	—

Key
— Data not available   (a) 1990   (b) 1970–93   (c) including re-exports

Sources: Maddison, 1995; United Nations, 1994; United Nations Development Programme, 1995; World Bank, 1995a; World Bank, 1995b

Table 1.2 **Comparison of South Korea in 1992 with Britain in 1912 and 1992**

	South Korea 1992	Britain 1912	Britain 1992
Total GNP (1992 international US$ bn)	436	207	910
GNP per head (US$)	10010	4868	15738
Rate of growth of GNP per head in previous 20 years (%)	8.2	1.1	2.3
Exports as % of GNP (a)	17.8	20.9	25.2
Foreign owned capital as % of total	19.3	1 (est)	17
Total international assets/liabilities 1988 (US$ bn)	24/35	—	2033/1998
Form of government	Recent presidential democracy	Parliamentary democracy, only male voters	Parliamentary democracy, universal adult suffrage
Form of capital	Dominated by a few giant conglomerates	Firms of many sizes	Firms of many sizes
Government spending as % of GDP	17.1	13.3	43.4
Position of trade unions	Small, growing	Legal but under legal attack	Legal but under legal attack
Agriculture/Industry/Services as % of GNP	7/43/50	6/40/54 (1901)	2/33/65
Workers in Agriculture/Industry/Services as % of total	17/36/48	12/44/44	2/26/72
Participation of men/women aged 15-64 in paid labour %	76/41	85/34 (aged 10–69)	91/59
Women in labour force as % of adult labour force	34	30	43
Productivity (output per hour worked) (1990 $ per hour)	8.48	4.4	23.98
Education enrolment rate %	79	—	77
Life expectancy at birth	71	51	76
Fertility rate (children per woman)	1.7	—	1.8
Infant mortality (per 1000 live births)	12	95	6
Hours worked per year (full time worker average)	2800	2624 (1913)	1491

Key

— Data not available   (a) including re-exports

Sources: Maddison, 1995; Mitchell and Deane, 1962; United Nations, 1994; United Nations Development Programme, 1995; World Bank, 1995a; World Bank, 1995b

The East Asian countries are usually compared with other developing countries. In the context of this chapter, however, it is interesting to see how a country like South Korea compares with the country where industrial capitalism first put down its roots – Britain at an earlier stage in its history.

Question

On the evidence of the variables shown in Table 1.2, was Britain in 1912 more or less developed than South Korea today?

Comparing the data in Table 1.2 for South Korea in 1992 with that for Britain in 1912 – just at the end of the period which nearly all historians regard as that of British economic and military supremacy in the world – the results are surprising. At that time Britain dominated an empire much larger than any the world had ever seen before, it was the world's largest exporter, accounting for about 16 per cent of the total, and had still not completely lost the title given to it nearly a century earlier as the 'workshop of the world'. South Korea today, with a population similar to that of Britain 80 years ago, is a country with no empire, it produces about 2 per cent of the world's exports and has only a very limited world political presence. Yet its national income, and also its national income per head, is about 50 per cent higher than Britain's in 1912; and its total exports – almost entirely of manufactures – are nearly twice as great in real terms as those of its illustrious industrial forerunner. When comparing 1992 data, life expectancy in South Korea is still five years below that of Britain's, but it is twenty years more than Britain in 1912. South Korea's educational level is already higher than that of Britain (Amsden, 1989).

Reflection

- Is capitalism running out of steam? Do developments in Asia represent a new area of dynamism that will lead the system to faster economic growth?

- Is a free market a necessity or a hindrance to economic development? Have the East Asian economies developed fast because of, or in spite of, their rather protective policies on imports and their apparently uncompetitive internal markets?

- How important is foreign investment to economic development? Have the East Asian economies developed because of, or in spite of, their relative resistance to foreign investment; and is China's relative openness to foreign investment changing the answer to that question?

- What is the effect of income distribution on economic growth? Has the fact that East Asian economies are among the least unequal in the world contributed to their economic success?

- Is capitalism as a world economic system inevitably polarized between developed and underdeveloped countries? Does the success of the East Asian countries suggest that it is open to any country to cross the gulf between underdevelopment and development, or are they a special unrepeatable case?

Maddison's long-term national income estimates allow us to make a detailed comparison between South Korea's recent growth and the historical growth of Britain.

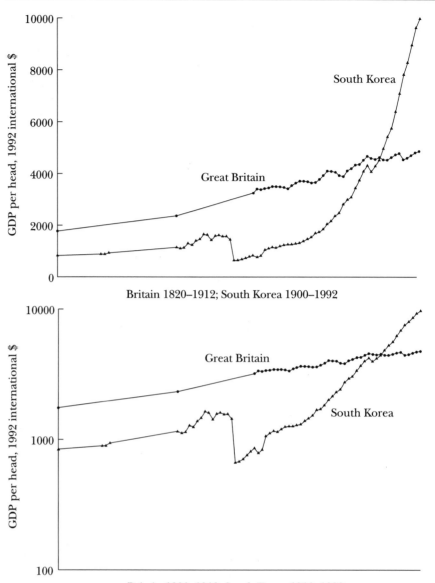

Figures 1.9a and 1.9b
Comparative levels of GDP per head: Great Britain 1820–1912; South Korea, 1900–1992
a) arithmetic (normal) scale
b) logarithmic scale

Source: Maddison, 1995

Figures 1.9a and 1.9b show the growth of GNP per head for South Korea from 1900 to 1992 and that of Britain from 1820 to 1912 on a normal and a logarithmic scale. (If you are not familiar with the use of logarithmic scales in graphs you should read pages 31–32 before proceeding). The slopes of the two lines on the logarithmic scale (Figure 1.9b) show that South Korea's rate of growth since about 1950 has been strikingly faster than that of Britain during the time in which it was still the world's leading industrial, trading and financial nation.

In 1992, national income per head in South Korea was still only 63 per cent of that of Britain, but if both countries maintain the rate of growth they had during the 1980s, then South Korea will overtake Britain's income per head around the year 2000. All but the poorest fifth of the South Korean population have already overtaken the British 1912 average; and since South Korea has a considerably more equal distribution of income than Britain, that poorest fifth of its population has the same level of income as the poorest fifth of Britain's population today.

As you try to explain East Asia's recent economic success yourself, or consider explanations given by others, examine what kind of explanations they are. Where do they put their primary stress? On historical, cultural, economic or other factors? How do these explanations relate to the issues of time and space raised in this chapter? If you had to explain the nineteenth century growth of Europe would you give the same kind of explanation as you give for rapid growth in Asia today? Try also to look at the proposed explanations in reverse. What do they say implicitly about the reasons for the different, often very unsuccessful, recent economic experiences of many of the countries in Africa?

As we have seen, the case of South Korea is not unique. The reason for the unprecedented capitalist growth of this region is one of the most debated topics in economics today. It is an experience used to vindicate several (often conflicting) theories and one of which many countries would like to find the secret. Efforts to adopt the East Asian way, however, have not been very successful in different social and economic climates. Some would say that this is simply because the formula has been wrongly transcribed. The strong suspicion exists, however, that it is more probably because East Asia's special economic circumstances arise from its particular history and that cannot be transferred. Difference and change are interrelated; space and time are interlocked.

Arithmetic and logarithmic scales: charting growth

You should already be familiar with the plotting of economic data on graphs to show changes over time. Time-series graphs help us to appreciate trends in data more clearly than tables of numbers. But with ordinary graphs some problems arise. If we graph data over a very long period it is possible to see the smaller values on the graph only if the scale is unmanageably large or, to put it another way, if we have a manageable size of graph, the larger values are clear but the smaller values are too small to see.

We can get round this problem by using a graph with a logarithmic scale instead of an arithmetic scale. Logarithms are a form of code into which real numbers are transformed into other numbers to make calculations easier. They are based on the power of a number, such as 10^2 or 15^3, the powers being 2 and 3 in these two cases.

Because $100 = 10^2$ we say $\log_{10} 100 = 2$. Putting this in words, 100 equals 10 squared, so log 100 to the base 10 equals 2 . The logarithm of 10 to the base 10 is 1; that of 100 is 2, that of 1000 is 3 and so on (10 is a commonly used base for logarithms).

The sum of the logarithm of two numbers, when translated back into a real number, gives the same result as the multiplication of the two original real numbers. For example:

$$\text{Log}_{10} 100 = 2$$

so

$$\text{Log}_{10} 100 + \text{Log}_{10} 100 = 2 + 2 = 4$$

In other words, translating

$$2 + 2 = 4$$

back into logarithms gives 10,000 – which is what you get by multiplying 100 by 100.

a) Arithmetic (normal) scale

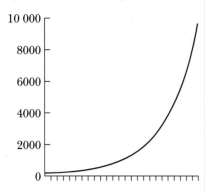

b) Logarithmic scale

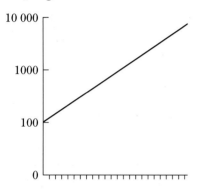

Figure 1.10

Before electronic calculators and computers, logarithms were very commonly used by anyone who had to do complicated calculations. The slide rule is based on the principle of logarithms. The logarithmic scale of a graph represents a form of coding or compressing data. But it is not uniform compression: as numbers increase in size so they are increasingly compressed. This compression is carried out in such a way that there is a constant distance on the graph between two numbers according to their ratio and not, as in the case of an arithmetic graph, according to their absolute value. On an arithmetic graph an increase from 10 to 100 will be represented by the same distance as an increase from 1000 to 1090; the increase is 90 in each case. On a logarithmic scale an increase from 10 to 100 will be represented by the same distance as an increase from 1000 to 10,000; the increase is 10 times in both cases.

Consider a graph in which we measure an economic variable over a period of time, with the variable increasing at a constant rate of 20 per cent each period. At the first date the value of the variable is 100, at the second period 120, at the third period 144 and so on. On an arithmetic scale the graph of this variable will be an upward sloping line with the slope constantly increasing (see Figure 1.10a). If we graph the same figures on a logarithmic scale the line still slopes upward but with a constant slope (Figure 1.10b). This fact gives us the second extremely useful characteristic of logarithmic scales: their slope indicates the rate of change of a variable. Hence, if we see a line on a logarithmic scale in which the slope is a straight line, we know that the rate of growth of the variable is constant; if the slope increases then the rate of growth is rising, and if the slope is getting less steep then the rate of growth is falling.

The disadvantage of the logarithmic scale is that, unlike the arithmetic scale, the visual relationship between two numbers is not equivalent to the real relationship. We must learn, therefore, when reading such a scale to translate it (or decompress it) in our minds so that the visual convenience which it provides for looking at rates of growth does not, at the same time, reduce our appreciation of other aspects.

6 Time and space: change and difference

In this chapter on some aspects of the history of capitalism, I have frequently mentioned change and difference – in other words contrasts in time and contrasts in space. The purpose of this is twofold. Partly it is designed to draw attention to those differences in themselves as a warning against simplistic attempts to describe the workings of capitalism by a set of invariable laws. The nuances are important in understanding what happens in the world. But at the same time, the idea of difference should not be carried too far. There are important common features which justify the use of the word 'capitalism' to describe the prevailing socio-economic system. To use a gastronomic analogy, there is an enormous range of extremely contrasting cheeses (especially if you live in France) but none of them is as different from the others as chalk, or even yoghurt. The growing internationalization of capitalism also means that, although national capitalisms are different from each other, each of them is part of a world capitalist economy.

Keeping the general and particular in balance is not always easy, especially when contributions to economics, as to all the social sciences, range from the highly abstract and theoretical to the extremely concrete and empirical. Theoretical economics tends to look for general propositions with the danger that the differences between different times and places are lost; it is, so to speak, more concerned with the differences between cheese and chalk. On the other hand, empirical economic studies may reveal the differing realities very well but underemphasize general principles, to continue the gastronomic analogy, they are more concerned with the differences between Camembert and Stilton.

The second purpose in addressing temporal and spatial change is to see how the two are related to each other. Has capitalism in all countries developed in the same way? Are past patterns in one country predictive of future patterns in other countries? Or is a feature of economic history that it can never be exactly repeated? And, if so, are different histories questions of chance and whim, or do the differences exhibit some pattern and order?

One approach to answering such questions is to look at cross-section relationships between economic variables today and to judge whether or not their pattern conforms with what we know about historical patterns. We saw from Figures 1.3 and 1.4, for instance, that the cross-section pattern of relationship between level of income today and the size of the industrial labour force conforms, in a rather rough way, to the historical pattern followed by the industrialized countries. Probably the same is true of the relationship between income level and the total fertility rate (Figure 1.5). But state expenditure as a share of GDP is currently much higher in poor countries than it was in the developed countries when they were at a similar level of income (see Figures 1.7 and 1.8).

One of the most fervent debates in modern economics has been about this question of the relationship between change and difference. Rostow in his book, *The Stages of Economic Growth* (1960), postulated that all countries passed through five stages in their passage from 'traditional' to 'modern' economies. The third and central stage he called, in a famous phrase, the 'take-off' into self-sustained growth and he dated the take-off of a large variety of countries. Rostow's ideas have aroused many different critiques but some of the first raised exactly this question of temporal and spatial change (Baran and Hobsbawm, 1961; Frank, 1966). Rostow believed that history would continuously repeat itself in one country after another. He was, therefore, in effect, reducing space to time. According to Rostow's theory, China was different from the US simply because it was further back on a road that it, too, was destined to travel. The 'traditional' society of a poor country today is basically no different from the 'traditional society' of Britain before the Industrial Revolution. Marxist and radical critics of Rostow argued that the very fact that industrialized countries had passed along that road made it impassable for those coming afterwards (Baran and Hobsbawm, 1961). History could not repeat itself because it had transformed what was possible. Instead, they argued, industrial capitalism had split the world into two parts; a small number of rich, industrialized and economically independent countries, and the majority of poor, non-industrialized and economically dependent countries, with increasing polarization between the two. In other words the 'traditional society' common to all countries was a myth: the 'underdevelopment' of today was not an original state but was created as a result of capitalist industrialization in the developed countries (Frank, 1966).

The economic historian Gerschenkron, in his book, *Economic Backwardness in Historical Perspective* (1962), argues in a similar vein that each of the European countries adopted a different route to industrialization according to their level of backwardness on the eve of their 'big spurt' to industrialize. More backward nations, with more to 'catch up' on were obliged to use different methods and institutions. So, for example, in place of the small individual capitalists of Britain we find the big industrial investment banks of Germany or the state as an agent of industrialization in Russia. This is an interesting theory because it links temporal and spatial differences. And, although Gerschenkron devised the theory for Europe only, it is intriguing to wonder whether it explains part of the rapid industrialization of East Asia, where in nearly all cases, as we have seen, the state has played a decisive role in the process, despite the prevailing ideology in the West that the state should be rolled back.

At the opposite end of the scale from Rostow's assertion of a universal pattern of economic growth, many accounts of the economic development of countries have been given which stress only the peculiarities of that particular experience, in effect denying the historical interrelationship of different countries' economic development experiences. This approach might be seen as the elimination of time from the story in the exclusive concern for differences in space.

Both views are unsatisfactory oversimplifications. It is necessary, but difficult, to see interrelations between time and space: to see, for example, that some spatial differences have been reduced through time, whereas others have been sharpened. The economic world contains both convergent and polarizing tendencies. In some respects South Korea has already reached a higher level of capitalist development than Britain had reached in 1912. But the difference of time (less than a second on our condensed world history calendar) is enough to make similar levels of economic attainment have completely different consequences in other respects. Britain's economy in 1912 allowed it to be a superpower; South Korea's larger economy today does not yet allow it more than a modest presence in the world.

7 Conclusion: How many more seconds?

We have seen something of the past and the present; what about the future? If we still live in the age of industrial capitalism as the dominant economic system of human society, then do we live near the beginning of that age or near the end of it? If modern industrial capitalism has so far lasted three seconds out of a planetary history of twenty-four hours, for how many more seconds will it be able to continue?

Many believe that industrial capitalism is still in its cradle; that it has a long future and is neither in danger nor in need of being replaced. Among those who think this way are those who hold the orthodox economic belief in the virtues of the market mechanism (see Chapter 2). Any problems with capitalism in practice, they argue, will be put right by more application of the principles of the free market.

The demise of twentieth century experiments in socialist economics in the USSR and its satellite countries, and the apparent conversion of the Chinese Communist Party to capitalist economics has also lent weight to the argument that capitalism still has a long life expectancy. Francis Fukuyama in a provocative essay interpreted the collapse of communism as the 'end of history' meaning that the basic struggle over the destination of humanity had, in some sense, been settled (Fukuyama, 1992). Robert Heilbroner, no less provocatively, reflected that '[l]ess than seventy-five years after it officially began, the contest between capitalism and socialism is over: capitalism has won' (Heilbroner, 1989).

Events in a group of countries relatively new to capitalist industrialization have revived expectations for the future of capitalism. The exceptional growth of East Asia, which we looked at in Section 5, has led to predictions that capitalism is embarking on a new period of expansion, this time socially and geographically based on the east and not the west, the Pacific and not the Atlantic.

At the same time the view that industrial capitalism is heading for the grave has been common almost since its birth and is not going to disappear. Perhaps the most powerful exponent of the idea that capitalism has a short life expectancy was Karl Marx and other members of the theoretical and political school which he pioneered. Marx believed capitalism would expand the productive power of human labour enough to liberate humanity from the need to dedicate almost all its available time to physical survival and would produce, in the proletariat, a new revolutionary class who would lead the way for a truly egalitarian and culturally advanced human society.

Critics of industrial capitalism point out that, despite the enormous development produced by capitalism, it has failed to solve the material problems of humanity. Competition may produce rapid growth of productivity but it also causes human life, of both capitalists and workers, to be constantly insecure with the danger of a sudden loss of livelihood. Even after two hundred years of generally rapid growth, most countries of the world continue to be poor and underdeveloped. No system so manifestly unfair and incomplete in the spreading of its gains and benefits can possibly survive in the long run, say its socialist and egalitarian critics. Except in parts of Asia there is little evidence that the polarization is being reversed.

Reflection

Look carefully at Figure 1.11. Consider what it suggests about the different experience of people in different regions of the world during the capitalist epoch. Does it justify the view that the capitalist world is divided into two parts: rich and poor? Is the world becoming more divided?

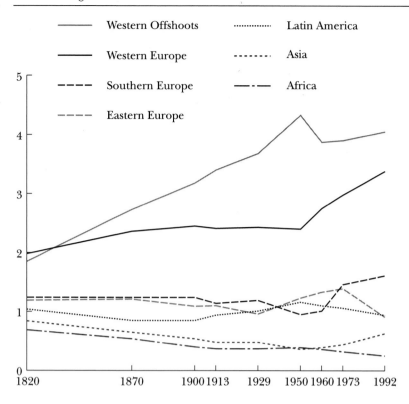

Figure 1.11 **Income per head of groups of countries related to the world average, 1820–1992**

Source: Maddison, 1995

Recent decades have seen the flowering of another equally fundamental critique of industrial capitalism. To environmentalists, the industrial capitalism of the last two hundred years has prepared the way for technological and economic disaster for humanity. The sixtyfold increase in the production of goods and services has created an equivalent increase in pollution and the wasteful use of irreplaceable natural resources. They see industrial capitalism as the system which has shattered a rough equilibrium between humanity and the rest of nature. And to some the rupture is enough to endanger the habitability of the planet.

So, there is no agreement on how many more seconds capitalism has to run. For some theorists, one second would seem exaggerated, while others think in terms of minutes. We cannot know exactly how long, but it seems unlikely that capitalism, being no more natural than the human social and economic orders which preceded it, will go on forever.

Further Reading

Armstrong, P., Glyn, A. and Harrison J. (1991) *Capitalism Since 1945,* Oxford and Cambridge, Mass., Basil Blackwell: provides a view of the nature of the capitalist economy and its post-war development.

Gerschenkron, A. (1962) *Economic Backwardness in Historical Perspective,* Cambridge, Mass., Harvard University Press: attempts to explain the differences in national processes of industrial capitalist development.

Hobsbawm, E.J. (1969) *Industry and Empire,* Harmondsworth, Penguin: draws attention to the way in which Britain's industrialization was affected by the country's position in the international economy.

Landes, D. (1969) *Prometheus Unbound*, Cambridge, Cambridge University Press: presents a view of the process of industrialization which stresses technological change.

Maddison, A. (1995) *Monitoring the World Economy 1820–1992*, Paris, OECD: offers an overview and comparison of present day economies with those of the past.

I am grateful to Paul Auerbach for the condensation of history used in the first paragraph of this chapter and also to members of the course team and consultants who generously commented on drafts of the chapter.

CHAPTER 2

THE ECONOMICS AND ETHICS OF MARKETS

*by Vivienne Brown
and Graham Dawson*

1 Introduction

The previous chapter demonstrated the immense dynamism of the capitalist system and of many market economies within it over the last two hundred years. In this chapter we shall be looking at some models that economists from different schools have developed to explain how markets work and why they have been so successful in many ways. Economic theories differ not only in how they characterize what markets do, but also in the criteria they use to assess the success of market economies. We shall be examining both these issues in this chapter.

The neoclassical interpretation of what markets do is that they solve 'the economic problem'; that is, they provide a way of allocating scarce resources among competing ends. There are other ways of doing this, such as voluntary co-operation and central planning. Milton Friedman's son David, a libertarian or 'anarcho-capitalist' thinker, set out these alternatives rather neatly: 'under any institutions, there are essentially three ways that I can get another person to help me achieve my ends: love, trade and force' (Friedman, 1978, p.18). In this view, the market is seen as the arena for, as it were, 'pure' trade conducted in isolation from the influences of love and force alike. Perhaps Thomas Love Peacock, the nineteenth century satirical novelist and friend of the utilitarian philosopher Jeremy Bentham (see Section 5.1), was giving succinct expression to the motive for 'pure' trade when he put these words into the mouth of one of the characters in *Crotchet Castle*, his satirical work on the economics of his day:

> The Rev. Dr. Folliott: My principles, sir, in these things are, to take as much as I can get, and to pay no more than I can help. These are every man's principles, whether they be the right principles or no. There, sir, is political economy in a nutshell.
> *(Peacock, 1831; 1969 edn, p.136)*

However, there is more than one way of doing economics. The aim of this chapter is to examine some of the answers which economists from different schools have given to the question of how markets work, focusing on three theoretical perspectives – neoclassical, Austrian and institutionalist. Neoclassical economic analysis is the dominant perspective and many economists regard its supremacy as unchallenged. But the Austrian approach is an established alternative tradition, while institutionalist (and related feminist and Marxian) research programmes continue to flourish, albeit away from the mainstream.

Our purpose in analysing these rival schools of thought is twofold; we are interested not only in how markets work but also in the different ways in which economists think about markets.

Section 2 begins with the established favourite, neoclassical economics, and introduces its theory of competitive general equilibrium, which examines the conditions required by and properties of an economy composed entirely of competitive markets, all of which are in equilibrium. A rather different approach to understanding markets will be discussed in Section 3. The Austrian school of economic thought has a distinctive understanding of the role of knowledge in competitive markets which focuses on market processes rather than equilibrium states. In Section 4 we introduce some of the main principles of institutionalist economics. The neoclassical and Austrian traditions agree in seeing individual economic agents as the fundamental building blocks of the economy, in the sense that economic processes and structures can be explained only in terms of the behaviour of individuals. The institutionalist perspective reverses this order of understanding, starting with institutions and then analysing individual behaviour within this broader context. For institutionalists, the behaviour of individuals cannot be understood without analysing the framework of institutions, norms, traditions and customs within which economic agents act.

In Section 5 our aim is to raise some of the ethical issues concerning a market economy. The neoclassical perspective uses the criterion of Pareto efficiency to answer questions about the welfare implications of competitive general equilibrium analysis. In this section, we examine how far this criterion captures the ethical appeal of markets and consider what alternative criteria we might adopt. This helps us explain why some economists find the idea of an economy entirely composed of competitive markets ethically appealing, while others find its ethical implications fundamentally uncongenial.

2 Neoclassical economics

2.1 Introduction

Neoclassical economics is a potentially confusing term. One problem is that it is named with respect to something else: 'neo' literally means 'new'. It suggests that neoclassical economics is to be differentiated from the earlier 'classical' approach whilst also being similar to it in some respects. The main classical economists were Adam Smith (1723–90), David Ricardo (1772–1823) and John Stuart Mill (1806–73). Some would also include Karl Marx (1818–83), although his revolutionary stance differentiates him somewhat from the others. The economists whose work later came to be seen as the first concise statements of neoclassical economics were Léon Walras (1834–1910) and William Stanley Jevons (1835–82), although Vilfredo Pareto (1848–1923) was also an important contributor. These neoclassical economists built on the work of the classical economists, but they focused on one particular aspect of classical economics: the workings of the price mechanism in a competitive market system. Other aspects of classical economics, such as the connection between economic growth and the distribution of income between classes, are downplayed by the neoclassical economists, in favour of models based on the behaviour of individuals.

Another problem is that the boundaries of neoclassical economics are unclear. On a broad interpretation, neoclassical economics represents the mainstream and predominant approach within economics, which takes the individual as its basic unit of analysis and makes certain fundamental assumptions about how individuals behave. In Section 2.2 we shall look at this broad interpretation of neoclassical economics. On a narrower interpretation, however, neoclassical economics comprises a particular model of a competitive economy first formulated by Léon Walras (Walras, 1874). Sections 2.3 to 2.5 will concentrate on this particular model of competitive general equilibrium, outlining its key assumptions and examining the way in which it provides the basis for the neoclassical view of the market as the most efficient way to allocate resources.

2.2   The price system as an allocative mechanism

Neoclassical theory traces the need for markets to the 'general scarcity' of all resources relative to human desires. Each individual in the economy has a particular set of desires or wants for goods and services. These include the desire for food, clothing, transport, holidays, health care – a vast array of potential items of consumption. The economic problem, for the neoclassical economist, is that the resources available for providing these items of consumption are limited. The economy is characterized by scarcity.

Definition

Scarcity

Where time and other resources are limited and not sufficient to meet desired ends.

Scarcity involves an imbalance between two features of the world. On the one hand there are limited resources: these include human time, effort and ingenuity as well as the earth's physical resources. On the other hand there are desires for items of consumption arising both from the need to be properly fed, clothed and housed, and from all those aspirations for human flourishing which require resources in order to be satisfied. By assuming scarcity as a fundamental human condition, neoclassical theory presupposes that there is an inevitable imbalance between limited resources and the extent of human desires.

The neoclassical postulate of scarcity implies the centrality of a certain kind of choice for all economic agents: choices have to be made between competing ends which require alternative uses of scarce resources, and between alternative ways of achieving those ends. An influential statement of this position by Lionel Robbins put it like this:

> But when time and the means for achieving ends are limited *and* capable of alternative application, *and* the ends are capable of being distinguished in order of importance, then behaviour necessarily assumes the form of choice. Every act which involves time and scarce means for the achievement of one end involves the relinquishment of their use for the achievement of another. It has an economic aspect.

> Economics is the science which studies human behaviour as a relationship between ends and scarce means which have alternative uses.
>
> *(Robbins, 1935, pp.14 and 16; original emphasis)*

Note again that there are two aspects to this explanation of scarcity. First, the means for achieving ends are both limited and capable of alternative application; resources (including time) are limited and can be used in alternative ways. Second, there are various ends and not all of them can be achieved. In order that a choice can be made, Robbins assumes that the ends can be ranked according to their importance. This implies that people have stable preferences by which alternative economic outcomes can be ranked.

Scarcity, according to neoclassical theory, is the central economic problem and so there has to be some mechanism for allocating goods and services between agents in the economy. One mechanism is that a superior authority could decide by edict who should have what and who should perform the tasks that need to be done to produce the chosen goods. Such a system may be feasible if the society is small and relatively simple, and if economic authority is uncontested. Another method of allocating goods and services might be by reference to tradition and custom. This method of allocation may be possible in systems that are relatively static. Another method may be by forms of consensual or democratic decision making where members of the society can agree on objectives and priorities for the allocation of goods and services. A neoclassical economist would argue that it is hard to conceive of such a system working across large and complex societies.

Even in large and complex societies, however, these methods of allocation are still to be found in certain areas. Health and education services may be allocated by the state or by charities. A mixture of custom, state regulations and consensual norms influence, for example, the conventions regarding the appropriate age for schooling or the availability of health services such as immunization for at-risk groups, which vary from country to country. Similar methods of decision making may also predominate within many organizations, such as firms and households, where custom and practice, democratic decision making and obeying the authority of the boss or head of household are all prevalent methods of allocation (see also *Firms*, Chapters 1–3 and *Households*, Chapter 6).

In societies characterized by the private ownership of goods and labour services, however, the overriding method of allocation between owners is the price mechanism of the market. Goods, services and resources flow around the economy by means of an intricate web of market transactions entered into by economic agents. All agents make choices as to what to buy and sell, subject to constraints determined by market prices. Households make choices according to their preferences, subject to the budget constraint provided by the income they can receive from the labour services and other resources that they have to sell, and the prices of the consumer goods and services they wish to buy. Firms choose whatever combination of inputs and outputs is most profitable using available technology, subject to the constraints provided by the prices at which inputs can be bought and outputs sold.

It is through this web of constrained choices that the price mechanism works as a means of allocating scarce resources. The price mechanism exists because choices have to be made and these choices are necessary because of general scarcity. Figure 2.1 summarizes this relationship between scarcity and the price mechanism in a market economy.

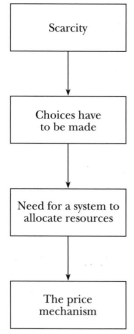

Figure 2.1 **Scarcity and the price mechanism in a market economy**

2.3   The competitive general equilibrium model

The previous section showed how individual choice as to what to buy and sell is central to the neoclassical view of the price mechanism. There are two main types of individual units in the neoclassical model of an economy: households and firms.

How does each of these types of individual units make its choices? For households, the basic psychological assumption of neoclassical theory is that they, and/or the people in them, are self-interested and rational. (*Households*, Chapter 6, explores the difference it makes whether households or people are taken as the decision-making agents and what effect the assumption of self-interest has.) Households choose between different courses of action according to a set of preferences. They also have a set of resources that they own and could sell; these are known as their 'initial endowments'. Like a calculating machine, households rank available options according to their preferences and so decide what goods and services to buy and which of their resources to supply to the market. In making those choices, households have to take account of the prices at which such transactions can be carried out.

Firms are rather similar. They do not need preferences because they are assumed only to be interested in profits. So firms choose from the available technological possibilities how to transform inputs (i.e. the resources they can purchase) into outputs (i.e. the goods and services they produce) on the basis of profitability. Again they operate like calculating machines, ranking different production possibilities by their profitability and choosing whatever feasible combination of inputs and outputs is the most profitable. In making this choice, firms have to take account of the prices at which they can purchase their inputs and sell their outputs. (*Firms*, Chapter 1 examines alternative objectives persued by firms; *Firms*, Chapter 8 examines conflicts of interest between people within firms.)

The basic insight of the general equilibrium model is that putting together all the choices made by households and firms will work only when all markets are in equilibrium simultaneously. If this occurs the choices made by all these economic agents are consistent with each other. In equilibrium every individual agent's plans are realized and so no one needs to change their plans.

Let us examine what has been said here in a bit more detail. First you may need reminding about how the concept of equilibrium applies to a market. A market equilibrium occurs when the amount demanded in that market is equal to the amount supplied. It is then that suppliers can sell exactly the amount they planned to sell, and purchasers can buy just the amount they planned to buy. Since both demand and supply depend on price, a market will be in equilibrium only at some prices, usually assumed to be just one.

An equilibrium in the market for one particular good can be represented using a demand and supply diagram. Figure 2.2 represents the market for a consumer good; the demand curve represents the decisions of households as to how much to purchase at each price, whilst the supply curve represents the supply plans of firms. The conventional assumption has been made in this case that, as price falls, the quantity demanded by households increases; that is why the demand curve is drawn downward

---

Definition

Equilibrium

An equilibrium is a situation in which the choices made by all agents are consistent with each other, so that all agents' plans can be carried out and there is no need for anyone to change their plans.

Definition

Market equilibrium

A market is in equilibrium when demand equals supply. In this situation all agents can sell or buy exactly what they had planned.

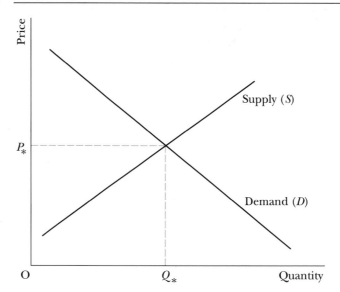

Figure 2.2 **Demand and supply in the market for a consumer good**

Definition

Competitive equilibrium

An equilibrium where all agents are price takers.

Definitions

Partial equilibrium analysis

Partial equilibrium analysis studies the conditions for equilibrium in a single market.

General equilibrium analysis

General equilibrium analysis studies the conditions for equilibrium in all markets simultaneously.

sloping. Similarly, the supply curve has been drawn upward sloping on the assumption of profit maximization, so that, as price rises, firms are willing to supply more of the good.

The equilibrium is where the two curves intersect. At the equilibrium price P_*, firms want to supply, and households want to buy, the equilibrium quantity Q_* of the good. This is a competitive equilibrium because all firms and households are price takers: that is, agents are not able to influence the price at which they can buy or sell the good.

But our focus here is not on single markets since that is the concern of partial equilibrium analysis. Here we are concerned with general equilibrium analysis which examines how prices are determined simultaneously in all markets and where what happens in one market can affect every other market too. To see this, consider what happens if the price of one good rises, say because of production problems. This means that households will adjust their purchase plans. In doing so, they will almost certainly change other aspects of their plans too, deciding either to buy something else instead, thus increasing their demand in some other market(s), or that they need a different amount of income and so adjust their supply to the labour market, for example. In general equilibrium, what happens in one market can have an impact on all others.

Consider, for example, the effect of discovering a new way of making steel. This cuts the cost of steel production thus shifting the supply curve for steel to the right. Figure 2.3 shows that the effect of a shift in the supply curve of steel from S_1 to S_2 is to lower the equilibrium price of steel from P_1 to P_2 and to increase the equilibrium quantity produced and sold from Q_1 to Q_2. But this in turn affects other markets, such as the markets for cars, cutlery and gardening tools. If steel can be bought for less, then all these products can be produced more cheaply and all their supply curves will move to the right, making their equilibrium prices lower too. This in turn may leave consumers with more money to spend on other things, so the demand curves for cardigans, crockery and daffodil bulbs may shift, changing the equilibrium prices in these markets too. Now these price changes may affect other markets, causing further adjustments to take place; for example, the change in the price of crockery may affect the

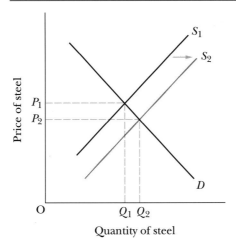

***Figure 2.3* The effect of an increase in the supply of steel**

demand for cutlery. Further, these changes may react back on the market in which the original change took place.

General equilibrium analysis recognizes that every market may have an effect on every other one, and thus that all equilibrium prices have to be determined simultaneously.

Exercise 2.1

Draw a supply and demand diagram to illustrate the effects of a fall in the price of steel on the market for cars. What are the possible repercussions in a general equilibrium setting?

In working through these repercussions, we tend to think of them happening as a sequence of events in the same way, for example, as a stone thrown into a pond causes a ripple of waves which follow each other. It seems natural for us to think about equilibrium adjustment in this sequential way, but the competitive equilibrium model is concerned only with analysing two equilibrium outcomes where, in each, all prices are in equilibrium simultaneously. This implies that competitive equilibrium theory takes the form of comparative static analysis where one simultaneous equilibrium in all markets is compared with another simultaneous equilibrium outcome. This takes account of all the mutual interdependencies between markets but does not analyse them in terms of a sequential series of adjustments.

When there is a change in demand or supply, this happens because there has been a change in one of the variables that was held constant when the demand and supply curves were drawn. These variables are sometimes described as falling under the *ceteris paribus* assumption which holds 'everything else the same'. These variables which are held constant are also referred to as the exogenous variables of the model in that they are determined outside the model and so are taken as given for the purposes of the model. Changes in the exogenous variables impact on the model from the outside, as we have seen in the example of the discovery of a new way of making steel. When there is a change in an exogenous variable, this results in changes in variables which are determined within the model; these variables are known as the endogenous variables. In the competitive equilibrium model, the endogenous variables are the equilibrium prices.

Definition

Comparative static analysis

Comparative static analysis compares two equilibrium outcomes.

Definitions

An exogenous variable

A variable whose value is determined outside the model and so is taken as given for the purposes of the model.

An endogenous variable

A variable whose value is determined within the model.

We have seen how equilibrium prices are determined by demand and supply, and how these prices change if there is a change in any of the factors that are held constant, that is, in any of the exogenous variables. Although equilibrium prices are determined within the model, remember that they are taken as given by each individual agent.

What are the exogenous variables in the competitive general equilibrium model? We have met some already. We have seen that a change in technology (a new way of making a product) will affect equilibrium outcomes by changing the conditions of supply. Technology is therefore an exogenous variable. We have seen that consumers have preferences and that it is in accordance with these preferences that they make their purchase plans. If those preferences change, then there will be a corresponding change in demand. Preferences are therefore an exogenous variable. Finally, households have a set of resources – sometimes called their initial endowment of resources – that they own and can sell to firms. These initial endowments include labour services and also all the other inputs available for production. The distribution of these endowments across households is taken as given for the purposes of the model in that it is determined by factors lying outside the model. If there is a change in the initial endowment of resources, there is a change in the income that households could earn from selling their endowments, and this constitutes a change in the conditions of demand. There is also a change in the supply conditions facing firms. The initial endowment of resources is therefore the third exogenous variable. In summary, the exogenous variables of the competitive equilibrium model are:

- preferences
- technology
- initial endowment of resources.

Figure 2.4 shows how the overall structure of equilibrium prices is determined by demand and supply, which are themselves the result of the particular set of preferences, initial endowments and technology which characterize the system at any point in time.

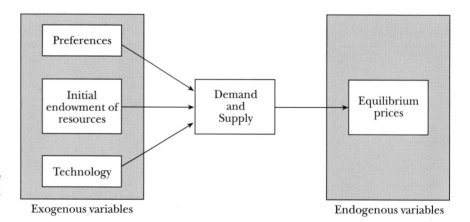

Figure 2.4 **The structure of the competitive general equilibrium model**

Exogenous variables   Endogenous variables

Since equilibrium prices are determined by demand and supply, which are in turn determined by the exogenous variables of preferences, resources and technology, the equilibrium set of prices will change only if there is a change in one or more of those exogenous variables.

Question

Can you think of examples of changes in each of the three types of exogenous variables that would change the equilibrium prices of a competitive general equilibrium model?

A change in tastes, a catastrophe that wipes out some resources, or a new invention that expands technological possibilities, will shift demand and supply and result in changes in the equilibrium price not only of one good but of many or even all goods simultaneously. It is this simultaneous adjustment of prices that gives the competitive general equilibrium model its flexibility and power, despite the very particular assumptions on which it is built.

Exercise 2.2

Which is the crucial assumption for an equilibrium to be competitive?

The competitive general equilibrium model is a model of a decentralized market system, without any overall plan or sense of direction, in which individual agents make their own choices and pursue their own plans in different markets. How is it that such a system can produce a co-ordinated outcome?

We have seen that an equilibrium occurs where agents' plans are consistent; in a market setting this means that demand equals supply in all markets simultaneously. If agents' plans are not consistent, some agents are not able to implement their plans. For example, if the demand for organic milk is greater than the supply then some consumers are unable to implement their planned purchase of organic milk. Conversely, if supply is greater than demand then suppliers are not able to sell all their output at the prevailing price. Demand equals supply in all markets if, and only if, all prices are at their equilibrium level. The task for competitive general equilibrium theory, therefore, is to establish whether there is a set of prices that will secure equilibrium in every market.

If there is such a set of equilibrium prices then a general equilibrium does exist and all agents' plans are mutually consistent. In this case, the system is in a state of balance, as there is no reason for any agent to revise those plans, unless there is an exogenous shock to the system. Here a decentralized system of markets results in an overall equilibrium that is not the intention or plan of any individual agent, but one in which all agents' plans are reconciled. If, however, there is no set of prices that can equilibrate demand and supply in all markets simultaneously, then equilibrium does not exist and agents' plans cannot be reconciled at any set of prices. If such a decentralized general equilibrium exists, it shows that orderly social outcomes do not have to be planned centrally but can be produced as the unintended consequences of individual agents pursuing their own goals.

The appeal of this notion of equilibrium has been enormously powerful within economics. Frank Hahn, a contributor to competitive general equilibrium theory, put it like this:

> ... the notion that a social system moved by independent actions in pursuit of different values is consistent with a final coherent

state of balance and one in which the outcomes may be quite different from that intended by the agents is surely the most important intellectual contribution that economic thought has made to the general understanding of social processes.

(Hahn, 1973, p.33)

Hahn traces the theoretical interest in the decentralized decision making of self-interested individuals to the work of the eighteenth century Scottish philosopher, Adam Smith, who argued that when a person 'intends only his own gain ... [he is] led by an invisible hand to promote an end which was no part of his intention' (Smith, 1776; 1976 edn, p.456). Smith's metaphor of the invisible hand refers to the process by which unintended beneficial consequences for society are the outcome of the decisions of individual economic agents who are simply attending to their own specific interests. The invisible hand ensures that the self-interested actions of individuals serve the public interest better than anything ostensibly designed to do so. The extent to which Adam Smith's economics can be captured by modern neoclassical economics is open to question as his arguments were the product of the concerns of an earlier period (see Brown, 1994). Nevertheless, neoclassical economics regards Adam Smith's *The Wealth of Nations* as a founding statement of the benefits of free market solutions to economic problems.

2.4   Competitive equilibrium analysis and efficiency

Smith's passage on the invisible hand refers to the idea that the public interest is best served by people pursuing their own private interest. This raises the question of the desirable properties of the equilibrium in a competitive general equilibrium model. Overall consistency, by which no person is frustrated in carrying out planned actions, may itself be considered a beneficial property of an equilibrium. However, neoclassical theory considers a competitive general equilibrium to have a second beneficial property: that the allocation of goods and services is efficient.

An economic outcome is regarded as efficient if no single agent can be made better off, in that agent's estimation, without making someone else worse off, in their own estimation. This definition was proposed by Vilfredo Pareto and is now known as Pareto efficiency. So, an existing economic allocation is regarded as Pareto efficient when any further improvement for some would have to be at the cost of a deterioration for others. This definition of efficiency has been widely adopted because it involves neither making judgements about an individual's real interests, nor assessing whether benefits to one individual might outweigh losses to another.

There is a very close relation between the neoclassical competitive general equilibrium model and Pareto efficiency. Intuitively this can be understood in terms of opportunity cost. (Chapter 7 will present a more detailed argument to show this result.) Whenever there is a choice to be made between goods, we can measure the opportunity cost of any one good in terms of the best alternative which has to be foregone (see also *Changing Economies*, Chapters 11 and 13). The notion of opportunity cost involves the idea of trading off one thing against another. For example, when you are considering whether to book a holiday, you will be balancing this against

Definition

Pareto efficiency

An outcome is Pareto efficient if it is not possible to improve the position of any agent (in that agent's own estimation) without at the same time worsening the position of any other agents (in their own estimation).

Definition

Opportunity cost

The opportunity cost of an economic good or action is measured in terms of the best alternative foregone.

the other ways of spending that money. The opportunity cost of the holiday is the best of those alternatives, whatever you would choose if the holiday had not been available. This is an example of a consumer's opportunity cost. But firms have opportunity costs too. When a car manufacturer is deciding whether to produce a family saloon, say, the opportunity cost of the family saloon is the best alternative model which could have been produced in that factory instead of the family saloon.

The outcomes of a competitive general equilibrium model can be shown to be Pareto efficient because both consumers and producers make their choices with respect to prices which accurately convey the true opportunity costs of their choices. It is worth thinking this through in terms of a specific example. Figure 2.5 represents a production possibility frontier (PPF) giving the maximum combinations of two goods, say, raspberries and carrots, that can be produced given the resources and technology that are available. (*Changing Economies*, Chapter 7, Figure 7.20 introduces production possibility frontiers.)

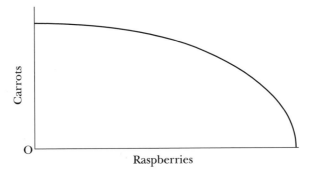

Figure 2.5 **The choice between raspberries and carrots**

A choice has to be made between these two goods since more of one means less of the other. Here more raspberries means fewer carrots and vice versa. The opportunity cost of extra raspberries is the carrot output that has to be foregone. Consider part A of the PPF in Figure 2.6. If raspberry output were increased by the small amount Δr, it would be necessary to reduce carrot output by Δc_A. The opportunity cost, in terms of carrots, of increasing raspberry output by Δr would be Δc_A.

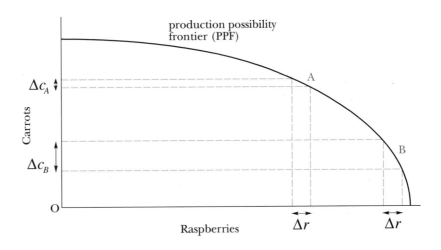

Figure 2.6 **Opportunity cost and the output mix**

Now consider part B of the PPF in Figure 2.6 where more raspberries and fewer carrots are produced. If raspberry output were increased by the same amount, Δr, as before, the output of carrots would fall by the greater amount of Δc_B. To increase raspberry output by Δr, the opportunity cost in terms of carrots is now Δc_B. Thus comparing A with B, the opportunity cost of producing raspberries in terms of foregone carrots has increased as more raspberries are produced.

Definition

Relative price

The relative price of a good is the ratio of its price to that of another good.

Now let us consider the choice between raspberries and carrots from the point of view of consumers. How much they buy will depend on their preferences and on the relative price of raspberries in terms of carrots, that is, on the ratio of the price of a unit of raspberries to the price of a unit of carrots. If consumers value raspberries highly relative to carrots, they will want to consume a high proportion of raspberries and will be prepared to pay a high relative price for them. Conversely, if consumers attach a low priority to raspberries relative to carrots, they will want to consume less and will be prepared to pay only a low relative price for them.

Putting together the production and consumption sides of the model, we find that, in equilibrium, consumers' preferences for raspberries relative to carrots equals the opportunity cost of raspberries relative to carrots. A high relative price for raspberries means that producers are encouraged to supply a large output relative to carrots, and also that consumers value raspberries highly and are therefore willing to purchase this large output at the high price. Conversely, a low relative price for raspberries calls forth only a low output relative to carrots and this is all that consumers want to buy. In either case, the equilibrium outcome will be one in which the relative price of raspberries equals both the opportunity cost of raspberries in terms of carrots in production as shown by the production possibility frontier, and consumers' preferences for raspberries relative to carrots.

This argument, when extended to all commodities, explains why a competitive equilibrium is a Pareto efficient allocation. Production is exactly tailored to consumer preferences through the mediating effect of prices reflecting the opportunity costs of producers and the relative preferences of consumers. It is impossible to reallocate resources in such a way that a different output mix would be more preferred by some consumers without at the same time being less preferred by others.

Consider a situation where consumers' relative preferences for one good in terms of another are not equal to the relative price of that good. If, say, the relative price is greater than the relative preference for an extra unit for any consumer, then that consumer would not want to purchase the extra unit. Conversely, if relative price is less than relative preferences, then a consumer would want to purchase more. The same holds for producers. If the relative price of one good is greater than the opportunity cost of producing an extra unit of that good in terms of the other, then it would be profitable to produce that extra unit. Thus all consumers and producers are doing the best they can only when relative prices throughout the model exactly equal opportunity costs for producers and relative preferences for consumers. In this situation there are no further gains from trade.

The condition that prices accurately reflect all opportunity costs is a very stringent one, however, and it will not hold if there are any market failures. This means, for example, that a competitive equilibrium is not Pareto efficient if there are any externalities. (Externalities are defined in *Changing*

Economies, Chapter 10, Sections 2 and 3.) If there are externalities in production or consumption, the private costs and benefits of an activity are not the same as the social costs and benefits of the activity, and relative prices do not reflect opportunity costs and relative preferences. For example, factories that emit harmful effluents for which they do not pay, will charge low prices that do not reflect the true opportunity cost of this production, and the allocation that results will not be Pareto efficient.

Further, we need to recognize that any competitive equilibrium outcome depends on the exogenous variables of technology, preferences and initial endowments of resources. This section has shown how, provided relative prices accurately reflect opportunity costs and relative preferences, a competitive general equilibrium makes a Pareto efficient use of resources and available technology in meeting existing preferences. However, the outcome also depends on the distribution of resources across economic agents. In particular, a different distribution of initial endowments would result in a different Pareto efficient outcome. Pareto efficiency says nothing about whether the initial distribution of endowments is desirable. The Pareto criterion and the issue of distribution will be examined further in Section 5 of this chapter.

2.5   Neoclassical economics and equilibrium

It has been argued in this section that the neoclassical model emphasizes the importance of the role of prices in a world of scarcity. A competitive general equilibrium model results in a Pareto efficient outcome (assuming there are no market failures such as externalities). Each Pareto efficient allocation takes as given a particular initial endowment of resources, and so there is a different Pareto efficient allocation for each conceivable initial distribution. This model assumes rational, self-interested behaviour on the part of all economic agents.

It is a feature of the competitive equilibrium model that it is a comparative static model where equilibrium outcomes are compared. This has the important implication that the competitive equilibrium model does not address the question of the process of adjustment from one equilibrium to another. The comparative static approach may, therefore, be contrasted with an approach which does analyse the process of change during disequilibrium. This contrast may be illustrated using the notion of a journey from one place to another: the competitive equilibrium approach can compare the starting point with the final destination, but it does not analyse the journey. In Sections 2 and 3 of this chapter you will see that the Austrian and institutionalist approaches regard the issue of the actual journey as the important one.

Neoclassical economics tries to provide some content to what might be happening during the disequilibrium process by trying to imagine a process of adjustment that would be consistent with the competitive equilibrium model. One difficulty is that the model assumes that all agents are price takers. This implies that all agents are so small that no one is able to influence the price. The problem here is that it is hard to operationalize the model and describe a disequilibrium process of price adjustment when there is no mechanism by which any price can actually be changed. One attempt at resolving this is to specify all the conditions under which a real market would approximate to the competitive equilibrium model. This model is known as perfect competition (see *Changing Economies*, Chapter 7). It assumes that all agents are small relative to the market so that no one agent can have an influence on the price. All goods must be homogeneous (rather than differentiated) otherwise firms would have some control over the market. This model also assumes that all agents are perfectly mobile and can respond costlessly to market signals; there is freedom of entry and exit for firms. It is also assumed that all agents are well informed and that the existing technology is available to all firms. This model of perfect competition is an attempt to operationalize the abstract theoretical notion of a competitive equilibrium by rooting it in the required characteristics of actual markets. As all agents are price takers, the equilibrium outcome in the perfectly competitive model is also Pareto efficient, but there is still the problem of how prices actually change in a model where all agents are price takers. This is sometimes glossed over by saying that 'market forces' make the price adjustments.

The models of competitive general equilibrium and perfect competition have proved to be powerful theoretical tools in providing insights into competitive equilibrium outcomes and in showing the efficiency properties of these outcomes (under certain conditions). A weakness is that they are not easily interpretable as a description of actual markets. Thus, although they present a model of a decentralized market economy that many economists find intellectually rigorous, they have been criticized by other economists who feel that they leave out too many features of actual economies where the assumption of price taking cannot be sustained. Sections 3 and 4 describe some of these other approaches that have tried to break away from the neoclassical emphasis on equilibrium outcomes.

3 Austrian economics and market processes

3.1 Introduction

One of the distinguishing features of Austrian economics is its scepticism regarding the neoclassical concept of equilibrium. Austrian economists believe that a dynamic approach based on the idea of market or competitive process is more useful than the static perspective based on equilibrium. Market process refers to the constantly changing interaction among economic agents. The Austrian position is that markets never attain equilibrium but are always in a process of change; there is no destination or resting place, only an endless journey. Austrian economists argue that the neoclassical model of perfect competition is paradoxical in that its assumptions preclude almost all the ways in which firms actually compete. These are captured by the idea of competitive process, which covers advertising, improvements in product quality and innovation (new products or processes).

The assumption that economic agents are well informed has come in for particular attention from Austrian economists, notably Friedrich Hayek (1899–1992) and Ludwig von Mises (1881–1973). There are two main aspects to the Austrian critique of this assumption. First, economic agents have very limited knowledge to bring with them to their market transactions. Second, this deficiency is made good by the market process itself, in that the information agents need to make decisions is provided for them by price movements. Notice that the Austrian antipathy to equilibrium reappears here, for it is *dis*equilibrium prices that disseminate this information.

3.2   The market as a discovery procedure

This difference of view can be traced back to different assumptions about the nature of knowledge and the part it plays in the operation of markets. It is not that the Austrians reject the neoclassical approach to markets outright; they accept the importance of scarcity but they believe that the model places insufficient emphasis on the discovery of knowledge and the effect this has on people's behaviour in markets.

One of the assumptions of the perfectly competitive model is that economic agents are well informed and 'shop around' for the best possible deal (see *Changing Economies*, Chapter 7). Consumers are presumed to know the location of competitively priced goods, job seekers to know of vacancies and firms to know of skilled workers and supplies of raw materials. Such background knowledge enables economic agents to react appropriately to price movements. The Austrian approach, however, models market processes on the assumption that the background knowledge possessed by economic agents is incomplete. The surprising thing about competitive markets is how little information is needed for them to allocate resources in a way that is responsive to consumers' wishes and the production possibilities of the economy.

> The manufacturer does not produce shoes because he knows that Jones needs them. He produces because he knows that dozens of traders will buy certain numbers at various prices because they (or rather the retailer they serve) know that thousands of Joneses, whom the manufacturer does not know, want to buy them.
>
> *(Hayek, 1982, Vol. 2, pp.115–6)*

The manufacturer needs to know very little about the source of the demand for his product. For Hayek, one simple piece of information can have far-reaching effects:

> The marvel is that in a case like that of the scarcity of one raw material, without an order being issued, without more than perhaps a handful of people knowing the cause, tens of thousands of people whose identity could not be ascertained by months of investigation, are made to use the material or its products more sparingly.
>
> *(Hayek, 1945, p.523)*

Question

What do you think is the new information that has the consequences described by Hayek in the passage quoted above?

The answer, as I am sure you guessed, is a price change. All that economic agents need to know, if they are to economise on newly-scarce resources and make more use of newly-abundant ones, is the change in their relative (disequilibrium) prices. No time and effort need be expended in discovering the causes of changes in the conditions of demand or supply. From the point of view of individuals, there is no difference between a price movement caused by a natural event such as a harvest failure or an earthquake, and one caused by human agency such as a change in fashion or a technological breakthrough. Such considerations are not transmitted by price movements and are irrelevant to the efficient allocation of resources. Perhaps the fundamental proposition of Austrian economics is that knowledge is itself a scarce resource, and a competitive market uses it very efficiently, giving economic agents exactly the knowledge they need to exercise their freedom to choose and enabling the economy to run effectively with only that limited knowledge available to economic agents.

There is more to the Austrian conception of knowledge than the fact that the information available to economic agents is incomplete; there is also a dynamic aspect to knowledge. For Hayek, markets actually discover knowledge through disequilibrium price movements. This notion of the market as a discovery procedure is a fundamental departure from the neoclassical concept of equilibrium. In Section 2 we saw that in the neoclassical approach the preferences of economic agents, the resources available and the technology are exogenous variables, while equilibrium prices are the endogenous variables. The equilibrium is, therefore, determined by these preferences, resource endowments and technology, which exist prior to any transaction and independently of each other, waiting, as it were, to be 'matched up' by the market. We can imagine each household with a list of its preferences and the resources it owns, each firm with a list of possible technologies and both groups scanning a list of prices.

From the Austrian point of view there is a problem with this account. Our knowledge can never be perfect and complete in the way supposed by the neoclassical model of how markets work. The neoclassical model operates as if there were a central database recording every consumer's preferences and every producer's stocks. In reality, the Austrians argue, knowledge is disparate or localized. The world is full of isolated items of knowledge and, while each of them is useless on its own, together they are full of significance. Let us suppose that I am a sculptor wanting some interesting pieces of scrap metal to inspire me to create a new work and you are examining the heaps of decaying agricultural machinery at the bottom of the field you have just bought with your cottage in the country. I cannot specify exactly the source of the scrap metal I want, I just know the sort of material I need. And while you are pleased at the thought that the spiky pieces of rusty iron are probably marketable, you do not have me in mind as a potential buyer. Once we have got together, the neoclassical model can analyse our transaction. But from the Austrian point of view this takes the really interesting part for granted. What markets do supremely well is to provide incentives for potential buyers and sellers to search each other out; they are a procedure for discovering useful knowledge.

3.3 The market as a creative process

Buchanan and Vanberg (1991) suggest that the creative spontaneity of the market is a further reason – in addition, as they see it, to its superiority as an allocative mechanism and a discovery procedure – for preferring it as a principle of social organization to socialism or central planning. There is more to the Austrian view of the market than the Hayekian discovery procedure of bringing together pieces of knowledge that were already in existence but disparate and localized. Another Austrian theme is that the market is a creative process, itself bringing into existence 'new' knowledge.

Buchanan and Vanberg argue that, in principle, everything that the market can do as an allocative mechanism and a discovery procedure could also be done by an omniscient (infinitely knowledgeable) central planner. If consumer preferences and resources are given, as they are in the neoclassical perspective, and the central planner is benevolent (disposed to be kind), the 'matching up' function of the market is merely a technical problem. The existence of an omniscient central planner removes the need for the market as a discovery procedure by definition.

However, there is something else that the market does which could not be done by an omniscient and benevolent central planner. It is possible to discover something only if it already exists; even an omniscient central planner cannot know what is not there to be known. Preferences concerning what to consume and technological possibilities in production emerge only in the process of choice itself; economic agents do not know in advance what ideas their imaginations will yield, for example what new products will be created.

Reflection

Consider some new products you have seen advertised recently. Do any of them strike you as being more innovative than others? What meaning do you attach to the phrase 'more innovative' in answering this question?

For example, suppose that a drinks manufacturer launches a new brand of soft drink, called *Copy Cat Cola*. Such a move presupposes that a cola drink already exists; the problem is that there is not enough of it. The entrepreneur has identified an opportunity for profit in a market for an existing product. Since the aim is to match the characteristics of existing colas as closely as possible, *Copy Cat Cola* is new without being really innovative at all.

The Austrian approach suggests that genuinely innovative consumer goods, if they are to be successful, have to do more than match up to a prior specification. For example, I might compile a comprehensive and detailed list of the features I require in a car. But I will never dream up something that matches my specification in the uniquely attractive and unexpected way that, say, the Fiat Punto does. If I could do that, I would be a car designer.

So here, perhaps, is at least part of the creativity of the market; its products may go beyond everything that consumers might include in their product specifications and hence beyond consumers' existing preferences or localized knowledge. It is the element of the unexpected in a new product which may motivate choice, even (or perhaps especially) in a market like that for cars where products are sometimes said to be all alike. It follows that consumer wishes as expressed in an ideal product specification are not enough to determine actual choices. This is the sense, for Austrian economists, in which preferences only emerge in the process of choice.

Although we could compile a list of the features we want in a car, genuinely innovative consumer goods have to do more than match up to our 'wish list'

In this way, the idea of the market as a creative process seems to express a feeling of wonder at the capacity of markets in some manufactured goods to evoke an entirely unsuspected array of products. This idea captures an image of the market as a cornucopia, an emblem of abundance, not only in supplying goods to satisfy pre-existing wants, but in actually creating some of the wants it satisfies and then enabling people to act to satisfy those wants.

The creativity of the market does not end there, according to the Austrian approach, for markets create resources too. It is misleading to assume that the availability of resources can be known. The natural contents of the earth do not come handily labelled as resources. Until someone perceives their capability for being transformed into products, they are not resources. For example, animal and vegetable remains had been lying around crushed between the upper strata of the earth for many millions of years in the form of hydrocarbons before human ingenuity found a way of transforming them into carefully controlled explosions inside internal combustion engines. Moreover, what counts as, or is perceived to be, a resource depends in part on changes in prices. The search for alternative fuels in response to the oil price shocks of the 1970s is a case in point. This is an example of how the market provokes discoveries both of resources and the technologies to use them.

Question

Can you think of a reason why recognizing the impact of price changes on consumers' preferences and the availability of resources and technology might undermine the neoclassical concept of equilibrium?

If preferences, resources and technology are endogenous to the price system and thus keep changing, then markets may never reach equilibrium.

As soon as a pattern of relative prices emerges that might enable all economic agents to implement their plans, it is certain to provoke some of them to develop new preferences, create new technologies or discover new resources and to exploit them in a way that leads to the revision of many plans. There is always something unexpected around the corner waiting to be discovered. That is what markets are so good at, and why Austrians believe that markets can never be in equilibrium.

Austrian economists argue that the neoclassical model understates the achievement of the competitive market. In Hayek's view, competitive markets economise on information; they make a little go a long way. From scraps of knowledge in different agents' heads, markets discover new possibilities of matching up people's needs. In addition, the model of the market as a creative process shows how new uses for resources and new consumer desires are brought into existence along with genuinely innovative products. Equilibrium requires that all the relevant facts are known and that there is no unsuspected knowledge still to be discovered which will disturb that equilibrium. From the Austrian perspective, this is an impossible condition. Far from a balance between opposing forces, they would claim that 'the economic affairs of society ... may be compared to a sailing-boat in tempestuous and tide-swept waters' (Shackle, 1972, p.438).

4 Institutional economics

4.1 Introduction

As you saw in Chapter 1, the institutions within which economic agents operate vary substantially even between capitalist economies. It may, therefore, seem strange that the theories of the market we have examined so far in this chapter pay no attention to the institutional forms that markets take. The model of rational individual choice upon which neoclassical economics is based is presented as independent of any particular institutional context. However, since it implicitly assumes the institution of private property and a legal framework to enforce contracts, it can be argued that neoclassical theory takes these institutions for granted as though they were universal. Most neoclassical economists do not try to explain how these institutions come about.

Institutionalist economists, on the other hand, see an analysis of the institutionalist context as vital to any study of economics. Rather than individual behaviour being the building block out of which a picture of the economy can be built, the order of determination is turned the other way around. Institutionalists would assert that the behaviour of the individual can only be analysed within an institutional context. This means that they have a different view of what markets do and how to analyse them. Warren Samuels, a prominent institutionalist, puts it like this:

> ... Institutionalist economists assert the primacy of the problem of the organisation and control of the economic system, that is, its structure of power. Thus, whereas orthodox (i.e. neoclassical) economists tend strongly to identify the economy solely with the market, institutional economists argue that the market is itself an institution, comprised of a host of subsidiary institutions, and interactive with other institutional complexes in society.
>
> *(Samuels, 1987, p.864)*

A number of things are worth noticing from this quotation. First, if the market is only one of a number of interacting institutions, its analysis cannot be conducted in isolation from that of other 'non-economic' institutions. Institutionalist economists do not, therefore, base their theories on a single type of economic behaviour, such as maximization, which is assumed by neoclassicists to pertain to all 'economic' decisions. Instead they see the study of markets as requiring an interdisciplinary approach, within which it can be expected that people behave differently in different institutional contexts. In the institutionalist approach, other social science disciplines, such as sociology and political science, are given equal standing alongside economics.

Further, this means that institutionalists focus less on particular issues of price formation and resource allocation, and more on the organization and control of the economy. They are interested in the ways in which different economic systems vary and in the institutional histories of different economies. When compared with the neoclassical approach, institutionalists see more variables as endogenous to their economic system and, moreover, they see this system as not a purely economic one. Unlike the neoclassical system, in which preferences, resource endowments and technology are variables exogenous to the economy, an institutionalist view sees individual preferences, resource endowments and technologies as formed within a socio-economic system, and therefore endogenous to it. For example, within institutionalist theories individual preferences depend on the interactions between individuals in society; people define their social standing and differentiate themselves from others by their consumption behaviour (see *Households*, Chapter 2). Institutionalists would, therefore, replace the neoclassical order of determination of Figure 2.4 with a more complex picture of interactions in a socio-economic system as shown in Figure 2.7.

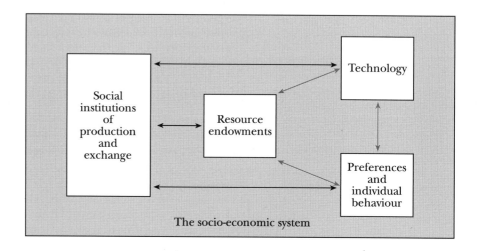

Figure 2.7 **The institutionalist model of a socio-economic system**

Source: Adapted from Hodgson, 1988, p.16

4.2   An interdisciplinary approach

Institutionalist economists see different markets as characterized by different sorts of institutions. As a result, the type of behaviour exhibited by consumers in markets cannot be expected to be all of one type. This has facilitated a more interdisciplinary approach in which economists have drawn on approaches taken in other social sciences. Hirschman's comparison of 'exit' and 'voice' is such an example, where insights from political science have been used to analyse market processes.

Hirschman (1970) defined 'exit' and 'voice' as two methods by which consumers express dissatisfaction and thereby set in motion efforts by firms to adjust their standards of performance, for example, by changing the products they produce. The concept of exit is related to one of the defining characteristics of competitive markets, the freedom of consumers and producers to enter and exit the market at will. In Hirschman's analysis, exit is exemplified by the 'customer who, dissatisfied with the product of one firm, shifts to that of another' (p. 15). If, for example, you decide that beef will damage your health, you can simply stop consuming it – you exit the market for beef. In doing so, the customer may set in motion 'market forces which may induce recovery on the part of the firm that has declined in comparative performance' (p.15). To continue the beef example, you may induce beef producers to sell meat from healthy cattle only. Exit is not a 'fuzzy' concept; it is an all or nothing affair; customers either exit or they do not. It is impersonal in not necessitating any direct communication of a customer's decision to switch suppliers. And the recovery or collapse of the firm, whichever occurs, comes about as an unintended consequence of the customer's action 'by courtesy of the Invisible Hand' (p.15).

Voice, on the other hand, has its origins in the political or non-market realm. You may, for example, voice your concern for the health risks associated with beef by taking part in a radio phone-in programme or by voting against the government. Voice is a much more ambiguous concept than exit and this fuzziness is exhibited along three dimensions:

1 The exercise of voice is matter of degree, in that the force with which it is exercised varies from 'faint grumbling to violent protest' (p.15).

2 Voice takes a variety of forms, from the ad hoc, unstructured or informal episodes exemplified by grumbling and protest, to institutionalized activities, such as participating in the design of a product or the negotiation of conditions of work.

3 Unlike exit, the process of voice is not an all-or-nothing affair (one either exits or one does not) because it typically involves compromise. Neither side gets everything it wants (or nothing at all); instead, having sacrificed something of what they wanted at the outset, they both come away with what is left.

Hirschman draws attention to another important characteristic of voice: 'it implies articulation of one's critical opinions rather than a private, "secret" vote in the anonymity of a supermarket' (p.15).

Question

Identify whether the following types of behaviour represent exit or voice:

- buying a can of baked beans from Tesco's rather than Sainsbury's
- picketing lorries carrying veal calves to France
- choosing a personal computer.

Switching supermarkets is straightforward exit behaviour; the picketing of veal calves is a strong case of voice. Buying a personal computer can involve both exit and voice; the enquiries you make about the characteristics of

Definition

Exit

An agent exercises exit behaviour by leaving a particular market in response to an unsatisfactory standard of performance by a supplier.

Definition

Voice

An economic agent can exercise voice by communicating an opinion to a supplier in a particular market without necessarily leaving that market.

different computers is a form of voice, but, ultimately, when you choose to purchase one brand rather than another, it is exit behaviour with respect to the rejected brand.

The concepts of exit and voice exemplify the interdisciplinary approach favoured by institutional economists, bringing insights and methods of analysis from political science to bear on economic issues. Recognizing that exit and voice may interact in the same market allows the analysis of markets which exhibit elements of both monopoly power and competitive pressure. For example, in some circumstances the threat of exit is one way of making the exercise of voice effective; the supplier is more likely to respond to a customer's complaint if the alternative is the loss of future business. Hirschman also identifies some situations in which the possibility of exit undermines the effectiveness of voice. If exit is possible, the potentially most vociferous may be the first to exit. Competition may, in fact, be collusive, with 'competitors' taking each other's dissatisfied customers rather than adjusting their behaviour. The optimal mix of exit and voice in such a situation is, Hirschman concludes, elusive; but it is that optimal *mix* which constitutes the solution, not just the freedom of exit which is all that perfect competition permits.

The importance of voice in markets is illustrated by Okun's analysis of the 'customer market as an institutional form'. In customer markets, the assumptions of perfect competition, for example that potential purchasers react only to price and that all suppliers are identical, do not hold. The characteristic features of customer markets can be described in these terms:

> Customers are valuable to sellers because of their potential for repeat business ... The firm comes to recognize its ability to discourage customers from shopping elsewhere by convincing them of the continuity of the firm's policy on pricing, services, and the like. It can encourage them to return to buy, or at least to shop, by pledging continuity of that offer.
>
> *(Okun, 1981, p.141)*

The transactions typical of customer markets involve recurrent rather than once-in-a-lifetime purchases, with the consequence that consumers believe that 'the experience of their last shopping expedition conveys relevant information for their next one' (p.140). Shopping around to find the lowest price or the most satisfactory price–quality combination incurs costs. Shoppers, therefore, have an incentive to stay with a previous supplier, provided they can be confident that no lapse in quality or rise in price has occurred. For example, it is inconvenient to keep switching between Tesco's and Sainsbury's, since it is easier to find where things are kept by sticking to one supermarket. For the owners of such supermarkets, it is therefore imperative that customers are retained on a regular basis. This is why they seek to encourage repeat business by using devices such as loyalty cards, discount vouchers or special offers that are available only to regular customers.

In customer markets, relationships between buyers and sellers typically involve the exercise of voice rather than exit. Such relationships are far from impersonal, involving direct communication of a customer's decision to switch suppliers. Moreover, in an effort to avoid this outcome, sellers try to convince customers that repeat shopping will be worthwhile and they pledge continuity on pricing and services. Repeat business also offers opportunities for customers to be consulted on the range and quality of services provided by sellers. Exit may be used to reinforce such exercises of voice, when customers threaten to end an extended relationship on the grounds of unsatisfactory performance.

4.3 New Institutionalism: rational action and institutional context

We have shown that the institutional approach is usually seen as a critique of neoclassical theory. However, there is also a 'new' institutionalism in which it is assumed, as neoclassical theory does, that individuals are self-interested and rational. This approach is both institutional, since it examines a variety of institutions beyond the competitive market, and neoclassical, since individuals are rational in pursuit of their own interests. This approach can be used to attempt to explain the emergence, existence and performance of particular types of institutions. For example, let us consider what difference it makes if the institutional context is such that firms can collude with each other and make legally binding agreements on pricing policy. Such agreements are illegal and therefore unenforceable in many countries. The US has particularly stringent, though not always effective, 'anti-trust' legislation.

Let us suppose there are just two oil firms, A and B, in the market who make an 'agreement' to keep their price high. One set of possible outcomes of this situation is given in Figure 2.8. (See *Changing Economies*, Chapter 5 if this type of diagram looks unfamiliar to you.)

If the agreement holds, so both firms charge a high price, then the firms get a profit of 5 units each – they settle at the top left quadrant of the pay-off matrix.

Firm B / Firm A	high price	low price
high price	5 \ 5	8 \ 0
low price	0 \ 8	2 \ 2

Figure 2.8 **Pay-off matrix for firms A and B: a prisoners' dilemma game**

Question

Faced with the pay-off matrix in Figure 2.8, should firm A charge a high price?

Consider first the scenario in which firm B charges a high price. Firm A will earn 8 units of profit if it charges a low price and only 5 units of profit if it charges a high price; so in this case it is better for firm A to charge a low price. Second, consider the scenario in which firm B charges a low price. Firm A will again prefer to charge a low price since this will result in a profit of 2 units, compared to 0 units if it charges a high price. Regardless of firm B's decisions, firm A's dominant strategy is to charge a low price. Check that you can see that firm B's dominant strategy is also to charge a low price.

If the agreement to charge a high price is not legally enforceable, both firms will be tempted to break the agreement. Whether or not the other firm's prices are high or low, each one will do better from charging the low price. This situation in which independent self-interested decision making leads to an outcome which is not optimal for either party is an example of a prisoners' dilemma game.

Now let us suppose the agreement is legally enforceable. For example, let us suppose that any firm that breaks the agreement has to pay 10 units to the other firm. This changes the pay-off matrix.

Exercise 2.3

Draw up the pay-off matrix for the situation where, if either firm breaks the agreement, they have to pay the other firm 10 units.

The technique used in this section is known as game theory. It can be used in any situation where the best course of action for an individual depends on what others do – situations when strategic planning is necessary. Strategic planning is not necessary in the model of perfect competition since no individual has the power to influence the market on their own. Where markets are not perfect, however, game theory can be used to explain how the pursuit of self-interested objectives might lead to particular institutional forms being set up.

For example, in the case of the two firms considered above, the benefit to firms of the collusive high price strategy can be used to explain why firms try to set up institutions which enable them to follow this strategy: whether through enforceable contracts, or through some other institutional form such as 'gentlemen's agreements' or observed norms of behaviour or strategic alliances (*Changing Economies*, Chapter 5; *Firms*, Chapter 4 considers strategic behaviour by firms in more detail). New institutionalism uses its analysis of the best strategy for individuals in particular institutional forms to explain why those individuals might find some institutional forms more to their advantage than others, and therefore have an incentive to set them up. In this way, new institutionalism, although starting from the individualist assumptions of neoclassical theory, produces an explanation of some aspects of the institutional structure of the economy.

Game theory is also used by new institutionalists considering policy issues to model the effects of different institutional frameworks. For example, in the case of firms A and B considered above, consumers will prefer the outcome in which such contracts to collude are not enforceable (or are illegal). Game theory, therefore, provides an analytical framework which could be used to develop industrial policies which might benefit the consumer.

5   Ethical issues concerning markets

5.1   Utilitarianism

In Section 2, we noted that many neoclassical economists have been enormously impressed by the result that the general equilibrium allocation of final outputs is Pareto efficient, so that it would be impossible to make anybody better off except by making someone else worse off. At first sight, Pareto efficiency may seem an uncontroversial objective; it has, however, some serious implications in relation to ethics. In some cases a Pareto efficient outcome might not be considered to be the moral outcome. In this section we will discuss the role of Pareto efficiency in answering two questions about the ethical implications of competitive general equilibrium analysis. First, what do many economists find so appealing about perfectly

Definitions

Ethics

Ethics can refer either to the set of principles governing the moral behaviour of a group of people (for example Christian ethics, business ethics) or to the philosophical analysis of such principles.

Utilitarianism

Utilitarianism is an ethical theory which states that an action or a rule is right if it produces more utility (or good consequences) that any alternative action or rule.

competitive markets? Second, why do many other economists find the ethical implications of such markets so uncongenial?

The principle of Pareto efficiency was put forward as a response to perceived difficulties with utilitarianism. Utilitarianism is usually summed up in the phrase 'the greatest happiness of the greatest number'. These words so inspired Jeremy Bentham (1748–1832), when as a young man he read them in a political pamphlet by Joseph Priestley, that he devoted his life to building a systematic philosophical defence of them. When Bentham published his *Introduction to the Principles of Morals and Legislation* in 1789, utilitarianism was received by his contemporaries as a radical philosophy. Bentham argued that the greatest happiness principle, as Priestley's words came to be known, should be the foundation on which we approve or disapprove of 'every action whatsoever' (Bentham, 1789; reprinted in Warnock, 1962, p.34). The radicalism of Bentham's ideas came from his concern with laws and legal systems, which at that time were not widely questioned, but accepted on traditional or religious grounds. Bentham, however, proposed to scrutinize the consequences of every law in order to discover whether or not it promoted 'the greatest happiness of the greatest number'.

The greatest happiness principle was also called the principle of utility, and Bentham was careful to distinguish utility from happiness. 'By utility is meant that property in any object, whereby it tends to produce benefit, advantage, pleasure, good, or happiness' (p.34). For example, utility is not happiness itself but the tendency of the goods we consume to produce happiness (among other things, as Bentham noted); it is the benefits or satisfaction from consumption (*Changing Economies*, Chapter 7; for further discussion of issues surrounding the concept of utility see *Households*, Chapters 1, 4 and 7).

For the moment let us turn our attention to the other half of the principle of utility – 'the greatest number'. Bentham was very clear about the importance of this aspect of utilitarianism: it is 'the *number*, of the interests affected ... which contributes, in the largest proportion, to the formation of the standard' (p.33) – the 'standard' here is the principle of utility. The appeal to the happiness of the greatest number solved a problem for Bentham's project of evaluating government legislation. A system of laws applies to every member of a community; the community is the party whose interest – whose happiness, for utilitarians – is in question. But what is a community, and how can we make sense of the idea of a community's happiness? 'The community is a fictitious *body*, composed of the individual persons who are considered as constituting as it were its *members*. The interest of the community then is what? – the sum of the interests of the several members who compose it' (p.35).

In 1789, the principle of utility was a radically democratic idea in its assumption that a community consisted of individual persons, each one's happiness counting equally in calculating the happiness of 'the greatest number'.

However, a century later it was precisely this reliance on the happiness of the majority that provoked Vilfredo Pareto to express his disquiet about utilitarianism. Pareto argued that the principle of utility entails the sacrifice of the interests of the minority to those of the majority. For example, social institutions widely believed to be unjust, such as slavery, might, on investigation, be found to promote the greatest happiness of the greatest number: '... is slavery moral or not? If the masters are numerous and the slaves are few, it is possible that the agreeable sensations of the masters form a larger sum ... than the painful sensations of the slaves' (Pareto, 1927; 1971 edn, p.48).

Pareto's response to this perceived weakness in utilitarianism was to formulate the definition of Pareto efficiency you met in Section 2.4, according to which a situation is efficient if it is impossible to make any agent better off (in his or her own estimation) without also making one or more other agents worse off (in their own estimation). At first sight this looks an attractive solution to the problem Pareto saw in utilitarianism. Suppose a community is considering the introduction of slavery for a minority of the population, in order to improve the well-being of the majority. This would be permitted by utilitarianism, because it promotes 'the greatest happiness of the greatest number'. But it would not count as an improvement on Pareto's criterion, because the increased well-being of the majority would have been achieved by making the minority who are designated slaves worse off.

However, a difficulty arises for Pareto efficiency if we change the example so that the institution of slavery is already in existence. The abolition of slavery is not an improvement, by Pareto's criterion, which specifies that no one be made worse off. In other words, slavery is a Pareto efficient outcome if its abolition would lead to a deterioration in the well-being of some economic agents, in this case the slave owners. In general, Pareto efficiency imparts a conservative bias to ethical judgements, placing a severe restriction on changing the structure of the economy. For example, it might have the effect of perpetuating hardship and injustice for some agents on the grounds that the amelioration of their conditions would entail a loss of well-being by other agents, in this case the privileged sections of society.

Another issue for Pareto efficiency arises out of the qualification that agents must not be made worse off *in their own estimation*. This proviso makes the Paretian approach a subjectivist ethical theory, in the sense that what is good for a person depends upon their own judgement of whether it is good for them. What could be wrong with that? Well, perhaps people can make mistakes about what is best for them. A market exchange might lead them to give up something which it was not in their real interest to give up. In the next section we suggest that the criterion of Pareto efficiency does not safeguard people against such unwise trade, and discuss the idea that there are certain goods to which people have an inalienable right, implying that such goods ought not to be the subject of market exchange.

5.2   The ethical appeal of Pareto efficiency

In neoclassical economics, the competitive market is seen as a reliable way of allocating resources to their most highly valued uses. As you saw in Section 2, in an economy in which all markets are in equilibrium Pareto efficiency is achieved and it is impossible to reallocate resources to make someone better off without making someone else worse off. The competitive model has, therefore, exerted a powerful influence on policy, the emphasis being on a market solution in which competition is encouraged. The following extract from David Henderson's 1985 Reith Lectures shows very clearly why some economists believe that economic agents left to their own devices in a competitive market will, on certain assumptions, make a better job of allocating resources than a central planning agency. In this passage a hypothetical system of licences for purchasing petrol is envisaged as a method of organizing a centrally planned resource allocation system. The government then decides to permit the resale of these licences, as a way of moving towards the ultimate ideal of a competitive market.

> At the time of the second oil crisis of 1979–80, a suggestion was made by the UK Road Haulage Association that the British government should adopt a new policy in relation to petroleum, and 'consider reducing or abandoning its use for non-transport purposes.' The argument was twofold: first, that other users of oil could get by without it, albeit with difficulty, while transport could not; and second, that transport was an essential service ...

> Suppose that a government accepted this line of argument. What could it then do? It could issue regulations forbidding the use of petroleum products for certain specified purposes. It could go further, by allowing petroleum products to be bought only under licence, and arranging that over time these licences to buy were increasingly issued only for transport uses.

> Consider the case where there is a comprehensive licensing system, which establishes a particular allocation or pattern of usage for oil – an allocation which has been decided centrally, according to the government's assessment of priorities. Is there any way of deciding whether a better allocation is possible? Yes, there is. If a particular user X found it worth while to buy some extra tons of oil at the going price, and if at the same time another consumer Y found it worth while to sell that same amount, then both would be better off, in their own estimation at least, if the exchange between them took place ... Since no one else would be made worse off by such private transactions, the new allocation can be judged ... to be better than the initial one. Moreover, it would still be judged better even if it so happened that X did not use this extra amount for transport, while Y would have used it for transport if the transaction had not taken place. The fact that some minister or high-level committee has decided that one use is essential, premium or high-priority, while another use is inessential, non-premium or low priority, is beside the point. The point is that the new allocation, based on demonstrated willingness to pay, makes a given amount more valuable than it was before.
>
> *(Henderson, 1986, pp.28–9)*

Question

Do any of the points made by Henderson remind you of the concept of Pareto efficiency?

Perhaps two phrases suggest that the passage is informed by the concept of Pareto efficiency. First, Pareto's definition of efficiency in terms of economic agents' judgements of their own well-being is recalled by the phrase 'in their own estimation at least'. Second, the phrase 'no one else would be made worse off by such private transactions' brings to mind the implication of Pareto's definition that a situation is Pareto *in*efficient if it is possible to reallocate resources in such a way that at least one person is made better off and no one is left worse off.

Let us think carefully here about the significance of the condition that a series of transactions may be said to improve the allocation of resources only if no one is to be made worse off by it. Economic agents will continue to buy and sell until all the gains from such trade have been achieved, that is, until it is no longer possible to make anyone better off without making someone else worse off. And no economic agent will engage in a voluntary transaction which makes her or him worse off. If people will only take part in exchanges which make them better off, it seems reasonable to infer that it is wrong to prevent them from doing so, as banning the use of oil for non-transport purposes would do.

Voluntary exchange in a competitive market is Pareto efficient because it ensures that:

1   every transaction which benefits both parties will eventually be made

2   none of the participants is made worse off by such a transaction.

As we have seen, the condition that no one be made worse off is a conservative principle of distribution, in the sense that it places a restriction on changing the structure of the economy. Are we sure that this is always a reasonable thing to do?

Question

Let us reflect for a moment on the starting point of Henderson's thought experiment. Was anything said about the initial distribution of petroleum licences?

Well, the distribution of licences was not described or stipulated in any way. We do not know, for example, whether a rich businessman has a licence which allows him to buy more or less petrol than an unemployed bricklayer. Whether or not we support the Paretian principle that the government should only adopt policies by which no one is made worse off depends on what we think of the initial distribution. If we assume that the initial distribution of licences was fair and equitable, then adopting the Pareto criterion and allowing voluntary exchanges may seem a reasonable course of action.

5.3   Are there intrinsic rights?

Is the Pareto criterion always applied in such uncontroversial circumstances as those stipulated in Henderson's thought experiment? In December 1991, Lawrence Summers, an economist with the World Bank, circulated a memorandum to some of his colleagues. It was leaked to the press.

Just between you and me, shouldn't the World Bank be encouraging *more* migration of the dirty industries to the less developed countries (LDCs)? I can think of three reasons:

(1)   The measurement of the costs of health-impairing pollution depends on the foregone earnings from increased morbidity and mortality. From this point of view a given amount of health-

impairing pollution should be done with the lowest cost, which will be in the country with the lowest wages. I think the economic logic behind dumping a load of toxic waste in the lowest wage country is impeccable and we should face up to that.

(2) The costs of pollution are likely to be non-linear as the initial increments of pollution probably have very low cost. I've always thought that under-populated countries in Africa are vastly *under* polluted; their air quality is probably vastly inefficiently low compared to Los Angeles or Mexico City. Only the lamentable facts that so much pollution is generated by non-tradable industries (transport, electrical generation) and that the unit transport costs of solid waste are so high prevent world-welfare-enhancing trade in air pollution and waste.

(3) The demand for a clean environment for aesthetic and health reasons is likely to have very high income-elasticity. The concern over an agent that causes a one-in-a-million chance of prostate cancer is obviously going to be higher in a country where people survive to get prostate cancer than in a country where under-5 mortality is 200 per thousand. Also, much of the concern over industrial atmospheric discharge is about visibility-impairing particulates. These discharges may have very little direct health impact. Clearly trade in goods that embody aesthetic pollution concerns could be welfare-enhancing. While production is mobile the consumption of pretty air is non-tradable. The problem with the arguments against all of these proposals for more pollution in LDCs (intrinsic rights to certain goods, moral reasons, social concerns, lack of adequate markets, etc.) is that they could be turned around and used more or less effectively against every Bank proposal for liberalisation.

(Hausman and McPherson, 1996)

A number of reactions to this memo are possible. Moral outrage at the injustice of what is being considered is certainly one possibility. Let us see if we can reconstruct the economic argument for transferring dirty industries to LDCs, and then try to clarify what the grounds might be for believing such a policy to be unjust.

Questions

1 Suppose that there is a system of licences for the dumping of toxic waste, similar to that envisaged by Henderson (1986) for the purchase of petroleum products. Explain briefly why high wage countries will charge more for issuing the licences than low wage countries.

2 What would the outcome of such a pricing policy be? How does this illustrate the impeccable economic logic behind dumping toxic waste in the lowest wage country?

3 The migration of dirty industries to LDCs imposes health-impairing pollution on their populations. However, if this movement of dirty industries is in accordance with economic logic, as Summers suggests, the people who live in the recipient LDCs are not made worse off by it. Do you agree?

The polluter (the company dumping the waste) would have to pay a very high price to buy a licence from a high-wage country. The increased mortality and morbidity caused by the pollution would lead to a substantial loss of earnings, and so it would be rational for the government of the high-wage country to accept the pollution only if the licence fee provided adequate compensation. The government of the LDC would be behaving rationally in selling the pollution licence for a lower price, because its population will suffer a smaller loss of earnings from the health impairment it causes, and would, therefore, need lower compensation.

Economic logic refers to the principles which operate in a perfectly competitive market to guide it towards a Pareto-efficient allocation of resources. Just as economic goods such as petroleum products ought to be allocated to their most highly valued uses, so economic 'bads' such as pollution ought to be allocated to the locations where they will cause least damage. A system of licences for the dumping of toxic waste would, in principle, allocate dirty industries in this way. Firms would buy their licences where they are cheapest and therefore dump their toxic waste in the lowest wage economy.

Turning to the second question, it seems at first sight surprising that the people who live in the recipient LDCs are not worse off. Their environment is more polluted than it was before the migration of dirty industries and their health has deteriorated. However, the government of a recipient LDC has made the voluntary decision that this is, so to speak, a price well worth paying for the new source of revenue. And the population of the recipient LDC, while worse off to the extent of the pollution, is better off by the amount of the licence fee. Abstracting from internal distributional issues, the LDC's population as a whole would not, therefore, be made worse off by the increased migration of dirty industries.

And yet there remains the stubborn intuition that something has gone terribly wrong. Well, one way of diagnosing the problem is to recognize that the Pareto criterion permits people in a weak bargaining position to engage in transactions which, while leaving them no worse off, deprive them of things that might reasonably be regarded as inalienable or intrinsic rights. These include the right to certain goods such as good health irrespective of earnings, or air that is sufficiently free of pollution to be 'pretty'. The Pareto criterion fails to differentiate different sorts of needs; any cause can be traded against any other if that is what a person chooses to do.

It is an implication of this definition of rights that the rights a person has do not depend upon what that person believes his or her rights to be. In this sense the concept of a right differs from the notion of what is good for a person which informs Pareto efficiency. As we saw in the previous section, Pareto efficiency represents a subjective approach to ethics in that judgements about a person's well-being are qualified by 'in his or her own estimation'. One way of interpreting the concept of a right is that it expresses an objective view of well-being, by identifying a set of basic needs which everyone has a right to have satisfied. It seems to be to some such principle that Summers is referring in the World Bank memo when he remarks in parenthesis that 'intrinsic rights to certain goods' constitute one argument against trade in pollution.

Rawls (1971, p.92) suggests that we think of human well-being as having access to 'primary social goods', where a primary good is defined as things

Definition

Rights

Rights are justified claims to the protection of a person's essential interests, which entail duties on the part of other people to refrain from damaging those interests.

a rational person would want whatever else he or she would want. This definition of a primary good is objective in the sense that it reflects what *any* rational person would want, not what a particular individual actually wants. Rawls recognizes that some of the things a rational person would want might be denied them by factors such as genetic endowment which cannot be rectified by social institutions. So the focus is on those aspects of well-being which can be affected by society, hence the term 'primary *social* goods'. Primary social goods 'in broad categories are rights and liberties, opportunities and powers, income and wealth' (p.92).

In the context of transferring polluting industries to LDCs, the concept of a right as a primary social good goes some way towards clarifying the sense of injustice at such a proposal. The licensing of pollution would be Pareto efficient in that the populations of the recipient LDCs would not be worse off in their estimation. But it would deny them access to certain primary social goods, including the right to unpolluted air and good health.

6   Conclusion

In this chapter we have introduced some of the questions economists ask about the ways in which markets work, and some of the theoretical frameworks they use in answering them. Our approach has been to discuss markets in general. However, as you work through the rest of this book, you will encounter a number of discussions of different kinds of markets, such as goods markets, labour markets, financial markets and markets in caring. This raises the possibility that a particular theoretical perspective, say, institutionalist economics, might be more helpful in understanding a certain kind of market, perhaps markets in caring services, than other approaches. Similarly, you might find that a broadly Austrian approach is particularly illuminating in connection with markets characterized by high rates of innovation (see *Firms*, Chapters 9 and 10). Both within the economics profession and in the wider public debate, which economic approaches are relevant to particular markets is the subject of intense controversy.

Further Reading

Neoclassical economics

Henderson, D. (1986) 'Soap opera in high places', Chapter 2 in *Innocence and Design: The Influence of Economic Ideas on Policy*, Oxford and New York, Basil Blackwell, pp.17–35: a brisk and readable exposition of the neoclassical theory of how markets allocate resources efficiently.

Robinson, J. (1963) 'The neo-classics: Utility', Chapter 3 in *Economic Philosophy*, Harmondsworth, Penguin, pp.48–70: a classic polemical piece on the philosophical foundations and ideological significance of neoclassical economics.

Austrian economics

Gray, J. (1992) 'The epistemic argument for the market', Chapter 2 in *The Moral Foundations of Market Institutions*, London, IEA Health and Welfare Unit, pp.5–17: an exposition and defence of the Austrian view of the market as a discovery procedure.

Institutional economics

Hodgson, G.M. (1994) 'Institutionalism "old" and "new"', in Hodgson G.M., Samuels, W.J. and Tool, M.R., *The Elgar Companion to Institutional and Evolutionary Economics*, Aldershot, Edward Elgar, pp.397–403: a brief and authoritative historical survey of institutional economics.

Economics and ethics

Sugden, R. (1992) 'Social justice', Chapter 18 in Hargreaves Heap, S. *et al.*, *The Theory of Choice*, Oxford, Blackwell, pp.259–85: a comprehensive survey of substantive ethical theories and their relevance to economics.

CHAPTER 3

DISCRIMINATION AND SEGMENTATION

by Robert McNabb

1 Introduction

Discrimination can manifest itself in all aspects of life. It may be evident in the type and location of housing available to certain groups, in their access to quality education and health care or how they are treated in the labour market. This chapter focuses on the last of these considerations and, in particular, why the labour market status of some groups of workers is significantly worse than that for the population at large. This does not mean that discrimination in the labour market is a more relevant consideration than other forms of discrimination, nor should it imply that labour market discrimination is independent from other forms of discrimination. Indeed, some economists would argue that a satisfactory explanation of labour market discrimination can only be developed when it is recognized that all forms of discrimination are related.

The fact that some people do better or worse than others in the labour market does not, in itself, signify the presence of discrimination. It would be more surprising if such differences were not observed. What is harder to explain, however, is why particular groups of workers are disadvantaged in the labour market. Why do women and members of ethnic minorities, for example, face significantly lower wages and poorer employment opportunities *as a group*? In this chapter we focus on the general observation that certain characteristics – gender, race, religion, age – actually matter in the labour market when there is no apparent reason why they should.

In the next section we outline the extent to which disadvantage in the labour market varies. There are, of course, many different dimensions to labour market disadvantage. The most obvious is differences in average earnings which may arise either because people from disadvantaged groups are paid less for doing a particular job or because they end up in (or are 'crowded' into) low paying jobs. A second dimension of labour market disadvantage is that the level of unemployment is higher for certain groups of workers than for others. Linked to this is the observation that disadvantaged groups are concentrated in jobs with higher turnover rates and greater job insecurity. Finally, some groups may be disadvantaged in terms of the type of work they have access to, with an emphasis on menial and repetitive tasks.

Since there are many different ways in which labour market disadvantage can be measured, it is perhaps not surprising that there are also different types of discrimination. The two main types are considered in Section 3.

The theories proposed to explain discrimination in the labour market are equally diverse. Differences are reflected not simply in terms of the underlying theoretical framework adopted but also in the particular aspects of labour market behaviour which are focused upon. Explanations which can be grouped under the heading of neoclassical theories focus mainly on the supply side of the labour market, such as the relationship between labour market disadvantage, low productivity and low levels of investment in human capital. We look in detail at such explanations in Section 4. Other, non-neoclassical theories, such as segmented labour market theory, concentrate on the limited access certain groups of workers have to 'good' jobs (independent of their human capital) and upon why there is segregation in access. We look at these alternative, institutional theories and related features in Section 5.

2 Labour market disadvantage

2.1 Gender-based disadvantage

The post-war period has seen a significant increase in the participation of women in the labour market, with women now making up around 45 per cent of the UK workforce. Although women still undertake the major share of family responsibilities and domestic activities, an increasing number of women are entering the labour market (see *Households*, Chapter 5). This increase is evident in many countries and has been associated with an improvement in the relative earnings of women. This trend towards greater equality is evident in Table 3.1, which shows the ratio of female to male earnings in a number of countries over the period 1960–1980.

Table 3.1 **The ratio of female to male hourly earnings in selected countries, 1960–1980**

	1960	1970	1980
Australia	0.59	0.59	0.75
France	0.64	0.67	0.71
Germany	0.65	0.69	0.72
Italy	0.73	0.74	0.83
Japan	0.46	0.54	0.54
Netherlands	0.60	–	0.71
Sweden	0.72	0.84	0.90
UK	0.61	0.59	0.75
USA	0.66	0.65	0.66
USSR	0.70	0.70	0.70

– data not available

Source: Mincer, 1985

Question

For the period 1960–80, identify:

1   the country with the largest reduction in inequality

2   the smallest reduction (or no reduction at all).

Sweden underwent the biggest reduction in inequality with the ratio of female to male wages increasing from 0.72 to 0.90. Both the USA and the USSR had no change in relative wages.

The labour market is complex and the two observations that more women now participate in the labour market and that there has been a narrowing of relative wage differentials reflect a number of possible relationships. On the one hand, it may be the case that more women participate because female wages have increased over time. On the other hand, the stronger commitment of women to the labour market could, in itself, increase female wages and narrow the earnings differential. Thus, if higher wages and higher participation are statistically associated, there are various views on causation which the labour economist must disentangle.

Despite the improvements that have taken place over time, however, it would be misleading to overemphasize the advances that have occurred in the relative position of women in the labour market. Nearly 45 per cent of working women in the UK, for example, are employed part-time, at pro-rata wages well below those of full-time workers. According to *People Management,* 'Women working on a part-time basis earn only 58% of male full-time workers' pay rates' (6 February 1997, p.8).

Data from the *New Earnings Survey* (1995) reveal that the earnings of women working full-time are also significantly below those of men in comparable jobs. As Table 3.2 shows, the average weekly earnings of women managers in 1995 was 68 per cent that of men. This ratio, earnings of women to men, of about two-thirds, was reported in six out of nine occupational groups.

Table 3.2   **Average weekly earnings by occupation 1995 (£)**

	Men (£)	Women (£)	Ratio: women/men %
Managers	537.00	367.80	0.68
Professionals	499.70	407.90	0.82
Associate professionals	442.90	333.30	0.75
Clerical and secretarial	269.90	230.40	0.85
Skilled manual	318.30	191.20	0.60
Personal services	296.10	198.70	0.67
Sales	310.30	199.90	0.64
Plant and machine operators	293.70	201.50	0.69
Other	250.50	170.80	0.68

Source: *New Earnings Survey,* 1995

Women may have to wait many years before they achieve equal pay with men. *People Management* state that, '... the average earning discrepancy between men and women remains at around 20 per cent. At the current rate of improvement, women will have to wait until 2040 before they achieve parity' (6 February 1997, p.16). Also, according to *People Management,* '... surprisingly, the gap remains widest of all in professional occupations. For example, women bank and building society managers earn 36 per cent less than men in similar posts' (*ibid*).

That women are paid less within even narrow occupational categories can arise for a number of reasons and does not necessarily involve women being paid less than men for doing the same job. It may reflect the nature of the organizations that employ women or the fact that women are typically employed at lower grades within occupational categories. For example, there is evidence that women academics are appointed at lower points on the university lecturer scale than comparable men and that they are less likely to become senior lecturers, readers and professors (McNabb and Wass, 1997). The failure of women to make significant progress in the professions and in senior management and administrative posts has led to the idea that there is a 'glass ceiling' which means that women are under-represented in positions of responsibility and influence.

In addition to this disparity in pay across all occupations, women tend to be heavily concentrated in occupations and industries that are characteristically low paying. The *1991 Population Census* (OPCS, 1992) recorded that just over 28 per cent of women were employed in clerical and secretarial jobs, 13 per cent in personal service occupations and 10.5 per cent in sales occupations (Table 3.3). The corresponding figures for men in these areas are much lower. In contrast, nearly 30 per cent of male workers are managers and professionals. These occupations employ only just over 19 per cent of women. Moreover, within broad occupational groups we find further concentrations. For example, two thirds of women in professional occupations are teachers whereas teaching accounts for only a quarter of professional males. Similarly, more than half the women in associate professional jobs are nurses.

Table 3.3 **Distribution of employment by occupation (%)**

	Men	Women
Managers	19.3	11.6
Professionals	9.5	7.6
Associate professionals	7.8	9.9
Clerical and secretarial	6.7	28.1
Skilled manual	23.1	3.5
Personal services	6.1	13.0
Sales	4.5	10.5
Plant and machine operators	14.3	5.1
Other	7.5	9.9
Not adequately described	1.1	0.8

Source: *1991 Population Census*, 1992, OPCS

2.2   Ethnicity and disadvantage

Detailed information on other disadvantaged groups in the UK is more limited. Recent studies of the labour market disadvantage faced by Britain's ethnic minorities indicate not only that they fare badly relative to white employees, but also that their relative position deteriorated throughout the 1980s and early 1990s. According to the *General Household Survey,* non-white employees in the UK earned 7.3 per cent less, on average, than white employees over the period 1973–9: this deteriorated to 12.1 per cent through the period 1983–9. The Campaign for Racial Equality reports an even larger disparity in earnings: using the *Labour Force Survey* (Eurostat, 1994) they found that the average hourly rate of pay for ethnic minority workers in Inner London was £5.62 compared with a figure of £9.82 for white workers.

A similar picture both of relative disadvantage and deterioration since the 1970s emerges in unemployment rates. Table 3.4 shows unemployment rates for different ethnic groups since 1979.

Table 3.4   **Unemployment rates for UK males in selected years**

Year(s)	White (total %)	Non-white (total %)	Indian (%)	Pakistani or Bangladeshi (%)	West Indian (%)
1979	4.0	6.0	4.8	8.1	7.3
1981	9.7	17.2	15.4	20.4	20.6
1983	12.0	22.0	17.0	32.0	28.0
1984	11.0	21.0	13.0	38.0	28.0
1985	11.0	21.0	18.0	28.0	23.0
1984–6	11.0	21.0	15.0	30.0	25.0
1985–87	11.0	20.0	15.0	29.0	24.0
1987–89	8.0	15.0	10.0	25.0	18.0
1989–91	7.0	13.0	10.0	21.0	16.0
1994	11.0	25.0	16.0	29.0	33.0

Source: Blackaby *et al.,* 1995

What is interesting about this table is that the information is also broken down by ethnic group. This enables us to highlight not just the differences that exist between white and non-white workers but also those that exist between ethnic minorities. Several points are worth noting. First, unemployment in all the years shown is lower for whites than for non-whites: in 1994 the unemployment rate among non-whites was more than twice that for white workers. Second, although the 1980s was a period of rising unemployment for all workers, the increase was much larger for non-whites than for white workers. Finally, there are significant differences within the non-white population. Workers of Indian descent fared significantly better than workers of Pakistani/Bangladeshi descent; workers of West Indian origin have faced the greatest deterioration in their chances of being in work.

Unemployment among young workers paints an even bleaker picture with 37 per cent of those from ethnic minorities unemployed in 1994: amongst young black workers the figure is 51 per cent (Blackaby *et al.*, 1995).

Young black workers face a bleak outlook; over half of them are registered unemployed

2.3 Other disadvantaged groups

Information on other disadvantaged groups, such as older workers or people with disabilities, is even harder to come by. The problems faced by older workers in the labour market have become an increasing cause for concern in recent years. The nature of the disadvantage faced by older workers is, however, much harder to uncover and the evidence is often anecdotal. One trend that has become evident during the past 15 years is the difficulty older workers have in obtaining any work and, in many cases, the jobs that are available often pay older workers significantly lower wages than they previously received. Job adverts can specify age limits (in contrast to race and gender) in the UK, though such practices have been made illegal in some countries, such as the US, Canada and France.

High general unemployment in the 1980s and 1990s had a significant impact on the employment opportunities for people with disabilities as they had to compete with large numbers of 'able-bodied' workers. The double discrimination facing people with disabilities from ethnic minority places them at even more of a disadvantage than white people with disabilities (Baxter *et al.*, 1990).

3   Forms of discrimination

Definition

Wage discrimination

Under wage discrimination an individual is paid less than another individual working at the same job.

We have already seen that labour market disadvantage can take various forms. Equally, discrimination in the labour market itself can manifest itself in different guises.

The most obvious form of discrimination involves women being paid less than men for doing the same or a similar job. This is what labour economists call wage discrimination, which has been addressed and formally eliminated in many countries through the introduction of equal pay legislation. Wright and Ermisch (1991) for example, report that 'the *Equal Pay Act* (1970), *Sex Discrimination Act* (1975), and *Employment Protection Act* (1975), contributed significantly to reducing discrimination in the British labour market' (p.508).

However, the ability of such legislation to improve the relative position of those workers facing discrimination is the subject of much debate. The following case study of performance-related pay shows how discrimination can be difficult to legislate for.

Merit pay scheme 'was discriminatory'

London Underground is changing the way its performance-related pay system is implemented after conceding a £60,000 racial discrimination case last month.

Consultants, Psychometric Research Development, will meet with London Underground in future to discuss any performance-related pay scheme as part of a settlement reached with 20 black station managers. The managers claimed that the scheme, in place for the three years between 1989 and 1992, indirectly discriminated against them.

Fatima Patwa, a solicitor for Brent Community Law Centre, which supported three of the 20 managers, told *Personnel Management* that the performance assessments left too much to the discretion of the senior staff carrying out the appraisals.

She said research found black managers were being awarded lower performance pay than their white colleagues. Some managers were failing to use the appraisal procedure correctly, making the same remarks on all forms while awarding different levels of pay, or ignoring the assessment entirely and simply making a judgement on salary.

In a statement agreed with the black managers, London Underground said that the indirect discrimination had been 'wholly unintentional'. It went on to say that it 'regrets the fact that its performance-related pay exercises for the three years from 1989 to 1992 were not carried out fully in conformity with its laid down procedures'.

The Commission for Racial Equality, which supported 17 of the managers, said the case was the biggest it had ever put to an industrial tribunal

The case was initially supported by the Transport Workers Legal Action Committee, which was formed by black workers within London Underground to deal with discrimination.

> Each of the managers will be paid £1,000 for financial loss plus £1,500 for injury to feelings and £650 for adjustment to voluntary severance payments.
>
> Source: *Personnel Management*, May 1993

Discrimination can also exist even where earnings are the same for all workers in a particular job. Employment discrimination occurs when workers from disadvantaged groups are employed in jobs for which they are over-qualified in the sense that they have higher levels of productivity compared with other workers doing the same job, and with the overall level of ability needed to undertake the tasks involved. This will arise either because members of particular groups face discrimination in recruitment, and so cannot gain access to better paid jobs, or because opportunities for promotion and selection for training are denied.

The definition of discrimination which underlies both wage and employment discrimination is the same. It involves the unequal treatment of individuals who are equally productive (sometimes described as 'of comparable worth') on the basis of characteristics, such as gender, race, age, religion, etc., that are not related to productivity and so should not affect earnings.

While wage and employment discrimination have been the focus of empirical and theoretical research, this should not be taken to imply that other forms of discrimination are less important nor that their impact is of less significance. Harassment at work, for example, is a form of discrimination which, although it has not received the empirical scrutiny of labour economists, is nevertheless an increasing cause for concern. It can affect an individual's performance at work and consequently his or her earnings and employment opportunities. To give one example: in a large-scale survey of junior barristers, 40 per cent of female respondents reported that they had faced some sort of sexual harassment at work (*Equal Opportunities Review*, 1995).

4 Neoclassical models of discrimination

Our earlier discussion suggested that to understand labour market discrimination we need to answer two principal questions. First, to what extent does the observation that, on average, some groups in society fare worse than others in the labour market actually reflect differences in productivity arising from differences in such things as education and training, and how much represents the unequal treatment of equally productive workers (i.e. discrimination)? Secondly, if discrimination in the labour market exists, what explanations are proposed to explain why it takes place? These two questions are, of course, not unrelated. The educational and training opportunities available to some groups in society may themselves reflect discrimination. As a result, labour market outcomes, which may or may not be discriminatory, may arise from discrimination that exists outside the labour market.

In this section we consider those explanations usually grouped under the neoclassical label, which build upon human capital theory (see Chapter 5, *Households*). No attempt is made here to provide an exhaustive coverage of all the neoclassical models and their variations, rather, we present two examples of neoclassically-based explanations. The first, Becker's 'employer taste' model, is based on the standard utility maximizing model and emphasizes the importance of market forces and competition; the second focuses on how imperfect information in the labour market can give rise to wage differentials even among comparable workers.

4.1 Becker's 'employer taste' model

The most prominent neoclassical explanation of discrimination is based on the work of Gary Becker and develops the idea that some workers, employers or customers do not want to work with or come into contact with members of other racial groups or with women (Becker, 1971). No explanation is given as to why this prejudice exists, rather it is simply assumed that there is a 'taste' or preference against people from disadvantaged groups and that this taste can be treated in exactly the same way that economists would analyse individual preferences between goods and services.

Suppose that an employer does not want to employ members of a particular group even though these workers are as productive as any others. If the firm has to pay all workers the same wage it will simply not employ members of the disadvantaged group. However, if it is possible to pay these workers less than those from other groups the firm then faces a trade-off: it can employ members of the disadvantaged group at lower wages and thus increase its profitability, or it can discriminate and employ only workers from the high wage group even though this will mean lower profits. Discrimination in the latter case therefore imposes a cost on the firm.

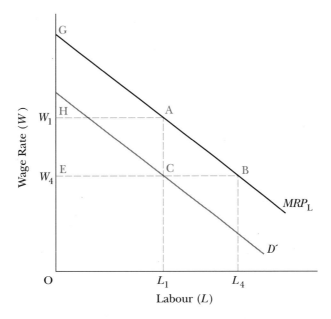

Figure 3.1 **Employer discrimination in the demand for labour**

Figure 3.1 can be used to show what happens in these circumstances. Let us assume for the sake of simplicity that there are no differences in productivity between different groups of workers. Since all workers have the same level of productivity, the marginal revenue product curve faced by the firm is the same, irrespective of which workers they employ. This is shown as MRP_L, the demand for labour curve (see Chapter 7, *Firms*). In a competitive labour market, a firm will employ labour up to the point where the wage equals the marginal revenue product of labour (which is why the MRP_L curve is also the firm's demand curve for labour). So, if the wage rate is W_1 the firm will employ L_1 workers. If the firm discriminates against members of a particular group, no workers from this group will be employed at W_1. This employer will simply exercise prejudice against them and, if this is a common practice amongst firms, the disadvantaged group will face unemployment.

What would happen if these workers were prepared to work at wages below W_1? Clearly, this will depend upon the extent to which the firm is prepared to discriminate since by employing disadvantaged workers at lower wages, the firm can lower its costs and thus increase its profits. Suppose that the firm is prepared to pay W_4 to L_1 workers from the disadvantaged group.

Question

Use Figure 3.1 to identify the volume of total profits which the firm would make from this discrimination.

For each unit of labour employed, the firm makes profits equal to the difference between revenue (MRP_L) and cost (W_4). At L_1 units of labour employed, total profits consist of the sum of differences between MRP_L and W_4 for each unit of labour employed between O and L_1. These total profits are represented by the area AGEC.

Now, if the firm only employed workers towards whom it is not prejudiced at a wage W_1, then total profits would be represented by AGH. Figure 3.1 shows that the firm gains additional profits from its discriminatory behaviour. By charging a discriminating wage of W_4 to disadvantaged workers, additional profits of ACEH are made by the firm. These additional profits compensate the employer for the prejudice held for disadvantaged workers.

This difference in wage rates paid to the two groups of workers results in a different demand curve for the disadvantaged group. This is represented by the line D' in Figure 3.1. For each level of employment the firm pays a lower wage rate to compensate for its prejudice against disadvantaged workers. This means that the demand curve for these workers is parallel but to the left of MRP_L (the demand curve for advantaged workers). Another way of looking at D' is to say that, at each wage rate, the firm is prepared to employ fewer disadvantaged workers than it will advantaged workers.

The problem, however, is that other firms may not hold the same prejudices. There could be another firm which has only one demand curve for all workers, as represented by MRP_L.

Question

Assume that a non-prejudiced employer hires labour at a wage rate of W_4. Using Figure 3.1, identify the following:

1   the total profits made by this firm
2   any additional profits made in comparison to the prejudiced firm.

The non-prejudiced employer, paying a wage rate of W_4, would employ L_4 workers regardless of their colour or creed. It would make total profits of BGE. By not being prejudiced this firm gains additional profits of BCA in comparison to the profits of AGEC made by the prejudiced firm. The problem, therefore, is that it is difficult for any one firm to indulge in prejudices without losing out to more profit-hungry non-discriminatory firms. Moreover, the additional amount of labour employed by these other firms would enable them to produce more output, thereby forcing down the prices of goods sold in the product market. This fall in product prices would drive the discriminatory firm out of business.

Although we have only considered a simple variant of the Becker approach to labour market discrimination, it is sufficient to highlight the most important conclusion. This is that discrimination can persist only if there are factors which limit the amount of competition in the labour market or in the product market. If these markets are competitive, the increased profitability of non-discriminating firms compared to discriminating ones will encourage non-discriminators to enter the market. This will put downward pressure on the price level and eventually force the higher-cost discriminating firms out of business. The extent of the inefficiency faced by discriminating firms is shown by the fact that, at wage W_4, discriminating firms employ L_1 workers, whereas a non-discriminating firm would employ L_4 workers and produce more output as a result. If, however, there are substantial barriers to entry which make it difficult for new firms to enter the market, competition will not erode discrimination.

The 'employer taste' model predicts that discrimination exists because employers do not want to employ certain groups of workers and will only do so if these workers are paid lower wages than those paid to workers in general. It thus provides an explanation of wage discrimination – equally productive workers being paid different wages. Other variations on this theme involve discrimination by workers and customers. The case study that follows provides an example of perceived customer discrimination by the Ford Motor Company.

Think global, act prejudiced?

Ford is better known for spraying its cars than re-spraying its employees. Indeed, in the bad old days when the company seemed to specialise in producing tinny boxes, the joke was that Ford's profits came from its skill in spraying metal onto paint rather than the other way around. But when an advertisement featuring line workers from its Dagenham plant in England was used in Poland, the black and brown faces of five employees were replaced with white faces (and hands).

The reason, according to Ford, was that the Poles are not used to seeing non-white faces, and it wanted to adapt its advertisement to suit local tastes. Unfortunately, when the original picture was reused back in Britain, the Polish version was used by mistake.

When they noticed what had happened, the line workers at Dagenham all walked out for three hours – a rare event in a British factory nowadays. Ford, which has apologised to the victims of the retouching and sent them a cheque for £1,500 ($2,320), blamed a

---

mistake by its advertising agency, Ogilvy & Mather. The agency cannot say who was responsible for the mistake, because it happened 18 months ago, and institutional memories in creative organisations clearly do not stretch back that far.

In some ways the Ford saga, which immediately provoked cheap jibes along the lines of 'Any colour you want as long as it's not black', unveils yet another problem of globalisation. In America and Europe, Ford is abolishing many of its regional fiefs and setting up transnational product groups. On the other hand, it has told its managers to demonstrate sensitivity to local peculiarities – particularly on the marketing side. Nobody at Ford seems to be apologising for what happened in Poland.

Source: *Economist*, February 1996

4.2   Statistical discrimination

Investment in education and training

Human capital theory has been used to show how investments in education and training lead to higher levels of earnings (see *Households*, Chapter 5). One reason why education and training are referred to as investments is because their benefits accrue over time and because training early in a career leads to higher earnings over the rest of an individual's working life. An important consideration, therefore, in the decision about whether to invest in additional human capital is the potential length of working life over which the benefits will be received. This would suggest that if certain groups of workers – most notably married women with family responsibilities – expect to have interruptions in their careers they will invest less time and energy in acquiring human capital. They thus face lower earnings as a result of having less training and lower skills. Because women themselves choose not to invest in skills and training, their lower earnings would not represent discrimination according to the definition used in this chapter. Of course, it could be argued that some women decide to focus on their family and domestic activities precisely because they perceive poor career prospects for women, prospects which are themselves a reflection of discrimination. This is an example of reverse causation.

The impact that career interruptions can have on the earnings profile of women can be shown using Figure 3.2. We shall initially assume that men come to the labour market with a certain amount of human capital and this determines their initial earnings. Subsequent training and promotion then result in their earnings increasing each year which is reflected in an upward sloping age–earnings profile. On the other hand, we shall also initially assume that all women expect to drop out of the labour force because of family responsibilities and, as a result, undertake less education and training before entering the labour market. Hence, their age–earnings profile is lower than that for men. For example, women may choose education and training courses, such as those providing clerical, secretarial or nursing skills, that enable them to enter occupations in which breaks from work incur the smallest penalty. Once they enter these occupations

Definition

Age–earnings profile

This shows how an individual's or group of individuals' earnings change over time.

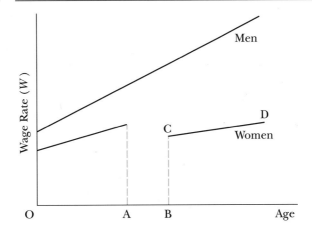

Figure 3.2 **The age–earnings profiles of men and women**

they receive less training than men because expected career interruptions reduce the returns from such investments and consequently their earnings profile rises at a lower rate than that for men. This is shown by the segment of the age–earnings profile up to age A. At age A, we assume that women drop out of the labour force and that when they enter the labour market again at age B, depreciation of their skills has resulted in a reduction in their potential earnings. In addition, the interruption has also resulted in a loss of seniority which has depressed their scope for earnings growth even further. This is shown by the segment CD.

Human capital theory therefore predicts that women will earn less than men because they do not expect to spend as long in the labour force. Intermittent work histories will also influence career choice. Fewer women will pursue skilled occupations and the professions, and more will be attracted to those jobs that enable them to more easily combine family responsibilities and labour market activity. Women are less likely to be promoted to higher level grades where these involve additional training since the monetary gains to the firm will, on average, be lower for women. The result is that promotions will be biased in favour of men.

We have, of course, made some very strong assumptions in painting the above picture of participation and occupational choice. Women now account for about half the total UK workforce (though women as a whole work shorter hours in employed labour and a larger proportion are part-time) and many women have as strong a commitment to their careers as men. The ability to combine family responsibilities and a career depends upon a number of different factors, not least of which will be the nature of the job and the availability and cost of such things as crèche and childcare facilities.

Productivity difference

The preceding discussion has only considered what would happen if all women undertake less investment in human capital than men. If men and women invest to the same extent, human capital theory suggests that no wage differences would be observed. What happens, however, if there are differences in skill levels both between genders and within gender groups? To consider this we will also make the additional assumption that firms do not know when recruiting workers who are the most productive. However, employers do know that, on average, women spend less time in the labour market than men because of career interruptions.

Figure 3.3 can be used to describe what will result. Since firms do not know each individual's potential productivity when hiring – both men and women may leave or may not be very productive once trained – they will set wages on the basis of what they do know, and that is the average level of productivity of each group. Since women have less training and work experience, their average level of productivity will be lower than men's. The two distributions show that there are variations in productivity among men and women. The fact that they overlap indicates that some women are more productive than some men. Let α be the *average* productivity of men and β the *average* productivity of women $(\alpha > \beta)$.

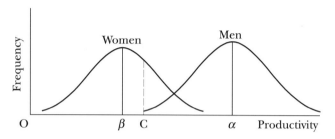

Figure 3.3 **The distribution of productivity for men and women**

For a man, individual productivity is equal to:

$$\alpha_i = \alpha + u_i$$

where u_i represents the differences in actual productivity above and below the average for all men.

Individual productivity for a woman is represented by:

$$\beta_i = \beta + u_i$$

The *average* level of human capital investment, and thus productivity, differs between men and women and this is reflected in the *average* earnings differential. On these assumptions, there is no discrimination, on average, against women. However, there is discrimination against *individual* women. Specifically, those women who have a productivity level to the right of the line above point C are being paid less than comparable men. It is also evident that the greater the variation in productivity within the female group, the more women will be underpaid compared with men who may be less productive. The curve showing the distribution of productivity would be wider, and, hence, there would be more overlap with the distribution curve for men. Discrimination here involves the unequal treatment of *individuals* on the basis of actual or perceived differences in the *average* characteristics of the groups to which they belong.

An additional point about potential productivity concerns the methods used by firms to try and identify which applicants are potentially the best employees. Firms use a variety of 'screening devices' when recruiting in order to establish the best potential employees. One such device is psychometric testing which many firms are now using to test applicants. However, it is possible that the very nature of these tests may be biased against women or ethnic minorities, adding further to the discrimination faced by individual workers.

Bringing selection procedures back on track

In early 1991 several ethnic minority guards at Paddington Station took British Rail to an industrial tribunal, alleging that the selection process for train drivers discriminated against applicants from ethnic minorities. In a settlement, BR agreed to work with the CRE to make the selection process fairer.

One element of this was a workshop with the Paddington guards to explore their test-taking behaviour. It became apparent that they were not, as the Americans say, test-wise. As a result, British Rail commissioned an open-learning pack which the guards could work on in their own time before retaking the test in September 1992.

The pack gave advice and tips on how to develop successful test-taking behaviour, as well as extensive practice materials to develop language proficiency. Six weeks were allowed, and the pack was supported with workshops at the beginning and at the end. The result? Five of the seven guards passed the tests and have gone forward for training.

Source: *Personnel Management,* December 1992

4.3   Empirical evidence

The neoclassical approach to discrimination produces a number of different explanations for why discrimination may exist in the labour market. Empirical analysis has tended, however, to focus not so much on testing these explanations but rather on establishing how much of an observed earnings differential between, say, men and women, can be accounted for by differences in their relative skill and education levels, their different work histories and differences in hours of work. That part of the actual differential that remains after allowing for these factors is usually attributed to labour market discrimination – it is the difference in earnings that cannot be explained by the productivity-related characteristics of the two groups. This decomposition is achieved using multiple regression analysis. The basic approach is as follows. Suppose that the earnings of men and women be determined by the following equations:

$$W_M = a_0 + a_1 E_M$$

$$W_F = b_0 + b_1 E_F$$

where W represents average earnings and E represents an education variable which determines earnings. In the first equation W_M represents the earnings of men, while E_M represents, say, the average number of 'A' levels held by men. In the second equation W_F is the average earnings of women, while E_F is the average number of 'A' levels held by women. The terms a_0 and b_0 are the intercepts of the two equations (see *Households*, Chapter 3). The observed average gender earnings differential – the difference in earnings between the two groups – can then be broken down by subtracting one equation from the other:

$$(W_M - W_F) = (a_0 - b_0) + a_1 E_M - b_1 E_F + (b_1 E_M - b_1 E_M)$$

The term $(b_1 E_M - b_1 E_M)$ has been artificially added to this equation. The equation can, as a result, be re-arranged to give us the expression:

$$(W_M - W_F) = (a_0 - b_0) + b_1(E_M - E_F) + (a_1 - b_1) E_M$$

The equation shows that the average wage differential – the difference in average earnings between men and women – is made up of three components.

The first term:

$$(a_0 - b_0)$$

is the part of the gender differential that is due to differences in earnings that take place on entry to the labour market. This will reflect differences in pre-entry human capital investments and/or pre-entry discrimination.

The second term:

$$b_1(E_M - E_F)$$

shows the contribution that differences in productivity-related characteristics between men and women make to the gender earnings differential. In other words, it shows the effect that gender differences in the average level of education have on the average earnings differential. This component represents that part of the earnings differential that does not reflect discrimination.

The final term:

$$(a_1 - b_1)E_M$$

measures the impact that unequal treatment has on the average wage differential. This is measured by the difference between the coefficients in the two equations on the variable measuring education. These coefficients show how education affects an individual's earnings. This term measures what happens when the labour market rewards productivity-related characteristics in different ways. It is this term, therefore, that is used as a measure of discrimination – women's productivity-related characteristics are treated differently from those of men for reasons that have nothing to do with the characteristics themselves. So, for example, suppose that women with 4 'A' levels earn less than men with 4 'A' levels (assuming all other things equal). This approach says that this can only come about because of discrimination. The extent of this discrimination is captured by the amount that the woman is paid less than her male comparator, which, in a model like the one above, is reflected in a smaller coefficient on the education variable in the female earnings equation compared with the earnings equation estimated for men.

The following example provides a demonstration of how the model can be estimated. Wright and Ermisch (1991) conducted an analysis of discrimination against women in the UK using data from the 1980 *Women and Employment Survey*. A total of 2094 employed women aged between 16 and 59 were interviewed in a nationally representative sample. Alongside this survey of women, husbands of those 1868 women who were married at the time were also interviewed.

Everyone was asked, among other things, their wage per hour, their place of residence, and any educational qualifications they had. Using a statistical procedure developed in a previous study (Wright and Ermisch, 1990), a variable for the potential experience of individuals was calculated. Since, unfortunately, information on the work experience of individuals was not collected in the survey, this was estimated using other information. Variables for education were specified to model the impact on wages of individuals holding CSEs, 'O' levels, 'A' levels, degrees or any other qualifications.

Unlike the model which was introduced at the start of Section 4.2, wages in this model are assumed to depend upon more than one variable. The method of multiple regression (see *Households*, Chapter 3; *Firms*, Chapter 5) is used by Wright and Ermisch to regress wages on a number of variables. It should also be noted that in this study, the logarithms of wages is taken as the dependent variable (see Chapter 1 for an explanation of logarithms). The wage equations for males and females are reported in Table 3.5. Note that for ease of exposition, a number of the additional variables used in the study, such as those representing the regions in which individuals reside, are not reported here.

Table 3.5   **Wage equations for males and females, Great Britain, 1980**

	Males (sample size 1868)		Females (sample size 2094)	
	Variable	t-statistic	Variable	t-statistic
Intercept	0.595	11.70	0.521	14.43
Potential experience	0.246	6.56	0.044	1.52
Education:				
CSE(s)	0.101	3.84	0.083	3.66
'O' level(s)	0.203	8.23	0.116	5.28
'A' level(s)	0.316	7.96	0.210	4.74
Degree	0.509	21.01	0.508	21.63
Other	0.099	1.60	0.062	0.58
R^2	0.249		0.224	

Source: Wright and Ermisch, 1991, p.516

On examining the two wage equations we need to check a number of features. First, we need to check the *sign* of the coefficients for each variable. In the wage equations for both males and females all the variables shown have a positive sign. This means that all these variables have a positive influence on wages. For example, the positive sign for potential experience means that potential experience is positively correlated with wages – there is a positive premium on experience. As potential experience increases, then, on average, both males and females should get a higher wage. The coefficients for all of the education variables are also positive for both genders. For example, the coefficient on the variable for males with 'O' levels is 0.203; this means that there is a premium in terms of higher wages for male workers obtaining 'O' levels compared to someone with no qualifications. The comparable value for females is 0.116.

Second, we need to check the statistical significance of the coefficients. To do this the t-statistics associated with each coefficient can be examined (see *Firms*, Chapter 5). A t-statistic greater than 1.96 for a particular coefficient means that we can have 95 per cent confidence in the statistical importance of that coefficient. In Table 3.5, with the exception of a t-statistic of 1.60 for 'Other' qualifications, all the reported t-statistics for males are higher than 1.96. A t-statistic of 0.58 for 'Other' qualifications and a t-statistic of 1.52 for potential experience are reported for females. Econometricians often estimate equations in which some coefficients have low t-statistics, but this reduces their confidence in the results obtained. We might also be somewhat cautious about the two wage equations in Table 3.5 since the R^2s are 0.249 and 0.224 for males and females respectively. This means that over 70 per cent of the variation in wages is not explained by these equations.

The key thing to note about these equations is that, in all cases, the coefficients for males are larger than the coefficients for females. Take, for example, the wage premium for 'A' levels. In the equation for males the premium on 'A' levels (the size of the coefficient) is 0.316, but in the equation for females it is only 0.210. The premium on potential experience shows an even wider disparity with a coefficient value of 0.246 for males and only 0.044 for females.

A formal measure of these differences in the size of coefficients is calculated by using the method of decomposition explained earlier in this section. Look back and make sure you have grasped that the differential between male and female earnings can be explained in terms of two main components:

1   the part of the earnings differential which is due to differences in productivity

2   the part of the earnings differential which is due to male and female workers of equal productivity being rewarded differently.

For the wage equations reported in Table 3.5 and the additional variables not reported in the table, Wright and Ermisch derive the estimate that 11.8 per cent of the wage differential is attributed to (1) and 88.2 per cent to (2). This means that unequal rewards for the same productivity are found to be more important when explaining wage differentials than differences in productivity. It should be noted, of course, that these results are qualified by the small R^2s of their wage equations. It should also be noted that Wright and Ermisch estimate a number of other wage equations with different specifications, which give less weight to the importance of discrimination. Nevertheless, even taking these cautious notes into account, the results reported in Table 3.5 provide a revealing insight into the extent to which discrimination takes place against women in the labour market.

It is more difficult to obtain empirical evidence about racial discrimination than for sex discrimination. Substantial earnings differentials have been found to exist between white and ethnic minority workers, with the latter earning about 10 per cent less than whites (Blackaby *et al.*, 1994). A significant part of this differential reflects the occupational and industrial segregation of ethnic minorities. Indeed, while there is evidence that ethnic minorities face wage discrimination and, in particular, face lower rates of return to education and general training, it is discrimination in terms of occupational access which is found to be of most significance (McNabb and Psacharopoulos, 1981).

However, this type of analysis only compares the earnings of people in work and, as we mentioned in Section 2.2, ethnic minorities are significantly more likely to be unemployed than white workers. This raises two issues.

1   Why do workers from ethnic minorities face worse employment prospects than white workers?

2   What impact does this have on the earnings differential between the two groups?

A study of unemployment among Britain's ethnic minorities (Blackaby *et al.*, 1995) found that although employees from minority groups had less favourable characteristics (in terms of the attributes that affect the likelihood of employment, such as age, education and so on), the main reason for their different unemployment experiences was discrimination. However, significant differences were found between the ethnic groups considered. For example, relatively high unemployment among workers of West Indian origin reflected their unfavourable characteristics rather than discrimination. In contrast, unemployment among workers of Indian descent was primarily the result of discrimination. They experienced relatively more unemployment even though their characteristics were, in fact, more favourable in terms of the likelihood of finding employment than those of white workers. Finally, the analysis indicated that discrimination against workers of Pakistani and Bangladeshi origin was greater than against those of Indian descent. The authors attribute the latter finding to the fact that workers of Pakistani and Bangladeshi descent, 'have reacted to discrimination in a different way by choosing to be more isolated and have adopted an economic structure which is more autarchic compared to other groups. Greater economic disadvantage is the consequence of this' (Blackaby *et al.*, 1995, p.25).

The same authors also examine the interaction between unemployment and wage discrimination among ethnic minority workers. They find that the limited employment prospects faced by ethnic minority workers is significantly more severe than the earnings disadvantage they face. As unemployment in Britain increased in the 1980s and early 1990s, ethnic minorities suffered disproportionately. Even ethnic minority employees with favourable productivity-related characteristics (those with better earnings potential than white workers) have become unemployed, thereby increasing the wage gap between white and non-white employees.

5   Segmented labour markets

In recent years different explanations of how labour markets operate have been proposed by a number of economists dissatisfied with neoclassical theory in general and its explanation for labour market disadvantage in particular. Some of these alternatives simply extend neoclassical models to include the effects of various institutional factors. Others, however, have sought to develop a new theoretical approach. All reject a predominantly competitive analysis and emphasize instead the fragmented nature of labour markets and the importance of institutional and social influences upon pay and employment. A common label for these alternative approaches is segmented labour market theory. The underlying theme of these approaches is that the labour market should be viewed as a collection of parts or segments. One segment may consist of high-waged, male, white workers, for example, and another of low-waged, female, non-white workers.

The concept of a segmented labour market has been applied in a variety of ways. Analyses differ in the outcomes of interest (pay, employment stability or mobility), in the delineation of segments (by job, industry, gender, race or age) and in the methodology of investigation, whether qualitative or econometric (McNabb and Ryan, 1990). There is, however, a consensus among segmentation economists about the way the labour market can be conceptualized and about how segments function. This convergence of views is primarily encapsulated in one particular variant of the segmentation approach, the dual labour market theory.

5.1   Dual labour market theory

According to this theory, the labour market is composed of self-contained sub-markets or segments. Segmentation economists argue that ignoring the different identities of these segments and the constraints they place on the workers makes it impossible to understand the nature of labour market disadvantage. Basically, the dual approach hypothesises that a dichotomy has developed over time between a high-wage primary segment and a low-wage secondary segment. Working conditions in the primary segment are generally favourable; there is steady employment and job security, and the rules that govern the organization of employment are well defined and equitable. The characteristics of secondary employment, on the other hand, are less favourable. Work here has little job security and there are high turnover rates. There are few opportunities for training or advancement and the work tends to be menial and repetitive.

Corresponding to this duality in the characteristics of jobs is a further distinction between primary (core) and secondary (periphery) industrial sectors. In the core sectors, firms have monopoly power, production is on a large scale, extensive use is made of capital-intensive methods of production and there is strong trade union representation. These establishments operate in national and international product markets. In contrast, employment in the periphery is located in small firms that employ labour-intensive methods of production, operate in competitive local product markets and have low levels of unionization. Although they are not entirely coincidental, there is a considerable overlap between primary jobs and core industries, on the one hand, and secondary jobs and periphery industries on the other.

In contrast to the supply side and individual factors which dominate neoclassical models of the labour market, segmentation theory emphasizes demand side and institutional factors. Specifically, segmentation in the labour market arises because of the characteristics of jobs rather than differences in worker attributes, such as education and training. Secondary jobs, however, are filled largely by groups whose attachment to paid employment has traditionally been weak, notably non-whites, females and youths. Primary segment jobs, on the other hand, tend to be the preserve of 'prime age' white males.

The segmentation that exists in the labour market primarily reflects the nature of internal labour markets within which primary and secondary jobs are found. Internal labour markets can best be thought of as the type of labour market that exists within an organization. At one extreme, the internal and external markets may be very similar: the structure of wages and the allocation of workers within the organization will be determined simply by external market conditions. In this case, the internal market is similar to what is happening outside the organization. At the other extreme

Definition

Internal labour market

This is the labour market that exists within a firm. It determines how wages are set and labour is allocated within the firm.

are organizations (usually large employers) in which wage structures and employment policies are set apart from external labour market conditions. Such internal labour markets will often be highly structured and regulated, and have employment systems that confer significant advantages to those already employed in the organization – 'insiders' – compared to outsiders. This is because access to jobs within the firm is granted preferentially, even exclusively, to existing members of the organization via promotion along well defined 'job ladders', often on the basis of seniority rather than productivity. Outsiders, on the other hand, have access to only a limited number of low level positions.

Pay rates within structured internal labour markets do not respond to demand or supply conditions in the external market but rather to the specific requirements and needs of the organization. Imbalances that develop over time in the supply and demand of particular types of labour *vis-à-vis* the external labour market are dealt with through a variety of non-wage adjustments, including recruitment and training, job redesign and subcontracting. Crucially, emphasis is on the institutional and social nature of internal labour markets rather than on any efficiency or economic considerations that may be proposed for their emergence. In order to provide an explanation of labour market disadvantage it is clearly important to understand why some organizations adopt employment systems that are protected from external market forces and why workers from disadvantaged groups have only limited access to the favourable conditions of work they provide.

Three features of the segmented labour market theory clearly differentiate it from neoclassical labour economics.

Job rewards

Segmented labour market theory views the labour market as systematically differentiating the job rewards achieved by comparable individuals. The high pay of primary workers cannot be explained simply in terms of their higher quality of labour since many secondary workers are capable of performing well, given the opportunity to do so. The labour market is thus seen as a key ingredient in the generation of economic inequality and not a passive mirror of the inequalities which people bring to it. Wage structures are differentiated by employer characteristics rather than worker attributes.

This is not to argue that all secondary workers are as good as all primary workers. Labour quality will, in general, be higher in primary jobs. The important point, however, is that differences in labour quality across jobs is less than that in pay and the direction of causality between pay and labour quality is reversed. Wage structures are taken as given, differentiated by employer characteristics rather than worker attributes. Under such conditions high-paying employers can take their pick from the applicant queue and rationally hire labour of high quality. The compensation, however, is only partial, with the differences in job rewards exceeding that in worker quality.

Labour quality and labour productivity must, therefore, be carefully distinguished. Productivity is an attribute of the job rather than the worker and depends upon the equipment available at the workplace and the product market served. Primary workers have higher productivity than secondary segment workers because of the jobs in which they work rather than because of who they are. Were they confined to secondary employment, with its labour-intensive techniques and unfavourable product markets, their productivity would be correspondingly lower. Worker quality, in contrast, is defined in terms of attitudes, behaviour and values.

In many instances, the skills that exist at the workplace involve learning by doing and are characterized by their informality in contrast to the more formal investment framework proposed by human capital theory. Acquisition of these skills involves being 'shown the ropes' by fellow workers and is not a distinct process within the firm. It is more a process of socialization that involves being accepted by existing workers, as well as the internalization of particular sets of norms and values, than a formal training programme. Certain groups of workers are thus segregated from better jobs because they are less acceptable socially rather than because they lack ability. Employers may also believe that particular characteristics, such as gender and race, correlate with those values and norms which characterize primary segment employment.

A similar divergence of interpretation also exists for employment stability. It is argued that the role in the family (for example youths and married females) or in society (for example inner-city, non-whites) of many secondary segment workers may mean lower intrinsic job stability than that displayed by primary workers. The segmentation approach, however, emphasizes the instability of jobs not workers. Many secondary workers, particularly married females, may be interested in and available for steady work but are denied access to it. Thus while the supply side does exert an influence, it is seen as less important than the demand side and social institutions in explaining the differentiation of outcomes in the labour market.

The role of market forces

The second distinguishing feature of the segmented labour market theory concerns the role of market forces in affecting labour outcomes. Although the impact of market forces is not denied, their role is seen to be in the product market rather than the labour market. The part played by labour market influences, particularly excess demand but also trade unions, is seen as subsidiary to such features of the product market as demand variability, employer power and production technology. Similarly, internal labour markets are thought to develop not so much as the result of the type of technology and the skills employed by the firm, as of the power relationships and control strategies that are required within the organization.

A key distinction employed in the segmentation literature is that between those jobs and workers in firms with structured internal labour markets and those in firms which are open to external labour market conditions. What, then, are the consequences of this distinction for the structure of wages? As we discussed earlier, jobs in the primary segment are generated by employers in core sectors whose ability to pay is boosted by large size, high capital intensity and high profitability, as well as a degree of monopoly power in their product markets. Secondary jobs are provided by firms located in the periphery, where firms are smaller and capital intensity is lower, and product markets are highly competitive on price. According to the theory, wages in the periphery will, as a result, be set at competitive levels which, since the secondary segment is characterized by an abundant supply of labour, will be low.

The advantages enjoyed by core firms do not, however, automatically result in favourable employment conditions for workers. Powerful employers can use their substantial resources to deny special advantages to employees through actions such as union busting and the relocation of production to low-wage, low-unionized regions. Conversely, even highly competitive product markets may yield core rather than periphery jobs if employees are well organized and able to fend off competition from home and abroad – as in parts of the coal, trucking and construction sectors in the US.

In any event, core employers need not extend primary jobs to all their employees. As a range of functions, particularly services such as cleaning and catering, is generally limited to secondary status either within the firm or in subcontractors, the contours of segmentation run through individual firms, not simply between sectors. Similarly, small firms may not offer just the low pay and job instability of the classic sweatshop, they may be the source of jobs with the high rewards offered by producers of speciality and high technology goods.

The differentiation of pay within internal labour markets is explained in neoclassical theories in terms of firm-specific skills which can only be developed through on-the-job training. The senior workers who possess such skills must be sufficiently well paid and secure in their jobs to ensure their willingness to train others. A sharper differentiation from neoclassical analysis, however, is achieved by elaborating a further factor, namely custom. The stability of work groups within internal labour markets is a favourable environment for the generation of norms or accepted ways of doing things. Employers must accommodate such norms if production is to continue without constant interruptions. Custom can be seen as both the accumulated total of norms which develop often quite informally as well as a norm in itself – the requirement that established practices be respected. Thus two groups of workers for whom the accepted practice is that they should be paid the same will often be paid the same, even if the presence of excess demand for one and excess supply for the other calls for different pay rates. Similarly, the job evaluation techniques that determine pay in many internal labour markets reward skill and responsibility in proportions which vary not with the relative availability of workers in the external market but with their relative position within the organization.

Tastes and attitudes

In contrast to the neoclassical assumptions of given tastes and attitudes, the segmented labour market theory treats both of these as endogenous. In other words, the prejudices that some groups hold against others, the attitudes that some disadvantaged groups have about work and so on are not taken as given. There are reasons why these prejudices and attitudes develop as they do and understanding these is essential in order to understand how the labour market operates to the detriment of these groups. Thus, on the one hand, unstable inner-city employment can be attributed to an adverse interaction between individual attitudes to work and to wider issues, while on the other hand, it may be attributable to the type of work which may be repetitive, menial and low paid. The experience of secondary jobs cumulatively leads to disadvantaged workers developing high quit rates and other bad work habits. Workers employed in bad jobs become bad workers. Similarly, the confinement of married women to secondary segment jobs reflects preferences that are moulded by their subordinate positions within both family and society. Finally, our understanding of discrimination can only be achieved once we recognize that some groups in society actually benefit from it.

5.2 The roots of segmentation

Why does segmentation occur? One approach to this question focuses upon the evolution of the product markets, from the competitive and the localized to the producer dominated, and from the national to an international market. Technological change makes capital-intensive methods of production possible. Employers, however, are unwilling to undertake large-scale investment unless the product demand is stable and predictable; when demand is variable, labour-intensive techniques are preferred. A growing division is found between firms which cater for stable markets and those in unstable markets. Firms with stable product demand create primary conditions of employment, including, notably, job security. Firms which face unstable demand operate in the secondary segment of the labour market.

The contours of segmentation, defined according to stability, fluctuate depending on the state of the economy. When labour markets are tight and product markets favourable, employers seek to tie workers to the firm by expanding the number of primary jobs. However, when there is a downturn, particularly one that proves longer and deeper than anticipated, employers seek to increase the share of secondary jobs, emphasizing the virtues of functional flexibility, in terms of workers being able to undertake a number of different tasks (multi-skilling) and numerical flexibility – varying the number of workers through lay-offs and short-time working.

The theory of segmentation advanced by radical economists (for example, Rebitzer, 1993) takes a different tack and focuses upon changing systems of organization within capitalist firms. The key to segmentation, they believe, is the strategy employers use for the control and motivation of their workforces. Chapter 1, Section 3.3 of this book briefly discussed systems of control within organizations. Systems of labour control that had been developed prior to the 1950s, notably the personalized discipline of 'simple control' and the impersonal machine-pacing of 'technical control', proved increasingly ineffective as some firms turned into large corporations and worker organization became stronger and more influential. These large employers turned instead to 'bureaucratic control'. As well as providing job security and career prospects in order to win the loyalty of employees, they developed impersonal discipline and monitoring procedures. Internal labour markets emerged and with them the differences between the job rewards of primary employers and those of employers who lacked the incentive to abandon the secondary segment.

The forces which led some employers to create primary jobs thus began with the emergence of the large corporation. Simple control, the open, highly visible, direct command rule by supervisors over subordinates, proved less viable in large plants; the interdependence between workers in mass production systems made it difficult to measure the output of individual workers. Additionally, the power wielded by large firms over product markets permitted them to take a longer view of the market and its likely level of stability. As a result they could offer superior job rewards. At the same time, worker solidarity was undermined by the introduction of job ladders to achieve status differentiation between workers. The rationale for the job ladders was to motivate workers and generate commitment rather than develop skills. The internal labour markets of primary employers represents a sophisticated version of the traditional capitalist strategy of 'divide and rule'.

Within the radical approach, the position of disadvantaged groups is seen as reinforcing the tendency toward segmentation. Segmentation limits the opportunities available to women and minority groups while the forces which support discrimination also help promote segmentation. The differentiation that exists between jobs is easier to maintain when it is associated with differences in workers' characteristics rather than the job itself.

In recent years there have been a number of changes in both product and labour markets in the UK which have led some researchers to rethink the nature of segmentation. Product markets have become more competitive, not simply in terms of increased pressure for lower prices but also in terms of demands for higher quality products and more frequent changes in product specification. In order to achieve and maintain a competitive advantage in these changing conditions, some firms have adopted employment policies which seek to motivate and promote commitment from workers. At the same time, there has been considerable deregulation in the labour market in Britain. This has allowed firms to be more flexible in determining the conditions under which they employ workers and some firms have taken the opportunity to directly reduce their labour costs thereby moving towards secondary segment employment. Other organizations, however, have used the opportunity to introduce innovations such as team-working, multi-skilling and quality circles. Attempts to promote motivation and commitment are based on the philosophy of human resource management, thus moving the organizations into (or further into) the primary segment. However, the types of organizations which benefit from employment practices that foster stability and commitment are not only those traditionally found in the core sector and the simplistic dichotomies that have traditionally underpinned the segmentation approach have given way to differences that are a matter of degree rather than of kind.

The following case study examines the consequences of deregulating the UK docks industry. This is an industry that has used deregulation in the labour market as a way to directly reduce its labour costs. In the process, however, it has moved from the organized, primary sector into the secondary sector.

Docks: The payback

Docks deregulation has led to more millionaire managers, more redundancies, and most alarmingly, more accidents at work. Recent events at Tilbury demonstrate this dramatically. Chief executive John McNab has just pocketed £5 million from the sale of the port to Forth Port Authority. The authority, incidentally, paid nearly four times for the shares than the price paid to the dockers who were made redundant. Forth paid £81.01 for each share whereas at Tilbury the dockers were forced to sell their share for a maximum of £22.72.

To make the sale of the port an attractive proposition, the number of dockers – or cargo handlers as they are now called – has been slashed from nearly 800 to about 300 since deregulation five years ago. And the accident rate among those left has more than doubled. Before deregulation, the national dock accident rate was 3.1 per cent. Since then it has risen to 7.2 per cent. And this figure probably understates the real rate because of the increased use of casuals workers, who are less inclined to report accidents.

At Tilbury, the accident rate is even higher – it stands at 7.8 per cent. This figure comes from statistics compiled by the Port Safety Organisation, to which the employers are affiliated.

Stress and fatigue are obvious factors in this increase. And that is hardly surprising when more arduous conditions of employment have been introduced at Tilbury, including compulsory overtime and double shift working. A recent Health and Safety Executive information sheet on dock work fatigue stated:

> The causes of fatigue can include not only severe physical effort but also the effect of working at times that are contrary to the body's natural inclinations, e.g. at night or on some systems of shift work, intense concentration and working continuously for long periods ... This can lead to stevedores failing to ensure that they are in a safe position with the result that they are hit by a falling object or struck by a swinging load.

John Connolly, national docks and waterways secretary of the T&G, commented on the similarities of what has happened at Medway:

> Tilbury was sold to the management and employees buy-out group for just £34 million and they have now sold it for £130 million ... The position is very similar to what happened in Medway where shares were sold to staff but were soon followed by an exercise of cutting staff numbers and reducing their terms and conditions of employment. When the men refused to accept these proposals they were made redundant and were paid just £2.50 for each of their shares. Six months later these same shares were sold for £38.50 each in a takeover.

> At Tilbury the signs have been evident for two years that the port has been consistently reducing the number of people employed and imposing more arduous conditions of employment, while bringing in casual labour.

> Earlier this year tenders to buy the port were asked for and the successful tender came from Forth Ports Authority who bought it as a low cost base, with a low workforce with reduced conditions of employment. This had been done on the back of casual labour and imposed conditions.
>
> At the same time there has been a significant increase in industrial injuries in the ports generally, despite the efforts of the Port Safety Organisation.
>
> Tug workers are also suffering from attacks on their working conditions. 'There has been reduced manning on tugs combined with increased working hours,' said John. 'The Health and Safety Executive has stated that the longer hours, use of casual workers, and worsening conditions has led to an increase in stress and fatigue in the industry.'
>
> Source: Pentelow, 1996

5.3   Empirical analysis

Three key hypotheses have been the focus of empirical evaluation of the segmented labour market theory. First, that the labour market can be represented as comprising at least two well-defined and self-contained segments. Second, that the labour market behaviour of workers and firms in each segment requires a different set of behavioural hypotheses. Finally, that there is limited mobility between the segments reflecting institutional and social barriers in the labour market rather than a lack of productive ability among lower segment workers.

The proposition that there is a clear and evident separation between a primary and secondary segment of the labour market represents a principal hypothesis of the dual approach. It is one, however, that receives only modest support in the empirical literature (see McNabb and Ryan, 1990). In general, there is little evidence of clusters of firms into core and periphery groups on the basis of the various characteristics that supposedly define the two segments. Recent work for the UK, however, has found that while firms do not cluster into distinct groups or sectors, there is clear evidence that some characteristics, in particular characteristics such as monopoly power, size of establishment and union density (variables that are associated with the core sector) are strongly correlated, and that the correlations identify features of the underlying industrial structure that are consistent with a segmented labour market approach (McNabb and Whitfield, 1996). Similarly, the employment of women and casual workers, and the use of part-time labour are also correlated, highlighting the importance of gender in identifying differences between firms. Moreover, the pattern of correlations that emerges from this work is also found to affect labour market outcomes such as the incidence of low pay, employment stability, and so on. Thus, while there is little evidence to support the notion of duality or even of identifiable segments, the industrial structure, the product market and its link with the labour market are consistent with a segmentation approach.

Much of the empirical work on the segmentation approach has, however, dealt with the unequal treatment of comparable workers between segments. Initial attempts to test this hypothesis focused upon whether incremental changes in labour quality are more highly rewarded in the primary segment than in the secondary segment. The basic empirical approach adopted to test this hypothesis involves two steps. First, a sample of workers is divided into two groups to represent the primary and secondary segments. Second, multiple regression techniques are used to estimate wage equations (similar to the ones considered earlier) so that the basic hypothesis can be tested. In general, the proposition that education is rewarded more for primary workers than for employees in the secondary segment is supported by the results of a number of studies (McNabb and Ryan, 1990). Typically, these find negligible gains in annual earnings among (variously classified) secondary segment workers from increases in years of schooling and work experience. This contrasts with the marked benefits recorded for both in the primary segment. Some contradictory evidence may, however, also be found in the literature. Several studies report that the returns to schooling and age, while lower in the secondary than in primary segment, are nevertheless economically strong and statistically significant.

The example detailed below, based on work by McNabb (1987), tests for segmentation using earnings functions estimated for core and periphery industry groups. The basis for this division is two variables typically associated with disadvantaged employment: the proportion of women employed and the proportion of employees not covered by a collective agreement. On the basis of these two variables, industries are defined as either being core or periphery.

The data in the example came from the 1975 *General Household Survey* in which male employees of ages 16 to 64 were interviewed. The key variables were:

Annual earnings	the dependent variable
Schooling	years of schooling
Experience	years of work experience
Experience^2	the experience variable squared
Weeks	weeks worked per year

The schooling and experience variables provide an indicator of the human capital of each worker. The more experience and education an individual has, the higher the quality of his labour. It should be noted that if the employee has worked for only a few weeks this will adversely affect his annual earnings, thereby giving a false picture of the relationship between these earnings and human capital. The weeks variable has been included to control for this.

Two of the wage equations reported in McNabb (1987) are shown in Table 3.6; the first is for the periphery segment, the second is for the core segment. The dependent variable is the logarithm of annual earnings. Note also that the weeks variable is expressed in logarithms (log Weeks).

For both segments of the labour market, the human capital characteristics of workers are positively correlated with earnings. In the periphery segment, for example, a coefficient of 0.67 shows the positive relationship

Table 3.6 **Industry earnings functions**

	Periphery segment	**Core segment**
Intercept	1.39	2.12
Schooling	0.67*	0.63*
Experience	0.65*	0.55*
Experience^2	−0.0009*	−0.0008*
log Weeks	1.21*	1.10*
R^2	0.4707	0.4517
Sample size	1641	3373

Note: * denotes that a coefficient is significant to the 1 per cent level or better (we can have 99 per cent confidence in its statistical significance)

Source: McNabb, 1987, p.262, Table 1

between years of schooling and earnings. Note that there is a negative sign on the Experience^2 term. This is a standard result in labour economics showing that beyond middle age, as workers get older, the effect of their experience has a diminishing impact on their earnings. Since a square of 50 years experience is much higher than the square of, say, 5 years experience, the squared term puts a greater weight on many years experience, thereby picking up the declining productivity of older workers.

It should be noted that all of the variables, apart from intercepts, are reported to be significant at the 1 per cent level, which means that we can have 99 per cent confidence in their statistical significance (see Chapter 5, *Firms*). In addition, the R^2s for both equations are just under 0.5, which means that nearly 50 per cent of the variation in wages is summarized by each regression equation.

We can now turn to a comparison of the coefficients for each equation. The dual labour market approach predicts that the return on human capital characteristics should be less in the periphery segment than in the core segment. In fact, Table 3.6 shows that the return on human capital is slightly higher in the periphery segment. The return on schooling is 0.67 in the periphery segment compared to 0.63 in the core segment. Similarly, the return on experience is 0.65 in the periphery segment and 0.55 in the core segment. In this example data, however, the coefficients are, in fact, very small, and it cannot be concluded that there is any significant difference between the return on human capital in the two segments. This particular evidence shows that a dual labour market does not exist for segments defined according to the proportion of women employed and the proportion of employees not covered by a collective agreement.

Evidence of segmentation can, however, be found if we look at the earnings of particular occupations. Table 3.7 overleaf, again based on the analysis of the 1975 *General Household Survey* data by McNabb (1987), reports wage equations for professional and semi-skilled manual workers.

Table 3.7 **Occupational wage equations**

	Professional	Semi-skilled manual
Intercept	−0.054	2.89
Schooling	0.047*	0.007
Experience	0.077*	0.034*
Experience^2	−0.011*	−0.0006*
log Weeks	1.79*	1.10*
R^2	0.556	0.500
Sample size	254	796

Note: * denotes that a coefficient is significant to the 1 per cent level or better (we can have 99 per cent confidence in its statistical significance)

Source: McNabb, 1987, p.264, Table 3

Exercise 3.1

Comparing the two wage equations in Table 3.7, examine the evidence that professional workers enjoy a higher return to their human capital than semi-skilled manual workers.

From Exercise 3.1 you can see that Table 3.7 provides some evidence for the existence of occupational segments. Workers in semi-skilled manual occupations are treated differently from professional workers. As they gain more human capital, in the form of schooling and experience, semi-skilled workers are not reimbursed, for each unit of human capital, to the same extent as professional workers. This confirms the insight of segmentation theorists, as discussed in Section 5.1, that workers are rewarded differently according to the jobs they do. Even if workers have the same human cognition characteristics, the amount they are paid depends on the job they do. This conflicts with neoclassical theory which predicts that workers will be rewarded proportionately according to their level of human capital

The final hypothesis that has received attention in the literature concerns the alleged lack of mobility between primary and secondary segments. This issue has received some attention in recent years as longitudinal data has become available. Concerning the rate of movement between segments, studies which impose clear frontiers between primary and secondary segments have generally found rates of upward movement in excess of the low levels suggested by the descriptive dual labour literature. Moreover, a considerable proportion of this upward mobility can be associated with the possession of increased labour quality.

6 Policy issues

There are several issues we need to address concerning anti-discrimination policy. The first involves the different policy prescriptions that can be derived from the theories we have considered. The various theoretical approaches provide different explanations for why discrimination occurs and it follows that these will produce different types of policies to deal with discrimination. Second, the empirical work that has been carried out to explain gender and racial earnings differences also provide significant insights into policy issues. Finally, we can examine the actual policies that have been introduced to deal with discrimination and the impact they have had.

The neoclassical analysis of discrimination points to two main issues that need to be addressed by anti-discrimination policy: the need to promote competition in product and labour markets, and the need to break down informational barriers that act against particular groups of workers. There are, however, divergent views as to how both can be achieved and not all neoclassical economists accept the efficacy of direct intervention in wage and employment determination. According to this approach, the aim would be to promote a 'market solution' for dealing with labour market discrimination and propose policies which enhance competition and reduce the restrictive practices of employers and trade unions. Such policies, they argue, will promote greater choice in education and housing markets, improve occupational mobility and provide the right environment for the elimination of discrimination through market forces.

Other commentators, however, stress the prevalence of market failure and the need for government intervention. Such intervention need not be direct, such as fixing wage levels, but could take place through compensatory public expenditure and legislation which offsets the disadvantages faced by particular groups in society. For example, we have already noted that the earnings of married women are depressed by intermittent work patterns due to family responsibilities. In part, this can be addressed by the extension of job protected maternity leave. Although Britain has had maternity leave legislation since 1976, it is far from universal. In addition, although it was traditional for women not to return to work when their children were young, this trend is declining. In 1979, 24 per cent of young mothers with children under the age of 9 months were in employment. By 1989 this had increased to around 46 per cent (Joshi *et al.*, 1985). In part this reflects changes in social norms about women with young children working. Increased financial pressures on families and a change in employers' attitudes have also contributed. The evidence indicates that women with job protected maternity leave have significantly higher earnings than women who do not, other things equal. Significant improvements in the earnings of women have also been found for policies aimed at improving childcare provision. These increase participation, enable women to work full-time rather than part-time and thus increase women's earnings: empirical analysis indicates that these effects are especially significant for lone parents. Other policy measures include retraining schemes which enable women returning to the labour market to come back to jobs similar to the ones they left and restructuring jobs to ensure that they can be done by people who also have domestic responsibilities.

Segmentation theory, in contrast, emphasizes occupational segregation and the inability of women and ethnic minorities to gain access to favourable jobs. This does not reflect a lack of ability on their part but, rather, barriers to entry to favourable employment. The most commonly advocated policies are those involving positive discrimination, such as job quotas for more favourable jobs or the disproportionate provision of more resources for education and training, and affirmative action policies which encourage the recruitment and promotion of disadvantaged workers.

Direct intervention in wage determination in Britain has primarily been achieved through the use of equal pay legislation. The efficacy of direct wage adjustment as a policy to overcome discrimination depends, in part, upon the impact it has on employment. Some economists argue that the relationship between wage increases and employment is such that the resulting job losses would be small. In addition, it is possible that increasing wage levels in secondary segment jobs would break the link which is seen to exist in a segmented labour market between low pay, job instability and the lack of access to better paid jobs. Paying higher wages in secondary jobs may encourage commitment on the part of secondary workers.

In Britain, the Equal Pay Act was passed in 1970 to ensure that people doing broadly similar work should be paid the same. The Act provided for a gradual move towards full implementation by 1975. In 1975, the Sex Discrimination Act was also passed which made it illegal to discriminate on the basis of gender and marital status in aspects of employment other than pay. The Sex Discrimination Act was supposed to check any tendency that the Equal Pay Act might have to make it harder for women to get jobs. In so far as women did different work from men – and there was evidence that some employers altered job content to ensure that dissimilar work was done (see Snell *et al.*, 1981) – then the Equal Pay Act would not impact on the gender wage differential. In 1983 an amendment to the Act was introduced that both consolidated the original legislation and extended it to cover equal pay for equal work within a firm. This extension of the law came from the EU and, among other things, sought to address the practice of re-defining jobs in order to pay women less than men. As far as racial discrimination is concerned, the 1968 Race Relations Act outlawed unequal treatment in terms of pay and employment practices.

Whether the introduction of equal pay legislation has had a positive effect on the relative earnings of women has been subject to empirical scrutiny (Zabalza and Tzannatos, 1985). It is certainly the case that the male–female differential narrowed during the five year implementation period, though some commentators attribute this to the impact of incomes policies which were also in effect during this period. However, the research indicates that the increase in relative female pay was only marginally affected by the operation of incomes policies at that time and it did not reflect a movement of female employment to higher paying sectors. Rather, the narrowing differential can be attributed to female earnings increasing in some jobs for which they had been previously underpaid. Moreover, what limited evidence is available does indicate that these changes had little negative impact on the employment of women.

7 Conclusion

In this chapter we have examined a number of explanations for why labour market disadvantage, such as low pay, unemployment, and so on, falls disproportionately on certain groups within the labour market. We have shown that these explanations basically fall into two broad schools of thought, the orthodox or neoclassical approach and institutional models of labour market segmentation. The former attempts to explain the distribution of disadvantage in terms of the standard tools of economic analysis with which you are already familiar, namely human capital theory and utility maximization. Human capital theory simply says that some people earn less than others and fare worse in the labour market because they invest less in education and skills and because they show less commitment to the labour market. In a sense, we are explaining labour market inequality in terms of factors found to be closely linked to labour market outcomes.

The neoclassical approach also recognizes that discrimination exists in the labour market. Indeed, the approach adopted by orthodox economists (based upon the early work of Gary Becker) has been used to estimate how much discrimination does exist. These estimates show how much of, say, the earnings differential between men and women reflects differences in productivity-related characteristics and how much is due to discrimination. The problem that proponents of this approach face is why does discrimination take place in the first place? Or, using the concepts employed by these economists, where does the 'taste' for discrimination come from? This is especially puzzling when, as you have seen, to discriminate actually imposes a cost on the economic agents who choose to discriminate.

The alternative approach, the segmentation theory, develops an explanation of discrimination and labour market disadvantage based on the premise that the labour market comprises non-competing groups of workers, some of whom have access to 'good' jobs and others who only have access to 'bad' jobs. The allocation to the low wage, secondary segment is not based on education or training but on the self-interest of dominant groups within the labour market. This approach, which seems to provide an analysis that derives more closely from the actual experiences of those who are discriminated against and marginalized in the labour market, does not perform well when subject to empirical scrutiny. Whether this reflects the nature of the tests employed to date by labour economists is an important question beyond the scope of this chapter.

Finally, we have touched upon a number of policy issues. The two approaches we have examined offer very different prescriptions. At one extreme, neoclassical economists support laissez-faire policies which promote competition in the labour market. At the other, segmentation labour economists see the need for intervention in the labour market to promote the interests of marginal workers. Many labour economists who see themselves as orthodox would, however, not disagree with the need for some form of intervention but would focus this on enabling disadvantaged groups to get access to better education and to training, and in the provision of such services as childcare facilities which can improve women's involvement in the labour market.

Further Reading

Rosenberg, S. (1989) 'From segmentation to flexibility', *Labour and Society*, 14, pp. 363–407: provides a useful survey of US literature on segmentation.

Rubery, J. and Wilkinson, F. (eds) (1994) *Employer Strategy and the Labour Market*, Oxford University Press, Oxford: describes recent developments in segmentation literature.

Polachek, S. and Siebert, S. (1993) *The Economics of Earning*, Cambridge University Press, Cambridge: a good analysis of orthodox models of discrimination.

CHAPTER 4   LABOUR MARKET POLICY

By Keith Whitfield

1 Introduction

Labour market policy has been a political battleground in recent years. By 'policy' in this chapter, however, I do not just mean the actions of governments. Rather, labour market policy can be defined as deliberate attempts by organizations to modify the manner in which the labour market operates. Many policy initiatives by organizations affect the manner in which the labour market works, but only as a by-product of some other main objective. What distinguishes labour market policy is a focus on improving the effectiveness with which labour is allocated, deployed and utilized.

Labour market policies take a variety of forms. They include those designed to improve the allocation and reallocation of labour, those that try to enhance and integrate education and training provision, and those that are principally concerned with creating jobs.

A wide range of organizations are involved in attempting to improve the effectiveness of the labour market. Among these are the International Labour Organisation (ILO), supra-national bodies such as the European Union, central governments, local governments, employers and their organizations, trade unions, religious bodies and charitable organizations. The activities of each of these has an impact on the structure of the labour market and the manner in which it responds to exogenous changes. They have been the subject of much debate between economists, politicians, policy advisors and those responsible for formulating and implementing labour market policy.

To date, the most important organization affecting any given labour market has been the national government of the country in which the labour market is primarily located. This is slowly changing as decision-making power gradually shifts to supra-national bodies such as the European Union, and product and labour markets increasingly extend across national frontiers. Indeed, much of the debate over the development of the single European market and the integration of European currencies has been concerned with the implications for labour markets and those whose well-being depends upon them. Nonetheless, even in the modern world, it is arguably still national governments that have the most profound impact on the way in which labour markets work.

National strategies to improve the effectiveness of the labour market vary substantially. There are two main areas of dispute. The first concerns the degree to which there should be government intervention in the labour market. The second concerns the degree to which policy should emphasize either the cost minimization approach, involving low wage costs as the main route to competitive advantage, or the productivity augmentation approach, which focuses on those conditions that promote the most rapid advance of productive potential, often irrespective of the effect on wage costs or even deliberately encouraging high wages as a spur to investment and/or technological advance.

A contrast can, for example, be drawn between British and German initiatives to increase the level of workforce skills. British policies in the recent past have focused on deregulating the labour market and have emphasized a market-led approach involving, *inter alia*, the devolution of responsibility for training provision from the highly centralized Training Agency to locally-based Training and Enterprise Councils (in England and Wales) and Local Enterprise Councils (in Scotland); training credit schemes, which allow trainees to fashion training packages to their own requirements, have been developed; and a national market in transferable skills has been encouraged via the National Vocational Qualification (NVQ) scheme. In contrast, the German government has been much more interventionist, supporting agreements between employers and unions to provide vocational courses for employees.

Attention can also be focused on the cost minimization approach of the British Conservative government of the 1980s and early 1990s. It pursued a relentless strategy of encouraging the conditions that promote low employment costs such as a series of employment acts designed to reduce union bargaining power, and opting out of the European Social Chapter. In contrast, the German government over the same period engaged in co-operation with unions and supported the Social Chapter.

Each policy intervention in the labour market is guided by a model of how the labour market operates, either explicitly or implicitly. The dominant model deployed by policy makers varies markedly across time and space, depending on the ideology of the policy-making body, the past experiences of policy making and the central issue of concern for policy makers. Britain has seen considerable shifts in this area, most notably the move away from the broadly structural/institutional model adopted during the quarter century immediately following the end of the Second World War towards the more market-led model introduced by the Conservative government in 1979. The effect has been a marked change in the nature of the UK labour market. Whether this has improved its operation or not is a hotly debated issue.

Labour markets are particularly distinctive in that they involve institutions, both formal and informal, that have profound effects on the exchanges within the markets. Examples of formal institutions are wage-fixing bodies, trade unions, legislation regulating the nature of the interaction between employers and workers, and the process of collective bargaining for settling the terms and conditions of employment. Informal institutions include implicit labour contracts and shared notions of fair wages. Such institutions need to be understood and incorporated in labour market models if effective intervention to improve labour market operation by any of those concerned with it (but especially national governments) is to be possible.

In this chapter I aim to develop a framework within which efforts to improve labour market performance, especially those by national governments, can better be understood. Section 2 builds on Chapter 3 and outlines a framework which can be used to analyse the labour market as a system. This will then be used to examine a number of issues that have been at the centre of the labour market policy debate in recent years. Section 3 looks at the case for the minimum wage and the European Social Chapter. Section 4 reviews the arguments for and against trade unions. The last section compares skill levels in Britain and West Germany, and discusses different types of government intervention that have been undertaken to ensure skill formation.

2   Models of the labour market

[handwritten margin notes: Wage competition. Can't work if it has a glass floor. Now too much. Overlying for neo.]

There are two main types of labour market model, both of which were discussed in Chapter 3. One is the neoclassical market model which is typically termed the wage competition or price–auction model. At its centre is the adjustment of prices (wages) to reconcile differences in labour supply and demand, and the high responsiveness of economic agents to the signals that are thereby given out.

The second model is based on the concept of the segmented labour market. It suggests that many of the processes emphasized in the neoclassical model do not operate in reality and that distinct segments, which operate according to different rules, can be identified in the labour market. In contrast to the wage competition model, the reconciliation of supply and demand in this second model is, at best, slow. Adjustment of quantities supplied and demanded is important in addition to, rather than instead of, price adjustment, and some markets might stay in disequilibrium for long periods. Consequently, there is much scope for other factors, such as custom and practice and administrative rules, to influence adjustment other than those central to the wage competition model.

These models differ in a number of crucial respects: the importance of wage flexibility in the adjustment process, the responsiveness of economic agents to changing incentives, the importance of institutional structures in directing change. The main consequence is that some models suggest that market processes will produce equilibrium between labour supply and demand in a reasonably short period of time, whereas others do not.

The key (but not the only) difference between the models from the standpoint of intervention to improve labour market performance is the process by which markets adjust to change. Vietorisz and Harrison (1973) introduced the notion of feedback effects. For example, an increase in wages has an impact upon the labour market such that, eventually, this change feeds back to influence wages once again. In markets that resemble the neoclassical model the feedback is negative; an increase in wages has a negative feedback effect – the initial increase in wages results in an induced fall in wages. Conversely, in markets which resemble the segmentation model there is positive feedback: the initial increase in wages has a positive impact which reinforces the initial wage increase.   *[handwritten: – last.]*

The differences between the two models can be illustrated by reference to Figure 4.1 overleaf which is based on Vietorisz and Harrison (1973). It shows the effect of an increase in wages in labour markets with tendencies to either positive or negative feedback. In part (a) where there is negative feedback, increased wages lead to the adoption of capital intensive techniques. This substitution of capital for labour leads to reduced labour demand and consequently there is a fall in wages. Thus the outcome is in the opposite direction to the initial change – there is negative feedback.

Definitions

Negative feedback   *[handwritten: neoclassical]*

When there is negative feedback, the initial and induced changes move in opposite directions.

Positive feedback

When there is positive feedback, the initial and induced changes move in the same direction.

Conversely, where there is positive feedback, increased wages lead to the adoption of more advanced technology, investment in higher skills, higher productivity and increased wages. In this case, the outcome is in the same direction as the initial change – there is positive feedback.

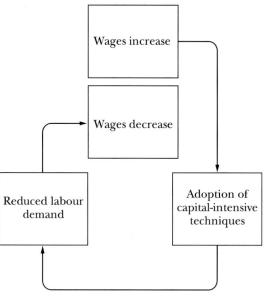

(a) Negative feedback

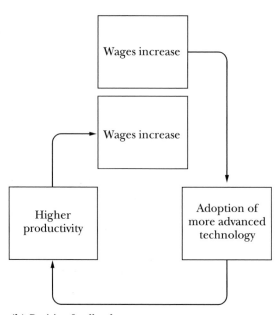

Figure 4.1 **Positive and negative feedback effects**

Source: Adapted from Vietorisz and Harrison, 1971, Figures 4 and 6, p.368

(b) Positive feedback

How, then, can negative feedback be generated by a neoclassical view of the labour market and positive feedback by the segmentation approach? This can be explained by looking at the market supply and demand for labour. Figure 4.2 shows an upward sloping market supply of labour curve (L_S) and a downward sloping market demand for labour curve (L_D). This market labour demand curve represents the summation of the individual long-run labour demand curves for each firm in the labour market (see *Firms*, Chapter 7, Section 2). For firms to adopt labour-saving innovations requires a long-run analysis in which both labour and capital can be varied.

The labour market starts at a position of initial equilibrium at A where L_1 units of labour are employed at a wage rate of W_1. Assume that this wage rate increases from W_1 to W_2.

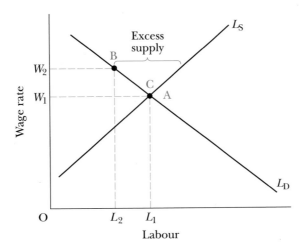

Figure 4.2 **An increase in wages with negative feedback effects**

In Figure 4.2, the initial impact of the increase in the wage is a movement from A to B. Firms cannot afford to employ the same number of workers at the higher wage rate so the amount of labour demanded is cut from L_1 to L_2. They replace workers with machines or, in the language of neoclassical economics, they substitute out of labour and into capital.

Eventually, however, this initial impact on the demand for labour is reversed. At point B in Figure 4.2 there is an excess supply of labour as there are not enough jobs to meet the amount of work which employees want to take. This means that in the labour market the wage rate will be bid down until demand and supply are in equilibrium. The wage rate falls from W_2 back to its initial W_1. Having moved from A to B, the market returns back to the initial equilibrium at C (the same point as the original point A). The initial increase in the wage rate has an induced effect which results in the eventual fall in the wage rate – there is a negative feedback from the initial increase to the eventual fall. Having substituted out of labour and into capital, the eventual reduction of the wage rate forces firms to reverse their substitution back to the more labour-intensive techniques of production.

For Vietorisz and Harrison this negative feedback scenario is decidedly neoclassical. First, the smooth substitution between labour and capital by firms is a feature of the neoclassical model. Neoclassical economists model this substitution by using isoquant analysis (see *Firms*, Chapter 7). Second, this view of the economy is static. The labour market must return to the static equilibrium at C after the wage increase. There is only one wage rate, W_1, which can clear the labour market, and hence only one equilibrium level of employment, L_1. Although there is a temporary movement from A to B and then back to C, in the long run the economy rests at the static equilibrium.

These characteristics of the neoclassical model are relaxed if the labour market is segmented. As you saw in Chapter 3, in a segmented labour market there are typically primary and secondary segments. Firms in primary segments employ workers at high wages and at a high level of productivity. Firms are typically large and enjoy some degree of monopoly power. Secondary segments, on the other hand, are characterized by low wages, low productivity and a large number of small firms.

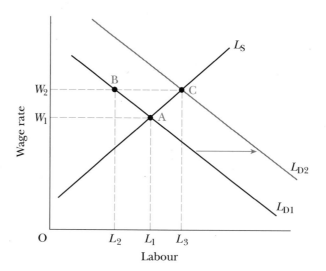

Figure 4.3 **An increase in wages with positive feedback effects: primary market**

To illustrate the positive feedback effects of a wage increase in the segmentation model, the demand and supply diagram can be further developed. In Figure 4.3, the initial wage increase is shown as before by the movement from A to B. As before, firms respond to this wage increase by adopting labour-saving techniques, substituting out of labour and into capital. Assume, however, that Figure 4.3 relates only to workers in the primary segment. Vietorisz and Harrison (1973) argue that firms in the primary segment will also react to the wage increase by implementing an innovation in technology: 'When the need to shift to a more mechanized or automated technology becomes pressing for the entrepreneur, he will exchange his existing productive structure – some years out-of-date – for one that is not only less labor-intensive but also more up-to-date' (Vietorisz and Harrison, 1973, p.369). As well as adopting new labour-saving techniques, in which existing technology is used to substitute capital for labour, firms also adopt labour-saving innovations in which the technology is changed. (This is discussed further in *Firms*, Chapter 9, Section 3.2)

This is a decidedly non-neoclassical view of the economy. Firms do not smoothly substitute between capital and labour as new techniques are adopted. They make decisions in fits and jolts when they move to improved technologies, that raise overall productivity in the primary segment. In Figure 4.3 this means that firms make higher profits since more output is produced for each unit of labour employed. At a given wage rate, more units of labour will be employed by firms and hence the labour demand curve shifts to the right. Firms still pay workers the wage rate W_2, but they now employ L_3 workers at C. After the initial increase in wages, from A to B, the induced effect sustains this increase at C. As was shown in Figure 4.1(b), there is positive feedback from the initial wage increase via an increase in productivity. This enables primary segment firms to continue paying this wage at the higher level of output.

This change in technology is possible because of the type of firm that operates in the primary segment. These firms are able to use their monopoly profits to invest in research and development. In response to a wage increase, they are able to change their technology to improve productivity. This contrasts with the neoclassical model in which many firms are assumed to have the same homogeneous technology which is given exogenously to all firms.

In allowing firms to change their technology in this way, the segmentation model is based on a dynamic view of the economy. Technology changes are not reversible as in the neoclassical model: a firm cannot adopt a less labour-intensive technique and then move back to its original technique. The change is historical in that a firm moves into a different stage of its development.

This dynamic change will not take place in the secondary segment. Wages in this segment will remain low, and the technology used by the small firms will remain unproductive compared with the primary segment.

Thus a crucial difference between the negative and positive feedback models lies in the way they treat the decision-making process within the firm and hence in the notion of time that they embody. The negative feedback model can be analysed within a neoclassical framework that constrains firms to varying capital and labour in response to a wage change on the basis of an unchanging isoquant map (Figure 4.2). Once wages return to their original level, the firm's labour-use decision will also revert to its previous position. The concept of time in this model is the formal, reversible concept of time found in comparative static analysis (*Firms*, Chapter 1).

The positive feedback model can be presented within the neoclassical framework, where a change in wage rates induces an innovation which shifts the labour demand curve to the right (as shown in Figure 4.3). But this is unsatisfactory. To understand the positive feedback process, we need to assume that firms can influence their own technology in response to wage changes. In the segmentation framework, the firms' influence over their own technology implies a more historical, non-reversible concept of time, where technological change becomes endogenous. (This view of technical change is explored in more depth in *Firms*, Chapter 10.)

Whether a labour market exhibits negative or positive feedback depends crucially on the behaviour of the economic agents within it. This is related to the institutional environments in which they are located and the incentives on offer. Thus the same agents faced with the same change will react differently in different institutional contexts. It is, therefore, imperative to understand how such structures vary and how they influence economic behaviour. The rest of this chapter considers different types of institutional environments and how they influence the direction of feedback effects.

3 Labour market regulation

One key factor which determines the behaviour of agents in the labour market is the way in which the labour market is regulated. If, for example, a firm wishes to lose workers in response to a wage increase, then such action has to be carried out in accordance with any redundancy or dismissal legislation. Governments regulate the way in which firms can fire workers. Similarly, if a firm wishes to cut wages then this, too, may be constrained by minimum wage legislation. In this section we look at the impact of minimum wage legislation and its abolition in the UK, and then turn our attention to a further source of labour market regulation, those regulations associated with the European Social Chapter.

3.1 Minimum wages

Until the early 1990s, part of the British labour market was regulated by Wages Councils. These were established early in the twentieth century to fix wages and other conditions of employment in industries such as agriculture, catering, clothing and retail trades, which had not developed appropriate collective bargaining mechanisms and where trade unions were not in a position to bargain collectively on behalf of workers. They were never intended to be permanent or even long-standing bodies but, over time, they became important institutions in a number of industries which traditionally had low pay and seemed unable to develop collective bargaining. Given the absence of a legal minimum wage in Britain, they were seen as a social safety net that protected the low paid. In 1986, however, the Wages Act severely constrained their role, reducing them to the setting of a single minimum wage rate (rather than a minimum rate for each occupational group) and excluding those aged under 21 from their scope. In 1993 Wages Councils were formally abolished in all but the agricultural sector.

The abolition of the Wages Councils resulted from a view that they were keeping the wages of some workers above market-clearing levels, thereby causing unemployment to be higher than would otherwise be the case. Such thinking reflects a neoclassical, negative feedback view of how labour markets work and is illustrated in Figure 4.4.

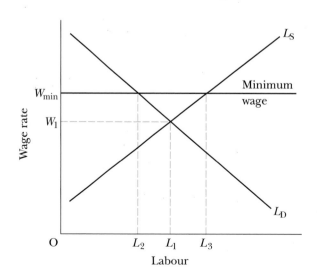

Figure 4.4 **Setting the minimum wage under negative feedback**

If the minimum wage (W_{min}) is set above W_1, the competitive level, there will be an excess supply of labour $L_3 - L_2$, the amount of labour units that workers are willing to supply at prevailing wage rates but unable to do so. In the negative feedback model any wage above the competitive rate will be whittled downwards. If, however, legislation ties the wage at W_{min} there will be an excess supply of labour in the long run.

Question

Assume that the minimum wage is imposed, as shown on Figure 4.4, for the primary segment of a segmented labour market. In Figure 4.4, what is the likely effect on employment of a positive feedback effect?

Under a positive feedback effect, the imposition of a minimum wage would force firms to invest in capital-intensive innovations, which would result in an overall increase in productivity. The labour demand curve would shift to the right, as shown in Figure 4.5. The minimum wage results in L_3 workers being employed, an increase in the number of labour units employed.

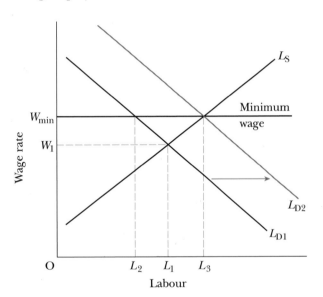

Figure 4.5   **The minimum wage under positive feedback**

The effect of a minimum wage on employment

We will now look at some empirical evidence of the possible impacts of the minimum wage.

The question of whether a statutory minimum wage causes a reduction in employment can be addressed empirically in three main ways – macroeconomic simulation, estimating the effect that Wages Councils had on employment before their abolition, and analysing the impact of abolishing the Wages Councils.

Macroeconomic simulation

This involves calculating the effect of a given change in the minimum wage on the average level of earnings, that is, the elasticity of the real wage with respect to the minimum wage. The value of this elasticity can then be entered into a macroeconomic model forecasting employment, which offers estimates of the elasticity of employment with respect to the real wage. The effect of this change on employment can then be estimated by comparing forecasts based on the pre- and post-change level.

Bazen (1990) provides a survey of the predictions made by a selection of macroeconomic models. These predictions are summarized in Table 4.1.

Table 4.1 **Employment effects of national minimum wage (NMW): macroeconomic simulation, main models**

Model	Employment loss from introducing NMW at half male median pay (000s)
City University Business School	124
HM Treasury (version a)	9
HM Treasury (version b)	259
Liverpool University	22
London Business School	29
National Institute of Economic and Social Research	41

Source: Fernie and Metcalf, 1996; based on Bazen, 1990, Tables 3 and 4

Each model simulates the impact of introducing a national minimum wage (NMW) in the UK. This minimum wage is set at half the median earnings of workers. As you can see, there is a very wide spread of results. The City University Business School model predicts the loss of 124,000 jobs, while the Liverpool University model predicts only 22,000 jobs being shed. Note that there are two versions of the Treasury model (versions a and b) – the latter being a revised version. These versions provide the widest variation – extremes of 9,000 and 259,000.

If even the Treasury's own model cannot provide a consistent result, it is difficult to take these predictions seriously. Bazen concludes that 'while these macro models have the merit of taking into account the various interactions in the economy, and explicitly incorporate the general policy stance adopted, the wide range of estimates is unhelpful' (p.224).

The approach used in studies of this type is also deemed to be inadequate by some commentators because it implicitly assumes that all sections of the labour market are similar, which, patently, they are not (Machin and Manning, 1993). An alternative macroeconomic simulation exercise (Garrard and Martin, 1996) overcomes this by examining six separate sectors of employment. This exercise estimated that, if the average Wages Council rate was uprated by the level of inflation since the Councils' abolition, then a loss of 40,000 jobs could be expected. This assumes that there would be no 'knock-on' effects from the influence of wage differentials of the minimum wage increase and is, therefore, a low estimate.

Wages Councils effects prior to abolition

Estimates of the effects that Wages Councils had on employment divide into two types. The first type, time-series estimates, investigate whether any change in the ratio of the minimum wage to average earnings (generally termed 'minimum wage toughness') through time was associated with change in employment in the industry concerned. This technique involves regressing employment change on the wage toughness variable and on a series of other variables, such as GNP growth, for influences on employment. The second type, cross-sectional estimates, are based on a toughness measure which compares the wage rate set by given Wages Councils with the average wage for workers covered by that council. Once again, the employment variable is regressed on the proxy for minimum wage toughness, and on a set of control variables for other influences on employment, such as foreign competition. Each of these regressions, therefore, offer an estimate of the elasticity of employment with respect to wages, other things being equal.

Table 4.2 shows a selection of studies that report on a range of elasticities of employment.

Table 4.2   **Impact of Wages Councils on employment**

Author	Sample (date of sample)	Elasticity of employment with respect to pay	
Kaufman (1989)	Sectors covered by statutory minimum wage (1971–79)	– 0.06	
Bazen (1990)	16 industries (1968–93)	– 0.60	
Dickens *et al.* (1994)	New Earnings Survey 12 Wages Councils (1978–90)	+ 0.15 to + 0.54	
Machin and Manning (1994)	New Earnings Survey 10 Wages Councils (1979–90)	Catering Retail Clothing Hairdressing	+ 0.99 + 0.60 + 0.27 – 0.45

Source: Fernie and Metcalf, 1996, Table 5

These studies indicate that, prior to 1980, there was a negative elasticity of employment in relation to the Wages Councils' wage. This means that a reduction in wages led to more employment. Kaufman (1989) reported an employment elasticity of – 0.06 for the period 1971–9, and Bazen (1990), in his study that started in 1968, an elasticity of – 0.60. After 1980, however, there was generally a positive elasticity, that is, a reduction in the wage rate led to less employment. The studies by Dickens *et al.* (1994) and Machin and Manning (1994) show positive elasticities, except for hairdressing, which vary from + 0.15 to + 0.99 for the post-1980s period.

> The weight of this evidence suggests that something changed in the 1980s and 1990s compared with the earlier period. In the last decade of their existence the wages councils succeeded in setting wages which gave a boost to jobs, whereas in the previous twenty or so years their activities cost jobs.
>
> *(Fernie and Metcalf, 1996)*

These positive elasticities have been the subject of much conjecture. They may indicate that the effects of an increase in the Wages Councils' wage might flow through more slowly than anticipated, or that Wages Councils' rates tended to increase at the same time as employment.

Impact of abolishing Wages Councils

An econometric study by Dickens *et al.* (1995) examined employment, unemployment and vacancies one year before and one year after the abolition of the seven largest Wages Councils and all Wages Council sectors. Employment changed little. Studies conducted in the 1980s by Craig *et al.* (1982) and in the mid-1990s by Crossman (1995) found no evidence of employment increasing following the abolition of Wages Councils. The studies reviewed by Fernie and Metcalf (1996) do not find any strong impact on levels of employment from the abolition of wage councils. Fernie and Metcalf state that '... the wages council sector's share of total employment was 11.7% prior to abolition and 11.8% afterwards' (p.17).

The impact of setting a minimum wage

The lack of consensus in the findings of these studies reflects how difficult it is to obtain precise empirical estimates of the impact of a change such as implementing a statutory minimum wage or abolishing the Wages Councils. They therefore require careful reading. The most detailed review of the British evidence to date presented by Fernie and Metcalf (1996) reaches two main conclusions. First, a national minimum wage at the same level as the average Wages Councils' rate at the time of their abolition (approximately £3.20 in 1996) would not have adverse employment consequences. Second, a rate set around half male median hourly earnings (approximately £3.70 in 1996) might cause job losses in some sectors, for example, catering and retailing.

3.2   The Social Chapter

A similar perspective to that promoting the abolition of the Wages Councils underpinned the British Conservative government's opt-out from the Social Chapter of the European Union in 1991. This Chapter, part of the Maastricht Treaty, offered a variety of employment rights to workers, relating to remuneration, disciplinary matters, consultation and information disclosure. The British Conservative government opted out of the Chapter on the grounds that it constrained employers and workers from negotiating employment rights which were appropriate to their particular circumstances, thereby increasing the costs of employment unnecessarily and harming their competitive positions. However, many firms operating in Britain and in other parts of the EU have an obligation to apply the rights embodied in the Social Chapter to all of their workers, irrespective of where they are located. Moreover, certain other EU initiatives, such as the Working Hours Directive, do apply to firms in the UK because they are seen to be matters relating to health and safety. The opt-out was, therefore, not total. It is interesting to note that one of the first acts of the incoming Labour government in 1997 was to sign the Social Chapter. At the time, this involved signing-up to two main provisions – one involving works councils, the other involving paternal leave.

The Social Chapter is just one of a large number of EU enactments which influence the level and nature of regulation in the UK labour market. The most important of these emanate from the 1989 European Community Charter of the Fundamental Social Rights of Workers – the Social Charter. This aimed to establish a framework for workers' rights which covered all EU countries. An action program was developed to implement these proposals and most of the original proposals have now been adopted, albeit considerably modified in some cases (Addison and Siebert, 1993). These have mainly focused on health and safety issues, but there have also been important initiatives relating to working time, the employment of younger workers, maternity leave and redundancy. These regulations now apply to all EU countries.

The aim of these provisions is to set a 'level playing field' for the development of the single European market and to ensure that no country is able to undercut any other by reducing workers' rights. This is deemed to be essential for the creation of a single European market. There have, however, been doubts expressed as to whether this policy will yield net economic benefits for the countries concerned. In particular, it has been suggested that it will slow down the process of job creation as it will become more expensive for firms to employ workers (Addison and Siebert, 1993). These job cuts could result in negative feedback effects on wage rates.

Furthermore, there is a feeling that some of the poorer countries of the EU will not be able to afford many of the provisions, especially those relating to pension rights in an era of an ageing population. Thus it has been suggested that the Social Charter will increase the costs of European production and will make European firms less competitive in international markets. Alternatively the provisions might move labour markets towards a positive feedback productivity augmentation process by making employers more creative about how they respond to exogenous shocks. To the extent that the countries of the European Union are predominantly producers of high value-added goods, this might be the most likely strategy. Once again, much depends on the responses of labour market agents to changes in their economic situations.

Not all the influences emanating from the EU, however, are likely to cause an increase in labour market regulation. Indeed, one of the main aims of creating the single European market was to reduce the restraints on trade in both product and labour markets. One consequence has been the development of Europe-wide labour markets and the increased mobility of workers across national boundaries. A classic example of this concerns the labour market for professional footballers, especially after the so-called Bosman Case, which eliminated regulations that reduced the incentives for players to move across national boundaries.

The Bosman Case

In the early 1990s, the labour market for professional footballers was heavily regulated by the transfer system which governed the movement of players between clubs and the rules governing the composition of teams in national and international club competitions. The transfer system required the club buying a player to pay a fee to the club selling him. If a satisfactory fee could not be agreed, the transfer would not take place. The composition of teams for national competitions typically involved a rule limiting the number of non-nationals who could be playing at the same time. Similar provisions concerned the composition of teams in European club competitions.

Jean-Marc Bosman was a player for RC Liège in the Belgian League and was prevented from leaving that club to join the French club US Dunkerque by the transfer rules operating in Belgium. He brought a claim against the club, the Belgian Football Federation and the European Football Association (UEFA) on the grounds that their rules were incompatible with the Treaty of Rome rules on competition and the free movement of workers. The European Court of Justice upheld his claim on the grounds that the transfer rules reduced players' access to the labour markets of other member states and thus impeded the free movement of workers. The nationality rules were also held to be against the Treaty of Rome in that they could impede a player's chances of being employed by a club from another member state.

The Bosman judgement has had a major impact on the nature of the labour market for professional footballers. In particular, it has reduced the bargaining power of employers *vis à vis* players. Those players who are at the end of their contract periods cannot be impeded from moving clubs by the imposition of a transfer fee. This has resulted in a substantial increase in the salaries of, at least, the best players. It has also resulted in clubs developing longer contracts with their key players, and often renegotiating these in mid-contract in an effort to reduce the players' abilities to act as free agents. More noticeably, it has markedly increased the proportion of non-nationals playing in the British football leagues. The same applies to other sports, such as rugby, in which the player is an employee. The implications are much wider than the sporting world and potentially affect all labour markets in which it can be said that a regulation restrains the ability of a worker to move freely between jobs.

Reflection

To what extent do you think that the Bosman case will affect labour markets other than those for professional sports players?

4   Unions and the labour market

The effect of unions on the operation of labour markets has long been controversial. The dominant view among economists, especially neoclassical ones, has been that unions are a market imperfection which prevent the labour market from attaining competitive equilibrium. This view has underpinned a number of attempts in recent years both to reduce the regulations that support the development of unions and to restrict their activities.

The alleged harmful effects of unions are argued to result from a number of activities, including the control of labour supply in the manner of a product market monopoly and the insistence on strict demarcation between jobs which causes overmanning and prevents the efficient use of labour. The consequences of these actions are said to be that the wage paid to union labour is above market-clearing levels and that the demand for certain types of labour is higher than it need be. This viewpoint can be analysed by looking at the monopoly supply model which is shown in Figure 4.6.

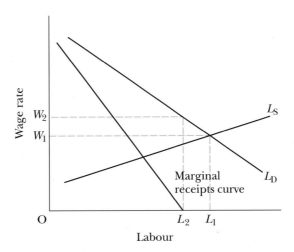

Figure 4.6 **The monopoly supply model**

Definition

Marginal receipts

These are additions to the total wage receipts resulting from the employment of additional units of labour.

In explaining the model I shall describe a particular labour market for workers producing a particular product. To simplify matters, I shall also assume a short-run situation in which capital is fixed.

Figure 4.6 shows the market demand for labour curve (L_D) and the market supply of labour curve (L_S). The market demand for labour curve shows the amount of labour demanded in this particular labour market at each wage rate. It is derived by adding up the (short-run) marginal revenue product (*MRP*) curves of each individual firm (see *Firms*, Chapter 7, Section 2). At the competitive equilibrium, L_1 workers are employed at a wage rate of W_1. Assume, however, that all the workers combine together in a trade union. In this situation the union will monitor the total receipts its membership receives for different levels of employment; these receipts represent the total wages paid to the workforce. One possible assumption is that the union might seek to maximize the total wage receipts. To model this behaviour we can draw a marginal receipts curve onto the labour market diagram. These marginal receipts represent the marginal returns to *all* workers when one additional worker is employed.

The marginal receipts curve shows the change in total receipts associated with each additional unit of labour employed. The curve is downward sloping because the wage rate falls as more labour is employed. Indeed, the fall in wages is not just for the extra unit of labour taken on, but for all workers employed. For this reason the marginal receipts curve is below the labour demand curve.

If the union seeks to maximize the total receipts of its workforce it will choose an employment level of L_2. At L_2 marginal receipts are equal to zero, there being no additional receipts to be had by increasing employment any further. This means that the union chooses a lower employment level (L_2) than the competitive level (L_1).

The result is that there are higher wages, W_2 instead of W_1, but fewer workers employed. This model shows that if there are many firms behaving competitively and workers combine together in a trade union there will be an adverse effect on employment.

The ability of unions to act as monopoly suppliers of labour can, however, be seriously questioned. A union can only act strongly in this way if it operates what is known as a pre-entry closed shop. This exists when available jobs can be allocated to existing members of the union only. Such closed shops have typically been the preserve of craft unions and professional associations. They have been based on the ability of such bodies to impose entry qualifications on certain jobs and to ensure that such qualifications are in short supply. Explicit use of the pre-entry closed shop has been made illegal in Britain and is no longer a strong base for union monopoly control.

A weaker form of the closed shop is the post-entry closed shop. This is where workers must either already belong to or agree to join a union if they are to undertake certain jobs. This type of closed shop exists either because the union is able to impose this condition on management or because of an agreement between management and unions. While it offers unions a number of advantages, in particular freedom from recruitment costs and a guaranteed income base, it does not, by itself, yield monopoly control over the supply of labour to the union. Furthermore, it has become increasingly difficult to operate such closed shops as so-called 'right to work' laws, particularly the 1980 and 1982 Employment Acts, have made it easier for workers to opt out of them.

Over and above such doubts about unions' abilities to act as monopoly suppliers of labour, there have been doubts expressed about whether unions impose costs on the market by enforcing closed shop agreements. This viewpoint is based on a notion that unions simply act as countervailing forces to the monopoly control of the labour market held by employers. In such a situation, where employers have such monopoly power, the theory of 'second best' (see *Changing Economies*, Chapters 7 and 13) states that it is not necessarily the case that the introduction of a monopoly on the supply side of the market will impose costs.

The theory of the 'second best' states that if one of the conditions for achieving an optimally efficient market is not fulfilled, the second best optimum might only be attained if some or all of the others are not fulfilled. Thus, in this case, if the employer's side was competitive, an efficient market would require the worker's side to be the same. But if the employer is a monopsonist, the solution nearest to that optimum might result from a union monopoly.

Consider the case where there is, in the extreme, only one firm employing labour of a particular type. It can be said to have monopsony power.

Definition

Monopsony power

A firm has monopsony power when it has some control over the price at which it buys labour.

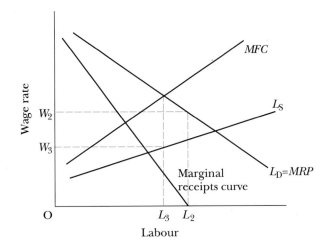

Figure 4.7 **Bilateral monopoly in a labour market**

It can be shown, as in Figure 4.7, that where an employer has monopsony power in a labour market, the introduction of a union can increase both wages and employment.

The main addition to this diagram, compared to Figure 4.6, is the marginal factor cost (*MFC*) curve (see *Changing Economies*, Chapter 21). The marginal factor cost of labour is the extra cost to the firm of employing an extra unit of labour. This cost to the firm is more than just the wage rate paid to the extra unit of labour. If the firm employs an additional worker, the *MFC* has two components which will make it rise. First, the wage rate for the extra worker increases, and second, the wage bill for all other workers increases. Hence, the *MFC* is above the market labour supply curve, which models just the increase in the wage rate.

Having set up this position of monopsony power we can now consider two extremes. The first is a monopsonist firm employing non-unionized workers. In this scenario the firm chooses the level of employment L_3 on Figure 4.7, such that its *MFC* is equal to its marginal revenue product (*MRP*). Instead of the market labour demand curve consisting of a number of *MRP* curves added together as in the case of a competitive market, in this case there is only one firm and one *MRP* curve. This firm maximizes profits at

$$MFC = MRP$$

by choosing to employ L_3 units of labour because any other level of employment would mean either that:

a)   more profits could be made by cutting employment (*MFC* > *MRP*), or

b)   more profits could be made by increasing employment (*MRP* > *MFC*).

Now, under the assumption that workers are non-unionized, they choose the amount of labour to supply according to the labour supply curve. The firm, therefore, can employ L_3 workers only by paying a wage rate of W_3. Because of its monopsony power, the firm can restrict the number of workers employed to maximize profits.

The other extreme is a monopsonist firm employing unionized workers. This is the case of bilateral monopsony where both firms and unions behave like monopolists. In this scenario, the union supplies L_2 workers for employment at a wage rate of W_2. Instead of the firm maximizing profits, the union maximizes the total wages received by its members by increasing employment up to the point where marginal receipts are equal to zero.

The conclusion from comparing these scenarios is that unions can generate more jobs and higher wages than a non-unionized labour market in a situation where firms have monopsony power. Of course, in practice, unions will possibly have some power to negotiate and firms will possibly have some monopsony power.

Given this balance of power, a process of bargaining has to take place between the different parties. Hence, an exact position of equilibrium cannot be precisely determined but will lie between W_2 and W_3 and between L_2 and L_3 on Figure 4.7, and will depend on the process of bargaining between employers and unions. In short, the introduction of a countervailing 'imperfection' moves the market towards its competitive equilibrium. It is not necessarily the case that unions can only gain wage increases at the expense of jobs.

As well as bargaining over wages, unions may also have a say over other issues such as skill formation. Using the long-run analysis in Section 2, the feedback model could be applied to this issue. Under positive feedback effects, the union may negotiate changes in the technical organization of production with the employer. If the higher wage negotiated by the union results in higher productivity, as shown in Figure 4.1(b), then this will depend on any bargain struck between the union and the firms.

An even stronger argument suggesting that unions may not necessarily be the 'bads' that many economists label them has been given by Freeman and Medoff (1984). They suggest, in line with much of the literature on high performance work systems (see *Firms,* Chapter 8), that organizations often fail to operate at levels of maximum efficiency because of a failure to develop mechanisms that can channel information from workers to management. In particular, workers may have grievances about how their jobs are being organized which they are unable to communicate to their employers. In response, they may reduce their work effort or even quit the job. Both involve costs to the organization.

Unions can act as channels of communication for such workers and can, thereby, promote the development of a less grievance-ridden workplace by providing a collective voice for the workers. The consequence of such a channel of communication could be a greater level of effort from workers and/or a lower quit rate, with the firm achieving more of its potential or, in other words, reducing its level of X-inefficiency (see *Firms,* Chapter 3).

Freeman and Medoff contrast two types of mechanism – 'exit' and 'voice' – through which workers can give vent to their grievance. (These concepts were first discussed in Chapter 2.) By using the 'exit' mechanism, workers withdraw either their effort or their labour; by using 'voice' the union represents workers' views and encourages constructive change in the workplace. Freeman and Medoff suggest that the latter offers major benefits to employers which, in many cases can outweigh the other, less benign, effects of unions on the firm. In particular, they argue that 'voice' is based on the views of the average union worker, whereas 'exit' is based on the views of the marginal worker. While 'exit' might be more effective when the firm simply wants to reduce the size of its workforce, 'voice' is more effective if the firm wants to increase the efficiency with which it organizes its workforce.

A labour market containing unions will operate in a different fashion from one which is union-free. There will be extra constraints on the ability of employers to use wages as an adjustment mechanism and it is possible that wages may remain in a disequilibrium position for substantial periods. Additionally, firms will be less able to adjust the number of workers by variations in hiring and redundancy/dismissal. This does not necessarily mean, however, that unionized labour markets are less efficient than non-unionized ones. It can be argued that variations in both wages and the number of workers have substantial long-run costs and that many employers (especially those attempting to develop high-performance work systems) can choose to avoid their use even when not constrained by unions. Moreover, a wide range of adjustment mechanisms, such as changes to recruitment practices, promotion rates and hours worked, is available and, particularly in the long term, these can be equal to or even more desirable than wage and numerical flexibility.

Only empirical investigation can establish the extent to which this positive view of unions pervades the labour market as a whole.

Empirical evidence of union effects on labour markets

The evidence of union effects on the labour market is mixed and the subject of much debate. This primarily reflects the complexity of disentangling the effects of unions and other labour market factors which are associated with them. The evidence on union wage effects indicates that unions generally obtain wages for their members which are significantly but not substantially higher than those of like workers in non-unionized firms and that this effect is greater where the firm has some monopolistic control over its product market (Stewart, 1991). In short, unions seem to be extracting a share of the super-normal profits obtained by such firms.

Evidence of the effect of unions on productivity and firms' financial performance is mixed. The effect on productivity is not clear; some studies point in one direction and others in the opposite direction (see Freeman and Medoff, 1984, Chapter 11; Addison, 1983, for example). The effect on financial performance is clearer, with the dominant view being that unions significantly reduce the financial performance of the firms in which they are located (Machin and Stewart, 1990). This reflects, in part, the ability of unions to extract wage premiums from firms, especially those firms in strong product market positions.

Unions, legislation and productivity in British manufacturing in the 1980s

The incoming Thatcher Government in 1979 promised to reform industrial relations in Britain and, in particular, to reduce union power. It introduced a wide range of initiatives which focused on banning the closed shop, constraining the right to picket, reducing the immunity of unions from being sued for damages and reforming trade union organization (Brown and Wadhwani, 1990). The stated objective was to reduce the perceived ability of unions to prevent employers from organizing employment in the most efficient manner. An increase in labour productivity (output per worker) was therefore expected to result from the reforms. Did this occur?

In two papers published in 1988, David Metcalf of the London School of Economics found considerable evidence that the UK labour productivity growth in manufacturing in the 1980s was double the 1970s rate and greater than in the 1960s. Furthermore, it was higher than that of the average of the seven major industrialized countries (USA, Canada, Germany, France, Italy, Japan and UK), the reverse of the previous periods. It is, of course, possible that the higher productivity growth in the years following the industrial relations reforms reflects factors other than the reforms themselves and/or the associated constraints on unions. However, Metcalf also reviewed studies examining the relationship between unions and productivity in Britain and concluded that they show that, 'Union presence is generally associated with lower labour productivity in a workplace' (Metcalf, 1988b).

Metcalf (1988b) concluded that the large increase in productivity in the 1980s rested on three industrial relations factors:

1   fear – productivity rose most in those industries with the greatest job losses

2   increased product market competition caused firms to pay more attention to labour costs

3   the decentralization of collective bargaining to the company or plant level resulted in more effective productivity bargaining, which involved the removal of restrictive practices, the introduction of new technology and the extension of shift work.

Nolan and Marginson (1990) objected to Metcalf's interpretation. First, they questioned whether the studies cited showed that productivity was generally lower in unionized plants. In particular, they showed that the relationship between unions and productivity was negative in small firms and those with a very low or a very high proportion of union members, and positive in larger firms and those with between 50 and 80 per cent of workers in unions. Second, Nolan and Marginson suggested that Metcalf was too keen to celebrate the gains in labour productivity which resulted from work intensification. This is seen to have short-term benefits in terms of increased output but long-term costs as the incentive for employers to undertake essential investment was eroded. Investment in plant and equipment in the 1980s was significantly lower than in the 1960s and 1970s.

Another assessment of the effect of the industrial relations legislation on unions and the economy by Brown and Wadhwani (1990) suggested that it reduced union power but did not seem to influence economic performance. The authors noted that in the early 1980s, unionized workplaces had larger falls in employment and higher propensities to engage in organizational change than non-unionized ones. The consequence was a much greater increase in productivity. This is interpreted as being the consequence of employers and unions bargaining away restrictions on working methods, primarily resulting from the pressure of increased product market demand and the increased bargaining power offered to employers by high unemployment, rather than the legislative reforms.

The effect of unions on the labour market is an emotive issue and it is clear from this debate that small differences in interpretation can yield strong feelings. Such is the nature of labour market debate. Such differences, however, should not obscure the fact that all three sets of authors suggest that part of the productivity growth in the 1980s came from work intensification. Whether you deem this to be a good thing or bad thing depends on who you are (the workers concerned, a consumer getting a cheaper product or service, or a shareholder getting bigger profits) and your underlying beliefs (a belief that unions protect workers from 'slave-driving' bosses or that unions have prevented employers from using their resources in the most effective way).

A corollary of this debate is that, as it was taking place, productivity growth was slowing markedly as Britain entered the late 1980s/early 1990s recession. Between 1987 and 1991 gross product per person employed grew by only 2.6 per cent. Thus, from the perspective of the early 1990s, the 1980s did not seem to have been such a miracle decade – more a deep recession followed by a strong recovery and a further deep recession. It was distinctive for the size of its fluctuations rather than its trend rate of productivity growth.

5   Skill formation

Recent years have seen increased attention paid to the linkages between skill levels and national economic performance. There is a growing perception that a strong causal link runs from the skill levels held by the workforce to the productive potential of their economies. The consequence has been a number of attempts by governments to increase the quantity and quality of skills held by their workers. This has been a particular concern of the British government due to the widespread perception that Britain's record has been particularly poor in this respect.

5.1   Comparing skills in Britain and West Germany

Prais (1995) compares the educational qualifications of the British workforce with those of a major competitor, West Germany. Using official surveys of households in both countries, a comparison is made between the proportion of the workforce in both countries with university qualifications and vocational qualifications such as City and Guilds craft certificates. This vocational type of training is referred to as an intermediate qualification. Table 4.3 overleaf provides a comparison of the two countries for manufacturing industries.

Table 4.3 **Qualifications of the workforce in manufacturing industries: Great Britain 1988, West Germany, 1987**

	Persons with stated qualifications as % of workforce in manufacturing industries			
	University		Intermediate	
	Britain	West Germany	Britain	West Germany
Chemicals and artificial fibres	14	9	26	62
Engineering: electrical and instrument	13	12	31	62
Engineering: mechanical	7	7	43	69
Food, drink and tobacco	5	2	21	65
Metal manufacture	4	3	34	64
Paper and printing	9	4	30	67
Petroleum products	13	12	39	65
Textiles, leather and footwear	3	1	16	60
Vehicles, transport equipment	7	7	41	66
Other manufacturing	4	3	28	66

Source: Adapted from Prais, 1995, Table 2.2, p.20

This table shows that the proportion of the workforce with university qualifications was very similar in the two countries in the late 1980s. In the petroleum products industry, for example, 13 per cent of the workforce in Britain had a university degree, compared to 12 per cent in West Germany. For intermediate qualifications, however, West Germany has a much higher proportion of its workforce trained up; 65 per cent of the West German workforce in petroleum products have an intermediate vocational qualification compared with only 39 per cent in Britain. This disparity in training is repeated across all manufacturing industries.

A key question to be asked is the extent to which these disparities in training impact upon productivity in the two countries. To give a detailed insight into this issue, particular attention can be paid to the clothing industry. Table 4.3 shows that in the textiles, leather and footwear industry (of which clothing forms a subset) the training disparity is particularly pronounced, with only 16 per cent of the British workforce having intermediate training, compared to 60 per cent in West Germany. The clothing industry is one of five industries reviewed in a comparative international study by the National Institute of Economic and Social Research.

Prais (1995) summarizes the findings of this study in which 160 establishments were visited over the period 1983–91. By matching plants that were of a similar size and produced similar items, this study was able to make detailed observations of British and West German workers. Of particular interest was the productivity of clothing machinists in British and West German plants.

> [They] probably provided the clearest examples of how training directly improved productivity. First, at the end of most lines of sewing machinists observed in Britain, someone was usually engaged in 'unpicking' faulty work – while this was never observed on visits to the matched German sample (not that

faulty stitching never occurred in German plants, but it must have been sufficiently less frequent to yield such an evident contrast). Second, a little more complex and more important: when putting a new style into production, an average of 2–3 days 'running-in' to reach full operating speed was required by German machinists, whereas the average British machinist required several weeks to reach full production speed. In that 'running-in' period German machinists were able to work directly from technical sketches, with only the occasional need for advice from their supervisor on difficult points; while in British plants very few machinists could work directly from technical sketches, and required their supervisors physically to demonstrate new operations. British plants thus understandably opted for the production of longer runs – with fewer changeovers – and for less elaborately stitched products; even so, two and a half times as many checkers ('passers') and supervisors were required per machinist in Britain than in Continental clothing plants (one for every twelve machinists in Germany, one for every five in Britain).

(Prais, 1995, p.65)

This is only a brief insight into the evidence collected by the National Institute survey, but the implication is that because the German machinists have more training, they are able to read technical sketches, produce more elaborately stitched products and make fewer mistakes. The National Institute survey found similar productivity differentials in engineering, wood furniture manufacturing, food manufacturing and the hotel industry.

5.2   Government responses

The main failure in the market for training is a consequence of the free rider or poaching problem. It results from a failure of the market to encourage people to invest in their skills. Two types of skills can be defined: general skills and specific skills. General skills can be defined as those skills that, for a group of different firms, increase their capacity to produce output by the same amount. The transferability of such skills between firms makes it unlikely that firms will pay for the costs of their acquisition, fearing that trained workers will move to other firms. These other firms will be able to pay trained workers a wage premium as they have not had to absorb the costs of training. The non-training firms in this case are called poachers or free riders

A contrast can be made with the acquisition of specific skills. These enable more output to be produced only in the firm in which they are acquired. As a result, firms are often more willing to cover costs of such training. However, workers trained in specific skills may leave before the firm accrues sufficient benefits to cover the cost of training. Firms, therefore, try to tie such workers to them. This is not easy due to laws prohibiting restraint of trade (as in the Bosman case discussed above) and typically takes the form of paying a wage premium to workers with specific skills. If this premium increases the supply of workers to the jobs in question, the firm may be able to reduce the wages offered for the initial training period and thereby effectively share the costs of training with the workers.

Definitions

General skills

These skills enhance the production capabilities of workers by the same amount in a number of different firms.

Free rider

A free rider benefits from something that someone else has paid for.

Specific skills

These skills only enhance the production capabilities of workers in the firm to which they are specific.

Question

The comparison of clothing workers in West Germany and Britain focused on a number of differences in skills. Identify any of these which you consider to be general skills.

Whether or not skills are general depends, to some extent, on your subjective judgement. Reading technical drawings may be a general skill which is transferable across industries, although there will be aspects to the manufacturing of clothing which are not transferable. Similarly, the number of mistakes made by a machine operator will not only relate to their level of general training but will also depend on the specific skills required to work a machine. This will depend, to some extent, on the idiosyncrasy of the job in question (see *Firms*, Chapter 8).

Under-investment in specific skills can exist in the market if firms and employees are unable to agree an optimal distribution of training costs. This can occur, for example, if workers do not trust firms to pay the wage premium after the initial training period or where firms are unable to reduce the wage offered in this period due to external forces such as collective agreements or minimum wages. The latter can also result in the sub-optimal investment in general skills.

Given these problems, a strong argument can be made for some form of regulation of training by governmental or quasi-governmental bodies. In many countries the main response to market failure has been to develop government regulatory arrangements which attempt to mitigate market failure. The prime example is the French legislation to ensure that employers spend a sum equivalent to a certain percentage of their wage bill on training. Such intervention is based on the hypothesis that market failures promote externalities which cause potential public benefits of training to exceed private benefits. An example is where there is an under-provision of general training. This reduces the productivity of the worker concerned and the scope for firms to use advanced technology. In such a case, government intervention can, potentially, internalize the benefits and thereby generate publicly optimal levels of skill.

There is, however, a strong body of opinion which argues that government intervention is not an appropriate response to perceived market failure. It is suggested that it is more appropriate to encourage market processes where they are deemed to be deficient. The principle underlying this approach is that the divergence between public and private net benefits caused by market imperfections have impeded the development of private markets. The encouragement of market processes is deemed to be more efficient than public intervention in the provision of goods because of the belief that, when the costs of government failure are taken into account, public intervention does little, if anything, to mitigate a market failure.

The main difference between the two schools of thought in this area can be illustrated by reference to general skill provision. The typical response to the under-provision of general training has been government intervention via the development of government supported training organizations. Increasingly, however, attempts have been made to develop markets which will encourage trainees to pay for their own training. The classic example is the replacement of student grants by student loan schemes in a number of countries.

Institutional reforms

In their efforts to foster higher levels of skill formation, governments have instituted processes of institutional reform which have directly addressed perceived market failures. Four main types of reform can be identified.

Encouraging market processes

Support for market-based training results from a belief that, while the public goods nature of training underlies observed deficiencies in skill formation, the most appropriate response is not to expand public provision but to develop private markets in those areas in which they are either currently deficient or non-existent. Such a philosophy underpinned many of the efforts of the governments of the UK and the US in the 1980s and early 1990s.

Policies for training provision have typically been allied to other policies, such as the privatization of public sector activities, which have attempted to increase the private provision of goods and services. Such policies have focused on encouraging private market structures and providing incentives to individuals and organizations to undertake activities previously considered to be in the domain of public enterprise. An example is the introduction of training credits for young people in the UK. This can be seen as a response to the criticism made of various youth training schemes that they did not satisfactorily respond to the needs of their client groups. The presumption is that the public administrators of these schemes do not possess the information necessary for the optimal distribution of public funds in this domain and that potential trainees do. Market failure is, therefore, caused by an imperfection introduced by an interfering government which is imparting a severe information deficiency into an otherwise satisfactory market. The question arises, however, whether the potential trainees have sufficient knowledge or capacity to make better decisions than the public administrators.

The major problem with market-led reform is that its potential for success is considerable only if the main constraint lies in the previous suppression of market activities. In those situations where market processes have simply been slow to develop, it is highly probable that their positive encouragement is, at most, only going to expand market processes into areas which are not naturally fertile for them. Some would argue that market-led reforms have not been hugely successful in raising overall skill levels. Moreover, such reforms can have a potential downside if they are introduced into a market that contains a potential for failure. For example, market-led reform in a market exhibiting widespread poaching is likely to expand the scope for free riding, thereby reducing the incentive for private provision.

Training levies

Training levies have been a contentious issue for many years. In essence they can be seen as an attempted public solution to the free rider problem. If private institutions or individuals are unable to provide sufficient training for national requirements, it is incumbent on national authorities to put in place mechanisms to provide training and to finance such training via a levy on the main beneficiaries.

The most direct form of training levy was that introduced in the UK following the Industrial Training Act of 1964. Large firms were compelled to pay a levy which was used to encourage training provision by Industry Training Boards (ITBs). This system was abolished following the ending of the levy in the 1980s and the ITBs were largely abolished. The main reason given for this curtailment was that employers felt they were not getting value for money from the system.

Training levies are, potentially, a way of internalizing the externalities in the free rider problem. In particular, they compel potential free riders to bear their share of the costs in developing an effective training system. In practice, however, they have not been given widespread support, especially from employer groups. Not only do they impose additional costs on employers but they are also seen to support the development of ineffective training bureaucracies.

Training expenditure legislation

Legislation requiring minimum levels of expenditure on training has been implemented in a number of countries, notably France and Australia. France initially required all firms with ten or more employees to allot 0.8 per cent of their wage bill to expenditure on training; since 1987 this has been increased to 1.2 per cent. Australia's legislation mirrored France's and required that firms over a certain payroll size (A$200,000 at its inception, index-linked to average weekly earnings) devote at least 1 per cent of their payroll to employee training. However, this scheme was subsequently abandoned on the grounds that, although it had achieved its aims, it had been subject to widespread criticism. In both countries, firms unable to meet the minimum requirement were obliged to pay a levy to the government that was used for increased expenditure on training.

The key principle behind such legislation is that the main cause of deficient training provision lies with employers. In short, they are seen to be either myopic in their provision of training or are in market positions in which the private incentives to spend on training are below levels which are sufficient for the public good. If the first is the case, the legislation could well make employers do 'the right thing' despite themselves and, increasingly, see the error of their ways. If, however, the second is a more accurate representation of the situation, employers will have strong incentives to evade the legislation and thereby subvert its intent. In this case a more direct addressing of the incompatibility of private incentives and the public good is needed.

It is clear that countries with such minimum requirements have levels of training expenditure which are high by international standards, but there is much debate about the efficacy of such legislation, both within the countries concerned and elsewhere. One of the main complaints is that much of the expenditure on training by firms operating near the legal minimum is 'pseudo training' and has little, if any, practical effect in improving the level of skill formation. It is also suggested that the rigid floor imposed by the legislation does not allow for differences in the training requirements of differing industrial sectors. On the other hand, analysis of the French legislation suggests that the minimum legal requirement has promoted the development of sectoral and regional training organizations which have made major contributions to skill formation (Verdier, 1994). Nonetheless, the need for frequent adjustments to the system also suggests that it is not regarded in France as the panacea to all its training problems.

Reforming educational provision

Reform of the educational system has been at the heart of most attempts to address the failure in the market for training. Evidence indicates that, at the very least, educational reform needs to be undertaken alongside other attempts to mitigate market inadequacy. Institutional reform which fails to incorporate the implications for educational provision is very unlikely to succeed, given the important role that education plays in the market for training.

In recent years, most industrialized countries have introduced reform in the provision of education, particularly vocational education, as part of an effort to improve international economic competitiveness. Among the most far-reaching of these changes are those which have attempted to introduce a greater vocational emphasis into the secondary and post-secondary curricula. The main aims have typically been to improve the quality of non-academic education, break down the academic/vocational divide and extend the period before young people need to specialize in their subject choices. The perception is that the major imperfection in the market for training lies in the public provision of education and, in particular, the over-emphasis on the education of an academic elite. The inevitable consequence is seen to be a failure to train sufficient numbers of people in the area of intermediate skills.

Among the countries which have gone furthest down this path are Denmark, France and the Netherlands. All have seen significant reforms which have concentrated on vocational preparation within the public education system. In essence, this has shifted much of the burden of vocational preparation from employers towards the government. As a consequence, there has been an increase in the level of public expenditure in these countries at a time when most industrialized countries have been attempting to make reductions in this area.

Have institutional reforms been successful?

Recent years have witnessed increased scepticism about the ability of either the governmental or market-led approaches to improve national training performance. This scepticism is based on a recognition that the market for training is located in a broader social and economic system, and that change in the former must be viewed in relation to its impact on the latter. Finegold and Soskice (1988), for example, contend that change in just one part of the socio-economic system is unlikely to be successful if the rest of the system remains the same. They illustrate this by reference to what they term the low-skill equilibrium. In this situation a number of mutually reinforcing mechanisms, emanating from a variety of sources, constrain the economy to a low skill level. Change in any one of these which is aimed at increasing the level of skill formation will not succeed because the other forces (many of which operate outside the training market) will mitigate its effect. They therefore recommend a broad approach to policy change rather than one focused on eradicating perceived failure/imperfections within the training market.

6   Conclusion

This chapter has compared two different ways of analysing the labour market, each with different recommendations for policy. In the first approach, a market which resembles the neoclassical model displays negative feedback effects. If, for example, there is an increase in the wage rate, this will initially result in reduced employment and eventually, because of excess supply of labour, the wage rate falls back to its original level. The upshot, if you take this view, is that there should be minimal intervention or regulation by institutions in the labour market. A minimum wage or Social Chapter would increase costs to employers and have an adverse effect on employment and wages, as would the intervention of trade unions in forcing up the wage rate. Similarly, legislation which commits employers to spend money on training will also adversely increase the costs of employing workers. In this view, interfering governments and trade unions only suppress market activity.

In the second approach, a market which resembles the segmented model displays positive feedback effects. An increase in the costs to firms of employing workers may be a good thing. Say, for example, a minimum wage is imposed. Firms are then forced to substitute capital for labour. To do this they have to revamp their production processes and invest in a more highly skilled workforce. As a result, their production processes become more productive and they can afford to employ more workers at the higher wages. The increase in wages is reinforced by the positive feedback effect. Intervention by trade unions in pushing for higher wages or by government forcing firms to pay for training can all have positive feedback effects on employment and wages.

As well as discussing the theoretical differences between these two views of the labour market, this chapter has provided an insight into some of the empirical evidence. It has been shown that economists and policy makers disagree markedly on how this evidence should be interpreted. Such disagreements about how the labour market should be regulated are not easily settled. The aim of this chapter has been to outline the main differences in the positions held by those attempting to understand how it can be made to work better.

Further Reading

Barrell, R. (ed.) (1994) *The UK Labour Market*, Cambridge, Cambridge University Press.

Keep, E. and Mayhew, K. (1995) *The British System of Vocational Education and Training: A Critical Analysis*, Oxford, Oxford University Press.

Philpott, J. (ed.) (1997) *Working for Full Employment*, London, Routledge.

CHAPTER 5

CAPITAL MARKETS

By David Gowland

1 Introduction

Finance is all-pervasive in the modern market economy. It is virtually impossible to carry out any transaction without using the financial system several times. If, for example, someone decides to buy a new car, they will have to make use of the payments system (cheque or credit card), and may very well have to borrow money to buy a car (use credit markets). Having made the purchase they are likely to need a third branch of the financial system to insure the car. So economic agents have frequent recourse to the financial system as part of other transactions, but inadequacies and imperfections in the financial system may prevent individuals from carrying out transactions. For example, the inability to borrow may prevent the purchase of a car at all. Hence, one is not only interested in the quality of financial services *per se* but also in their impact upon other industries and economic activities. Among the institutions in an economy, the financial system is central and can be considered the infrastructure of the infrastructure.

The importance of finance in facilitating transactions is not limited to capitalist societies. Indeed, money and credit pre-date capitalism by many centuries. They are institutions that are thousands of years old and have been important in almost all civilizations. However, finance plays an especially important role in a capitalist society. First, financial institutions facilitate physical investment and therefore the accumulation of capital, which, as you saw in the opening chapter of this book, is a central feature of the capitalist system. Second, well-functioning financial systems direct investment towards its most productive uses. It will only be by coincidence that a saver is the best person to make an investment and have the most productive opportunities for investing in the economy. Well-functioning financial markets, however, will permit the saver to lend physical resources to other individuals who are proposing productive investments. As a result of a financial transaction, both parties can gain from this exchange. The saver should receive a higher rate of return than would have been available from investing the capital in a project available to him, or holding capital in a sterile form, such as money. The investor may not be able to proceed with this project without access to finance.

If this form of financial market, a capital market, is working properly and there are no significant externalities associated with particular projects, society, as well as the individuals concerned, benefits because savings flow towards the investment opportunities with the highest rate of return.

Two distinctions are necessary at this stage. First, saving is frequently described as financial investment (buying saving certificates might be called investing in them). In this context, however, the term investment is used to mean the purchase of capital goods – durable pieces of physical equipment

Definition

Capital markets

Capital markets bring together those with surplus funds (lenders) and those who wish to invest in real assets (investors, entrepreneurs and borrowers).

and plant (*Changing Economies*, Chapter 2). Second, capital markets are *financial* markets where buyers raise the funds needed to buy capital goods; they are *not* the actual markets for capital goods such as machinery and equipment.

The need to study the interaction between savers/lenders on the one hand and borrowers/investors on the other was also emphasized by Keynes (see *Changing Economies*, Chapter 16). Indeed, it is central to the whole Keynesian macro-economic analysis that unemployment can arise if there is no mechanism to ensure co-ordination between savers and investors.

It is no surprise, therefore, that economists have increasingly paid attention to the structure and impact of financial institutions. Financial systems vary greatly from country to country. These differences are partly the product of history but they are also the consequence of deliberate policy choices by governments. In recent years, the financial structure has been reformed in many countries and considerable attention has been devoted to the issue of how financial markets operate and which is the best structure. These debates have been most intense in the context of capital markets.

This chapter looks at how capital markets work by drawing on the models of the market introduced in Chapter 2. As you will see, imperfect information and uncertainty, which characterize the Austrian and institutional models of the market, play an important role in the context of financial markets and various types of institutions have emerged to deal effectively with them. The next section introduces capital markets, which are subsequently classified into three forms (informal, formal and organized capital markets) in Section 3. The two main types of contract that characterize capital markets and their advantages and disadvantages are introduced in Section 4. Section 5 shows how institutions that promote liquidity and marketability facilitate the funding of long-term investment. Section 6 illustrates the various institutional forms in which capital markets are organized.

2 Capital Markets

Question

What mechanisms ensure co-ordination between the supply and demand for capital?

Starting with the neoclassical framework outlined in Chapter 2, the most obvious candidate is the price mechanism. As for any good, buyers of capital will pay a price to sellers. In the case of capital, this will take the form of an interest rate that co-ordinates the action of savers/lenders with borrowers/investors. Moreover, if we assume perfect information and perfect certainty, it will do this in such a way as to ensure that the amount and allocation of investment is optimal.

Suppose, however, that the demand for funds by borrowers exceeds the quantity offered by lenders. To attract the scarce funds of lenders, investors will have to offer an attractive rate of return. Funds will thus go to those investors who are able to offer the highest rate of return to savers. Those investors who are willing to offer the highest rate of return must also be those who perceive that their investment will offer the highest yield, otherwise they would be unwilling to offer such a high yield. Thus, one may equate willingness to pay by a borrower with his or her expected return. Hence rationing by price will ensure that the investment projects selected by the capital markets will be those which offer the highest prospective rate of return. To summarize, a properly functioning capital market will ensure that the investment projects chosen are those which offer the highest prospective rate of return. Thus the price mechanism should ensure that society receives the benefits of an optimal level and allocation of investment. Neoclassical growth theory has shown that the resulting level of investment will maximize consumption growth over time (under the assumption that externalities are not significant).

If there were perfect information and perfect certainty then this argument would be incontrovertible. However, the impact of imperfect (often asymmetric) information and of uncertainty has led some to criticize this neoclassical argument. Keynes (1936, p.161) referred to these as 'the dark forces of time and ignorance'. Since 1980, the economist Joseph Stiglitz has pioneered the application of the new economics of information to finance and argued that one can appraise the quality and performance of financial systems by their ability to cope with the problems generated by imperfect information – such as adverse selection and moral hazard (see Chapter 2, *Firms*). According to Greenwald and Stiglitz (1992) there are:

> ... basic differences between financial (capital) markets and other markets, in which goods are traded contemporaneously. In capital markets, money today is exchanged for a *promise* of returns in future.

> ... It is precisely this difference which explains why financial markets are not, and cannot be, run as auction markets: why lenders, for instance, do not simply lend to those who are willing to offer to pay the highest interest rates.
>
> *(Greenwald and Stiglitz, 1992, p.39, emphasis in the original)*

Question

Would you rather lend money to a flamboyant entrepreneur who offers to pay a high interest rate for a risky project or to a person with a reputation for probity who offers to pay a low interest rate for a low-risk investment? What considerations would contribute to your decisions?

Price considerations would certainly influence your decision, but I am sure that you would also evaluate the riskiness of the project that your money would fund. In particular, two considerations are important. First, the borrower/investor has a greater knowledge about the investment project than you (asymmetric information) and may cheat you. Second, even if the borrower/investor is completely honest about the investment, he or she could be wrong about the level of returns in the future (uncertainty).

> Thus in contrast to markets for homogeneous commodities, in which the role of institutions (firms and market makers) can reasonably be approximated by the interaction of supply and demand, in studying financial markets and the allocation of funds, the role of institutions is central.
>
> *(Greenwald and Stiglitz, 1992, p.39)*

Definition

Auction market

Auction markets trade in commodities that are homogeneous and have a large number of sellers and potential buyers.

Over time, economic systems have developed a range of financial institutions to deal with the uncertainty that surrounds financial transactions.

3 Informal, formal and organized capital markets

Capital markets are a mechanism which brings borrowers/investors together with savers/lenders. Historically, different institutions have emerged in capitalist systems to facilitate the transfer of funds from savers to investors, and marked differences are noticeable today across countries. In many developing countries, capital markets can be described as *informal*. Such markets still exist in parts of Europe and were predominant there until about 1960. Informal markets work in the following way. Suppose that an entrepreneur has a bright idea. He can approach local rich citizens and ask them if they are willing to back him. He will obtain finance only if he is sufficiently persuasive. Much of the Industrial Revolution in the UK was financed in this way. James Watt was able to proceed with his development of the steam engine because Matthew Boulton put up the required funds (see *Firms,* Chapter 9). In many societies this informal capital market centres on one or two local dignitaries. In the past in rural France, for example, this was usually a notary. Any local citizen with funds to spare would approach the notary and ask if he had any ideas as to how to invest their funds. Similarly, anyone needing funds would approach this functionary. This would include not only entrepreneurs but also young people anxious to purchase farms or houses. The role of a notary was an important step towards the development of a formal financial market.

Nowadays, specialized financial institutions provide venture capital funds for the modern equivalent of James Watt, so he would approach these rather than relying on the haphazard process whereby he met Mr. Boulton. Most formal markets, moreover, evolve into organized financial markets.

In the UK, this process began in the seventeenth century. Around 1690 those wishing to deal in shares in London started to congregate at Jonathan's Coffee House. This quickly became a formal market. However it took about one hundred years for it to develop into an organized market and develop a legal existence with a formal procedure. Part of this procedure was that would-be purchasers of shares had to approach the market through a broker.

Brokers had to be members of the Stock Exchange and satisfy various legal requirements. During the nineteenth century, the Stock Exchange assumed responsibility for any default by its members and, crucially, it provided a settlement system. This is the process whereby title is transferred to the purchaser and money is received by the seller. In the case of a pint of beer the settlement system is simple. The drinker hands over the cash more or less simultaneously with the receipt of the pint. In the case of finance, for example when buying or selling a financial instrument such as a share, the process is necessarily more complex. A financial instrument lacks the concrete nature of beer. Anyone can recognize whether or not they have been given a pint of beer whereas a piece of paper may or may not give valid legal title to the assets described therein. Lenders must be fairly confident that the 'promise' will be maintained, otherwise they could be deterred from lending.

Definition

Formal financial markets

Formal financial markets contain institutions and organizations which borrowers/ investors (savers/lenders) can approach to borrow (lend) funds.

Definition

Organized financial markets

Organized financial markets have a formal system of exchange with a legal existence and a formal procedure for settlement.

Definition

Broker

A broker brings buyers and sellers together.

In informal financial markets, trust and reputation usually ensure the enforcement of contracts. In such markets, 'financial transactions [are] often concentrated among members of a well defined ethnic group or community' (Greenwald and Stiglitz, 1992, pp.47–8) and therefore social sanctions effectively ensure the fulfilment of contracts.

However, when markets grow and become increasingly organized they also become impersonal, and therefore it is necessary to have a legal infrastructure to ensure the fulfilment of contracts and to combat fraud. A well designed legal system is very important for the functioning of a capitalist economy. Historically, the definition and the detection of fraud has been refined and improved; improved accounting standards have also helped in the reduction of fraud.

A crucial development in the legal infrastructure in capitalist systems, moreover, has been the existence of the principle of *limited liability*. This principle means that the lender's responsibility for the debts of a business is restricted to the size of the lender's investment in it. Since firms are legal entities separate from their owners, investors are not liable for the debts accumulated by the firms they own. This important institution removes constraints arising from the uncertain nature of investment as it rules out the danger that the investor may lose more than they commit.

4   Types of security

Definitions

Security

A lender/saver acquires a claim on a borrower as a consequence of a capital market transaction. Such a claim is usually referred to as a security.

Debt contract

Under a debt contract the amount that the borrower must repay is independent of both the outcome of the project and the borrower's net worth/income but it may depend upon the state of the world.

Equity contract

Under an equity contract the amount received by the saver depends on either the outcome of the project or the borrower's condition (income/net worth).

Key to the operation of financial outlets are the constantly developing types of 'promises', i.e. contracts, that are exchanged. These deal with the uncertainty inherent in financial transactions in different ways.

Securities can take many different forms but there are two principal varieties:

- (pure) debt instruments
- equity instruments.

Suppose that an entrepreneur borrows £2 million to dig a mine. The debt contract might specify a fixed amount to be repaid by the borrower/investor. Alternatively, the contract might specify that the amount the borrower/investor has to repay depends upon the general level of interest rates, that is, upon a state-of-the-world variable. Other variables that define the state of the world could be the exchange rate or the rate of inflation. The essential point is that, in pure debt contracts, the amount that the borrower/investor has to repay is independent of the future value of the mine and of his or her income.

In the above case, the amount that the borrower/investor has to repay does not depend upon either future income or the future movements in the price of the mine. The lender of an equity contract however, acquires a portion of the ownership of the mine and is entitled to participate in the company's profits.

Holders of equity are entitled to (but only to) all that is left after all the other claimants on the firm have been paid. In legal terms, an equity interest, i.e. a profit, is a residual claim, which is subordinate to the interests of all other parties. Other parties are the employees of the company (wages); suppliers of raw materials, intermediate and capital goods; debtors (interest) and the government (taxes).

Because of the difference in the nature of debt and equity, there are different risks and rewards involved in providing finance whether it is in the form of equity or in the form of a loan (pure debt finance). Companies usually fund their investments by a mixture of debt and equity.

4.1 Debt finance and risk

Question

What risks and rewards would you face if you lent money under a debt contract?

From the definition of debt we know that the reward is the (contractually defined) interest that is paid when the debt matures. The risk is that the borrower might default.

One characteristic of pure debt contracts that is attractive for investors is that these contracts fix a maximum amount that will be repaid. In consequence, borrowers/investors will wish to take greater risk than is optimal for a bank. Suppose that a borrower has a choice of two strategies, one involving more risk than the other. To simplify things, let us assume that the borrower sets up a firm in order to take advantage of limited liability. If the riskier strategy pays off, all the extra return accrues to the borrower, a necessary consequence of pure debt contracts. On the other hand, if the riskier strategy fails and the firm loses everything, then losses are divided between the bank and the borrower. It is possible that the extra return will more than compensate the borrower for the increased risk involved. However, the bank is bound to prefer the safer option since it stands to gain none of the extra return if the risky strategy pays off (the amount repaid does not depend on the return to the project). *Firms,* Chapter 1 explains how to calculate expected returns and the following example should clarify the argument.

Suppose that the interest rate is 8 per cent. The borrower/investor will have a positive return only if the return to the project is greater than 8 per cent because the first 8 per cent goes to the bank (debt has priority over equity).

A borrower has a choice between two projects, each with an expected return of 10 per cent. Project A offers a return of 10 per cent with certainty. In this case the bank will have a return of 8 per cent (the interest rate) and the borrower a return of 2 per cent (10 − 8 per cent).

The other project, B, offers with equal probability (probability = 0.5) a 20 per cent return if it pays off and 0 per cent if it fails. To simplify the arithmetic we shall assume limited liability and that the bank gets its principal back. Hence, the total expected return from the investment in Project B is:

$$(20 \times 0.5) + (0 \times 0.5) = (20 \times 0.5) = 10$$

The borrower will receive a net return of 12 per cent in the good state of the world and 0 in the bad. The borrower's expected return is therefore 6 per cent:

$$((20 - 8) \times 0.5) + (0 \times 0.5) = (12 \times 0.5) = 6$$

The bank will receive 8 per cent in the good state of the world and 0 in the bad state, so its expected return is:

$$(8 \times 0.5) + (0 \times 0.5) = (8 \times 0.5) = 4$$

Hence the more risky strategy gives an expected return of 6 per cent to the borrower and 4 per cent to the bank. The borrower might well prefer the more risky strategy as it yields an expected return of 6 per cent against a return of 2 per cent for the safe strategy. The bank, however, will necessarily prefer the safer one as it yields a return of 8 per cent against an expected return of 4 per cent. But the bank cannot determine which strategy the borrower will opt for, that is, it cannot ensure that the investor will choose the safe strategy because it has less information than the investor (asymmetric information) and it cannot determine the way in which the money is spent (lack of control).

When the interest rate is at 8 per cent, it is profitable for investors to borrow funds for both types of projects, safe and risky. If we assume that risky and safe investors/borrowers turn up with the same probability (probability = 0.5) and the bank cannot tell which is which, the expected return for the bank will be:

$$(8 \times 0.5) + (4 \times 0.5) = (4 + 2) = 6$$

and only one in four (25 per cent) borrowers will default (only 50 per cent choose the risky option, and, of those, half will default). The various events are summarized in Table 5.1.

Table 5.1   **Returns with interest at 8 per cent**

	Project A **Return** **(certain)**	**Project B** **Good state** **of the world**	**Bad state** **of the world**	**Return** **(expected)**
Return	10	20	0	10
Bank	8	8	0	4
Borrower	2	12	0	6

Exercise 5.1

What happens if the bank increases the rate of interest from 8 per cent to 11 per cent?

Calculate the expected returns for the bank and the borrower. You can proceed in two steps. First, calculate the expected rates of return for the investor for the safe project (A) and the risky project (B) investments. Remember that the expected return from the investment is the average of the returns weighted by their probabilities. Second, repeat the same procedure for the bank.

Now calculate the total expected return for the bank, keeping in mind that the assumption that investors/borrowers turn up with the same probability might not hold given the new returns for projects A and B.

The exercise shows that increasing interest rates is not a good strategy for the bank. At low rates of interest banks will lend to both safe and risky customers. As interest rates rise, the bank's customers will take more risks. This may represent the same borrowers taking greater risks (moral hazard) or merely that the safe borrowers are dropping out (adverse selection). Banks may find that if they increase their interest rate then a greater proportion of their customers default. Bank revenue is interest paid by those who repay less than the amount lost to those who default. If default rates are linked to the interest rate then there is a rate of interest which will maximize the banks' expected rate of return. Left to themselves, banks will never increase rates beyond this point irrespective of the amount of excess demand.

This means that the price mechanism does not always ensure that the excess demand for loans will be zero. Financial markets are not auction markets because uncertainty and information asymmetries exist. Banks do not know which strategy investors will follow. Moreover, pure debt contracts, like the one in the example, generally do not give lenders *control* over the use of assets. Banks, and lenders of debt finance in general, cannot ensure that the assets funded with the loans will be used in the best way.

Question

How do banks respond to the problems of lack of control and asymmetric information?

Banks respond in two ways: by screening borrowers and by rationing their funds. If you have borrowed money from a bank you have probably noticed that transactions are not impersonal. In general, in both the UK and the US, banks ask customers to fill in a form known as a scorecard. The bank then allocates points to the potential borrower, for example, for being in regular employment, owing a home, etc. Through this screening process, the bank collects information about the borrower and therefore reduces information asymmetries. The anonymity of standard commodity markets disappears.

On the basis of the total number of points scored, the bank offers the customer a loan of a certain amount at a rate determined by the bank. In some, but not all cases, this will be as large or larger than the borrower requests. Often, however, the prospective borrower cannot borrow as much as he or she wants and no expression of willingness to pay more will increase the amount available. The bank offers a fixed price–quantity package on a take-it or leave-it basis and borrowers can choose neither the quantity nor the price. Moreover, the credit market is marked by chronic excess demand. According to elementary economic theory, banks should respond to excess demand by raising the price – the interest rate – they charge. They do not do this for the reasons that we saw above. This behaviour is called credit rationing; borrowers are allowed only a certain quantity of the good they desire – hence they are rationed.

Rationing can take various forms. The bank may refuse a loan or may lend only a proportion of what the borrower wants. In addition, the bank may be willing to lend only if certain supplementary conditions are met. In particular, it may demand collateral or security, that is, it may lend only if the borrower can produce assets for full collateral (of equal value to the loan). The bank is given a charge on these assets so that it will acquire ownership of them if the borrower defaults. Loans may also have conditions imposed on the use to which they may be put. These forms of credit rationing are experienced by corporate as well as personal borrowers.

The existence of credit rationing throws doubt upon the neoclassical model of optimal allocation of finance through interest rates and suggests the need for deeper analysis that explicitly takes into account the issue of institutional design.

4.2   Equity finance and the managerial theory of the firm

Question

What risks and rewards would you face if you bought equity capital (ordinary shares) in a company?

Holders of ordinary shares receive the returns from their investment in two ways. If the company is profitable (and sometimes also if it is not) it pays a dividend to the shareholders. In addition, the value of shares in the stock market can grow, and investors can sell the shares at a higher value than the price of purchase and realize capital gains. The capital gain, however, can be negative (a loss) if the price of the shares declines. Another problem with equity investment is that managers may decide not to pay dividends at all and may use profits to finance new investment opportunities.

An advantage that equity has over debt is that it confers ownership rights, and usually, therefore, decision power, to shareholders. As we saw above, debt contracts do not confer control on the use of assets; they can only specify some constraints on the use of the funds borrowed. If somebody owns more than 50 per cent of the equity capital which confers a right to vote, they can decide how to run the firm. The control that shareholders can actually exercise, however, has decreased with the appearance of very large firms at the beginning of the twentieth century (Berle and Means, 1932). In many firms, ownership is dispersed among many small investors who are not involved in the running of the company as they only own a very small fraction of it. Large companies are usually run by professional managers. This implies that managers enjoy some freedom of action and they may abuse it. This phenomenon is called the management/public good problem. The effort that a few shareholders put into monitoring the actions of the managers generates benefits for every shareholder. Since, however, monitoring is expensive in terms of time and resources, shareholders may be inclined to free ride on the monitoring provided by others. If every shareholder behaves in this way the managers will not be monitored at all.

Even if groups of shareholders agree to monitor the management, the management/public good problem is compounded by the fact that the separation between ownership and control generates asymmetries in information between managers and shareholders. Managers know the firm and the external environment much better than the shareholders, and shareholders are aware of that.

Principal–agent theory (*Firms*, Chapter 2) can be used to analyse this phenomenon. The principal is the party providing the funds, in this case equity, while the managers are the agents. The existence of asymmetric information means that those who provide equity finance (the principals) are rarely in a position to discipline those who use it (the agents) because they don't know whether the agents are doing the best they can.

The managerial theory of the firm analyses this issue. Managers have considerable discretion to pursue their own goals, and these goals are likely, it is argued, to diverge from those of shareholders. This divergence may take two forms. Managers may pursue their own interests at the expense of shareholders if they believe that they will gain prestige or income through unprofitable growth or excess size. This line of reasoning was pioneered by Penrose (1959), Marris (1964) and Baumol (1967). An alternative line of argument was first pointed out by Hicks (1935) but is usually associated with Williamson (1964) under the title of 'managerial slack'. This is simply that managers may use their discretion to have a quiet life (work less hard) or to spend the firm's resources in ways that yield benefit to the management but not the shareholder, for example on items such as plush offices, chauffeur-driven cars, private jets and helicopters and subscriptions to exclusive clubs.

In the UK and the US, mechanisms have evolved in recent years which seek to remove the underlying divergence of interest between principals and agents. Such devices as stock options mean that managers stand to gain enormous sums of personal wealth if the company's share price rises. While stock options align the interests of managers and owners, the huge sums that managers gain as a result of the exercise of their stock options represent a cost for the owners. In the principal–agent literature these costs are referred to as bonding costs.

It is also often argued that, especially in Anglo-Saxon countries, stock markets constrain the freedom of managers through the takeover mechanism. Manne (1965) termed this 'the market in corporate control'. If managers do not maximize the interest of shareholders, then share prices will be lower than they could be, given the nature of the firm's assets. This gives an incentive for someone to purchase the company (buy corporate control) and maximize the company's profits. Buyers can pay a price in excess of the previous market price because they feel that the assets of the acquired company will have a higher value under their management. Both the seller and purchaser benefit from the takeover. Since managers know this, the *threat* of takeover is assumed to reduce the discrepancy between the actions of the agents and the interests of the shareholders.

The effectiveness of the takeover threat, however, has been challenged on various grounds. In particular, for the threat to be effective it must be easy and relatively costless to trade the shares. Shares of private companies (i.e. companies not quoted on a stock market) are not easy to trade. It is not easy to find a buyer, and there is seldom good quality, reliable information available on the company since it does not have to disclose as much information as companies quoted on stock exchanges. In other words, there is not an *organized* market for the shares of unquoted companies and, therefore, they are not easily marketable. Organized financial markets make *marketability* easier and reduce the agency problem that arises from the separation of ownership and control by enhancing the takeover threat.

Well-functioning, organized markets also generate other economic advantages by increasing the marketability, and therefore the liquidity of financial assets.

5   Liquidity and marketability

Definition

Liquidity

Liquidity measures the ease with which an asset can be converted into purchasing power.

5.1   Liquidity, marketability and the irreversibility of long-term investments

An asset is liquid if the lender can convert it into purchasing power in a short *time*, at low *cost* and with little *risk* (see *Changing Economies*, Chapter 11). Another aspect of liquidity is *depth*. This measures the quantity of an asset that can be encashed quickly.

Since people usually prefer liquid assets (i.e. it is better to have the funds available now than have them stuck in a long-term investment), it is more difficult to find funds for long-term irreversible investments. However, an otherwise illiquid asset may be rendered liquid if one can borrow against it. Organized financial markets provide liquidity through ensuring marketability.

Take the example of the Channel Tunnel. From a social point of view this is an irreversible investment and few investors would be willing to commit funds indefinitely or even for many years. The £5 billion spent on digging, lining and equipping the Channel Tunnel could not possibly be recovered if someone decided that it had been a mistake to construct it. However, the building of the Channel Tunnel was financed, in part, by the issue of ordinary shares that are traded on various stock exchanges. Holders of these shares may sell them on a stock exchange at any time they choose. Hence, individual investors can reverse their decision to invest in the Channel Tunnel, although, as in this particular example, marketability does not ensure against the risk of losses.

This is the greatest single social and private advantage of organized capital markets. Large quantities of investment funds are available to finance uncertain or highly illiquid investment projects because the fund providers know that they can reverse the decision on a highly organized capital market by selling the claims to a third party. Their investment remains relatively liquid because it is marketable and so they are willing to provide funds for socially irreversible investments, such as the Channel Tunnel.

5.2   Marketability and specialization in organized markets

There is little doubt that the Anglo-American capital markets provide greater depth and liquidity than any other. The UK and US authorities encouraged and fostered financial innovation throughout the 1970s and 1980s to increase the liquidity and marketability of virtually all assets. As a result, many previously highly illiquid assets became relatively easy to trade on organized markets.

During this period it became possible to develop many assets into various components and trade these separately. This was part of a process called securitization whereby a previously non-tradeable loan is made in a form that permits trading on a secondary market. Securitization offers the advantages of specialization, that is, financial institutions can concentrate on the activities in which they have superior competencies.

The introduction of securitized mortgages

Traditionally, house purchase in the UK has been financed by a long-term mortgage, typically for 25 years. This meant that the provider, usually a Building Society or bank, was committed to the loan for this period. During this time they had to administer the mortgage (collect interest etc.), bear the risk if the borrower defaulted and fund the mortgage, that is, they had to find an alternative deposit if the ultimate lender withdrew his or her funds. In the 1980s all these activities became separated through securitized mortgages. Mortgages were made in a form which meant that they could be re-sold by the original lender to someone else. A pioneer of such securitized mortgages was the Bank of Scotland. Suppose someone wished to buy a flat in Edinburgh, they would approach the Bank of Scotland who have considerable expertise in appraising both the value of the property and the creditworthiness of Scottish economic agents. However, the Bank of Scotland did not always have a competitive advantage in funding the mortgage. Hence it frequently made loans in securitized form which meant that they could be sold to, for example, Dai-Ichi, the largest Japanese insurance company. Dai-Ichi had a surplus of funds to invest and felt that UK mortgages were a highly attractive investment. The sale might leave the risk of default with the Bank of Scotland or with Dai-Ichi. A third possibility arose, however. The mortgage could be insured so that this risk was transferred to a third party, usually an insurance company (Eagle Star was the biggest provider of such insurance). In practice, the Bank of Scotland usually continued to administer the mortgage, collect interest and decide what to do when a payment was missed, however many mortgages were administered by a third party. The Skipton Building Society acquired a reputation for being exceptionally efficient at administering mortgages and frequently administered mortgages on behalf of foreign financial institutions, including various Saudi Arabian banks.

It is easy to see that the case study provides a classic example of competitive advantage. Dai-Ichi, the Bank of Scotland and the Skipton Building Society each have a chance to employ their competitive advantage in different aspects of a mortgage so that all the benefits of specialization can be achieved. Moreover, as a consequence of this specialization and the competition that it has engendered, mortgages have become less liquid obligations for the borrower in that they are now available for a period of 35 years. These and similar developments mean that lenders are far more willing to lend against the security of different assets.

5.3   Liquidity and short-termism

In the section above we saw that Anglo-American financial systems are very effective in mobilizing capital for socially irreversible investments by ensuring the liquidity and marketability of financial assets. In recent years, financial innovation, and the competition and specialization that it has engendered, has generated advantages to investors and savers. It is argued, however, that such financial systems are efficient only from a private point of view. Keynes (1936, p.155) argued that the 'fetish of liquidity', that is, excessive concern with returns in the short term and ignoring longer-term development, engendered what his successors called short-termism.

Definition

Short-termism

Investment projects with higher expected returns may be rejected because the returns are deferred.

One way in which financial systems that promote liquidity and marketability can generate short-termism is through an excessively competitive market for corporate control. The argument runs as follows. While in many cases the intervention of shareholders is desirable and leads to an increase not only in the profits of the company but also in its efficiency measured from a social point of view, in other cases it can push corporate management to be too anxious to please shareholders by pursuing strategies that generate high profits in the short-run but inhibit long-term planning. Again, the root of the problem lies in the existence of information asymmetries between managers and shareholders. Shareholders will lack the information necessary to decide if expensive investments that do not generate rewards in the short-term are wise or merely managerial aggrandisement (putting growth and size before profits). Furthermore, shareholders know that the board knows more than they do and that the board might use this extra information to put their interests before those of the shareholders. Hence, shareholders may rationally decide not to fund such long-term uncertain investment (a version of Akerlof's market for lemons, see *Firms,* Chapter 2).

Thus, it is argued that Anglo-Saxon managers have to pursue short-term objectives because of the pressure from the market for corporate control, while the German and Japanese financial systems provide managers with greater long-term security. Paradoxically, an organized stock market that makes it possible to collect funds for irreversible social investments could actually discriminate against long-term and innovative investment. Even if this is true, however, it is important to consider that such security might be abused, and managers might use the long-term security to make a series of disastrous decisions.

6   Forms of capital markets

6.1   Broker markets

Capital markets have to bring borrowers and lenders together. This necessarily involves transaction costs. Moreover, such transactions are likely to be bedevilled by uncertainty and asymmetric information, which may give perverse incentives to recipients of funds. In a seminal article in 1988, Oliver Williamson applied transaction cost economics to finance; Neave (1989) has subsequently extended this analysis. Williamson argued that there were three fundamental forms of organizing capital markets: broker markets, intermediary markets and internal capital markets. Each of these institutional forms has some merits and demerits.

As we saw above, a broker is a person who brings buyers and sellers together; a classic example is a stockbroker. Anyone wishing to purchase or sell shares in the UK would normally approach a broker. The term can also be used to describe other economic agents performing similar functions, for example estate agents. Williamson widened the definition to include the whole mechanism, including brokers. In particular, he applied it to a stock exchange. The crucial defining characteristic of a broker market is that individual economic agents acquire claims on the financial user of the funds. So, for example, suppose I use a broker market to finance investment in the Channel Tunnel, I acquire shares in the Channel Tunnel Company and have no direct claim on the broker.

We have seen in previous sections that formal and organized markets offer several advantages. They provide a locale for exchange, and favour the financing of long-term investment by promoting liquidity by marketability. However, markets can be inefficient when transactions are characterized by asymmetric information or severe uncertainty as we saw, for instance, in the case of credit rationing (Neave, 1991). The case study on mortgages, in addition, showed that intermediaries can accumulate competencies in particular areas of finance.

6.2   Intermediary markets

Financial intermediaries

The essence of an intermediary market is that the provider of funds acquires a claim not on the final user but on an intermediary; similarly, the user of funds acquires an obligation to the intermediary. A classic example is a unit trust (outside the UK this is known as an open-ended mutual fund). In this case, individuals who wish to purchase shares acquire units in the unit trust. Hence the investor owns, for example, 100 units in the M&G High Income Fund. This unit trust then uses the investor's money to purchase shares in companies. Thus the individual investor owns units while the shares are owned by the unit trust.

Using financial intermediaries offers advantages both to the individual investors and the companies in whom investment is made.

Economies of scale

Traditional analysis of intermediaries emphasized their inter-related advantages of economies of scale especially in managing pre-determined risk.

The administration of investments can be a time-consuming and expensive process as it involves the selection of an investment, its purchase and sale, the collection of interest and dividends and monitoring the investment's performance. Specialist intermediaries are likely to be doing this on a large scale and can so reap the benefits of economies of scale.

Risk reduction

Financial intermediaries reduce risk through investing in many companies. This is called diversification and can yield two main benefits.

If the investments are independent, a risk can be converted into a known amount, through the law of large numbers. For example, suppose you lend £100 to one person with a probability of default of 10 per cent. There is no way that you can eliminate the 10 per cent danger of losing your *entire* investment. Suppose, however, that you lend to 1000 individuals. If the probability of default remains at 10 per cent, you no longer face a 10 per cent risk of losing *all* your funds, instead you have a known contingency that you may lose 10 per cent of your investment. You can compensate for this by demanding, for example, a higher rate of interest (note that in this example there is no adverse selection because the investments are all equally risky). The larger the number of investments, the less the dispersion of possible returns.

The returns of some investments are not independent and in some cases they are negatively correlated, that is, some investments will do well while others do badly. As an example, investment in ice-cream companies will do well when the weather is hot and sunny and badly when the weather is cold and rainy. The opposite is likely to be true of umbrellas. Hence the risk of investing in ice-cream can be offset by also investing in umbrella manufacturing companies. Again one minimizes risk, that is, the dispersion of possible returns.

An individual investor is unlikely to have the funds to diversify on a sufficiently large scale; the cost of doing so would be prohibitive for small investors and very expensive even for large ones. On the other hand, an intermediary will be able to invest in a larger range of companies. Suppose there are 1000 investors, for example, and that each has £500 to invest. Each investor might invest in five companies – leading to 5000 transactions. Now suppose, instead, that each investor invests £500 with an intermediary. The intermediary then invests in 50 companies, investing £10,000 in each. There are now only 1050 transactions (1000 purchases of claims on the intermediary and 50 purchases by the intermediary) but each investor now has the benefits of diversifying into 50 companies rather than five.

Economies of massed reserves

Because of the high number of lenders and borrowers, financial intermediaries provide an alternative to the liquidity offered through a market. Through financial intermediaries, liquidity can be provided to lenders/savers without any obligation by borrowers/investors to repay their funds.

Because of the larger number of investors, the intermediary can calculate the likelihood that any individual investor will actually encash their investment on one day and the likelihood of being able to obtain new investments. So, if the intermediary holds a small cash reserve this should be sufficient to meet the encashments on any day and to deal with any timing discrepancies between purchases and sales. Hence it can guarantee that each individual investor has the option of encashing his investment without any need to redeem his claim on ultimate borrowers, that is, sell shares.

The quality of information flows

One may characterize all the above as a provision of insurance to investors. Diversification provides insurance against risk of default (and loss more generally); the liquidity mechanism provides insurance against the contingency that one may wish to encash the investment. This highlights the fact that they are both means of managing pre-given risk in a more efficient fashion. Since Stiglitz, analysis has switched to the better management of risk. The basic argument is that the intermediary may be better at assessing or reducing risk through greater/better information.

Financial intermediaries collect information about borrowers through the screening process. Another way of obtaining good information is through universal banking, whereby banks own significant equity stakes in companies. This banking form is common in Germany but has been illegal in the US since 1934 (the Glass Steagall Act) and is unusual in Britain.

In addition, German banks manage large blocks of shares on behalf of shareholders. Hence, many banks own and/or manage large stakes in companies to whom they provide funds. For example Deutsche Bank owns 25 per cent of Daimler-Benz and manages shares which normally amount to at least another 20 per cent. The chairman of Deutsche Bank is usually a member of the supervisory board of Daimler-Benz. Deutsche Bank is also a major provider of debt finance to Daimler-Benz. Hence, it is argued, Deutsche Bank has much greater knowledge of the company than would be the case for any individual shareholder or lender in the UK.

The divergent history of Jaguar since 1966, compared to German car manufacturers such as Daimler-Benz and BMW, is often cited as an example. Jaguar was taken over by the then British Motor Corporation in 1968 because it lacked the funds to develop its cars. The resulting company was later absorbed into British Leyland and subsequently nationalized. Jaguar was eventually privatized but was unable to retain its independence and was taken over by Ford. Those who admire the German system argue that German car manufacturers were able to obtain funds because prospective investors (such as Deutsche Bank) could obtain better and more information than their UK counterparts. They could, therefore, better appraise the risk involved in large-scale investment in luxury and sports cars. They could also ascertain the quality of management and the dangers that management would abuse the use of funds in either managerial/excess growth or in excessive risk taking through the provision of debt finance. Moreover, German banks and their satellite shareholders could take a long-term view of the company's prospects rather than being influenced by short-term movements in share prices. Indeed, there was no way that Deutsche Bank could walk away from its investment in Daimler-Benz whereas dissatisfied investors in Jaguar could sell their shares and abandon the problems.

6.3   Internal capital markets

Both broker and intermediary markets as described above are examples of *external* capital markets, this means that borrowers and lenders have access to the whole range of the market and are not part of the same legal organization (although Deutsche Bank is half-way towards being an insider in the above example). The simplest form of an *internal* capital market is a holding company such as the Hanson Group in the UK. A holding company is a company whose only assets are shares of other companies which it then controls. The fact that Hanson demerged in the late 1990s illustrates that there are weaknesses as well as strengths to internal capital markets. In its heyday in the 1980s and early 1990s, however, Hanson frequently vaunted the virtues of the internal capital market. In internal capital markets, funds for expansion have to be generated within the group. Hence if Chloride Batteries wished to expand then it could obtain the profits from the surpluses generated by the Imperial (Tobacco) Group.

In Japan large quantities of funds are generated within the *keiretsu*. These are normally household names such as Mitsubishi, successors to the pre-war *zaibatsu*. These giant companies were broken up by the American occupation authorities immediately after the Second World War. Hence Mitsubishi now consists of over 300 companies. However, the companies still retain legal links through cross-shareholdings and overlapping directorships. More importantly, they retain a strong sense of corporate ethos and in many ways all the companies in the group feel a common affinity. One of the members of each group is a bank. This bank is a major provider of funds to the other companies in conjunction with any other firm that is generating a surplus.

The disadvantage of an internal capital market is that it produces a large element of chance and arbitrariness into the capital market process. Suppose that someone in Mitsubishi has a good idea, for example, for an electronics project. This idea may never be pursued if Mitsubishi is not making profits from car manufacturing. At the same time, some other company outside the *keiretsu* might have funds available and might decide to invest in an electronics project that is clearly inferior to Mitsubishi's idea. Since the funds do not flow between the two companies, they are not allocated efficiently.

An internal capital market, however, has the advantage that the quality of information within a group (whether legal or social) is likely to be much higher; Mitsubishi executives are in a much better position to check on the quality of claims put forward by other members of the group. Moreover social pressures and obligations means that one might not mislead a fellow group member in the way that one might mislead a venture capital fund or an independent bank. Hence, it is argued that the quality of information is better and so investment funds can be allocated in a better fashion. Moreover, an internal capital market renders companies immune to the wishes and pressures of their shareholders, hence one can assume that there are no or few dangers of short-termism.

7   Conclusion

The function of the financial system, and in particular of capital markets, is crucial to a modern capitalist economy. A well functioning capital market facilitates the mobilization of funds for investment towards the most productive projects. However, transactions in financial markets are fraught with uncertainty and asymmetric information. Capitalist systems have, therefore, developed institutions that facilitate transactions between lenders and borrowers.

Developments in the legal framework have been central to the functioning of financial markets. The institution of limited liability, the fight against fraud and the establishment of organized markets have all facilitated the accumulation of capital. The institutional structure of capital markets varies greatly from country to country, and there are heated debates about the way in which such differences can influence economic growth. Capital markets can be organized through brokers, intermediaries or as internal capital markets. All of them have their advantages and disadvantages.

In recent years, financial markets have witnessed a significant number of developments in response to various events, such as the fall of communism in eastern Europe, pressures from the World Bank and the IMF, notably in Africa and Latin America, and from the globalization of financial markets. According to Greenwald and Stiglitz, the constant evolution of financial institutions has its roots in the imperfect nature of financial markets as there are constantly opportunities to exploit through the introduction of financial innovations.

> ... there will always be those who will seek to take advantage of existing and new contract forms for their own advantage, to define the boundaries of the fraud statutes, and to exploit common perceptions of contract interpretations, and the limitations of trust and reputation as contract enforcement mechanisms ...

> The process is best described as an evolutionary one, in which the deficiencies in the market give rise to new contract forms, in which some of those in the market gradually learn how to exploit the new contract forms, and in which the market gradually learns the deficiencies in those forms, giving rise, in turn, to still new arrangements.

> (Greenwood and Stiglitz, 1992, p.61)

CHAPTER 6

FINANCIAL SYSTEMS AND INNOVATION

by Andrew Tylecote

1 Introduction

You have seen in the previous chapter how, in capitalist economies, financial institutions play a central role in the process of capital accumulation as they facilitate the transfer of savings towards useful investment projects and limit the problems caused by uncertainty and asymmetric information which are substantial in financial transactions.

This chapter examines how, in different countries, financial systems deal with a particular category of investment projects, namely investment in innovation. Innovation is crucial to the competitive success of capitalist economies (*Firms*, Chapter 9), and an ongoing debate exists on which types of financial system are more successful in funding innovation. In this chapter, I set out a theory of how the institutional structure of financial systems affects innovation, and I present some empirical evidence that is consistent with this theory. I start, in the next section, by classifying financial systems into two main types, bank-based and stock market-based, according to their institutional characteristics. In Section 2, I analyse the different ways in which these systems perform their two functions of providing capital and exercising corporate governance, and how they have developed over time.

Section 3 joins in the debate on which type of system is better for innovation, and looks at how innovation can be funded. Funding innovation is a challenge for any financial system because it requires a special type of investment – investing in intangible capital. Knowledge is a very specific asset: it does not have much of a 'carcass value'. In addition, innovating firms may well not manage to *appropriate* all the benefits from their innovations.

Any general theory suggests a *research programme* – a programme of generating and testing rather specific hypotheses (*Firms*, Chapter 5). Some of the hypotheses that I derive from the theory outlined in this chapter in order to answer the question about funding innovation also help us to shed light in Section 4 on some 'stylized facts' that have been identified in studies on the national pattern of technological advantage.

Why, for example, is the UK strong in pharmaceuticals and weak in machine tools, while for Japan it is the other way round? Do these industries make different demands on the financial system? Industries vary in how appropriable innovation is, and in the main sources of uncertainty about it. Some sources of uncertainty can be reduced by tried and tested methods in bank-based economies, others cannot. Uncertainty that cannot be reduced is best tackled by what is called venture capital. I argue that, in principle, both types of system can provide venture capital, although the stock market-based economy of the US is way ahead at the moment.

2 Stock market-based and bank-based financial systems

2.1. The main features of the systems

In capitalist economies, various financial institutions have emerged over time to facilitate the transfer of funds from savers to investors. These institutions differ from country to country as the structure of financial systems is influenced by the historical development of a country in various ways.

The previous chapter showed that providers of funds have to be confident that borrowers will invest wisely, otherwise they may be deterred from lending. In addition, lenders face problems generated by the existence of uncertainty and asymmetric information, and their lack of control over investors' behaviour. The relationship between the provider and the user of capital, therefore, involves two elements: information and control.

Financial systems across countries show considerable differences in the way information asymmetries and control over the use of capital are dealt with. In this chapter, I distinguish between two types of financial systems, taking two examples of each: bank-based (Germany and Japan) and stock market-based (the UK and the US). This classification, although it is by no means the only one possible, has already been used in the literature, though with different labels (Berglof, 1990; Corbett and Mayer, 1991; Corbett and Jenkinson, 1994). In fact, every country has its own institutional characteristics, and important differences exist between the UK and the US and between Germany and Japan. However, I shall concentrate on the common features of the two systems in order to show how different financial structures can influence the performance of the economy.

Stock market-based and bank-based systems differ along three main dimensions. The first is the relative importance of long-term bank lending versus equity finance. The second is the nature of the relationship between banks and firms. This is *transactional* or arm's-length in stock market-based systems and *relational* in bank-based systems. In transactional lending each loan is seen as a one-off and is secured against collateral (the carcass value of the firm). In relational lending, by contrast, each loan is seen as being part of an ongoing relationship, in which the bank's risk is reduced by the bank having thorough knowledge of the firm's prospects. The third major difference is the nature of corporate control. In stock market-based systems there is a pronounced separation between ownership and control in large firms, which leaves greater scope for managerial discretion. In bank-based systems, various stakeholders, beside legal owners and managers, control the actions of the firm to a much greater extent than in stock-market based systems.

These dimensions are inter-related and evolve over time. Since the late 1980s, for instance, financial markets around the world have witnessed a great many reforms (partly due to the globalization of finance) and there is a lively debate about whether the institutional structures are converging and, if so, towards which system.

Table 6.1 summarizes the characteristics of the two systems.

Definition

Stakeholders

Individuals and groups with a stake in the success of the firm.

Table 6.1   **Properties of the two systems**

Stock market-based (US and UK)	Bank-based (Germany and Japan)
A large number of firms are quoted in the stock exchange	A small number of firms are quoted in the stock exchange
Dispersed ownership	Concentrated ownership and control
Separation of ownership and control	Association of ownership and control
Takeovers are often hostile and antagonistic (market for corporate control is active)	Absence of hostile takeovers (market for corporate control is not active)
Little incentive for outside investors to participate in corporate control	Control by stakeholders (banks, related firms, and employees)
Banks do not hold corporate equity and do not sit on boards of firms	Banks hold corporate equity and sit on the boards of firms
No cross-shareholdings between companies	Cross-shareholdings exist between companies
Low commitment of outside investors to long-term strategies of the firm	High commitment of the various stakeholders to the long-term strategies of the firm
Takeovers may create monopolies	Insider systems may encourage collusion

Source: Adapted from Corbett and Mayer, 1991, pp.63 and 65, Tables 3 and 4

In stock market-based systems, the economy is dominated by large firms that look to the stock market as a major source of equity and other finance, and also as a market for corporate control. Firms must seek to establish a good reputation and a correspondingly high share price so that they are not taken over. Banks are not used as a major source of risk capital, since their lending is transactional rather than relational.

In bank-based systems only a small number of large firms are public companies quoted on the stock exchange (see, for instance, the contrast between Germany and the UK in Figure 6.1 and they do not concern themselves with it as a market for corporate control – they do not fear takeover bids or seek to make them. Instead they and, *a fortiori*, other private companies look to banks as their main source of external long-term funding.

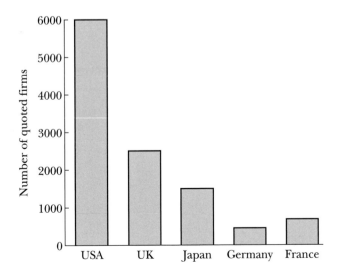

Figure 6.1   **Number of firms quoted on stock market**

Source: Corbett and Mayer, 1991, p.64

Firms' relationships with banks are accordingly close and lending is relational. This means that each loan is seen as part of a long-term relationship in which the firm is bound to inform the bank fully as to its position and prospects. The bank is committed to support the firm through bad times, in return for influence over its policy and personnel. Where a large firm borrows from more than one bank, one of them is normally recognized as the 'lead' or 'house' bank and this bank will maintain oversight of the firm's financial position (Henderson, 1993).

The relative importance of the stock market in stock market-based economies is illustrated by Figure 6.2 which shows that the total value of all firms quoted on the stock exchange (the market capitalization) is highest in the US and UK, once the size of the economy (GDP) is taken into account.

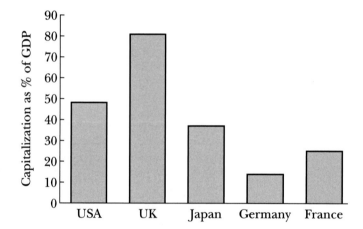

Figure 6.2 **Capitalization as a percentage of GDP**

Source: Prowse, 1994, p.30

The differing role of banks and stock markets is only part of the story. The key distinction between the two systems is in their mechanisms of corporate control. While in the UK and US ownership is dispersed among a large number of shareholders and, therefore, ownership and control are separated, in countries with bank-based systems, such as Germany and Japan, stock ownership is concentrated, although in different ways. For example, Table 6.2 shows that in Germany 59 per cent of large firms have a single owner holding over 50 per cent of the equity.

Table 6.2 **Ownership concentration in large firms: percentage by share of largest owner**

Largest owner's share	France	United States	Japan	United Kingdom	Germany
>50%	55	9	17	2	59
10-50%	42	39	42	14	41
<10%	2	52	25	84	

For each country, the table shows the percentage of large firms in each ownership category

Source: Berglof, 1990

In the continental European countries, founding families have a tendency to insist on retaining control; a tendency which seems to have cultural roots. There is a corresponding insistence on the obligations of ownership, including the exercise of control (Schneider-Lenne, 1992; Kester, 1992). In Germany, for example, few owners of middle-sized companies seek stock market flotation:

> They are not particularly interested in money ... They are more concerned not to lose their special position within their local community ... If they sell, they become merely rich – as the proprietor of a company they really are somebody. Even when a family decides to list, it rarely abandons control to the vagaries of the stock market. Thus the BMW group – majority-owned by the Quandt family – can enjoy the benefits of the stock market without changing its essential character as a (very large) family business.
>
> *(Waller, 1994, p.21)*

To retain control, owners must avoid diluting their share stake too much by mergers or by raising new voting share capital. If that means staying small, then banks are likely to be the best external source of capital.

Question

What possible obstacles do firms face if they want to raise debt finance, and in what ways can firms and banks overcome such obstacles? Look back to Chapter 5 when thinking about this.

You saw in the previous chapter that banks usually respond to lack of control and asymmetric information by rationing and screening. This suggests that companies in Germany and Japan might face financial constraints on investments. However, this does not seem to be the case since the level of investment per unit of output is higher than in the Anglo-Saxon countries (see Figure 6.3).

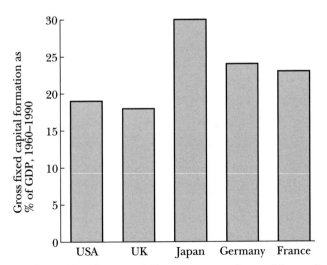

Figure 6.3   **Investment intensity in selected industrialized countries**

Source: OECD, TSM database

Relational lending partially overcomes the problem of asymmetric information as banks get to know firms and industries in more depth over time. The development of a close relationship and the acquisition of reliable information from banks, in turn, depend on the fact that in Japan and Germany banks also hold equity of non-financial firms and exert corporate control in various ways.

For example, since the 1870s German company law has insisted on two-tier boards. The upper, supervisory board is expected to keep a close eye on the lower board which runs the firm. The members of the supervisory board are elected by the shareholders and, under recent co-determination legislation, by the employees. Nonetheless, in large companies with heavy bank borrowing, the chairman of the supervisory board has traditionally been a bank official. The bank's power on this board might arise simply from 'loan leverage', but there is another source. From the beginning, small shareholders have usually deposited their shares with the bank, which has the right (with their agreement) to use their votes at shareholders' meetings. Over time, the banks have built up substantial industrial shareholdings of their own. As long as their survival depended upon the health of the companies to which they had lent, the banks appear to have done a good job of 'corporate governance' in the large companies which were no longer controlled by their founding families.

The role of family shareholders in Japanese industry has been less influential, first because, culturally, there is a tendency to regard firms as communities over which control by outsiders is illegitimate, and second because the great *zaibatsu* holding companies were split up and largely purged of family ownership after the Second World War. From the early 1950s, precisely because of the distrust of outside control, a network of cross-shareholdings grew up among companies with banks and other financial institutions participating so that stable shareholdings became dominant and hostile takeovers impossible (Kester, 1992; Prowse, 1992).

Although in Japan a single bank can only own up to 5 per cent of a firm, the influence of the 'main bank' (the bank that both holds equity and manages the company's cash flow and loans) on corporate control is substantial. 'In 1980 listed firms with bank borrowing had main banks as largest or second largest shareholders in 39 per cent of cases and in the top five shareholders in 79 per cent of cases' (Sheard, 1985, quoted in Corbett and Mayer, 1991, p.63).

Officials of the main bank gain detailed information about the firm through the management of the firm's financial activities and through direct contact with top management and business partners. This enables them to act early when the existing managers are under-performing and to replace them, usually by other existing employees (Aoki, 1990).

As well as the banks' influence, trade associations, suppliers, customers, competitors and employees also have some say as to how companies are run in Germany and in Japan. In these two countries, industrial managers can put pressure on their fellow managers in related firms. As for the workers, in Japan the life-time employment system for managers and other core workers of large firms helps to ensure that top managers feel an obligation to their fellow employees. In Germany, the co-determination system, in which employees are given a share of control by law, has the same effect. Pressure may also be informal as firms are usually embedded in local communities. In short, the parties that have a stake in the firm – the stakeholders – effectively contribute to corporate governance in bank-based economies. As you will see later in Section 3.2, the existence of such enfranchised stakeholders can make a difference in the innovation process.

In the organization of corporate control, bank-based systems contrast sharply with stock market-based systems. In the Anglo-Saxon economies, with their liberal traditions, wealth has been seen essentially as a commodity rather than enmeshed with rights and obligations, and, accordingly, family shareholders have been more ready than elsewhere to give up control. This is particularly true in the UK, where according to one influential economic journalist: '... successful British capitalists, politicians and officials have always been driven by the social goal of becoming gentlemen, apeing the lifestyle of the English aristocrat, and aiming to have the same kind of effortless, invisible income' (Hutton, 1995, p.114).

Stock exchange flotation has provided a means of exit from owner control. This led first to fragmented individual shareholdings and, more recently, to increasing concentration in the hands of financial institutions, now (especially in the UK) mainly pension funds. These institutions, however, do not behave like the banks of Germany and Japan, rather they have deliberately avoided any control relationship with management, acting as traders rather than investors, with highly diversified portfolios (Tylecote and Demirag, 1992; Porter, 1992).

Because of the widely dispersed shareholding, corporate control rests with management in stock market-based systems, and shareholders rely on the market for corporate control, i.e. *outsiders* are expected to discipline managers. Hence, in the UK and US hostile takeovers are more common.

2.2. Corporate governance and economic efficiency

The differences in corporate governance affect the ways in which the interests of the providers of funds are protected in the system. While the stock market-based system relies on *outsiders* to crack down on the sources of inefficiency, the bank-based system relies on *insiders*. The outsiders are the institutional investors (investment trusts, pension funds etc.) who dominate the US/UK system and are the main actors in the market for corporate control. You saw in Chapter 5, however, that a stock market which does not value shares properly can give rise to short-termism, and that control devices, such as stock options, can be an expensive way for outsiders to provide managers with the right incentives.

In the bank-based system, the insiders (family owners, bankers and other industrial managers) are the disciplinarians. They are much less likely than outsiders to generate myopic (short-termist) behaviour because they are much less likely to be ignorant about the firm's activities. Where, however, the key problem is to overcome conservatism, that is, an attachment to old products, processes and ways of doing things, a stock market-based system has an edge. In the bank-based system it is up to a specific group of insiders to crack down on bad management; if they fail the situation can slumber on until the firm runs out of cash. Anglo-Saxon capitalism, with its market for corporate control, means that managers of large firms are never safe to go on with out-of-date routines, because they are never safe from a hostile takeover. If the prospect of such a fate does not keep them on their toes, then the changes needed may take place through a takeover.

2.3 A historical perspective on the systems

You may have noticed that the stock market-based system is characteristic of the economies that developed earlier, the UK and the US, while Germany and Japan are 'younger' advanced economies. Does this mean that 'mature' economies present the others with the image of their own future? When they 'grow up' will they look more or less like the Anglo-Saxon systems? If you create the same circumstances (in this case economic maturity, in some sense) will you produce broadly the same result? Or is it that economies are path-dependent: does their history count?

So far as financial systems go, there seems to be something in both views. Perhaps the most important reason why history does count is the speeded-up nature of late development. Economies like Germany's in the early nineteenth century and Japan's in the late nineteenth century did not simply grow as Britain's had a century previously. They tried to strike out towards where Britain (and other leaders) then were, and close the gap as rapidly as possible. That meant that they needed massive infusions of capital, particularly into their heavy industries, and that key firms had to grow very quickly. The process involved a great deal of risk for the firms involved. The equity markets in these countries were as underdeveloped as the rest of their economies. The only way to get the capital together that was needed for industry was to 'hoover up' the savings of the landowners and the middle class, who would most certainly not entrust them to the stock market as it then existed. With luck and good regulation, however, banks might be trusted. In Japan the tradition was to fear all private financial institutions and stock markets equally. This led people to save in the government-backed institutions such as post offices: the public sector then acted as banker to the rest, including the privately owned banks. But how, then, could the banking system be protected from the riskiness of its investments?

There were broadly two solutions to the fragility of the bank-based system. The first solution was to devise arrangements that gave the major banks such good information about industry, so good an understanding of it, and so much control over it that the risk was drastically reduced. The central bank would back up smaller banks as the lender of last resort in a real crisis. The second solution was for the state, in some way, to take over the risk of lending to industry.

In Germany there was a particularly successful example of the first solution, devised mostly in the 1870s. Since 1945 this has been supplemented by a strong system of public-sector banks built up by regional and local government to lend to small and medium enterprises. In Japan, too, the state broadly prefers to support privately-owned banks rather than replace them, but state finance has also played a more direct role, particularly in the aftermath of the Second World War. In addition, the existence of *keiretsu*, that is, diversified industrial groups, helps to bring providers and users of funds closer. Italy and France, on the other hand, have preferred the second type of solution. Over the last half century in these two countries, the state has borne most of the risk of industrial finance, mostly through public sector banks. In any event, in all these cases, the financial systems that developed were essentially bank-based, rather than stock market-based, and to a large extent they have stayed that way.

It is interesting to note that both the UK and the US used to rely much more heavily on banks than they do today, and in both countries there was an apparently conscious decision to change the system. Will Hutton (1995) shows how provincial banks in the industrial areas of Britain were developing a system of 'relational lending' up to the late 1870s. The crucial moment came in 1878 when the City of Glasgow Bank and the West of England and South Wales District Bank both faced liquidity problems. They appealed to the Bank of England for support to tide them over, were refused and collapsed. After that, the main British banks withdrew from lending to industry. In the US, however, as in Germany, industry went on being able to depend heavily on bank finance, which helps to explain why they succeeded where Britain failed in the new, capital-hungry electrical, chemical and motor industries that grew up in the first part of the twentieth century. In the US, the crucial turn away from bank finance came in the 1930s, when Congress imposed restrictions on it in the aftermath of the Wall Street Crash (Roe, 1994). What these Anglo-Saxon retreats from bank finance had in common is that they were decided by central institutions – the Bank of England in one case, Congress in the other. Both institutions prioritized financial stability over fast industrial development.

Whether the central institutions in bank-based systems will follow in the footsteps of the US and UK is still a matter for debate. The increasing integration of financial markets in the global economy opens many possibilities as large multinational firms can seek funds from wherever they want in the world.

3   Financial systems and innovation

3.1   Gains and losses from reducing uncertainty

Now that we have seen how financial systems may differ it is time to ask how we might judge which type works best. Because technological progress is so important in the modern economy (*Firms*, Chapter 9), we shall focus on what works best for one particular area, technological innovation. Innovation requires investment, and financial systems provide capital for investment, so we will compare the efficiency of the two systems in this role.

In order to make things simpler, we shall start by assuming that the outcome of the project reflects the benefits to the economic system as a whole. We shall then go on to see what happens when we relax this assumption.

In the case of new products and processes, both lenders and borrowers have to live with a lot of unquantifiable uncertainty about the outcomes of investment projects; so one great challenge to the financial system is to reduce that uncertainty as far as possible. A well-organized and expert financial institution may be able, using its expertise, to reduce the uncertainty that surrounds, say, a thousand projects or firms which appear, at first glance, to have a high level of 'downside' risk and choose, perhaps, a hundred or so that seem to have the best chance of success. The remaining risk attached to the chosen projects can then be substantially reduced through diversification.

Expertise requires specialization of some kind and not all financial institutions will be able to assess the prospects of all types of innovative projects. Instead of having many different banks competing to lend to it, all of whom use some neat, quick and cheap way of reckoning its creditworthiness, a firm may find only one or two prospective lenders available. These may be lenders who know the firm already, or know its industry, or know its locality. This situation is more typical of the bank-based system and it suggests an advantage this system may have. Where innovation is concerned it will be a particularly telling advantage over a stock market dominated by outsiders because it takes a great deal of knowledge of the firm, the industry and the technology involved to judge the prospects of any project.

However, there is a price which may have to be paid for this specialization: the economy may suffer from monopoly power as banks do not have to compete for funds. Monopoly power allows monopoly profits and other abuses – for example, finance given or refused on one person's whim, slackness and conservatism.

The Anglo-Saxon financial system allows each large firm access to capital on the same basis as every other, but it does this by having the shares of each firm held by a large number of individuals and institutions. In the bank-based countries, the concentration of ownership, even in large companies, means that shareholders have an opportunity, and the incentive, to become familiar with the company and its industry. However, there is a flip side: there are no large pools of 'impartial' capital slopping about. This means that a cash-rich firm which is on good terms with its major shareholders will, in effect, have a lot of cheap capital available to it. Firms that are short of cash and do not have major shareholders with a lot of cheap capital available to them will probably find equity funding hard to come by.

3.2   Tackling the problem of appropriation

The difficulty of *appropriating* advances in knowledge is a problem that often inhibits innovation (*Firms*, Chapter 9). The first firm to introduce a new product or pioneer a new process can expect to benefit from it, but others almost certainly will too – its customers particularly, but also its suppliers, its competitors perhaps, and firms in other industries and countries to which its innovation is relevant. And when we say the firm itself will benefit, we don't usually mean only the shareholders via higher profits; its employees, for instance, can expect higher pay, better job security, better chances of promotion. Even the state and local government share in the benefits, through higher tax revenues and lower needs for unemployment benefits. The upshot of all these *spillovers* is that the social return on investment in innovation is likely to be substantially higher than the private return to the shareholders of the innovating firm. If investment is only motivated by that private return, there will be less investment than there should be.

There is one way, however, in which the gap may be narrowed. Those gainers who are close to the firm, or within it, may have an influence over it, and they may make a contribution of some kind to the finance of the investment. They are the enfranchised stakeholders, and the gain to them will count, in effect, as part of the private return which the firm is trying to achieve. In any large Japanese firm there has been an (implicit) deal between the permanent workers and the firm: work hard, show flexibility and accept relatively low pay in your early years, and we will see to it, if we possibly can, that you will have a well-paid job until you retire. In current world market conditions the only way the firm can hope to deliver on that promise is by continuous innovation. In effect, the programme of innovation is being 'financed' by the junior workers, and when they become senior workers they share in the returns. Business customers and suppliers in Japan are also considered to be 'part of the family': in various ways they contribute to the investment, have influence over the firm, and enjoy the gains later.

German firms have a somewhat similar relationship with their workers, who, unlike Japanese workers, have legal rights (from the co-determination laws) to influence management. In Germany, there are also strong inter-firm links. All the firms in an industry share in certain common activities: they will be members of its employers' association, trade association and research association. Sharing the costs and output of research obviously helps to narrow the appropriability gap. So does co-operation within the employers' association. To overcome the free rider training problem (discussed in Chapter 4, Section 5.2), the 'deal' among employers in Germany is that all companies train; none poach others' trained workers. This increases the incentive to train, which is part of the investment in innovation.

To sum up, if there is some set of formal or informal arrangements for relating what stakeholders get out of innovation to what they put into it, this will narrow the appropriability gap and push the rate of innovation up nearer to what is socially desirable. The institutional arrangements in Germany and Japan appear to have this effect.

4 Innovation: differences among industries

In this section, I take into account the fact that innovative activities differ across industries (*Firms*, Chapter 9). So far as the finance of innovation is concerned there are three sorts of differences which are of vital importance.

- The *visibility* of innovation. How easy is it for someone who is not closely involved in managing the development of a new product or process to judge what resources are being devoted to it and how well they are being spent? This is at the heart of the problem of short-termism that was introduced in Chapter 5.

- The *appropriability* of innovation. Can the firm ensure in a straightforward way (for example by patents) that the bulk of the returns on it do accrue to the shareholders; or does innovation in the industry naturally tend to involve large spillovers to other stakeholders?

- The *novelty* of innovation. How far does a product or process innovation involve or need radically new ways of organizing its development or production, radically new technologies, and/or radically new markets or selling methods?

I will be arguing that the stock market-based system is at a particular disadvantage in industries where visibility and appropriability are low. The balance of advantage in coping with a high degree of novelty is not so clear.

4.1 Visibility, appropriability and firm-specific perceptiveness

Innovation involves a variety of different types of investment – not just the research and development (R&D) spending which is normally associated with it. Physical investment, design and engineering, employees' training and marketing costs are all necessary for the success of an innovation. The different types of expenditure will make a very different impression on an industry analyst. Spending on physical capital appears in the accounts as acquisition of a capital asset, which means that it does not have to be subtracted from profit. The same is true of some elements of R&D, which is obviously an investment of a sort, however risky or unwise the industry analyst may think it. The same may be said of training, though much of it is informal and impossible to account for separately. The least visible expenditure is innovative expenses within production (which is where a lot of engineering is likely to be done, including the sorting out of 'teething troubles' after production starts) and marketing. It is very difficult to show to anyone who does not have detailed knowledge of the firm, that the higher costs resulting from such changes are not due to sheer inefficiency.

There are wide variations among industries in the pattern of spending on innovation, as Figure 6.4 shows.

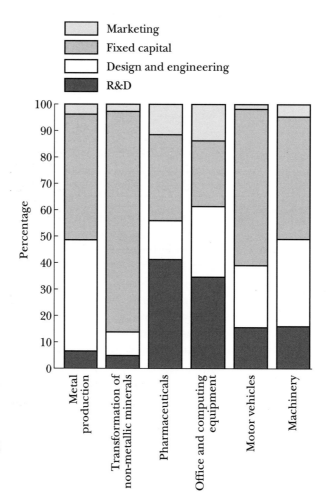

Figure 6.4 **The percentage share of spending in different innovative activities, for selected industries, Italy 1981–85**

Source: ISTAT, 1988, Table 11

Visibility also depends on the way the innovation and the firm are organized. The more centralized the process, the more visible it is to the outside. In a divisionalized firm with several tiers of profit centre, it is not easy even for the finance director, let alone outside analysts, to tell the difference between unnecessarily high costs in the operating companies, and a big innovative effort which will pay off in future. Again, industries vary in how far the firms within them tend to control the process of innovation centrally. It is much easier to centralize the process (or most of it) when it largely revolves around basic and applied research, than when it revolves around development. So another indicator of visibility is the fraction of R&D that goes to research, as opposed to development.

Figure 6.5 illustrates the types of research undertaken in different industrial sections of the UK.

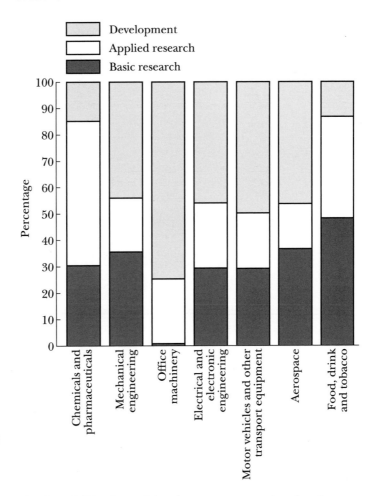

Figure 6.5 **Distribution of R&D activity in the UK, 1985**

Source: ISTAT, 1988

The less visible the activity, the more perceptive the observer must be in order to judge whether the firm should be funded, and to monitor progress. In general, this perceptiveness needs to be firm-specific, although a general knowledge of the industry will help too. A bank-based economy with enfranchised stakeholders can be expected to have a lot of insiders with good firm-specific perceptiveness; the outsider-dominated financial systems cannot.

We have already seen that systems with enfranchised stakeholders generally cope better with problems of appropriability. Industries vary in how much stakeholder enfranchisement can help, and how far there is a problem anyway. In the pharmaceutical industry, for example, it is less of a help because the firms involved do not have particularly important suppliers and they do not sell to industrial customers. So in this industry there is little scope for getting strong customer–supplier groupings to share the effort and the returns. Anyway, the problem can be quite well controlled by patenting new drug discoveries. An example of such a patent is that of Glaxo's anti-ulcer drug, Zantac, where the patent turned out to be worth hundreds of millions of pounds.

There is a connection between visibility and appropriability. The easier it is to protect appropriability by patenting, the freer the firm is to explain and publicize its innovations to outsiders. The pharmaceutical industry can and does do that in the UK and the US, by holding regular briefings for stock exchange analysts on the progress and prospects of its drugs. This industry happens to have other advantages in achieving high visibility. An unusually high proportion of its innovative expenditure is on R&D which is conducted in centralized departments and is not devolved to profit centres several tiers down. The mechanical engineering industries, on the other hand, are at the opposite extreme: they are decentralized, their innovations are dependent on low-visibility activities and any innovations are difficult to protect by patent. They tend to have close relationships with their industrial customers and suppliers of components and equipment. This analysis helps explain why, while the US and the UK lead the world in pharmaceuticals, they have become steadily weaker since the 1950s by comparison to Germany and Japan in the main areas of mechanical engineering.

4.2   Dealing with novelty: the stock exchange strikes back?

The advantage of the insiders in the bank-based, stakeholder-enfranchised system arises largely from a continuity of relationships. For example the firm-specific perceptiveness of a bank may arise through it having known an innovating firm for many years – a specific manager in the bank may even have known the firm's chief executive for a long time. In a new or rapidly-changing industry, however, continuity may be impossible or dangerous. Established firms may be able to succeed only by learning to do things in a radically different way, in terms of organization and technology. Accordingly, new start-up firms may have an advantage as they have nothing to unlearn. Conversely, however, they cannot have knowledgeable insiders to provide finance and corporate governance. The established firms can – but will insiders give the firms the kick they may need to change their ways?

It follows that the sort of industry in which one would expect the Anglo-Saxons to excel is one where visibility and appropriability are not a great problem, but novelty is. The US excels in pharmaceuticals and electronics, the UK in pharmaceuticals. Both these industries are highly technology-based and, thus, likely to be high in novelty. We have already seen that pharmaceuticals have little difficulty with visibility and appropriability. So the facts are reasonably consistent with the theory.

If, in a new industry, firm-specific perceptiveness is hard to come by, how can any financial system do a good job for that industry? The best hope is that someone within the system with access to capital has a high degree of industry-specific expertise. Capital can then be put into selected firms, all or most of it as equity, and the industry-specific expert can take a hand in corporate governance in at least the early stages of the firm's development. When the firm is older and established enough to engage with the ordinary providers of capital – the stock exchange and/or banks, as the case may be – the start-up capital that has been put in can be liberated and put into new start-ups.

The US is one country which seems to have developed an effective way of financing its high-technology industries. In the US, venture capitalists are now an established part of the financial system, and a large fraction of the capital they provide has gone into high technology industries (65 per cent in 1994, according to the Bank of England, 1996, p.21).

The investment is usually in equity and often the venture capitalists expect to share in governance as well as finance. In 1995 the flow of new venture capital in the US was estimated at $3.85bn., but that was only what was called 'formal' venture capital (Authers, 1996). More important, but harder to measure, is 'informal' venture capital provided by 'business angels'. These are rich individuals who use their own personal funds, industrial knowledge and contacts. Estimates of their rate of investment in high-technology sectors have been put as high as $20bn. per year (Coghlan, 1996). Venture capital tends to be concentrated in certain sectors and localities. In the US in 1995, for example, 47 per cent of 'formal' investments went into California, with Massachusetts and Texas receiving another 12 per cent between them (Authers, 1996). High-technology and informal venture capital is even more concentrated – for example, in information and communication technology in northern California – thus enabling venture capitalists to be expert in their industry and to be effective in corporate governance.

Since the US has a stock market-based financial system, venture capital there has grown to be part of that system. After all, a well-functioning stock market is essential for venture capitalists as they reap their reward when the company is either floated or acquired by existing large firms. Formal venture capital institutions are commonly subsidiaries of the financial institutions – mutual funds, pensions funds and insurance companies – which dominate the stock exchange. The UK, having a similar financial system, was the quickest to follow the US lead and by the mid 1990s had the largest venture capital industry in Europe (47.5 per cent of total European new investments in 1995, according to Fazey, 1996). However, the UK, in borrowing the term, has redefined it to include the funding of management buy-outs of established firms. By 1995 this use of venture capital absorbed 73 per cent of the total; only 4 per cent was going into 'early-stage' financing.

Technology-based firms in the UK receive a much smaller share of venture capital than in the US, and business angels are also less patient in the UK (Bank of England, 1996). Why is this? On the one hand, ignorance of technology is a particular problem for UK financial institutions; on the other hand, 'many would-be technology entrepreneurs are naïve in areas of financial and other management. This appears to be much less of a

Definition

Venture capitalists

A venture capitalist is an organization (or individual) that is prepared to invest long-term risk finance for the start-up and development of small unquoted companies that have significant growth potential.

problem in the United States, given the more frequent contact between university science departments and their business schools. There appears to be an important cultural difference between the two countries in their attitude towards the commercialisation of research' (Bank of England, 1996, p.26). It appears that bringing the financial, academic and business communities closer together is a priority for UK innovation policy, and the Technology Foresight programme has focused on bridging this gap (see *Firms*, Chapter 12).

Although the UK has the largest venture capital industry in Europe, not enough goes to technology-based firms.

Bank-based economies have developed their own versions of venture capital. In Germany in 1994, for example, funds owned by the banks provided most venture capital. The government also contributes significantly. The German venture capital funds are, as you would expect, in less of a hurry to get their capital out. While, on average, US venture capitalists take advantage of stock exchange flotation to get out after five years, and the impatient British do so after only three or four years, in Germany the average period of investment is seven years, and they often continue to hold the firm's shares after the initial public offering (OECD, 1992). However, in Germany, as in Britain, a very low proportion of venture capital (only 7 per cent, according to Deutsche Bank) has gone into early-stage financing in high technology areas (Bank of England, 1996).

5   Conclusion

A well-functioning financial system is essential for economic development as it channels savings towards the most productive investment projects. However, financial transactions are fraught with uncertainty and information asymmetries. The level of uncertainty is particularly high in the case of innovative investment as the capital accumulated is mostly intangible (knowledge).

Over the years, countries have developed different institutional structures to facilitate the accumulation of capital. In this chapter, I have classified financial systems in two main categories, stock market-based and bank-based. From the historical discussion it emerges that a key characteristic on which they came to differ is the priority that the state and the central bank have given to industrial development. This priority seems to have been much higher in the bank-based economies.

The two types of financial systems can reduce uncertainty in different ways. The bank-based system has the edge in reducing the uncertainty which arises from low visibility and low appropriability of innovation because these problems can be much alleviated by 'enfranchised stakeholders'. This led us to go back and broaden the notion of financial systems to include all those, including employees, who in some way, cash or kind, might contribute to innovation, and benefit from it: stakeholders in innovation. However, there is another sort of uncertainty which arises from the novelty of an innovation. Here it is open to either system to develop the industry-specific expertise required, but the stock market-based system of the US is currently far ahead. Since industries differ in the degree of appropriability, visibility and novelty, we can deduce that some industries will be favoured by the structure of the financial system in some countries but not in others. In other words, we can explain some patterns of technological specialization by understanding the nature of the financial system.

The main aim of this chapter, then, was to set out a rather general theory of how financial systems affect innovation. Any general theory which is worth having suggests a research programme – a programme of generating and testing rather specific hypotheses. In this case, the hypotheses would be that an economy whose financial system had such and such scores on characteristics a, b and c would tend have such and such a performance in innovation in industries x, y or z. Such a programme requires empirical work to establish what the scores and performances are. When we test our hypotheses, however, we have to take into account that there may be other factors that help to explain the patterns of technological specialization observed, such as the strength of a country's scientific research, the natural resources available and the size of the market.

On this important topic, the programme has only just begun. Many of the empirical statements about financial systems and industries made in this chapter were rather tentative, based on the information available at present. Over the next few years, researchers in this field hope to generate much more cross-country evidence of the impact of financial systems on industrial innovation.

Further Reading

There is quite a lot of recent readable work on the differences among financial systems and their implications for corporate governance and management. Some of the best is in the *Oxford Review of Economic Policy* (*OREP*). A complete issue of *OREP* in 1992 was devoted to this theme, with articles by Kester on Japan and Schneider-Lenne on Germany, and an overview by Jenkinson and Mayer:

Jenkinson, T. and Mayer, C. (1992) 'The assessment: corporate governance and corporate control', *OREP*, 8 (3), pp.1–10.

Kester, W.C. (1992) 'Industrial groups as systems of contractual governance', *OREP*, 8 (3), pp.25–44.

Schneider-Lenne, E. R.(1992) 'Corporate control in Germany', *OREP,* 8 (3), pp.11–23.

There is also an later overview in *OREP* by Sussman:

Sussman, O. (1994) 'Investment and banking: some international comparisons', *OREP,* 10 (4), pp.79–93.

Masahiko Aoki offers a more formal analysis of stakeholder enfranchisement (without using that term) in large Japanese firms in 'Toward an economic model of the Japanese firm', *Journal of Economic Literature*, vol. XXVIII, March 1990, pp.1–27.

Michael Porter criticizes the short-termism of the US financial system in his 'Capital disadvantage: America's failing capital investment system', *Harvard Business Review,* September/October 1992, pp.65–82.

The British financial system has similar effects on innovation. The impact on innovation in the pharmaceuticals and engineering industries is explored by Tylecote, A. and Demirag, I. (1992) 'Short-termism: culture and structures as factors in technological innovation', pp.201–25 in Coombs, R., Walsh V. and Saviotti, P. (eds) *Technological Change and Company Strategies*, London, Academic Press.

In case you had written off the US system as hopelessly short-termist, you should read the Bank of England's 'The financing of technology-based small firms', October 1996, which shows how superior the US venture capital system is to all the competition.

Another very readable overview of corporate governance and some of its effects is Charkham, J. (1994) *Keeping Good Company: A Study of Corporate Governance in Five Countries*, Oxford, OUP. (The five countries studied are Germany, Japan, France, the US and UK).

Chapter 5 of Will Hutton's *The State We're In,* London, Jonathan Cape, is a brief but persuasive attack on the effects of the British financial system on the British economy over the last century.

If you find the historical approach to the understanding of the modern economy interesting, there is a whole journal devoted to it. *Industrial and Corporate Change (I&CC)* has carried some excellent articles on the evolution and effects of financial systems, such as:

Lazonick, W. and O'Sullivan, M. (1996) 'Organisation, finance and international competition', *Industrial and Corporate Change*, vol.5, no.1, pp.1–49.

Mowery, D. C. (1992) 'Finance and corporate evolution in five industrial economies, 1900–1950', *Industrial and Corporate Change*, vol.1 , no.1, pp.1–36.

Rather out of character for *I&CC*, because it is not historical, is one of the seminal articles for the New Keynesian approach to finance:

Greenwald, B. and Stiglitz, J.E. (1992) 'Information, finance and markets: the architecture of allocative mechanisms', *Industrial and Corporate Change*, vol.1, no.1, pp.37–63.

CHAPTER 7

COMPETITIVE GENERAL EQUILIBRIUM

by Vivienne Brown

1 Introduction

One of the most significant aspects of economic change in the last decades of the twentieth century has been the resurgence of economic liberalism – the belief that decentralized markets promote economic prosperity more effectively than state planning or intervention. This has contributed to the break-up of the Soviet bloc in eastern Europe and also to the many changes seen in mixed economies, such as the UK, where the economic frontiers of the state have been pushed back in a number of ways. These policies have included various combinations of liberalization, deregulation and privatization (*Firms*, Chapter 6). In the UK, for example, organizational changes have been introduced within the public sector in an attempt to replicate the market and introduce more commercial practices (*Firms*, Chapter 7). Some aspects of such 'social markets' will be discussed in the following chapter. At the same time as these organizational changes have taken place, the traditional legal protections which supported trade union activities have been taken away in order to make the labour market closer to the ideal 'flexible' market which responds to market forces. Chapter 4 examined some of the effects of such labour market policies.

These changes are the result of a complex interweaving of many factors, but economic arguments have played their part. In the UK, the apparent failure of Keynesianism in the 1970s to deliver non-inflationary growth contributed to the increasing disenchantment with state intervention in the economy, and provided a new platform for anti-Keynesianism to play an influential role in the shift towards economic liberalism. These liberal economic arguments grew out of a long-running debate about the merits of a decentralized market economy as opposed to state planning, and about the virtues of competition. Neoclassical economics has contributed to this debate.

Chapter 2 sketched in a preliminary way the important result that a competitive general equilibrium is a Pareto-efficient outcome. This result has been used by many economists to argue for the merits of a decentralized market economy and explains why neoclassical economics is generally assumed to represent a free market orientation. On the other hand, the model of the competitive economy that underpins this result is a highly abstract one which is based on very restrictive assumptions. Many economists have questioned whether it does, in practice, provide such a strong case for decentralized market economies. In this chapter we shall investigate this issue. We shall look more deeply into the model of competitive general equilibrium and its links with Pareto efficiency. In the course of this, we shall also find that the model of competitive general equilibrium does not give us any simple or straightforward advice on the extent to which decentralized economic policies should be pursued, and that its actual role in economic debates in the past illustrates the equivocal nature of the policy conclusions that can be drawn from it.

How a decentralized, unplanned competitive market can produce orderly outcomes is a question that has fascinated economists since at least the eighteenth century. As you learnt in Chapter 2, the idea that the unintended consequence of individuals behaving with only their own interests in mind may be an outcome that is orderly – even beneficial – for society as a whole, has been encapsulated by the idea of the 'invisible hand'. The paradoxical nature of the idea that economic outcomes which are unplanned at an economy-wide level may be better than planned ones seems to fly in the face of common sense. The invisible hand becomes even more extraordinary when this beneficial outcome is seen as the result of the pursuit of self-interest on the part of individual economic agents. Somehow the invisible hand transforms private self-interest into overall economic well-being.

HOW MANY ECONOMISTS DOES IT TAKE
TO CHANGE A LIGHTBULB?

– NONE, THE INVISIBLE HAND DOES ALL
THE WORK !

This apparent paradox has led economists to ask two different sorts of questions. The first question concerns the operation of the invisible hand: just how does a competitive market function? How are prices set in a competitive market, and how is equilibrium restored after a disturbance? The second question concerns the allegedly beneficial outcome of a competitive market: how is it that competitive outcomes promote overall economic well-being? What is meant by 'well-being' and are there different gainers and losers in competitive markets?

These questions are explored in the following sections which together build on and extend the model of the competitive market you first met in Chapter 2. In Section 2 we shall examine the competitive general equilibrium model first put forward by Léon Walras to explain how a decentralized system of markets can cohere without any overall plan. In Section 3 we shall consider how equilibrium prices are determined in this model. In Section 4 we shall look at a different version of this model, drawing on neoclassical analysis of consumer and firm behaviour. Section 5 considers what is meant by beneficial outcomes. It looks at the normative or welfare properties of competitive equilibrium outcomes, and the policy conclusions that might be drawn from this.

In addition to addressing the issue of competitive markets, we shall also be reviewing and pulling together different aspects of the neoclassical model that you have met in various parts of the course. We shall be building on the preliminary groundwork of Chapter 2 of this book and linking together the neoclassical analysis of consumer behaviour and household labour supply from Chapters 1 and 5 of *Households*, with the neoclassical theory of the firm and labour demand from Chapters 3 and 7 of *Firms*. We shall pull together these different parts of the neoclassical theory so that you can see how they all fit together to form a coherent model of the interrelated way in which markets work. In this way I hope to show you something of the overall theoretical power of the model of competitive equilibrium, while also discussing some of the unresolved issues concerning it that continue to trouble economists.

2   The Walrasian model

2.1   Introduction

When the BSE crisis hit the British beef industry in 1996, in the wake of scientific evidence that beef might not be safe to eat, the price of beef plummeted as consumers lost confidence in beef and cut down their consumption of it. The fall in prices hit retailers, the beef products industry and beef farmers. As their incomes fell, all those involved in the various stages of producing and retailing beef had less money to spend on purchases. Beef farmers in particular were badly hit as it was suddenly not worth taking their animals to market, yet it was costly to keep them until prices increased. The fall in farmers' incomes in turn affected the value of farming land. Many consumers turned to substitute products and increased their demand for other meat, poultry and fish, while others increased their purchases of vegetarian substitutes such as vegeburgers and vegesausages. The increased public awareness of, or misinformation about, farming practices led to an increased demand for organic produce, while food manufacturers who used beef derivatives started looking around for non-beef substitutes. The original crisis in the beef market thus had a number of ramifications throughout other markets.

Some of these effects may have been short-lived, but the BSE crisis was a highly dramatic example of the sorts of changes that are happening all the time in the economy. Fashions come and go, new products are invented as old ones die out and new sources of raw materials are discovered. The economy is like a kaleidoscope of shifting demand and supply, ever restless and changing as shifts in one market have repercussions in many other markets far removed from it. Faced with these intricate interconnections between markets, economists want to explain whether and how order is possible in this kaleidoscope of activity. They want to see whether people operating atomistically as consumers or producers are part of a wider co-ordination of economic activities in which all choices can be realized. Can this complex interplay of different markets cohere as a consistent intermeshing of individual choices, or is the kaleidoscope simply a picture of chaos? Does this kaleidoscope need a visible guiding hand, in the shape of some other kind of institution, to co-ordinate economic activities, or is the invisible hand working efficiently?

2.2 Competitive general equilibrium

The competitive general equilibrium model was first outlined by Léon Walras (1834–1910), who was born in France but became professor of economics at Lausanne in Switzerland where he was a pioneer of the mathematical approach to economics. Walras' interest in economics was part of a methodological desire to apply the methods of the physical sciences to economic theory that resulted from a broad concern with social and political issues. He took a keen interest in social justice and proposed the nationalization of land and natural monopolies. He described himself as a 'scientific socialist' (Walker, 1987).

As we saw in Chapter 2, the Walrasian competitive general equilibrium model is based on the individual choices of economic agents in response to given market prices and the exogenous variables of preferences, resource endowments and technology. The kaleidoscope of economic activity is held fixed for a moment to see whether, given the exogenous variables, the sum of the choices of all individual agents are consistent, so that consumers' plans to purchase coincide with producers' plans to supply. This requires equilibrium in every market, so finding out whether individual choices are consistent implies that we have to find whether there exists a set of equilibrium prices at which demand and supply are in balance everywhere.

Walras' work laid the foundations for an analysis of competitive general equilibrium and his insights have since been developed in advanced mathematical models. We can get some of the flavour of this model by using partial equilibrium analysis of one market in which the prices of other goods are held constant. Figure 7.1(a) shows a demand and supply diagram like the ones you met in Chapter 2, where the prices of all other goods are held constant. Remember that the demand curve derives from utility-maximizing behaviour by households, and the supply curve derives from profit-maximizing behaviour by firms. At the equilibrium price, P_E, quantity demanded equals quantity supplied, Q_E. If price is below the equilibrium price, say at P_a, then the quantity demanded, Q_a^D, is greater than the quantity supplied, Q_a^S. If the price is above the equilibrium price at P_b, the quantity demanded, Q_b^D, is less than the quantity supplied, Q_b^S.

As we wish to focus on the determination of the equilibrium price, it is helpful to represent this in terms of an (own-price) excess demand curve which shows the difference between the quantity demanded and the quantity supplied of a good at each level of its own price, again on the assumption that all other prices are held constant. This is shown in Figure 7.1(b). The vertical axis shows price and the horizontal axis shows excess demand which is positive when demand is greater than supply and negative when supply is greater than demand. At the equilibrium price P_E, excess demand is zero because demand and supply are equal; this is the point at which the excess demand curve intersects the price axis. At prices below P_E there is a positive excess demand; this is shown for P_a where the excess demand is Z_a which is equal to the distance $Q_a^D - Q_a^S$ in Figure 7.1(a). At prices above P_E there is a negative excess demand since demand is less than supply. This is shown for the price P_b by Z_b which is equal to $Q_b^D - Q_b^S$ in Figure 7.1(b).

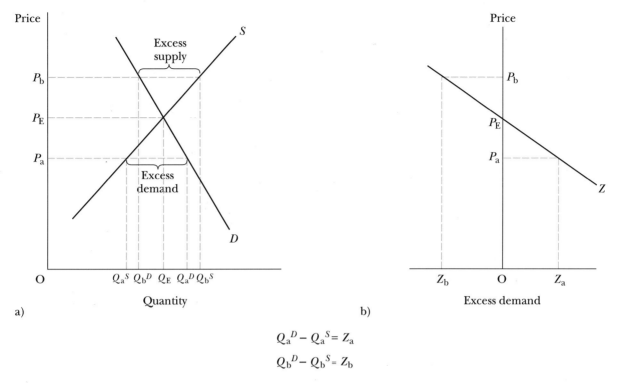

$$Q_a^D - Q_a^S = Z_a$$
$$Q_b^D - Q_b^S = Z_b$$

Figure 7.1   **Demand, supply and excess demand in a single market**

Figure 7.1 shows just one market with its (own-price) excess demand curve. The exogenous variables here are the prices of all other goods as well as preferences, resource endowments and technology. If any of these changed there would be a shift of the excess demand curve. In a general equilibrium model, however, we are looking at all markets simultaneously and so the excess demand for any good is dependent on all prices, not just on its own price. For example, the excess demand for vegeburgers is dependent not only on the price of vegeburgers, but also on all other prices.

One task for general equilibrium theory is to establish the conditions for the existence of a competitive equilibrium. This requires finding out whether a set of equilibrium prices exists for all markets simultaneously, bearing in mind all the ramifications implied in the notion that all the excess demands depend on all the prices. Certainly, some of these ramifications might turn out to be very small, but finding the total effect of all these interdependencies requires that none is overlooked. Establishing the existence of an equilibrium for the model as a whole involves finding a set of prices where all excess demands are simultaneously equal to zero.

As it is not possible in two dimensions to draw excess demand as a function of many prices, general equilibrium analysis cannot be represented in diagrams in the way that partial equilibrium analysis can. For a mathematical formulation of the problem of the existence of competitive equilibrium, you might like to read the technical box overleaf.

The existence of competitive equilibrium

The competitive general equilibrium model is composed of n goods and services. The ith good has an excess demand function:

$$Z_i = Q_i^D - Q_i^S$$

where $i = 1, 2, ..., n$

As explained in Chapter 2, the variables which are held constant for this model – the exogenous variables – are the initial endowments of resources owned by households, the preferences of households and the available technology. The variables that are to be determined by the equations of the model – the endogenous variables – are the equilibrium prices.

There is no money in this model, and demand and supply levels depend only on relative prices. An equilibrium set of prices is, therefore, a set of relative prices. If we choose any good, say the nth good, as a numeraire good or unit of account in which the prices of all other goods are expressed, then its price $P_n = 1$. This means that the prices of all other goods, $P_1, ..., P_{n-1}$, are just their prices relative to the price of the nth good, because:

$$P_i = \frac{P_i}{1} = \frac{P_i}{P_n}$$

Since P_n is always 1, there are just $n{-}1$ relative prices to be found.

How do we write the excess demand function for the ith good? We know that the excess demand for the ith good is a function of all the exogenous and endogenous variables. As it is a general equilibrium – and not a partial equilibrium – model, we must recognize that every excess demand Z_i will depend not only on its own relative price, but on all other relative prices as well. The excess demand for the ith good can, therefore, be written as:

$$Z_i = f_i(U, R, T, P_1, P_2, ..., P_{n-1})$$

$U =$ preferences

$R =$ initial endowments

$T =$ technology

where the excess demand, Z_i for the ith good, is a function of preferences, initial endowments, technology and all $n{-}1$ relative prices.

The plans of all economic agents are consistent when all excess demands are zero, that is, all goods and services offered for sale have a purchaser and all potential purchasers are able to find the goods and services they want to buy. To establish whether an equilibrium exists, we therefore need to find the set of prices at which all the excess demands are equal to zero. As it happens, we only need to do this for the excess demands for $n{-}1$ goods. This is because each agent spends all their available income (there is no saving) but no more than their income (there is no borrowing either), whether or not the system is in equilibrium. For each

Definition

Numeraire good

The numeraire good is the good in terms of which all prices in the model are expressed. All prices are therefore relative prices.

individual agent, the total amount planned to be spent on purchasing goods and services equals the total amount expected in income from supplying goods and services. If this holds for each agent, then it must hold for all agents taken together, so that the value (in terms of the numeraire) of the sum of all excess demands must equal zero. This implies that the following expression must always hold, not just for equilibrium prices:

$$P_1 Z_1 + P_2 Z_2 + ... + P_{n-1} Z_{n-1} + Z_n = 0$$

where $P_n = 1$, because n is the numeraire good.

This property of excess demand functions is known as Walras' Law.

As a result of Walras' Law, if the $n-1$ excess demands $Z_1 ... Z_{n-1}$ are zero, then the nth excess demand, Z_n, must also equal zero. This can be seen more clearly by reformulating Walras' Law as follows:

$$P_1 Z_1 + P_2 Z_2 + ... + P_{n-1} Z_{n-1} = -Z_n$$

This implies that we need only find a set of prices such that $n-1$ excess demands are equal to zero. In other words, in a system where there are n goods, an overall equilibrium exists when $Z_i = 0$ for all $i = 1, 2, ... , n-1$. This implies a system of $n-1$ equations:

$$Z_1 = f_1(U, R, T, P_1, P_2, ..., P_{n-1}) = 0$$

$$Z_2 = f_2(U, R, T, P_1, P_2, ..., P_{n-1}) = 0$$

...

...

$$Z_{n-1} = f_{n-1}(U, R, T, P_1, P_2, ..., P_{n-1}) = 0$$

We have here a model in $n-1$ equations and $n-1$ unknown prices. Mathematically, finding the equilibrium prices amounts to solving these equations simultaneously. If these equations can be solved, then equilibrium exists.

Definition

Walras' Law

Walras' Law states that the value of the sum of all excess demands must equal zero whether or not the system is in equilibrium.

Walras' approach to competitive general equilibrium has fundamentally influenced the way that economists now think about it. Mathematical refinements of Walras' insights have deepened economists' understanding of the conditions required for the existence of a competitive general equilibrium, but there is one issue which remains something of a conundrum – and that is the process by which prices are determined. This is the subject of the following section.

3   The determination of prices

3.1   Introduction

When economists talk about the determination of prices, this has (at least) two distinct meanings, although in practice it is hard to keep them apart. One meaning applies to equilibrium models such as the one in the technical box above where equilibrium prices are determined by a system of equations; here 'determined' implies a logical outcome. The other meaning concerns the process by which prices are determined in actual markets; 'determined' now refers to a real process of change through time. The value of any formal model lies in the insights that it provides into real economic situations, but the model may sometimes be a rather 'idealized' version of real events. A conundrum that has puzzled economists is how the determination of equilibrium prices in the mathematical model relates to the process of price determination in real markets. This conundrum is the subject of this section.

3.2   The Walrasian auctioneer

Because the Walrasian model is an equilibrium model, it does not consider what happens if the system is out of equilibrium. This raises a question as to how equilibrium prices are actually arrived at in real situations where markets are out of equilibrium. This question is made more complicated by the competitive assumption that all agents are price takers, that is, agents accept the going equilibrium prices and make their plans subject to these prices. In the formal model this is straightforward as the equilibrium prices are simply the solution to the system of equations. In the real world, however, this introduces a problem. If all agents are price takers, how do prices ever actually get changed in real markets?

Walras himself tried to show how actual competitive markets could arrive at the equilibrium prices by a process of trial and error, by what he called 'groping' or 'tâtonnement' in his original French. Walras suggested that a competitive market process of price adjustment could be imagined as an auction or a place where prices are openly announced by brokers or criers, and where agents make provisional bids to buy or sell goods on the basis of these prices (Walras, 1954, pp.83–4). This process goes through a number of different rounds; prices are called out and agents make their bids, and then, without any trades taking place, another set of prices is called out and further bids are made, and so on, until a set of prices has been reached at which all the excess demands are equal to zero. Thus agents are able to keep revising their plans with each new price called out until excess demands are eliminated. Only when offers to buy equal offers to sell will trade actually take place at the announced prices. One crucial aspect of this process of groping or tâtonnement is that trades do not take place at disequilibrium prices. It is thus a highly stylized account of price adjustment and it is hard to think of any real world counterpart. Walras recognized that this ideal version of a competitive market was not the norm, but he felt that many markets, such as stock exchanges and trading markets, approximated closely to it. He also argued that it was an acceptable scientific procedure to start off with a theoretical ideal and then work from that, because this was the method used in physics (p.84).

Later economists have tried to make sense of the process of tâtonnement as an account of how prices adjust in competitive markets, by adopting the idea of a central 'auctioneer' who calls out prices and who works out, from the bids provided by all agents, the excess demands at each set of prices called out. The Walrasian rule for price adjustment, which the auctioneer implements and which competitive markets operationalize, is that price should be increased if there is positive excess demand at that price, and reduced if there is negative excess demand. This process of price adjustment continues until all excess demands have been eliminated. This notion of a central auctioneer following the Walrasian rule for price

Definition

Walrasian rule for price adjustment

The Walrasian rule for price adjustment is that price should be raised if there is positive excess demand and reduced if there is negative excess demand.

adjustment is really a 'fiction', it is not supposed that competitive markets work in this way but it tries to catch the essence of how anonymous markets seem to work. This auctioneer is sometimes referred to as the Walrasian auctioneer.

The Walrasian rule for price adjustment can be illustrated using Figure 7.2, but remember that the auctioneer is not meant to have the information given by the excess demand curve, only the bids to buy and sell at the prices that are called out.

If P_a were called out, the auctioneer would discover that there was positive excess demand at that price equal to Z_a. Following the rule, the auctioneer would then increase the price, maybe to something like P_b. When P_b is called out, the auctioneer discovers that excess demand would now be negative at Z_b which implies that the price change was too great. Now the price needs to be reduced again, but as P_a was too low, the next price should be higher than that. Perhaps now P_c is called out but there would still be excess demand of Z_c, so the price needs to be increased, and so on. Eventually after groping about in the dark we see that the price should eventually converge on the equilibrium price of P_E.

By examining the properties of excess demand functions such as that illustrated in Figure 7.2, economists have developed mathematical models of the process of Walrasian price adjustment. They have discovered that if an excess demand curve is negatively sloped throughout its range, then the Walrasian rule for price adjustment will result in convergence on a single equilibrium price. If an excess demand curve does not have this shape, the Walrasian rule may not converge on an equilibrium price and/or there may also be more than one equilibrium outcome. This is explored further in the technical box overleaf.

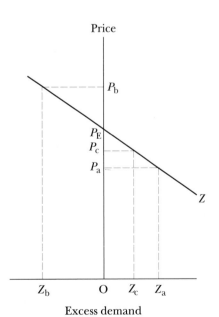

Figure 7.2 **Tâtonnement: following the Walrasian rule for price adjustment**

Exercise 7.1

Try to imagine yourself as the Walrasian auctioneer in a very simple situation – say a single market – just to get a flavour of what is involved. Remember that you are not meant to know what the excess demand curve looks like. Look at the steps below and describe how they follow the Walrasian rule for price adjustment.

1   If a price of 120 were called out, the excess demand would be −100.
2   If a price of 70 were called out, the excess demand would be 50.
3   If a price of 100 were called out, the excess demand would be −40.
4   If a price of 90 were called out, the excess demand would be −10.
5   If a price of 80 were called out, the excess demand would be 20, etc.

What might the next step be?

Where might the equilibrium price lie?

Instability and multiple equilibria

If an excess demand curve is positively sloped throughout its range, the Walrasian rule for price adjustment is unable to converge on the equilibrium price. This is illustrated in Figure 7.3.

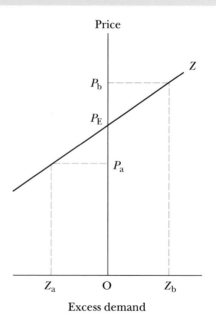

Figure 7.3 **Unstable equilibrium: an upward-sloping excess demand curve**

In Figure 7.3 the equilibrium price is P_E but the Walrasian rule for price adjustment would not converge on this price if it started from any other price. If P_a were called out, there would be negative excess demand of Z_a. According to the Walrasian rule, a negative excess demand requires a reduction in price, but if a price below P_a is called out, this would result in an even larger negative excess demand. This in turn would prompt the auctioneer to call out an even lower price, and so the price would diverge further and further away from the equilibrium price. Similarly, if P_b were called out, there would be positive excess demand of Z_b.

According to the Walrasian rule, a positive excess demand requires an increase in price, but if a price above P_b is called out, this would result in an even larger positive excess demand. This would prompt the auctioneer to call out an even higher price, and so again the price would diverge further away from the equilibrium price. Thus, although an equilibrium price exists at P_E, this is an unstable equilibrium because any movement away from it would result in further movements away from it. By contrast, the equilibrium in Figure 7.2 is stable because any movement away from it results in convergence back on the equilibrium.

If an excess demand curve has a positively sloped section as well as a negatively sloped section, then instability can be combined with more than one equilibrium. This is illustrated in Figure 7.4.

In Figure 7.4 the excess demand curve is negatively sloped at low prices and positively sloped at high prices. There are two equilibrium prices, P_E^1 and P_E^2. An unstable equilibrium price is shown at P_E^1, whereas P_E^2 is a stable one. You can see this by starting from any price below P_E^1 and showing that the Walrasian rule results in convergence on P_E^2. Starting from a price greater than P_E^1 does not lead to a convergence on P_E^1 but results in greater and greater price increases with greater and greater levels of positive excess demand. Figure 7.4 therefore illustrates both an unstable equilibrium, at P_E^1, and multiple equilibria, at P_E^1 and P_E^2, one of which, P_E^2, is stable and one of which, P_E^1, is unstable.

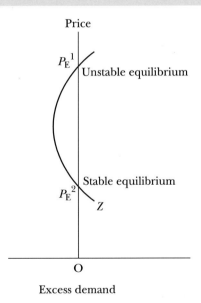

Figure 7.4 **Instability and multiple equilibria**

How might excess demand curves have upward-sloping sections? They are caused by the presence of strong income effects which outweigh the substitution effects of a price change, and so produce demand or supply curves which have the 'wrong' slope for some prices. *Households*, Chapter 1, Section 3.2, discussed Giffen goods for which demand increases as their price rises, and in *Households*, Chapter 5, Figure 5.5 showed how the presence of strong income effects in the labour market produces a backward bending supply curve of labour. Either of these cases could result in the excess demand curve shown in Figure 7.4.

Exercise 7.2

Figure 7.5 shows the market demand and supply curves for a good that is a Giffen good at some prices. Derive the excess demand curve for this good. Identify the stable and unstable equilibrium prices for this good. (See *Households*, Chapter 1, Section 3.2, for the derivation of this diagram.)

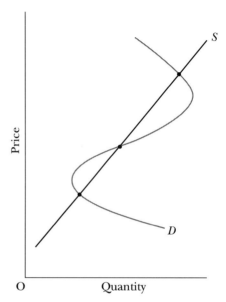

Figure 7.5 **Market demand and supply curves for a Giffen good**

I have argued that a competitive process of price adjustment may be thought of in terms of the fiction of the auctioneer, but the auctioneer is really some way from being a good image of the invisible hand. The auctioneer represents a centralization of the process of price adjustment that accords little with the notion of decentralization that is implicit in the invisible hand. In addition, tâtonnement implies that no trades take place until the equilibrium price has been announced by the auctioneer. This, too, is hardly a realistic picture of a decentralized market where equilibrium prices, arising from the give and take of everyday market transactions, emerge gradually out of disequilibrium prices (Hahn, 1987).

3.3   Competitive markets

One of the very few real world instances of tâtonnement is the fixing of the price of gold in London. This occurs at twice daily meetings which are chaired by a representative of N.M.Rothschild & Sons Ltd, and are attended by dealers who are in telephone contact with their dealing rooms who, in turn, keep in touch with customers. At these meetings, the chairman functions as the Walrasian auctioneer by announcing an opening price and then receives bids at that price from the dealers in consultation with their dealing rooms. If the buying and selling bids do not 'balance' the chairman announces another price and a second round of bids are made. This process continues until a balance is achieved and then the chairman announces that the price is 'fixed'. This 'fixed' price then provides a published benchmark price for gold.

The London Gold Fixing

The fixings are meetings held twice daily at 10.30 and 15.00 hours in the City of London to establish the market price for gold. These meetings provide market users with the opportunity of buying and selling at a single quoted price.

Each member of the fixing sends a representative to the fix meeting who maintains telephone contact throughout the meeting with his dealing room. The chairman of the fixing, traditionally the representative of N.M. Rothschild & Sons Limited, announces an opening price which is reported back to the dealing rooms. They in turn relay this price to their customers, and, on the basis of orders received, instruct their representative to declare as a buyer or seller. Provided both buying and selling interests are declared, members are then asked to state the number of bars in which they wish to trade. If at the opening price there is either no buying or no selling, or if the size for the buying and selling does not balance, the same procedure is followed again at higher or lower prices until a balance is achieved. At this moment the chairman announces that the price is 'fixed' ... The fixing will last as long as is necessary to establish a price which satisfies both buyers and sellers. In general this will be about 10–20 minutes, but in exceptional circumstances may take more than an hour.

A feature of the London fixing is that customers may be kept advised of price changes throughout a fixing meeting, and may alter their instructions at any time until the price is fixed. To ensure that a member can communicate such an alteration, his representative has a small flag on his desk which he raises and, as long as any flag is raised, the Chairman may not declare the price fixed.

The fixing provides a published benchmark price, which is widely used as a pricing medium.

Source: Rothschild pamphlet

The example of fixing the gold price is instructive as it shows the institutional requirements for a tâtonnement process to work in practice; the fixing involves a small group of dealers and their customers within a highly specialized market setting. It is hard to imagine this process working in large markets that involve many buyers and sellers, let alone working across all markets simultaneously in a general equilibrium framework. The gold fixing also shows that any particular institutional setup requires its own resourcing and does not come free; a number of individuals have to give up time in order to attend the gold fixing meetings twice each day. This reminds us that, in practical situations, markets are not simply disembodied forces that cost nothing, but represent particular institutional settings that require their own resources in order to function. Financial markets are a good example of this. These markets are often seen as good approximations of competitive markets, but they are not costless. For example, the size of salaries in major financial centres is legendary – quite apart from the champagne lunches! – and a striking reminder of the resource costs of even highly competitive market institutions.

The gold fixing is also a highly centralized way of determining equilibrium prices, again illustrating the conundrum that the process of tâtonnement seems to require a centralized rather than a decentralized method of fixing prices. This is also illustrated by the argument, originally made in the 1930s, that tâtonnement could be used to carry out a form of socialist central planning! It was suggested by Oskar Lange and Abba Lerner that a central planning board could act like a Walrasian auctioneer in setting the prices of capital goods and state-owned resources and so bypass the need for an actual market in finding equilibrium prices. Against this Hayek argued that the informational assumptions of such planning overlook the way in which information is produced as part of the market process, and that it is precisely the ability of markets to economise on information that enables them to function more efficiently than any plan, making it impractical to try to imitate the Walrasian process of tâtonnement. As you saw in Chapter 2, Hayek also rejected the neoclassical notion of equilibrium itself, arguing that the notion of tâtonnement towards an equilibrium was itself misconceived. (Vaughn, 1980, summarizes the socialist calculation debate.)

Thus, in trying to operationalize the notion of tâtonnement, some economists saw the Walrasian system as a blueprint for socialist planning rather than decentralized markets. And in arguing against socialist planning, Hayek also argued against Walrasian economics as a theoretical system. A root problem, recognized by neoclassical economists, is that competitive analysis assumes that all agents are price takers, but this leaves unresolved the issue of how prices are changed when the system is out of equilibrium.

Although this problem remains unresolved at a theoretical level, at the practical level of real markets it is clear that the direction in which many prices change does conform to the Walrasian rule for price adjustment, in that positive excess demand leads to a rise in price and negative excess demand leads to a fall in price.

Reflection

As an illustration of this, think about a local market where you do your shopping. Can you think of cases where the goods with a negative excess demand are sold off cheaply at the end of the day? Alternatively, house and flat prices in your area might be a good example of competitive prices. To what extent does the local estate agent perform the role of the Walrasian auctioneer?

In spite of these theoretical difficulties, experiments in economics have also confirmed many times over that there is a rapid convergence on the equilibrium price in various kinds of competitive markets. In particular, there is one trading structure in which the competitive equilibrium price is attained especially fast in experimental situations, and that is the 'oral double auction' (Hey, 1991, p.198). The oral double auction has been described in the following manner:

> This envisages the market participants to be either physically present in the same location or telephonically linked so that they can all communicate with each other. There is an auctioneer

who administers the auction process but who otherwise takes a passive role. The active role is taken by the agents themselves, who are free to call out bids (offers to buy) or asks (offers to sell) depending upon whether they are potential buyers or potential sellers ... The process of calling out, and accepting, bids or asks continues until no new bids or asks are forthcoming and trade has ceased.

(Hey, 1991, p.185)

With oral double auctions, market clearing is a dynamic disequilibrium process in that deals are finalized at going prices rather than waiting until an equilibrium price has been discovered as in the case of the Walrasian auctioneer. And unlike the case of the Walrasian auctioneer, it is a form of competition that is commonly found in real markets, for example the London International Financial Futures Exchange (LIFFE).

Thus, in spite of the theoretical difficulties which have perplexed theoretically-minded economists, for practical purposes many economists accept the usefulness of the insights of the Walrasian model in explaining some real markets. In spite of its strict assumption of price taking and no trading at disequilibrium prices, the Walrasian auctioneer model is regarded as a benchmark illustration of the convergence of competitive markets on the equilibrium price.

4   Some more models of general equilibrium

4.1   Introduction

We have seen that the question of the existence of general equilibrium comes down to the question whether there is a set of prices at which all excess demands are zero. This is a very complicated question for many goods, but if the idea of a competitive economy is simplified to just two goods and two consumers, it is possible to use Edgeworth box diagrams to represent a competitive general equilibrium and to show that, under certain conditions, equilibrium prices do exist. These diagrams are named after Francis Edgeworth who, like Walras, was one of the founders of general equilibrium analysis. Edgeworth (1845–1926) was born in Ireland and eventually became a professor at Oxford. He was a classicist and linguist, but he also pioneered a mathematical approach to economic analysis, as well as publishing work in ethics and in statistics (Newman, 1978).

In this section I shall use the Edgeworth box diagram first to represent a general equilibrium in a competitive exchange economy in which there is consumption but no production, and then I shall add production to present a general equilibrium of exchange, consumption and production.

4.2   General equilibrium of exchange and consumption

Chapter 1 of *Households* showed how the behaviour of individual consumers explains the shape of the demand curve. Each consumer's preferences may be represented using an indifference map.

A single indifference curve is shown in Figure 7.6 which is based on Figure 1.6 in *Households*, Chapter 1. It is assumed that indifference curves are convex to the origin. If the budget constraint is shown by the line BC, then the consumer maximizes utility by consuming the bundle where the budget line is tangent to an indifference curve. This occurs at point A.

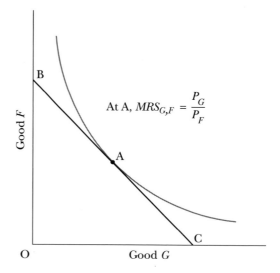

Figure 7.6 **Utility maximization**

The horizontal axis measures the units of good G, and the vertical axis measures the units of good F. At point A, the marginal rate of substitution of good G for good F, $\text{MRS}_{G,F}$, is equal to the relative price of G in terms of F, $\dfrac{P_G}{P_F}$, that is:

$$\text{MRS}_{G,F} = \frac{P_G}{P_F}$$

In other words, the rate at which a consumer would give up F for G and still remain on the same indifference curve is equal to the price of G in terms of F.

We can use this principle of utility maximization to develop a simple general equilibrium model of exchange and consumption in a competitive economy comprising two individuals and two goods. This model may seem very restrictive, but we shall see that the results generalize to many consumers and many goods. This simple economy can be illustrated using the Edgeworth box diagram in Figure 7.7. There is no production in this economy, but each individual receives a bundle of goods as an initial endowment. The economy's initial endowment of two goods is just the sum of the individuals' initial endowments. Let us say this sum is 50 kilos of figs (good F) and 60 kilos of grapes (good G); this gives the dimensions of the box shown in Figure 7.7. Figs are measured vertically and grapes are measured horizontally on the sides of the box diagram. By reading the axes from the bottom left hand corner for one agent and from the top right hand corner for the other agent, any point in the box can be understood as representing two bundles of goods, one for each agent, such that the two bundles together equal the economy's initial endowment. Such a point is shown as point A in Figure 7.7.

Reading Figure 7.7 from the bottom left-hand corner with the origin at O_x, one agent, Xerxes, has 40 kilos of figs and 10 kilos of grapes at point A. Reading the figure from the top right-hand corner with the origin at O_y the other agent, Yvonne, has 10 kilos of figs and 50 kilos of grapes at point A. (If you find this hard to follow, try turning the page upside down to see Yvonne's quantities. Note that Xerxes' axes are in black and Yvonne's are in red.) The sum of the two bundles of goods comprise the total endowment of the economy. Moving to any other point within the box keeps the same total endowment of the two goods but distributes them differently between the two consumers, Xerxes and Yvonne.

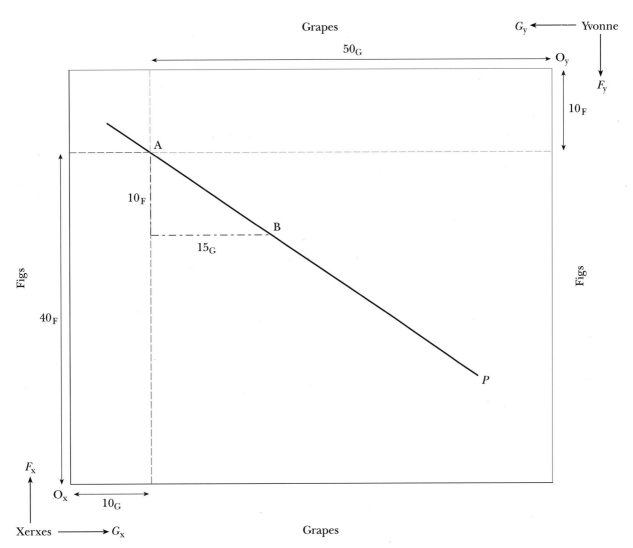

Figure 7.7 **An Edgeworth box diagram showing an initial allocation of two goods between two consumers, and a price line**

In this exchange economy, the only way for individuals to increase their utility is by exchanging some of their goods with each other. Exchange enables the two individuals to consume different combinations of the commodities that are available in this economy. We can represent the bundles that can be reached by exchange at a particular relative price by drawing a price line in Figure 7.7.

For example, all the bundles on the price line, *P*, in Figure 7.7 can be reached by exchange from A at the relative price:

$$\frac{P_G}{P_F} = \frac{2}{3}$$

That is, the price of grapes in terms of figs is $\frac{2}{3}$. This implies that, trading along the price line from A to B, 10 kilos of figs would be exchanged for 15 kilo of grapes. Xerxes' consumption bundle at B would contain 15 kilos more of grapes and 10 kilos less of figs than at A; Yvonne's consumption bundle at B would contain 15 kilos less of grapes and 10 kilos more of figs.

The question for general equilibrium analysis is whether, given the agents' preferences, there exists a relative price between the two goods such that, if the individuals were to trade with each other at this price, excess demand for both goods would be zero. (Note: since there are only two goods, there is only one relative price and, by Walras' Law, if there is zero excess demand for one good there must be zero excess demand for the other good too.)

In order to examine the exchange that Xerxes and Yvonne will choose, we need to show their indifference maps in the Edgeworth box diagram. This is shown in Figure 7.8 where the indifference maps are represented by just four indifference curves for each consumer.

The Edgeworth box diagram in Figure 7.8 shows the indifference maps of both individuals, but Yvonne's is turned upside down because her consumption is measured in the opposite direction to Xerxes'. Xerxes' indifference map extends from the bottom left-hand corner up and to the right with the origin at O_x and is shown in black. His indifference curves are labelled U_{x0}, U_{x1}, U_{x2} and U_{x3}. Yvonne's indifference map has been flipped over so that it reads from the top right-hand corner down to the left with the origin at O_y and is shown in red. Again you may find turning the page upside down helps you to see this. Yvonne's indifference curves are labelled U_{y0}, U_{y1}, U_{y2} and U_{y3}. The initial endowment, A, is at the intersection of the indifference curves U_{x0} and U_{y0}.

Looking at the two indifference maps in Figure 7.8, we can see that there are a number of points of common tangency between the two sets of indifference curves. These points represent positions of simultaneous utility maximization by Xerxes and Yvonne, subject to different common prices which are shown by the different price lines, P_1, P_2, P_3 and P_4. For example, with the price line P_2, Xerxes is maximizing utility on indifference curve U_{x1}, and Yvonne is maximizing utility on indifference curve U_{y2}. When all the points of common tangency of all the indifference curves have been joined up, they form a line, *CC*, which is known as the contract curve. Note that, as utility maximization for any consumer implies that the MRS equals the ratio of prices, simultaneous utility maximization for both consumers, subject to a common price ratio, implies that Xerxes' MRS is equal to Yvonne's MRS.

Definition

Contract curve

The contract curve shows all the points of tangency between the indifference curves of two consumers. These are the points at which simultaneous utility maximization is possible for the two consumers, subject to different prices.

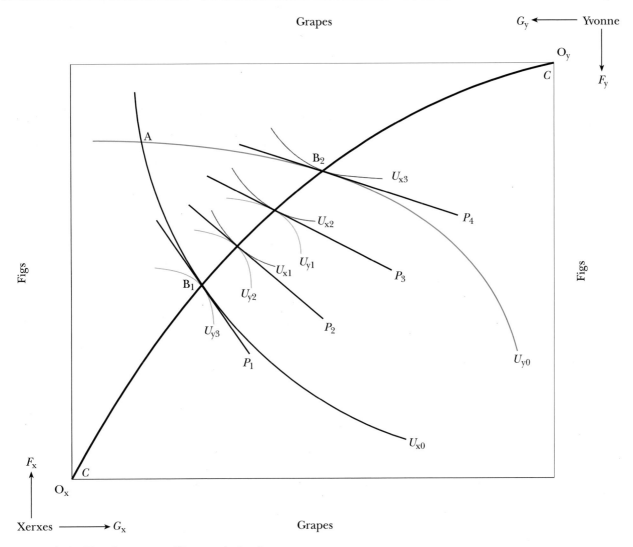

Figure 7.8 **Simultaneous utility maximization**

We have seen that simultaneous utility maximization is possible only at points on the contract curve. Given the initial allocation at A, however, not all points on this contract curve represent an improvement for both Xerxes and Yvonne, since there are some points on the contract curve which represent a worse outcome than at A. Xerxes would not want to trade to a point on the contract curve below and to the left of B_1 as this would put him on a lower indifference curve than U_{x0}. Similarly, Yvonne would not want to trade to a point on the contract curve above and to the right of B_2 as this would put her on a lower indifference curve than at U_{y0}. With an initial endowment at A, only points which lie on the portion of the contract curve between points B_1 and B_2 are preferred to A by both Xerxes and Yvonne. This portion of the contract curve, which lies between the two indifference curves corresponding to the initial allocation, is known as the core

Starting with an initial allocation at A, the equilibrium outcome must lie within the core, but where within the core? Any point within the core qualifies as such a competitive equilibrium outcome if, at some given price ratio, both consumers would choose to trade to that point from the initial allocation at A. In terms of the Edgeworth box shown in Figure 7.9, such a point must be one at which a price line P, drawn to it from A, is tangent to both consumers' indifference curves. Such a point is shown at E in Figure 7.9. In moving from A to E, Xerxes and Yvonne are trading figs and grapes at the price ratio given by the price line, with Xerxes exchanging figs for grapes and Yvonne exchanging grapes for figs.

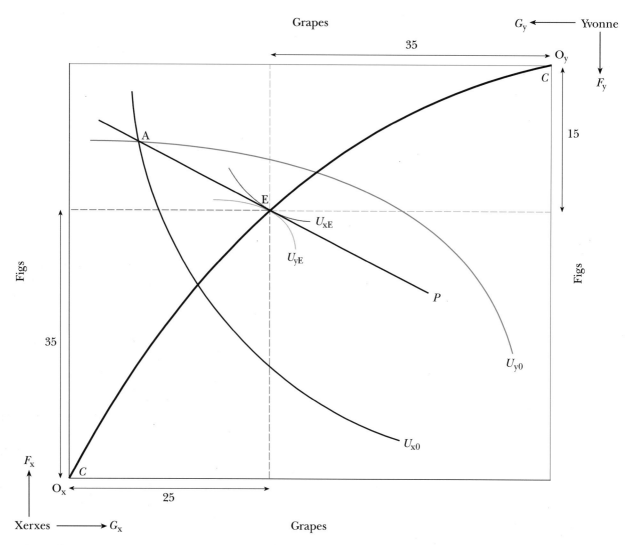

Figure 7.9 **A competitive equilibrium**

At E, the amounts demanded and supplied by Xerxes and Yvonne are equal, given the price line, *P*, and so excess demands are zero. At A, if faced with the price line *P*, both Xerxes and Yvonne would trade along it until they reached their highest indifference curve at point E, where each would be maximizing utility. Xerxes would be on his highest indifference curve, U_{xE}, and Yvonne would be on her highest indifference curve, U_{yE}, given the price line *P*. At the equilibrium point E, Xerxes consumes 35 kilos of figs and 25 kilos of grapes, and Yvonne consumes 15 kilos of figs and 35 kilos of grapes. Comparing this consumption with the initial allocation at A, we find that Xerxes has traded 5 kilos of figs for 15 kilos of grapes, and Yvonne has traded 15 kilos of grapes for 5 kilos of figs. Xerxes is now consuming more grapes and fewer figs, and Yvonne is consuming more figs and fewer grapes, but note that Xerxes' offer to sell figs equals Yvonne's offer to buy figs (5 kilos), and Xerxes' offer to buy grapes equals Yvonne's offer to sell grapes (15 kilos). Thus demand equals supply. These trades imply that the price of grapes in terms of figs is:

$$\frac{P_G}{P_F} = \frac{1}{3}$$

Note that at equilibrium both consumers' MRS, as expressed by the slopes of their indifference curves, are equal to relative prices, that is:

$$\mathrm{MRS}_{G,F} = \frac{P_G}{P_F} = \frac{1}{3}$$

Exercise 7.3

Consider an economy in which there are two consumers, Brenda and Colin, and two goods. At the initial allocation, Brenda has 30 kilos of figs and 20 kilos of grapes and Colin has 20 kilos of figs and 40 kilos of grapes (Note: in this example the total endowment for the economy is still 50 kilos of figs and 60 kilos of grapes). Brenda and Colin trade until an equilibrium is reached at which Brenda's consumption bundle is 25 kilos of figs and 35 kilos of grapes.

1   What is Colin's equilibrium consumption bundle?

2   What trades have to take place to reach this equilibrium from the initial allocation?

3   What must the price ratio, $\frac{P_G}{P_F}$, be?

4   Draw an Edgeworth box diagram to represent this.

Disequilibrium and multiple equilibria

Disequilibrium

To check whether you understand why Xerxes' and Yvonne's MRS must be equal to the relative price at equilibrium, try thinking through a different situation where it does not hold, where their indifference curves are not tangent to the price line and so there is disequilibrium. This possibility is illustrated in Figure 7.10 where the price line cuts the contract curve at point H which is in the core but where the price line is not tangent to an indifference curve of either Xerxes or Yvonne at this pont.

In Figure 7.10, at point H, the price line, *P*, is not tangent to either Xerxes' indifference curve U_{xa} or Yvonne's indifference curve U_{ya}. You can see this because both indifference curves cross *P*. This implies that at H both Xerxes and Yvonne would prefer to move to a higher indifference curve. Xerxes would prefer to move to H′ on indifference curve U_{xb} and Yvonne would prefer to move to point H″ on indifference curve U_{yb}, but this is not possible because to get from H to H′, Xerxes wants to exchange figs to get more grapes but, unfortunately, Yvonne wants to do the same to get to H″. The amounts offered in exchange by Xerxes are not consistent with the amounts offered by Yvonne, and so there is disequilibrium.

Question

Why are the consumption bundles at H′ and H″ inconsistent?

At H′ Xerxes wishes to consume 13 kilos of figs and 45 kilos of grapes, but at H″ Yvonne wishes to consume 12 kilos of figs and 40 kilos of grapes. If Xerxes wishes to consume 13 kilos of figs and Yvonne wishes to consume 12 kilos, their total consumption would be 25 kilos, this is less than the total initial endowment of 50 kilos of figs. Similarly, if Xerxes wishes to consume 45 kilos of grapes and Yvonne wishes to consume 40 kilos, this is more than the total initial endowment of 60 kilos of grapes. Given the initial allocation at A where Xerxes has 43 kilos of figs and 15 kilos of grapes, and Yvonne has 7 kilos of figs and 45 kilos of grapes, the amounts offered in exchange are inconsistent and so demand and supply are not equal.

Xerxes wishes to trade 30 kilos of figs for 30 kilos of grapes whereas Yvonne wishes to trade 15 kilos of grapes for 5 kilos of figs. At this relative price of:

$$\frac{P_G}{P_F} = 1$$

There is a positive excess demand for grapes of 25 kilos and a negative excess demand for figs of 25 kilos.

So the relative price shown by the price line *P* cannot be an equilibrium price. If there is positive excess demand for grapes and negative excess demand for figs, the Walrasian rule for price adjustment says that the price of grapes should be raised relative to that of figs.

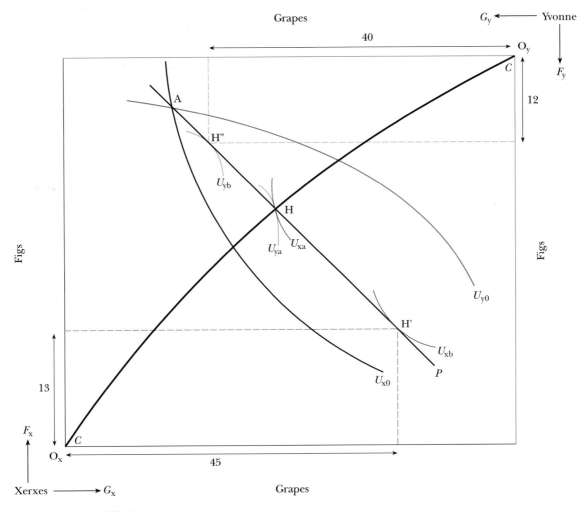

Figure 7.10   **Disequilibrium**

Exercise 7.4

Should the price line pivot around A in a clockwise or anti-clockwise direction in order to get to an equilibrium from A?

Multiple equilibria

There can be more than one equilibrium point and this can be represented using an Edgeworth box diagram. Multiple equilibria occur when it is possible to draw more than one price line through the initial allocation at A which is tangent to a pair of indifference curves in the core. This possibility is shown in Figure 7.11 overleaf.

Excess demands are zero at each of the equilibria marked as E_1, E_2 and E_3. Note that at each equilibrium, both consumers' MRS are equal to the relative price:

$$\text{MRS}_{G,F} = \frac{P_G}{P_F}$$

but the relative price and corresponding MRS are different for each equilibrium.

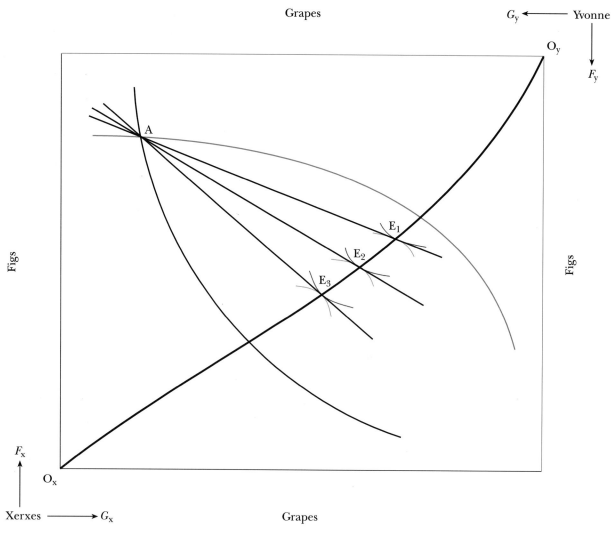

Figure 7.11 **Multiple equilibria**

Exercise 7.5

On Figure 7.11, is the price of grapes relative to figs higher at E_1 or E_3? What does this imply about the $\text{MRS}_{G,F}$ at these two equilibria?

We saw an example of a competitive equilibrium at E in Figure 7.9, but it is important to remember that the equilibrium reached at E depends on the initial endowment of resources between Xerxes and Yvonne as shown at point A. Different initial allocations of resources would result in a different equilibrium. This is shown in Figure 7.12 where the initial endowment at point A' is more unequal than it was at A in Figure 7.9, as Yvonne has more figs and more grapes than she had at A (and also more at A' than Xerxes has). The resulting equilibrium at E′ enables her to consume more of both goods than she could at E (and also more at E′ than Xerxes can).

The indifference maps for Yvonne and Xerxes are the same in Figure 7.12 as in Figure 7.9, and the total endowment of 50 kilos of figs and 60 kilos of grapes is also unchanged. The only difference lies in the distribution of this endowment between Yvonne and Xerxes at A′. Yvonne now has 42 kilos of figs and 50 kilos of grapes, and Xerxes now has only 8 kilos of figs and 10 kilos of grapes. With a relative price of $\frac{4}{5}$, the equilibrium is shown at E′. At this point Yvonne consumes 38 kilos of figs and 55 kilos of grapes and Xerxes consumes 12 kilos of figs and 5 kilos of grapes. Thus we see in this case how a different initial endowment results in a different equilibrium.

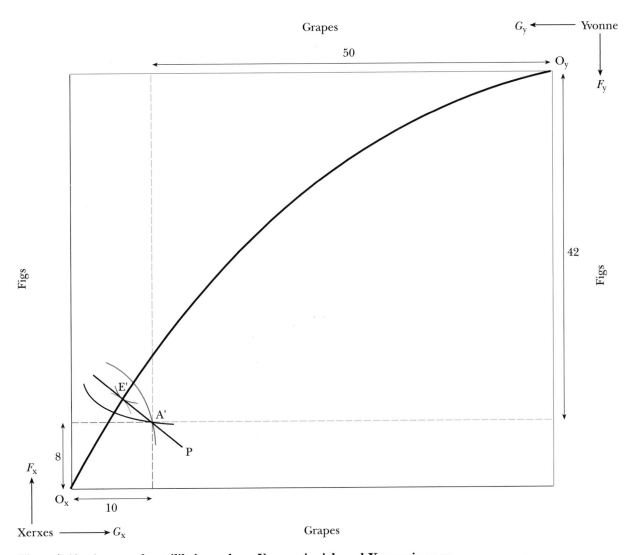

Figure 7.12 **A general equilibrium where Yvonne is rich and Xerxes is poor**

This section has presented a very simple model of an exchange economy with only two consumers, two goods and no production. In spite of this, the results using the Edgeworth box diagram illustrate an example of a competitive equilibrium, based on utility maximization by price-taking consumers. The features of a competitive equilibrium which it illustrates hold even when there are many consumers and many goods.

- All excess demands are zero: at equilibrium, Xerxes' offers to buy and sell grapes and figs exactly match Yvonne's offers to sell and buy grapes and figs.

- Until equilibrium is reached, trade between agents can allow all agents to increase their utility, i.e. trade is a positive-sum game: both Xerxes and Yvonne increase their utility by trading with one another. This holds even when the original distribution between the consumers is very unequal.

- The equilibrium outcome depends on the distribution of the initial endowment between the two consumers: the competitive equilibrium at E depends on the initial allocation at A, and a different endowment of goods between Xerxes and Yvonne results in a different equilibrium with different prices and different equilibrium consumption bundles for each of them.

In this section I have focused on a pure exchange economy where there is consumption but no production. In the next section I will look at the production side of an economy, so that in Section 4.4 I can combine the two to give a general equilibrium of exchange, consumption and production.

4.3   Equilibrium in production

To represent the production side of the economy on a diagram, we keep to a simple model of two final goods, but, as with the two-person exchange model, the results generalize to many commodities. Our aim is to find out the amounts of the two goods produced and the price at which they are sold. The first step involves considering all possible combinations of quantities of the two goods that could be produced given existing technology and different techniques of production. The production possibility frontier (PPF), which you met in Chapter 2, shows all the maximum combinations of two goods that are feasible given existing technology. Figure 7.13 shows a production possibility frontier in which kilos of grapes are measured on the horizontal axis and kilos of figs are measured on the vertical axis.

Given the existing technology, every point on the production possibility frontier shows the maximum possible output of one good, given the output level of the other good. For example, point B on the PPF shows that if the quantity of grapes produced is G_B, the maximum amount of figs that it is possible to produce is F_B.

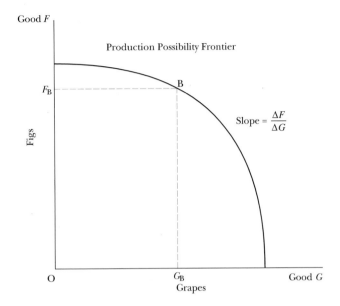

Figure 7.13 **The production possibility frontier for figs and grapes**

The slope of the PPF, $\dfrac{\Delta F}{\Delta G}$, is negative and its magnitude shows the rate at which figs have to be sacrificed (or foregone) in order to produce one more unit of grapes. We have met this idea before too: it is a version of the notion of opportunity cost that you met in Chapter 2 and is called the marginal rate of transformation (**MRT**) as it measures the rate at which one good can be 'transformed' into another by reducing the output of one and increasing the output of the other, assuming that all resources are fully employed:

$$\text{MRT}_{G,F} = -\frac{\Delta F}{\Delta G}$$

An important feature of the PPF is that its slope is different at each point. The slope of the PPF at any point can be found by measuring the slope of a line which is tangent to it at that point

Definition

The marginal rate of transformation (MRT)

The marginal rate of transformation of good G for good F measures the rate at which the output of F has to be reduced to obtain an additional unit of G. It is given by the magnitude of the slope of the production possibility frontier:

$$\text{MRT}_{G,F} = -\frac{\Delta F}{\Delta G}$$

On Figure 7.14 compare the slope at point B with that at B′ which is further to the right along the PPF. At point B′, the tangent is shown by the line T′ and is steeper than the tangent T at B. This shows that the slope of the PPF becomes more steeply negative along its length from left to right; that is, the MRT of good G for good F increases as more of good G and less of good F is produced. The MRT of a good increases as more of it is produced because the opportunity cost of producing it increases as more resources are transferred into its production.

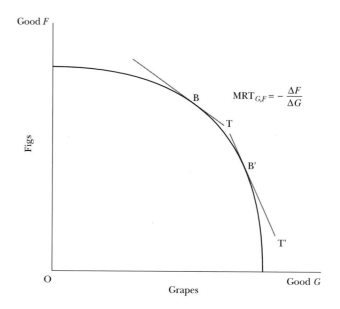

Figure 7.14 **The MRT equals the magnitude of the slope of the PPF**

We can see that the MRT between two goods measures the rate at which production of one has to be reduced in order to increase production of the other by one unit, and that this is equivalent to the notion of opportunity cost. We can put this in terms of their relative marginal costs (MC). The marginal cost of a good is the cost of the last unit produced (*Changing Economies*, Chapter 4, Section 4). In a many-good economy, we think of this as measured in terms of money. In our two-good model, cost can only be measured relative to the other good. So the marginal cost of producing one extra unit of good G, is simply the amount of good F it costs to produce that unit of good G, that is, the opportunity cost of that last unit of G in terms of F. But this is just the marginal rate of transformation of good G for good F. In other words:

$$MC_G = \text{MRT}_{G,F}$$

If there were more goods we would have to talk in terms of ratios of marginal costs, and the marginal cost of one good in terms of another would be equal to the ratio of their marginal costs. So in general:

$$\text{MRT}_{G,F} = \frac{MC_G}{MC_F}$$

However, if we are measuring costs in terms of good F, then $MC_F = 1$. For example, if the marginal cost of grapes is twice that of figs, this means that one more kilo of grapes costs two units of figs. In this case also, the $MRT_{G,F} = 2$, because two kilos of figs have to be given up in order to have one more kilo of grapes.

In a competitive economy, however, profit maximization implies that firms produce at that level at which marginal costs are equal to output prices (*Changing Economies*, Chapter 7, Section 4; *Firms*, Chapter 3). This means that in equilibrium, the ratio of the marginal costs of the two goods will be equal to their relative price, that is:

$$\frac{MC_G}{MC_F} = \frac{P_G}{P_F}$$

This implies that the marginal rate of transformation between the two goods is equal to their relative price in a competitive economy, that is:

$$\mathrm{MRT}_{G,F} = \frac{P_G}{P_F}$$

This is an important result because it shows that profit maximizing under competitive conditions results in the relative output price being equal to the magnitude of the slope of the production possibility frontier. This can be illustrated by adding a price line to the production possibility frontier as shown in Figure 7.15. If the relative price of grapes in terms of figs is shown by the price line, P, the profit maximizing output mix under competitive conditions will be at the point E. This is the point at which the price line is tangent to the production possibility curve, making the magnitude of its slope, $\mathrm{MRT}_{G,F}$, equal to the price ratio, $\frac{P_G}{P_F}$.

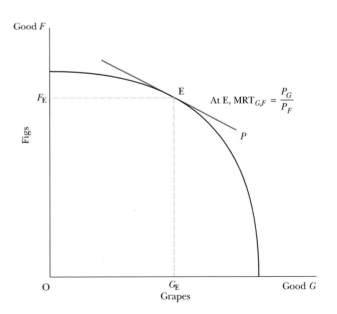

Figure 7.15   **Competitive output**

We have now derived a production possibility frontier for the economy which shows that, under competitive conditions, the economy's MRT between the two goods is equal to their relative price. We are now ready to expand our model of the exchange economy to include production so that we can find out whether there exists a relative price that will support a general equilibrium of exchange and production simultaneously. This is the subject of the next section.

4.4   General equilibrium with production

We are now ready to examine a simultaneous equilibrium for exchange and production. In this economy, both figs and grapes can be produced. Our task is to find the equilibrium relative price and the output mix of figs and grapes, together with the amounts consumed by Xerxes and Yvonne.

We know that consumer optimization under price taking results in the marginal rate of substitution of grapes for figs being equal to the ratio of prices for both consumers:

$$\mathrm{MRS}_{G,F} = \frac{P_G}{P_F}$$

We have also seen that profit maximization under price taking results in the marginal rate of transformation of grapes for figs being equal to the ratio of prices:

$$\mathrm{MRT}_{G,F} = \frac{P_G}{P_F}$$

This implies that, in equilibrium in a competitive economy, the marginal rate of substitution must be equal to the marginal rate of transformation, that is:

$$\mathrm{MRS}_{G,F} = \frac{P_G}{P_F} = \mathrm{MRT}_{G,F}$$

This can be illustrated by combining the box diagram of exchange and consumption with the production possibility frontier diagram. This is shown in Figure 7.16.

The production possibility frontier shows the competitive profit-maximizing output mix, E, where F_E of figs and G_E of grapes are produced, subject to the price line P. These amounts of figs and grapes then provide the dimensions for an Edgeworth box with the competitive utility-maximizing consumption bundles of figs and grapes at E′, subject to the price line P. This is a competitive equilibrium because excess demands for figs and grapes are zero at E′, given the price line P. Note that the MRS for each consumer equals the MRT because both equal the relative price. This implies that the MRS and MRT lines are parallel because they have the same slope, that is:

$$\mathrm{MRS}_{G,F} = \frac{P_G}{P_F} = \mathrm{MRT}_{G,F}$$

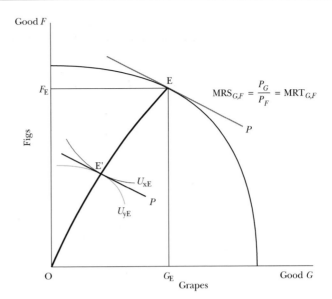

Figure 7.16   Competitive equilibrium in exchange, consumption and production

A complete general equilibrium model also needs to include an analysis of Xerxes' and Yvonne's endowment of the factors of production which are used to produce the final output, and whose sale gives them the income required to buy their respective consumption bundles at E'. Thus the competitive equilibrium in Figure 7.16 depends crucially on the initial endowment of factors of production between Xerxes and Yvonne, although this is not shown on the diagram. With a different distribution of the initial endowment, the relative incomes of Xerxes and Yvonne would be different and so we would expect the output mix and consumption bundles to be different as well. For example, if Yvonne received a greater initial endowment she would be able to consume a larger bundle than before, that is, she would be able to consume more of both figs and grapes. Thus, the output mix at E and the consumption bundles at E' in Figure 7.16 represent just one possible competitive equilibrium. In general, we would expect there to be as many different equilibrium output mixes and consumption bundles as there are different initial endowments of factors of production, assuming that each initial endowment leads to a unique equilibrium. Multiple equilibria would, of course, make this more complicated.

Exercise 7.6

If the equilibrium price of grapes in terms of figs were higher than shown in Figure 7.16, what would this imply about the equilibrium output mix of figs and grapes, and the consumers' MRS?

4.5   Conclusion: prices again

This section has examined the existence of competitive general equilibrium in two-person, two-good models which can be illustrated using Edgeworth box diagrams. As with the Walrasian model, we have found that the existence of equilibrium is dependent on there being a relative price that will yield zero excess demands. Note, however, that the issue of how the equilibrium price is actually set is still unresolved. The two agents are price takers, but the process by which the equilibrium price might have been discovered by actual agents falls outside the model.

Edgeworth was aware of this issue and, like Walras, he proposed a way around it. His solution was to think of price setting in terms of a series of contracts made directly between agents which can be renegotiated right up until the moment when the equilibrium outcome is reached. This process of 'recontracting', as Edgeworth called it, ensures that contracts that do not result in the equilibrium outcome are not adhered to, that is, that there is no 'false trading'. It is the equivalent of Walras' idea that no actual trades take place until the process of tâtonnement has finished and the equilibrium prices have been called out. If there are two agents negotiating a price, then the final equilibrium can be anywhere in the core. As we have seen, the core is the part of the contract curve that is preferred by both agents to the original endowment, but the actual point reached within the core depends on the negotiations between the two agents. Edgeworth showed mathematically that the equilibrium outcome negotiated by agents will converge on the competitive outcome of a Walrasian model as the number of agents becomes very large. In this large numbers case, the core of the contract curve shrinks to a single point representing the competitive outcome. (This cannot be illustrated using a box diagram for the same reason that excess demand curves in a general equilibrium setting can not be illustrated diagramatically: a two-dimensional surface is incapable of representing the multi-good, multi-person case.) The process of recontracting thus attempts to solve the problem of how the equilibrium outcome is actually discovered in real markets without a Walrasian auctioneer. Recontracting means that contracts are made directly between maximizing agents, but to explain how the equilibrium is arrived at we still need to rely on the device that no false trades are concluded. It therefore does not solve the theoretical conundrum of how equilibrium prices in real world markets can be determined as the outcome of ordinary trading relations where 'false', that is disequilibrium, trades are the norm.

5 Competitive equilibrium and welfare economics

5.1 Introduction

In the Introduction to this chapter we saw how arguments for economic liberalism have been linked with the neoclassical analysis of competitive markets. In this section we come to consider the argument that a competitive equilibrium promotes economic well-being, by which I mean Pareto efficiency. This was presented intuitively in Chapter 2, but we will now trace this argument more rigorously. (See *Households*, Chapter 4 for a discussion of different notions of well-being.)

5.2 Efficiency and competitive equilibrium

The notion that a competitive equilibrium promotes economic well-being is based on the argument that a competitive equilibrium is Pareto efficient, in that it is impossible to improve any agent's situation without making someone else worse off. We can examine this argument by looking back at Figure 7.16 which showed how, in the general equilibrium of exchange and production, the same price line P is tangent to both the economy's production possibility frontier at E and the consumers' indifference curves at E'. This means that the relative price represented by P is equal to both the economy's MRT and consumers' MRS at these points, and therefore that:

$$MRT = MRS$$

This implies that the opportunity cost of grapes in terms of figs in production is equal to consumers' preference for grapes relative to figs. To demonstrate that this competitive equilibrium is Pareto efficient, we now need to show that it is impossible to reallocate production or consumption to make either Xerxes or Yvonne better off without making the other worse off. We do this by showing that $MRT = MRS$ is also the condition for Pareto efficiency.

First consider whether in Figure 7.16 there is any other consumption bundle on the contract curve that is more preferred than E' by either Xerxes or Yvonne, which does not make the other worse off. Any other consumption bundle on the contract curve will be more preferred than E' by either Xerxes or Yvonne, but less preferred by the other. Points to the right of E' on the contract curve would be more preferred by Xerxes as lying on a higher indifference curve than U_{xE}, but less preferred by Yvonne as lying on an indifference curve below U_{yE}. Similarly, points to the left of E' would be more preferred by Yvonne but less preferred by Xerxes. Thus, all points on the contract curve are Pareto efficient in an exchange economy. This may be contrasted with all those consumption bundles that are off the contract curve and which are not Pareto efficient because moving from them to some point on the contract curve would increase utility for one agent (without reducing it for the other) or for both agents. For example, looking back to Figure 7.9, a point such as A is less preferred by both Xerxes and Yvonne to any point in the core. Another way of saying this, as we have seen, is that it is only on the contract curve that both consumers are maximizing utility, given their preferences and the relative price ratio, and where they have the same MRS of one good for the other.

All points on the contract curve are Pareto efficient in an exchange economy, but in a production and exchange economy, only point E' is a Pareto-efficient consumption bundle when output is at E. This is because consumers' MRS at E' equals the MRT at E. If the rate which consumers would give up units of F for an additional unit of G equals the rate at which the output of F has to be reduced to obtain an additional unit of G, then it is impossible to reallocate production or consumption to make either Xerxes or Yvonne better off without making the other worse off. Consider the case where the MRT of good G for good F is greater than the MRS of good G for good F. In this case, the amount of F given up to produce the last unit of G is greater than the amount of F which a consumer would give up for that unit of G and still remain on the same indifference curve. This implies that reducing the output of G by one unit would increase the output of F by an amount that would place one or both consumers on a higher indifference curve. Changing the output mix by reducing G by one unit and increasing F would, therefore, be a Pareto improvement. Similarly if the MRT of good G for good F were smaller than the MRS of good G for good *F*, then increasing the output of *G* would put consumers on a higher indifference curve and so would also be a Pareto improvement. It is only when the MRS = MRT for every pair of goods and for every consumer, that it is impossible to reallocate production or consumption in such a way as to make any consumer better off without making some other consumer worse off. The equality between MRS and MRT for all goods and all consumers is, therefore, the condition for Pareto efficiency.

The reason a competitive equilibrium is Pareto efficient is that, in the absence of externalities, the Pareto condition MRS = MRT always holds. Firms set marginal costs equal to prices and this implies that the economy's MRT equals relative prices; consumers adjust their consumption so that their MRS equals relative prices. The outcome is that MRS = MRT. This result, that, in the absence of externalities, a competitive equilibrium is Pareto efficient, is known as the First Welfare Theorem.

There are two points to notice about the First Welfare Theorem. The first is that it is silent about the issue of distribution. When we considered the exchange economy above, we saw that a competitive equilibrium depends on the initial endowment, and so there is a different equilibrium for each initial endowment. This is also true when we include production – there will be many competitive equilibria depending on the initial endowments of productive resources. Each of these equilibria is Pareto efficient but the final allocation of consumption is different in each. The second point is that the First Welfare Theorem contains a proviso that there are no externalities. Externalities occur where private costs/benefits differ from social costs/benefits (*Changing Economies*, Chapter 10, Section 3.1). If there are externalities, then firms and consumers are setting their private costs and benefits equal to prices, and this means that competitive prices will not reflect social costs and benefits. If there are externalities, this means that competitive prices fail to equate the true social MRT with the true social MRS, and so the competitive outcome is not Pareto efficient.

Definition

First Welfare Theorem

The First Welfare Theorem states that, in the absence of externalities, any competitive equilibrium is Pareto efficient.

Externalities mean that a competitive equilibrium is not Pareto efficient

Production externalities

In the case of pollution from a factory, for example, the social costs of production exceed the firm's private costs as the latter do not take into account the effects of the pollution on the environment or on people's health. Competitive firms will carry on producing until the private marginal cost equals the market price. If the marginal social cost exceeds the marginal private cost, this means that the social cost at the margin exceeds the market price, and so the true social MRT exceeds consumers' MRS in a competitive equilibrium. This implies that consumers are not paying the full cost of the activity and that there is more than a Pareto-efficient quantity of the polluting activity being produced.

Consumption externalities

In the case of contagious diseases, for example, other people benefit from a person's inoculation against the diseases in addition to the immediate consumer of the inoculation, and so the marginal social benefit is greater than the marginal private benefit. In this case, the true social MRS is greater than the MRT in a competitive equilibrium, and so the quantity consumed is smaller than the Pareto-efficient quantity.

We have seen that the First Welfare Theorem shows that any competitive equilibrium is Pareto efficient, under certain conditions. Is the converse also true, that any Pareto-efficient allocation can be achieved as a competitive equilibrium? The answer to this question is complicated by the problem of nonconvexity. So far in this chapter I have assumed that the production possibility frontier bows outwards and that consumers have convex indifference curves, so I have avoided the problems posed by nonconvexities (*Households*, Chapter 1; *Firms*, Chapter 1). The presence of nonconvexities means that a competitive equilibrium may not exist. I will trace through the implications of this for the case of nonconvexity in production, that is, in increasing returns to scale.

A technology is nonconvex if there are increasing returns to scale. These increasing returns to scale are associated with imperfectly competitive firms, not competitive firms (*Firms*, Chapter 1; *Changing Economies*, Chapters 6 and 7). This is because, under increasing returns to scale, large firms may outcompete small firms until the number of firms becomes so small that other strategic considerations will start to apply (see *Firms*, Chapter 4). The presence of increasing returns therefore means that a competitive equilibrium may not exist. For this reason, it is not the case that every Pareto-efficient allocation is also a competitive equilibrium because the competitive equilibrium might not exist. Pareto efficiency is possible even in the presence of increasing returns, but the increasing returns may prevent that outcome from being a competitive equilibrium. This brings us to the Second Welfare Theorem which states that, if there are no nonconvexities, every Pareto-efficient allocation can be achieved as a competitive equilibrium.

The Second Welfare Theorem shows that, if there are no nonconvexities, any Pareto-efficient allocation can be achieved by competitive markets from some initial allocation of resources. Note the importance of the initial endowment again. We have seen that every Pareto-efficient competitive outcome is based on an initial endowment of resources distributed among the economic agents. The converse is that any Pareto-efficient outcome is feasible as a competitive outcome but the initial distribution has to be the appropriate one. This result is significant as it shows that, theoretically, the issues of efficiency and distribution are separate. Competitive prices secure an efficient outcome (in the absence of externalities and nonconvexities) from any initial endowment, but an appropriate initial endowment is needed to secure any particular distributional outcome. Thus, the competitive market itself can be said to be distributionally neutral. The policy implication is that issues of efficiency and distribution are better kept separate. Policies to promote competition can be used to secure efficiency, unhindered by distributional considerations, because these can be looked after by adjusting people's initial endowments – preferably by lump sum taxes or benefits that do not distort relative prices or choices at the margin.

How does this result affect the case we considered in Section 4.2 for the exchange economy where Yvonne is rich and Xerxes poor, as was illustrated by the initial endowment A′ in Figure 7.12? If it were decided that Xerxes should have a larger consumption bundle than that shown at E′, what would be the best policy?

Definition

Second Welfare Theorem

The Second Welfare Theorem states that, in the absence of nonconvexities, every Pareto-efficient allocation can be achieved as a competitive equilibrium.

Question

Look again at Figure 7.12. If you were to introduce a policy to increase Xerxes' final consumption bundle so that he could consume more of both figs and grapes than at E', how might you do it?

The implication of the Second Welfare Theorem is that distributional issues should be resolved by changing the initial endowments, and not by changing the competitive pricing mechanism. The solution would be to change the initial endowment at A', by giving Xerxes more and Yvonne less, and then letting the market mechanism work to produce an equilibrium price at which both Xerxes and Yvonne maximize their utility by trading until their MRS equals that price.

This separation between efficiency and distribution is clear-cut in theory, but it is not so easy to make in practice as we shall see in the following section. The policy implications of the two welfare theorems are considered in the next section.

5.3   Welfare policies

We have seen that, at a theoretical level, there is a strong link between competitive outcomes and Pareto efficiency. This has been used to suggest that a decentralized economy with competitive markets and an absence of government intervention is the one that works most efficiently. According to this argument, government intervention in the form of taxes, subsidies, regulations and the direct provision of services, distorts the role of prices in allocating resources and so introduces inefficiencies into a market economy. The policy issues are, however, more complicated than this would suggest.

Improving efficiency

If the world we live in corresponded to the assumptions required for the two welfare theorems, there would be little need for government economic policy. As, however, the assumptions do not, in general, hold in the real world, it has been argued that the welfare theorems provide a rationale for certain types of government intervention to improve efficiency.

It is clear that many externalities exist in real economies. The problem with externalities is that market prices do not reflect the true social costs or benefits of an economic activity because economic agents set their private MRS or marginal costs to market prices. By doing this they leave out of account the additional external social implications of their actions. One policy response is to introduce a tax or subsidy which reflects the additional social costs or benefits of the economic activity. In this way, it is argued, the market price (including the tax/subsidy) will convey the true social cost/ benefit of the activity. This is the economic rationale behind the calls for polluting activities to be taxed, for example. Such taxes are known as 'green taxes'. If the tax reflects the amount of pollution caused, then polluters have an incentive to find ways of reducing the polluting side-effects of their economic activity. This should result in levels of pollution that are Pareto efficient in that the social costs of the products of a polluting activity are made equal to the private costs faced by producers, and the prices consumers pay for the products also reflect these costs (*Changing Economies*, Chapter 10, Sections 3 and 5).

In the real economy, increasing returns clearly exist. This implies that the scope of the Second Welfare Theorem is limited in practice. *Firms*, Chapter 6, discusses some policies for regulating those industries in which increasing returns to scale are prevalent.

As we have seen, the notion of 'competition' in competitive general equilibrium theory is a highly specific notion that is hard to operationalize given the requirement that all agents are price takers. In many real world markets, it is clear that firms do have a degree of control over prices. Thus, in many real markets, the kind of competition that is relevant may be a far cry from the one needed by the Walrasian model and may be closer to the disequilibrium process emphasized by Austrian economists (see Chapter 2) or strategic behaviour in oligopoly markets (see *Firms*, Chapter 4). Policies to encourage competition may, therefore, be encouraging not so much Walrasian price taking but other market forms in which prices diverge from marginal costs, especially in markets where there are significant returns to scale.

Furthermore, competitive models of markets tend to see 'market forces' in abstraction from the institutional settings within which these markets actually operate. We had a glimpse of this in the example of the London Gold Fixing in which the benchmark price of gold emerges not from the interplay of impersonal market forces, but as a result of twice daily meetings of a group of dealers with a chairman who acts as a Walrasian auctioneer. This example reminds us that, unlike the model of price-taking competition, information is not a free good. In the real world without a Walrasian auctioneer, both transaction costs and information costs may be considerable.

Thus, in terms of practical policies, the choice is not whether to make markets work so that agents take prices as given, but whether markets can be made to work more competitively in a broad and pragmatic way. This, however, may not bear a close relation to the Walrasian model taken strictly, especially in a world of imperfect competition and increasing returns.

Definition

The Theory of the Second Best

The Theory of the Second Best states that the satisfaction of some marginal conditions for Pareto efficiency in the presence of the failure of others will not necessarily improve consumer well-being. In cases where the first-best policy is not possible, the second-best policy is to have uniform distortions across the economy, rather than eliminating distortions in only some sectors.

Second-best policies

The policy problems we have considered derive from the fact that a real economy does not meet the strict conditions required for the welfare theorems. This suggests that we live in a 'second-best' world. What should be the guidelines for policy in a second-best world? It has been argued by some economists that the satisfaction of some marginal conditions for Pareto efficiency in the presence of the continued failure of others, will not necessarily improve consumer well-being. For example, if an economy is composed of many monopolists and prices, in general, are greater than marginal costs, then forcing one monopolist to price at marginal cost but leaving the others free to price as they wish may introduce a greater distortion between the prices of different goods. In these circumstances, the best policy – although it is a second-best policy – is to try to ensure that distortions across the economy are kept in balance as much as possible.

As the real world is a second-best world, this implies that the best policy would involve trying to balance out the various distortions in the marginal conditions for competition and Pareto efficiency. Transport policy offers an example of the difficulties involved. In a price-taking Pareto-efficient world, different methods of transport would compete equally and all market prices would reflect true social costs. The actual mix of bikes, trains, cars, buses and planes would, therefore, reflect consumer preferences in the face of true social costs. But how should transport policy be arranged when some forms of transport have received more subsidies than others? The problem is exacerbated by the problem of defining and measuring social costs. Proponents of rail transport, for example, argue that road users are subsidized by the enormous public expenditure on roads and motorways. In a second-best world where, despite vehicle and petrol taxes, it is politically infeasible to argue that road users should pay the full cost of their road use, rail supporters argue that railways should be subsidized to create more of a 'level playing field' across transport services. The argument that railways should be subsidized to counteract the inadequacy of green taxes on road pollution is an example of a second-best argument. (Cyclists can argue that cycling is the most under-subsidized of all forms of transport, especially in view of the absence of pollution from cycling.)

This approach to a partial improvement in the marginal conditions, however, requires considerable knowledge, skill and a disinterested public spirit on the part of the government. The question of knowledge and skill brings us back to the paradox raised earlier, where the Walrasian tâtonnement seems a far cry from the notion of the invisible hand in a decentralized market economy. We are back to the notion of a more active central agency which uses the Walrasian model as a planning tool to make markets work more effectively than they can unaided. It also brings us to the issue of the 'economics of politics', and whether governments are able to operate – like the auctioneer does – as disinterested players who stand outside the game, uncontaminated either by their own interest in being re-elected or by the special interest groups (such as road and rail users) which lobby the government in support of their own interests (*Changing Economies*, Chapter 10, Section 4).

Distributional policies

The Pareto criterion states that there is a welfare improvement only if someone is made better off (in that person's estimation) without making someone else worse off (in that other person's estimation). This implies that the Pareto criterion is not always relevant when choices have to be made on distributional grounds. For example, the Pareto criterion cannot help in making choices between different initial endowments. Nor can it provide a way of choosing between different Pareto-efficient points on the contract curve, although it may sometimes be helpful in choosing between points off the contract curve compared to a point on the contract curve. This is illustrated in Figure 7.17.

The consumption bundle at J is Pareto efficient and is preferred by both customers to the bundle at K, since both are on a higher indifference curve at J. But what if we want to compare K with L, a very unequal distribution, similar to the distribution we saw in Figure 7.12? L is Pareto efficient because it lies on the contract curve, but it is an unequal distribution

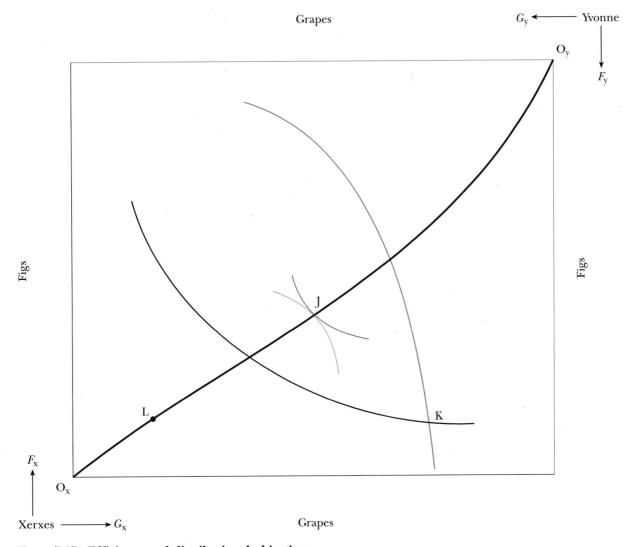

Grapes

G_y ⟵ ─── Yvonne

O_y

F_y

Figs

Figs

F_x

O_x

L

J

K

Xerxes ───⟶ G_x

Grapes

Figure 7.17   **Efficiency and distributional objectives**

compared with K which is not Pareto efficient. Yvonne would prefer to be at L than at K, whereas Xerxes would prefer to be at K than at L. If a society has mechanisms for making collective economic choices, then it might prefer a point such as K to one such as L on distributional grounds, thus choosing to trade-off efficiency for a distributional objective of, say, a more equal society.

Efficiency and distribution

A feature of the Second Welfare Theorem is that it separates efficiency and distributional issues, although, as we have seen, a society may choose to trade efficiency for the sake of distributional objectives. In practical issues of welfare policies, however, it is not easy to keep them separate. The reason for this is that prices perform two functions simultaneously:

- they allocate resources between alternative uses
- they influence agents' budget constraints.

This distinction is sometimes expressed in terms of the allocative and distributional function of prices. Welfare policies that affect prices will therefore have both allocative and distributional implications.

As an example of this connection between the allocative and distributional implications of welfare policies, consider again the case of transport policy. Any transport tax/subsidy, as we have seen, will affect the choices made at the margin by consumers and producers. In this respect it is an allocative policy, but it also has distributional effects because it increases the real incomes of those who use the subsidized service at the expense of those who pay taxes. Or consider health policy. Changes in the prices charged for medical services will have both allocative and distributional effects: demand will fall for a service whose price is increased, and users of this service will experience a fall in their real income, either by having to pay more for it or by failing to benefit from the medical service if they can no longer afford to purchase it.

5.4   Conclusion

This section has examined the First and Second Welfare Theorems which summarize the close connection between competitive equilibrium and Pareto efficiency. In spite of these theoretical results, we have found that there are some welfare arguments for government intervention in the presence of externalities. In addition, in a second-best world there are arguments for government policy to balance out the various distortions in the marginal conditions for Pareto efficiency and so try to make markets work more efficiently than they can unaided. On the other hand, these welfare arguments raise difficult issues about the knowledge and skill available to governments. We also saw that the separation between efficiency and distribution implied by the Pareto criterion is not always possible in practice and that once distributional objectives are taken into account, an efficient outcome may not always be the most desirable one.

6   Conclusion

This chapter has analysed two different versions of the model of competitive general equilibrium, and has examined the argument that competitive outcomes are Pareto efficient. The chapter has shown that, although the notion of competition as an 'invisible hand' has an intuitive appeal, economic models that analyse the way competition works are complex and highly abstract. These models are useful in showing precisely the assumptions that are required for competition to function, but their significance for contentious policy debates is double-edged. The models have been used both to argue for decentralized policies of non-intervention, as well as for more interventionist policies ranging from socialist central planning in the 1930s to social-democratic tax/subsidy policies that have resurfaced in recent years in connection with 'green' issues, but which have a longer history in connection with welfare policies of income redistribution and the provision of health and education services. The moral, if there is one, is that economic models, by themselves, rarely provide definitive answers to social and political questions, although they are sometimes claimed to do so in public debates.

CHAPTER 8   SOCIAL MARKETS

by Maureen Mackintosh

1   Introduction

1.1   The social boundaries of the market

Questions

Should sex be bought and sold?

Can love be bought and sold?

The above questions are designed to illustrate some difficult issues about the social boundaries of the market. Make some notes on your answers before you read on. Do not just write 'yes' or 'no'; put down some reasons for and against your answers.

Most of the commonly heard arguments for legalizing brothels and soliciting concentrate on the welfare of the individuals involved. Two chief constables in Northern England restarted a public debate in 1996 when they argued that licensing brothels would help to protect prostitutes from abuse and mistreatment, and help to protect under-age girls from being drawn into the business. Health workers supported them, arguing that it would also mean better treatment for sexually transmitted diseases, including Aids (*Financial Times,* 31.7.96). These views assume that a market for sexual services will always exist, and that illegality merely puts the women and men involved at more severe risk than they experience in legal exchange. Conversely, arguments against legalization generally take a more absolute ethical position. Opposition in 1996 was particularly sharp from some religious groups, who identified undesirable moral implications of a society's formal acceptance of prostitution (*Guardian,* 30.7.96).

The second question also invites philosophical answers. English common parlance counterpoises 'marrying for love' and 'marrying for money'. The question, as phrased, suggests that there may be a logical or definitional problem about buying and selling love. If it is not freely given, is it love? The same kind of question could be asked of friendship. If we buy our friends' commitment to us, are they friends? Chapter 2 quoted David Friedman distinguishing three methods of influencing another's actions, love, trade and force, implying thereby that love and trade are alternatives.

The philosopher Elizabeth Anderson suggests that the problems we have with the sale of friendship and love arise because these are members of a larger category of *shared goods* (Anderson, 1990). A shared good is one which is enhanced by sharing. We cannot, for example, easily experience affection or commitment alone; both are enormously enhanced if they are reciprocated as part of a shared experience. Other personal examples are conviviality, which needs the participation of others; companionship; and sexual relations, which many people feel are enhanced by reciprocated emotion and devalued without it.

These examples suggest that some things should not be or cannot be bought and sold, because the sharing relationship they embody is thereby changed and devalued. The debate on legalizing soliciting illustrates the point. Proponents see their opponents' arguments as irrelevant, arguing that what would be legally advertised, commercial sex between adults, is not a shared good but is a commodity which is already widely traded. It should not be confused with reciprocal emotional relations.

Doubts about buying and selling certain goods extend, furthermore, beyond the category of emotional relationships. Markets in some goods may seem not so much ethically wrong, as plain dangerous. Mercenary armies are a good example, though the word 'mercenary' has a derogatory as well as a cautionary content, carrying the suggestion of a profession of arms devalued by being put to wholly financial ends. Indeed, many activities defined as professions offer services in which we would not wish the motivation of the supplier to be wholly mercenary. We hope that our lawyer has our best interests – and not merely his or her pecuniary interests – at heart when advising us. Doubts on that point about professionals are at the heart of many cautionary tales.

Other doubts about buying and selling certain goods (including services) relate to the exclusionary effects of markets. Consider public green space in cities: a less personal good with some of the characteristics of shared goods. Not everyone enjoys well-used urban parks on sunny days – some prefer solitude – but those who do enjoy these spaces find their pleasure enhanced by the enjoyment of others. Some might not feel quite the same, however, if only those small children whose parents could pay were allowed in. Charging for a public park means that it ceases to *be* a wholly public park. Similar doubts can apply to the market supply of other goods to which access is a strong emotional issue, such as health care.

These examples are sufficient to establish that there is a wide range of goods and services which are problematic market commodities. Buying and selling them seems to risk a loss of worth to society. In the economic and broader social science literature there are two main lines of explanation for why this is so.

1.2   Values and market efficiency

The first sort of explanation of why we might set some social boundaries to the market is based in questions of ethics and values. From her reflections on shared goods, Anderson draws out the general point that there seems to be, entangled with our ideas about these goods, a notion of a hierarchy of values. A characteristic of many shared goods seems to be that the motives of the participants matter to the quality of these goods. Friendship can only be given, it cannot be coerced; and if it is provided instrumentally for an financial purpose, it is suspect. So we seem to have a hierarchy of values here which sets the motives for participation in shared goods – such as generosity or trust – above the financial motives of market exchange. Some things are above money.

We only have to put it that way to see that it is controversial. The argument depends on assumptions about the values expressed through, and embodied in, market exchange, and on our ranking of those values. Anderson conceives of market exchange as impersonal and self-seeking, a conception defined in contrast to the values of sharing. A suitable commodity is then a good or service, the value of which is not undermined by impersonal and self-seeking exchange. To 'commodify' other goods – to subject them to market exchange – devalues them.

There are two kinds of counterargument to this on the terrain of values. One is to claim that market exchange is misrepresented in this contrast. Markets, it is argued, require such social values as trust and a certain level of honesty to work at all, and they may actively develop such values, for example through the self-reinforcing effects of reputation and repeat business in 'customer markets' (Chapter 2, Section 4). It would follow that Anderson's assumption that the market undermines such values is at least partly incorrect. The other line of criticism is to argue that market exchange embodies other important values, notably freedom of choice, which are not of lesser worth than values such as generosity and commitment, but are of equal or greater importance in a value hierarchy.

In public debate, competing values or value hierarchies collide, and 'freedom' is a key focus of disagreement. Public space is a good example. Some people in Britain have expressed uneasiness about local developments of US-style fenced and guarded residential areas, on the grounds that it is wrong – a reduction in freedom and community – to close off previously public space in this way. Others see fenced private property as an expression of freedom. A similar debate on the freedom to trade *versus* the freedom of access, in the context of health care, is discussed later in this chapter.

All of these arguments concern values: what kind of society and human relationships do we want? An alternative approach to tackling the difficulties encountered in buying and selling some goods and services is to treat the problem as a *technical* one: what goods can be marketed efficiently, how can efficiency be improved, and does a category of goods exist which cannot be properly commodified in this sense at all?

This is the standard approach of neoclassical economics. In this framework, values are a matter for the individual. The boundaries of the market are a matter of the technical features of goods and services: notably, whether they can be packaged as pure private goods.

Pure private goods in this technical sense are goods which are *rival* and *excludable*. If a good is 'rival', then more for you means less for me. Excludable goods can be supplied to you without also supplying me. The converse, pure public goods, are non-rival and non-excludable (see *Firms*, Chapter 9). The predicted problem with public goods is 'free riding': people will conceal their true willingness to pay, hoping that others will provide a good from which they cannot be excluded. The result will be underprovision (*Changing Economies,* Chapter 10). In theory, therefore, public goods provide one boundary to the market.

It is not easy to think of examples of pure public goods. But large numbers of goods have some public good characteristics, including externalities, which make market provision inefficient. Consider the provision of

Definitions

Private goods

A pure private good is rival and excludable.

Public goods

A pure public good is non-rival and non-excludable.

drinking water to households. Drinking water has many characteristics of a private good: it is a rival good (once I have drunk some, it is not available to you) and an excludable good (your water supply may legally be cut off in England and Wales if you do not pay your water bills).

On the other hand, there are a number of public goods aspects of water supply. Clean water has public health benefits, not only to those who drink it, but also to their neighbours by reducing the risk of transmitted infections. For example, the introduction of a clean water supply was the main way in which cholera was eradicated in western Europe. The water supply process also produces environmental externalities: reservoirs which may be beneficial (lakes to walk beside) or damaging (farm land drowned); rivers dried out and the depletion of aquifers. The market price mechanism does not capture either of these types of external effects. So drinking water might be under-supplied because of public health externalities or over-supplied because of negative environmental effects (*Changing Economies,* Chapter 10, Section 3).

The ethical and the technical approaches to explaining the social boundaries of the market are not mutually exclusive. It is quite possible to find the technical arguments illuminating and also to regard the debate on values as relevant. The two lines of thought, however, suggest different explanations for:

- the emergence of regulation and of non-market forms of supply for many goods
- the social resistance to the commodification of some goods and services.

Commodification – the shaping of goods and services into a form approximating private goods and available for market sale and purchase – is a complex historical process. For example, the public goods aspects of the supply of water on tap in houses have led to its public provision in many parts of the world. However in countries such as India, well-off people resort widely to private supply, and water supply in England and Wales was privatized in 1989. It may have struck you that neither of the two theoretical approaches just discussed displayed much sense of this history. Both the technical and the value aspects are typically presented as static, embodied in the goods themselves. But historically, views on what *should* be bought and sold, and the practice of what is, in fact, marketed, have interacted and changed over time. In other words, the social boundaries of the market shift, and are historically and socially constituted.

I will use the term 'social good' in this chapter to refer to the diverse set of goods and services for which, at any historical moment, commodification is regarded as problematic. The central objective of the chapter is to explore some characteristics of markets in social goods: the 'social markets' of the chapter's title. I have chosen examples where ethical and technical issues interact in current debate. Section 2 examines markets in health care, Section 3 uses the example of social care to explore public contracting for the supply of social goods and Section 4 considers how norms of ethical behaviour can improve the operation of social markets. The focus of the chapter is on understanding markets, not on policy formation. Much of the analysis, however, has an evaluative content. It looks not only at how markets work in specific contexts, but also at how well or how desirably they work, and with what social effects.

<table>
<tr><td valign="top">

2 'Managed markets' and 'quasi-markets' in health care

</td><td valign="top">

2.1 Health care as a social good

In Section 1, I identified the class of social goods in two ways: goods the commodification of which is felt to be problematic for value reasons, and goods with characteristics which appear to pose technical economic barriers to full commodification. The extent to which health care is a social good by either criterion is a matter of sharp debate, with substantial policy implications. I will begin with the technical arguments.

The World Bank, for example, argues that in low income countries, governments should fund only primary and preventative health care. This includes diagnosis, pre- and post-natal care, vaccinations and health advice, as well as a small range of medicines for common conditions. Such services, the Bank notes, have strong 'public good qualities'. The Bank contrasts preventative care with curative treatment after diagnosis, by medicines or surgery. It argues that 'individuals can capture the full benefit of curative care interventions so economic efficiency is not reduced by the government not funding this type of care' (World Bank, 1996, p.15). Work through the following exercise, to explore the World Bank's technical argument, and at the same time review some key concepts.

</td></tr>
</table>

Exercise 8.1

1   What are the public good qualities of primary and preventative health care?

2   Draw a diagram to illustrate the effect of these public good qualities in reducing economic efficiency if primary health care were traded on a competitive market. (*Changing Economies*, Chapter 10 will help here.) Would primary health care be under- or over-supplied?

3   With reference to the diagram, explain the World Bank's reasons for arguing that competitive markets in curative care are fully efficient. Do you agree with their argument?

The exercise established that, in technical terms, health care is neither a pure private good nor a pure public good. Much of it is capable of being sold on a market as a private good, but because of externalities – and for other reasons to which I return below – economists predict that health care markets will tend to be allocatively inefficient.

The World Bank's arguments furthermore focus on efficiency rather than access. But many people see access to health care as a matter of social concern, even as a basic human right. The division is illustrated by a much cited exchange between the philosophers Bernard Williams and Robert Nozick. Williams (1973) argued that the only proper criterion for medical care is medical need. Nozick (1974), in reply asked why then it did not follow that 'the only proper criterion for barbering services is barbering need'?

Question

Stop a moment and think about this for yourself. Are haircuts different from health care? If so, why?

One possible reply is that health care is simply more basic than haircuts: we can do without the latter, but the former is central to the quality of life, one of our basic needs. So we may accept more readily that the rich have better haircuts than that they have better medical care. Michael Walzer (1983, p.87) reflecting on this debate in a book on justice, adds that societies change over time in what they regard as a socially recognized need. He argues that, 'In Europe during the Middle Ages, the cure of souls was public, the cure of bodies private'; hence in the Middle Ages 'eternity was a socially recognized need' and the aim was a church in every parish. As medicine improved, and religious belief declined, the 'socially recognized need' came to be not eternity, but longevity: a new social meaning given to widening access to health care.

Societies differ across space as well as time in the extent to which health care is thought suitable for commodification. Besley and Gouveia (1994) argue that people in the US seem to accept more readily than western Europeans that those with more money to spend should get more health care. John Elster (1992, p.13) puts a US-based point of view clearly: 'I see no reason, for instance, why the rich should not be allowed to buy medical treatments that are not available to others, provided they pay the full social costs. To refuse them the right to do so would be a form of sumptuary legislation, based on barely disguised envy.' This argument treats health care as a consumption good like any other for the purposes of economic analysis.

Conversely, western European public opinion and opinion-formers are more apt to take the view that access to health care should be determined solely or largely by need, a view likely to be influenced by experience of comprehensive social insurance-based or tax-financed health care systems. In this context it is relevant that Williams was writing in Britain, and Nozick in the US. In some cultures, health care appears to have developed features of a shared good, for which access – publicness – is valued. And for that reason, people may be willing to pay for health care in forms which are redistributive: where those who can pay also pay for those who cannot.

The argument that health care can express social solidarity – and be devalued by exclusivity – was most famously developed by the sociologist Richard Titmuss in a passionate defence of the economic efficiency and ethical desirability of unpaid blood-doning:

> ... the ways in which society structures its social institutions – and particularly its health and welfare systems – can encourage and discourage the altruistic in man; such systems can foster integration or alienation; it can allow the 'theme of the gift' – of generosity towards strangers – to spread among social groups and generations. This ... is an aspect of freedom in the twentieth century which, compared to the emphasis on consumer choice ... is insufficiently recognized.
>
> *(Titmuss, 1970, p.225)*

The reference to 'gifts' suggests one final sense in which health care may have shared goods qualities. Health services rely for their quality, in part, on the relationship between practitioner and patient. The quality of care depends greatly, for example, on the patient conveying clear information (since diagnosis relies very heavily on this), on the ability of the practitioner to listen and interpret, and on the co-operation of the patient in the treatment. Furthermore, the experience of being cared for is part of the service expected; in some areas, such as terminal and long-term chronic care, a very substantial part of it. It is, therefore, an interesting test of Anderson's arguments to ask if paying for care – and any particular form of payment – threatens the caring relationship. I come back to this issue in Section 4.

2.2   Private market dilemmas in health care

The technical economic problems of health care as a commodity imply that private health care markets will display static inefficiencies. Over time, the markets may also generate dynamic inefficiencies through strategic behaviour by participants. (The distinction between static and dynamic efficiency is explained in *Firms,* Chapter 3.) The sources of static market failure include not only externalities, but also *asymmetric information.* Patients tend to find it very hard to judge the quality of the health care they are receiving because of their lack of medical knowledge, compounded by personal vulnerability at the time when they most need the service. Superior knowledge and control, in turn, create *moral hazard* (or incentives to cheat) for care providers, since they can influence the quality of provision without penalty. (*Firms,* Chapter 2 and *Changing Economies,* Chapter 23 explain these two concepts.)

Potential health care users also cannot predict the care they will need, so the attempt to reduce risk generates a demand for insurance in private markets for health care. If health care is insurance-financed, this implies that the market is characterized by *third party payment*: neither provider nor client is paying at the time the service is received, so neither have an incentive to keep down costs. Taken together, these market failures create some characteristic 'pathologies' of private health care markets.

The first 'pathology' is a tendency to rising costs.

Exercise 8.2

Assume that in a private and imperfectly competitive health care market, doctors are reimbursed on a fee-for-service basis by insurers, that is, they are paid for each separate service they provide. Explain why this may lead to rising unit and total costs of health care.

The US is the only industrialized country where private medical insurance predominates (*Changing Economies,* Chapter 23). Until recently, its health care market was dominated by fee-for-service provision, and its health care system is the most expensive in the world. Studies in a number of countries show that a switch towards fee-for-service payments increases the number of treatments (Donaldson and Gerard, 1993). A telling comparison is between costs in the US and in Canada where there is a universal tax-funded health care system, with far fewer fee-for-service payments. With similar levels of average income, the US had fees around three times higher than Canada in the mid-1980s (Donaldson and Gerard, 1993, p.106). Doctors' incomes were much higher in the US, as was the proportion of spending on administrative costs; and the intensity of treatment was greater (Ham *et al.,* 1990).

Furthermore, the US has a much more hospital-based system than Canada, with poor primary care. This second 'pathology' of private health care markets also raises unit costs, since hospitals and specialists are more expensive than primary practitioners.

Question

In addition to the World Bank's arguments in Section 2.1 about the under-provision of public goods, can you think of other reasons why private health care markets tend to under-provide primary care?

Doctors tend to have market power. This is sustained by their semi-monopoly of information, by the barriers to entry to the profession created by long training and exclusion of the untrained, and by professional collusion. Doctors may use this market power to develop the better paid and more prestigious specialities, relative to primary health care, and may also keep other practitioners, such as nurses, out of primary care, thus biasing the supply of care towards hospitals.

The third main 'pathology' of private health care markets is the exclusion of some of those in need. Some of that exclusion is the result of market failure, since private insurance, like the market for second-hand cars, is subject to *adverse selection* (*Firms*, Chapter 2). This is another result of the asymmetric information in health markets: in this case the *patients'* private information. The health insurance companies know less than each client about that client's likely needs.

Exercise 8.3

Suppose that clients with high expected needs for health care successfully understate their needs to insurance companies, and therefore pay less than their expected costs of treatment. Explain how this may, through a process of adverse selection, lead to some people who would have been prepared to pay the full cost of insuring themselves being excluded from medical insurance. (The 'market for lemons' analysis in *Firms*, Chapter 2 will help with this exercise.)

The response of medical insurance companies to the adverse selection problem is to seek more information: to get better at identifying good risks and charging them low premiums. The better they get at this, the more expensive insurance becomes for high-risk people, because risk pooling is being reduced. (It also further pushes up administration and monitoring costs.)

At this point a nasty interaction sets in between the insurance market and poverty. Poor people will not, in any case, be able to afford average insurance premiums. But the poor also tend to fall into high-risk categories requiring more expensive insurance. They are more likely than the middle classes to be ill and to have chronic and congenital conditions against which one cannot get insurance, or for which insurance cover runs out. Under-consumption in private health care markets is driven by the interaction of income- and risk-based exclusions with rising costs.

2.3   Private 'clubs' in social markets

The development of regulated health care markets

The pathologies of unregulated private health care markets imply a need for regulation and intervention. Most industrialized countries, apart from the US, fall into two groups, those that run most health care as a tax-funded public service – notably the UK and the Scandinavian countries – and those that organize it through some form of compulsory state-subsidized social insurance, such as Germany. All industrialized countries, except the US, achieve virtually universal access to health care through these means (*Changing Economies,* Chapter 23). In recent years, reforms in the organization of health care in some of these countries, for example in Britain and in Finland, have introduced more market-like processes into the tax-funded systems. In the US, the fee-for-service or 'indemnity' insurance system that pays the bills of health care providers who are consulted by those insured, is rapidly being replaced by a health care system dominated by health maintenance organizations (HMOs) which seek to combine insurance and health care provision. It is sometimes argued – controversially – that industrialized countries' health care systems are 'converging' on a model of 'managed markets' or 'managed care' or, sometimes, 'managed competition' (Chernichovsky, 1996).

This section and the next explore some aspects of these highly regulated social markets. An explicit aim of many health care market reforms has been to increase – or in the US case sustain – patients' choice of health care provider, while keeping – or in the US case putting – a lid on costs. The key idea in both the US and the UK reforms, despite the very different contexts, was to ensure that finance (insurance) and provision were in the same set of hands, while allowing potential patients some choice of provider.

The US vehicle for this, the HMOs, are independent commercial or non-profit organizations. The defining feature of the HMO model is that an HMO contracts to provide, for an agreed fee per person, access to a predetermined range of health care over a given period. Unlike fee-for-service insurers, the HMO is also responsible for providing the care. The HMO may contract with groups of doctors to provide the care, or it may employ doctors itself; it will also contract for specialist and hospital care.

The British National Health Service (NHS) has always combined finance and provision in one organization. The 1990 organizational reforms somewhat weakened that link, separating 'purchasers' (funders) from 'providers' (such as hospitals and primary doctors). But they also established 'fundholding' groups of general practitioners (GPs, primary doctors) within the tax-funded service which had some resemblances to HMOs. In this model, a group of GP practices holds a budget, for some or all of the care for their patients, for which they contract as necessary with hospitals. The budget is tax financed, and based on a mix of patient numbers and indicators of need, such as local levels of deprivation. Patients may move between GP practices and GPs may accept or reject patients, but unlike HMOs, patients make no direct payment to the practices.

In both the HMOs and NHS fundholder models, the organizations accept the risk of providing care within a budget fixed by a 'capitation' charge, that is, a fee per person.

Question

Why should the integration of finance and provision solve the problems identified above of cost escalation and adverse selection?

The providers of care are working to a known budget for a given population of patients in any year. They therefore have a strong incentive to keep costs down, since they retain the benefits for the organization either to spend on their patients or as profits for commercial HMOs. Third-party payment is removed, which should deal with tendencies to over-supply, so long as the organizations face reasonably strong negotiators for those paying. The private buyers of health care in the US are mainly employers, not individuals, and in parts of the US, employers have organized buying groups to negotiate with HMOs over price and the range of provision. The problem of adverse selection is also reduced because employers pay a 'capitation' fee per employee, so HMOs pool risk over quite large groups.

In addition to cost control and widened risk pooling, health care reformers have sought to increase or retain provider competition and patient choice. Economists such as James Buchanan, who are particularly critical of the lack of scope for 'exit' by consumers where the state is a monopoly supplier, have long argued that goods that are neither wholly private nor wholly public goods could be provided by voluntary associations of consumers in 'clubs' (Buchanan, 1965). Models of provision of social goods through clubs are attractive to market-oriented economists and policy makers because they appear to overcome one of the key economic arguments for state provision: the tendency of the market to underprovide public goods. Indeed, on some stringent assumptions which are discussed below, it is possible to reach a Pareto-efficient general equilibrium in which certain types of semi-public goods are provided by voluntary clubs through a market-like mechanism.

These economic arguments for voluntary provision have been developed alongside the growing political attraction in many countries of the idea of social provision through associations outside the state. The political theorist Paul Hirst, for example, argues in an influential book (Hirst, 1994) that, 'Voluntary association is an alternative to top down bureaucracy in the competent provision of services'. And European research documents the rise of 'stakeholder co-operatives' for self-organized provision of welfare (Borzaga, 1996). One way to analyse HMOs is as a set of health care 'clubs' with people shopping around between them. (Fundholders, as we shall see, fit the model rather less well.)

Definition

Club goods

Club goods are excludable but at least partially non-rival.

The economics of clubs

In economic theory, club goods are goods with partial public goods qualities, being at least partly non-rival, but excludable. The central idea of club goods models is that public goods that are excludable – through distance or institutional exclusion – do not pose the same problems for voluntary provision as pure public goods. In theory, the private provision of public goods leads to under-provision because of 'free riding' (Section 1.2). If the good is excludable, 'free riding' can be prevented, since a club can charge an agreed entry fee to provide a desired level of a good for its members. People reveal their preferences by joining a club that offers the mix of good and cost they prefer. If they change their mind they can 'vote with their feet' and join another club.

The image, then, is of a social market of clubs providing choices of level of consumption of club goods at various entry costs. Shared goods, such as conviviality and sports played with others, are natural 'club' goods. Swimming pools are often used as the example in explaining the models, since (until crowded) they are non-rival, but easily excludable. But the model can also be applied to goods which – although rival in provision (more for me, less for you) – are best financed through insurance of some kind. HMOs provide health care risk pooling, which can be seen as a good which is non-rival in the sense that more risk poolers do not, just by joining, reduce the effectiveness of risk pooling for existing members, often quite the contrary. The HMO may also be providing the non-rival benefit of health care cost-control.

For a social market to work by satisfying preferences, consumers must be able to join a club that maximizes their utility, given their preferences for club goods and other goods. The economic analysis of clubs proceeds in two stages. It first analyses how a voluntary association of consumers can design their preferred club, by making the dual decision about the amount of the club good to be provided and the number of club members to share its consumption. Having shown how the optimum membership and scale of such clubs is determined, from the point of view of the members, the analysis then goes on to consider the conditions under which such voluntary associations can result in economy-wide allocative efficiency.

I will tell the story in terms of a non-profit health club (of the swimming pool and exercise-machines type) and begin by considering the choice of number of members for a particular club.

Optimal membership for a given scale

Assume that the individuals wishing to join this club have identical tastes and incomes. A small group of founder members of the club are considering how many additional members to let in. Suppose the founders have already committed themselves to a given level of services of the club, in terms of the size of pool and range of facilities: I will call this the 'scale' of the club. You will have to think of scale as uni-dimensional; members can choose a larger or smaller scale but not, for example, more expensive tiles for the same sized pool. All members pay the same fee. This type of club is called a 'homogeneous club' (Cornes and Sandler, 1996).

The decision on the number of members will then take the form shown in Figure 8.1. Consider the marginal financial benefits to an existing member of adding one more member. Figure 8.1 shows these marginal financial benefits, *MB*, as large at first and then declining sharply.

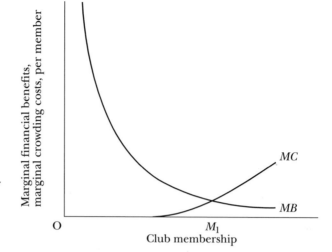

Figure 8.1 **Optimal membership for a given scale of club**
Source: based on Mueller, 1989, p.151

For example, if we think of all the club costs as fixed costs then, given the decision on scale, increasing membership from one to two would halve those costs for the first member, a huge financial benefit. Later, the marginal financial benefit to each member of adding one more member becomes smaller, since the cost is already spread over a larger membership. Now consider the marginal cost curve *MC*. This shows the marginal loss in utility to an existing member of adding one more, in terms of crowding in the pool or waiting for machines. *MC* will be zero for the first few members (it might even be negative for those who come for conviviality as well as exercise). But eventually, the crowding effect of new members starts to irritate, and the marginal costs of crowding by new members starts to rise. There will come a point where the extra irritation from an extra member is no longer worth the financial benefits (point M_1), and this is the optimal club membership.

The optimal membership of the club is therefore limited by the costs of crowding. Club goods, unlike pure public goods, are only partially non-rival. As the number of consumers rises, additional consumers start to reduce the utility of others. A pure public good displays no crowding: the *MC* curve would lie along the horizontal axis and the optimal membership of the club would be infinite.

Question

Figure 8.1 is drawn for a club of one scale. How would the *MB* and *MC* curves shift if the founders decided on a larger scale club?

The *MB* curve would move upwards, since the fixed costs would be larger, hence the marginal financial benefit of a new member to an existing member rises. The *MC* curve will shift rightwards: with a larger scale club, crowding will begin at a higher membership. Hence, as we might expect, a larger scale club will have a larger optimal membership. So we can draw a line such as M_{opt} on Figure 8.2 that shows how optimal membership rises as club scale increases.

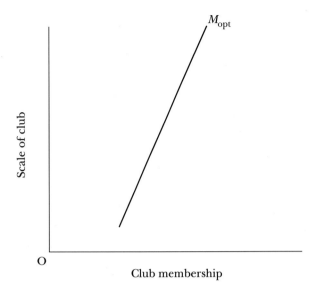

Figure 8.2   **Optimal membership for each scale of club**

Optimal scale for given membership levels

That is one part of the dual decision. Now look at the problem the other way around. Suppose a fixed number of people decide to form a club. They will want to pick a club scale which maximizes their utility (remember I assumed identical tastes and incomes). If they share the financial costs equally between them, they will increase the scale of the club until the extra financial cost to each outweighs their enjoyment of the extra facilities.

Exercise 8.4

Draw a diagram illustrating that last argument.

Exercise 8.4 shows how a given group of members will choose their preferred club scale. If the group of members is enlarged, the marginal cost curve in Figure 8.8 will shift downwards, and the preferred scale of club will increase. We can draw a line, S_{opt}, showing the optimal scale of club for each size of membership group. I have added S_{opt} to Figure 8.2 to give Figure 8.3 overleaf.

The optimal health club

Figure 8.3 shows the outcome of the dual decision on club scale and membership. The point where M_{opt} and S_{opt} cross defines the optimal club, with scale S_* and membership M_*, given the assumptions about members' tastes and incomes and financial costs of clubs. At this point, the members are each satisfied that no other scale of club would be preferred, nor are there any benefits from adding or ejecting members. This is a welfare maximum *for this club* (not for society as a whole).

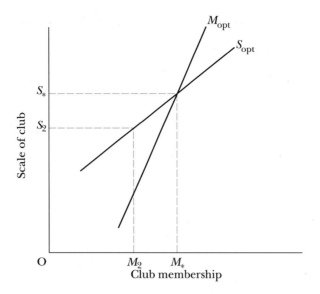

Figure 8.3 **The optimal health club**

Exercise 8.5

To check your understanding, consider a club of scale S_2 with membership M_2 on Figure 8.3. Why is this not the optimum club?

Exercise 8.5 showed that a club of scale S_* and membership M_* on Figure 8.3 forms a stable equilibrium: clubs of different sizes converge towards that optimum size and scale. For such a stable equilibrium to exist, M_{opt} must be steeper than S_{opt} as shown in Figure 8.3.

This model of a homogeneous club shows that such a club can have an optimum size and scale derived from the costs of provision and the tastes of the members, including their dislike of crowding. Club goods can, in principle, be provided by voluntary associations. The expanding club good literature has gone on to consider what happens once we drop the assumption of uniform tastes and allow people of like tastes to form clubs. This allows the voluntary emergence of diverse mixed goods provision to satisfy diverse tastes, potentially raising welfare above that achieved, for example, by uniform public supply.

Charles Tiebout, a US economist, was the first to point out in the 1950s that we could think of local government jurisdictions as clubs – small relative to the national government – and imagine people migrating between them to find the mix of public good provision and cost which suited them best (Tiebout, 1956). He showed that on a set of very stringent assumptions, such a 'voting with the feet' process will produce a Pareto-efficient general equilibrium through voluntary association without the intervention of the state. These conditions include perfect knowledge and the freedom of 'migration' between clubs. There also have to be enough diverse clubs available to serve all preference patterns and an absence of spillovers or externalities between clubs (Mueller, 1989, p.155). Note particularly the last assumption. The club model assumes that all the benefits and costs of consumption are captured within the club. If not, then such externalities prevent an economy reaching a general equilibrium that is a welfare optimum, just as they do in competitive trading of private goods (Chapter 7, Section 5.2)

Club goods and health care provision

The 'voting with the feet' metaphor is interesting in the context of applying the club goods model to health care. Is this movement between clubs a market process? The model certainly relies on 'exit' as well as 'voice' (Chapter 2, Section 4) to arrive at an equilibrium, and its political attraction appears to be the element of voluntarism. HMOs and GP fundholding have both been 'sold' politically as offering diversity and choice. In the UK, it was argued that fundholding GPs could offer increasingly diverse types of provision (adding clinics or a range of home nursing care to core primary doctoring, for example). It is also suggested that patients can 'shop around' when choosing a GP, although their choice of GP does not affect the taxes they pay for health care. So the social market of clubs will 'sort' potential patients into 'clubs' of homogeneous tastes, thus raising welfare and increasing freedom.

What, however, of income levels? I smuggled in above, when discussing a single type of good, the assumption that members have identical incomes. If we consider now a diversity of clubs and a diversity of incomes, then these models predict that clubs, as voluntary associations, will tend to become homogeneous as to income levels as well as tastes (Ricketts, 1994, p.321).

Question

Can you explain intuitively why this is likely to be so?

The theory of clubs identifies an optimum which depends on preferences, the characteristics of the good, and willingness to pay. Willingness to pay will tend to differ between income levels since ability to pay varies. Hence a rich person will generally find the facilities in a poor members' club too basic, while a poor person is likely to find a rich members' club too expensive.

With purely social clubs, this result may be seen as just an extension of the private benefits of high income in terms of the private goods it buys. But health care? A health care 'club' which includes members of different income levels provides a common level of service to all. If different health care clubs offer different levels of service and charge different fees, then they will tend to differentiate themselves by income level.

Question

Can GP fundholding avoid this outcome?

In principle it should do so. GP fundholders in the UK do not fit the 'clubs' model to the extent that GP budgets are financed from general taxation. So people can join clubs they could not pay for if the payment were a fee. The budgets are set on the basis of the numbers of patients registered plus various allowances for greater than average predicted need, for example for high numbers of elderly patients or high indicators of local social deprivation. Inner-city GPs have claimed, however, that these supplements are too small to even-out provision, and fundholding spread most rapidly in wealthier areas where the demands on GPs are lower than in the inner cities.

Nevertheless, the principles of GP fundholding, in contrast to HMOs, should largely sustain the redistribution from richer to poorer which occurs when any public good is provided to a community of mixed incomes financed by proportional or progressive taxation. This kind of redistribution through public and semi-public goods is a very important mitigator of private income inequality in many societies, which is no doubt one reason why the highly regressive poll tax was so resented in the UK. Dennis Mueller, an American economist who specializes in 'public choice' issues, puts the point this way:

> A given distribution of private incomes might be considered just when individuals reside in communities of heterogeneous income strata, so that the relatively poor benefit from the higher demands for public goods by the relatively well-to-do. The same distribution of income might be considered unjust if individuals were distributed into communities of similar income and the relatively poor could consume only those quantities of public goods which they themselves could afford to provide.
>
> *(Mueller, 1989, p.172)*

We can make an analogous point for health insurance. If a shift occurs from central to local or 'club' provision of health care, or if 'voting with the feet' becomes more pronounced in an existing system, then any existing income inequality is likely to be made worse.

2.4   The behaviour of health care 'clubs'

How do health care clubs behave in practice? This discussion draws on experience in the US of HMOs, and also considers GP fundholders in the UK, who do not fit the formal clubs model (since they do not charge patients directly) but offer some interesting comparisons.

Ownership

The clubs model of social markets is associative, based in voluntary agreement and shared ownership, so the model club is a non-profit organization for its members' benefit. But as Martin Ricketts (1994) points out, many 'clubs', including many health clubs of the type I used for my example, are profit-seeking firms, and they do differentiate themselves, as predicted, into high price, high quality provision and more basic, cheaper clubs. Ricketts suggests that where investment funds are a constraint, profit-seeking clubs are more likely to emerge, whereas clubs where the social environment is the product – 'social' clubs where the main product is the shared good of conviviality – are more likely to be, and to remain, non-profit making.

In this context, the evolution of HMO ownership is interesting. Early HMOs in the US tended to be non-profit making organizations. In the 1980s, many non-profit HMOs converted to commercial status and most new HMOs were profit-seeking firms. Langwell (1990) attributes this shift to a search for better access to equity capital and the end of Federal incentives to non-profit HMOs. Most HMOs are now commercial finance organizations who contract with providers. In California, large organized groups of doctors integrate finance and provision, but these HMOs, too, tend to be profit-seeking (Robinson and Casalino, 1996).

In principle, one would expect the behaviour of non-profit making and profit-seeking organizations to differ in response to the same incentives (*Firms,* Chapter 2). I will return to this issue in Section 4.

Cream skimming

Consider the following set of incentives. You are a group of doctors with a known budget with which you provide comprehensive care for a population of patients. You can exert some, but relatively little, influence over the prices you face for the care you buy-in rather than provide yourself. The care any individual will need is uncertain, but some patients are in higher risk categories than others and hence have a high probability of costing more to care for than others. You can make a well-informed estimate of which patients are high risk.

Question

If you can select your patients, how will you be tempted to do it?

You may seek to refuse patients in high risk categories. This means either that you will keep a larger financial surplus for yourselves, or that you can provide a better service to your remaining patients. If you are an HMO you can also lower premiums and increase your enrolees. Refusing potentially expensive patients in this way is called 'cream skimming' or 'favourable selection', and has a serious exclusionary effect. The behaviour occurs in both HMOs and GP fundholding, but is poorly researched. In the US, HMO premiums tend to rise in a region as HMO coverage increases, because early opportunities for competition through favourable selection are exhausted (Wholey *et al.,* 1995). In the UK there is some relevant anecdotal evidence, for example of seriously mentally ill patients being excluded from lists because of the cost of their drugs, but, as yet, no systematic research is available on the extent of cream skimming.

Quality shaving

Now turn to the following scenario. A government health care purchaser or a financial HMO is seeking to contract for hospital and community services. They have a fixed budget, and genuinely wish to do well by the population for whom they are responsible. They also, however, wish to satisfy their principals' objectives. In the UK, these are the government targets for the health service, notably more services at lower unit costs and shorter waiting lists. In the US this may be the HMO's shareholders' desire for reasonable revenues, and employers' desire to keep premiums down.

Health care providers, such as hospitals, are bidding for contracts to provide the services. The contracts pass some of the risk to the providers, by giving them a fixed budget, though with some scope for renegotiation. The contracts cover both cost and quality; they state how much the service should cost for a particular quality of service. Providers bid a proposed price/quality package, and the contracts must include information on outputs that can be fairly easily monitored.

Finally, this bidding process happens each year, and each year the same mix of objectives is in place. Both sides know this.

Question

Describe the incentive structure in this bidding process. On which issues will each side's sticking points be likely to emerge, and what will be sacrificed?

The purchasers have 'sticking points' set by their principals: notably price control, plus 'throughput' in the government case and profits in the shareholder case. The providers, to win the contracts, therefore need to keep a grip on unit costs. Quality is something everyone genuinely cares about, but it is no one's sticking point. Furthermore, quality of treatment, as opposed to numbers treated and costs, is hard to measure and monitor since it relies heavily on professional judgement.

In the UK before the NHS reforms that divided 'purchasers' from 'providers' came into effect (Section 2.3), there was an experimental simulation of the reforms known as the 'Rubber Windmill'. The report on this simulation noted that the logic of the new system implied that, 'Providers are, to an extent, freed from direct responsibility for health outcomes'. Given the pressures on providers, it went on, '... there exist circumstances in which both purchasers and providers may walk away from quality issues' (East Anglian Regional Health Authority, 1990, p.11).

In other words, the outcomes of contracting will depend on the priorities of the participants under pressure. If the purchasers focus on 'throughput' or profits above quality of care – and that is what they monitor – and if providers have a choice between lower 'throughput' or profits and lower quality, then there are shared incentives to let quality slip. Whether this is happening is hard to know precisely because quality of treatment is so hard to monitor.

---

3 Private provision through public contracting: auction markets in social goods

3.1 Auctions and franchising in social goods

It is not only in health care that the incentives embedded in contracting for social goods are becoming a matter of public concern. The 1980s saw the beginning of an international wave of 'privatization' of public monopolies, including both the wholesale transfer of firms to the private sector, and increased contracting-out of government-financed services that had previously been directly supplied. As Martin Ricketts noted in *Firms*, Chapter 6, goods and services for which competitive markets with large numbers of buyers and sellers are hard to establish include infrastructure networks which display large economies of scale. Power and water supply networks are excludable through connections and charging, but their services are non-rival below capacity output. Other industries, too, display economies of scale and local monopolies. An ambulance service for a medium-sized city, for example, may be most efficiently run through a centralized dispatch system, and such a city may need only one general hospital providing a full range of specialisms. These features tend to create monopoly power for suppliers.

Social polices also create supplier power. Decisions not to exclude people from a service, by providing it free at the point of use – examples include public libraries, parks, primary education, clean water, as well as emergency and primary health care – tend to create local monopolies whether funding is public or voluntary. Such policies add the 'public' quality of free access to goods which would technically be excludable. They also change people's experience of using those services, generating a concept of access to certain services as a right rather than a market choice. This social understanding of certain goods as primary goods from which people should not be excluded – especially in countries where average incomes are well above subsistence levels – applies to a number of the services provided by the utilities. The classes of goods which have tended to be public monopolies for technical (network) and social (access) reasons therefore overlap. Dieter Helm, an industrial economist who writes on regulation, argues that privatized utilities will always remain under public scrutiny because they 'provide basic social primary goods' (Helm, 1995).

Whether public or private, monopoly power can lead to X-inefficiency and unresponsiveness to consumers: supplier-led rather than user-led services (*Changing Economies,* Chapters 8 and 10; *Firms,* Chapter 6). One solution now frequently proposed is to institute competition *for* the monopoly, through a separation of financing and provision, with competition to provide the service. Such attempts to make local monopolies contestable through auctions and franchising are now widespread internationally (*Firms,* Chapter 6). Competitive tendering by independent contractors (or indeed by separately constituted public enterprises) for a time-limited licence to operate the monopoly is now used over a wide range of services. In this section we examine the application of this form of market mechanism to social goods.

3.2   Bidding to supply local services

The aim of an auction for monopoly power is to try to achieve the cost benefits of supply by a single firm while avoiding some of the associated problems. Such auctions result in the transfer of some property rights and initiative to the contractor for a fixed period (*Firms,* Chapter 6). The competition may be to manage the service, with the assets remaining with the public authority; or it may involve a transfer of assets to a contractor; and it may involve various levels of contractor obligations concerning investment in the service. In the case of Private Finance Initiative (PFI) in the UK, the contractor bids to build and run a facility with some local monopoly power for a fixed number of years, gaining a return on the investment from charges or government revenue payments.

Bidding for public monopoly contracts has many similarities with franchising in the private sector. Franchising is quite common in retailing; McDonald's is the most famous example and many petrol service stations are run in the same way. It is often found where there are different economies of scale at different stages of production and distribution. The franchiser develops the intangible asset of the brand name, since economies of scale in advertising the brand name are considerable, and may also provide wholesaling. The outlets, which have few scale economies, are franchised, and the franchisee uses the brand name subject to conditions on the nature of the product. Would-be franchisees bid for each local franchise.

In Britain, local government has become something of a test-bed for competition for local monopolies. Legislation until mid-1997 enforced competitive tendering within local government for construction, cleaning, catering, roads, building and grounds maintenance, refuse collection and street cleaning, vehicle maintenance, management of housing and leisure facilities, construction-related services, and personnel, legal, information technology and financial services. Financial and policy pressures have also led to extensive contracting-out of social care. Enforced tendering was also instituted in the 1980s for cleaning and catering in the health service, and for many central civil service activities, including prison management (Walsh, 1995).

Bidding for franchises in the public sector is typically done through what is called a Chadwick-Demsetz auction (*Firms*, Chapter 6). Edwin Chadwick was a Victorian social reformer who originally advocated this kind of public auction, later formalized by the American economist, Demsetz. Prospective contractors are invited to bid on price to provide a specified quantity–quality package or to bid a price–quality package. The bids can only be put in when the public authority has decided on the extent of asset transfer to the bidders.

Social care, by which I mean such services as long-term physical care and support for the frail elderly and the disabled, offers an example. Firms (commercial or non-profit) that wish to supply residential or home-based (domiciliary) care tender prices and quality levels in a bid to be included on an 'approved list'. The list will then be used to place those needing care who are supported by public funds. This is, therefore, quite close to the private sector franchising model, since the approved list gives those included a 'marque' of approval by the authority. In this model, suppliers undertake their own investment and own their assets. The same is true in refuse collection, where private contractors normally supply collection vehicles in their own livery, while authorities continue to provide waste treatment, which has much higher scale economies and requires more specific fixed assets. I will use the similarities and contrasts between refuse collection and social care to illustrate some of the strengths and problems of franchising in social goods.

Refuse collection and social care have some similarities. Both have some economies of scale and both are technically excludable. Both generate demands for open access for those who cannot pay: refuse collection because of the health effects and environmental externalities, and social care for social and ethical reasons.

Reflection

You can probably also think of some other differences! Make a list of these before working through the discussion that follows.

The aim of the auction process is to drive down costs for given quality levels. To achieve this, there must be some X-inefficiency to be exploited, some way of paying less for inputs, or some scope for innovation in working methods which the previous public supplier was not pursuing because of their monopoly position. The effectiveness of auctions is also influenced by the nature of the assets required and the scope for monitoring quality, as the following examples show (see also *Firms*, Chapter 6, Section 3).

The winner's curse

Competitive auctions have been fruitfully explored by game theorists, and the so-called 'winner's curse' offers a reason why potential competitors may be reluctant to bid against an incumbent firm. Usually presented as an analysis of *over*-bidding for natural monopolies such as North Sea oil drilling concessions (Kreps, 1990, pp.83–5), it can be adapted to explain why outside firms may bid too low in social auction markets.

The game can be conveyed intuitively with an example from social care. Suppose that six firms are bidding for a single contract to provide meals at home to people unable to cook for themselves. All the firms have imperfect information (as does the local authority letting the contract) about the likely costs of providing the service, because neither delivery conditions nor demand can be wholly known in advance. Furthermore, each firm's internal cost structure is different.

On this basis, each firm makes a private estimate of their expected costs of fulfilling the contract. They must then bid a fixed price per meal to the authority, up to a maximum number of meals. The firms' estimates of expected costs will vary, with some being more optimistic than others about their ability to keep costs down. Each firm will bid a sum which represents their expected costs plus a mark-up to provide them with a profit.

Question

Stop here a minute and think about this story. Which firm will win? Why may that firm regret that it bid as it did?

The most optimistic firm will win, that is, the one that makes the lowest estimate of expected costs and bids accordingly. However, each firm has different partial information, so if all the firms shared all the available information, then the best estimate of expected costs would be higher than the most optimistic firm's estimate. Hence, the winning firm is likely to have underestimated its costs. The winner's curse is to win the contract but lose money in those circumstances.

In the case of public auctions, it is likely that the incumbent firm has the best information; and the more uncertain the demand and technical conditions, the more likely that is to be true. In those circumstances, outside firms may be discouraged from bidding: they will think it only too likely that if they win, they will suffer from the winner's curse. Hence, competitive bidding may not occur or, if it does, the winning firm may reduce quality or find it hard to operate profitably.

The hold-up problem

Now consider a situation where several firms are bidding for a welfare meals contract in a situation where a local authority has a run-down and inadequate set of kitchens to produce the meals, and wishes to expand the service. It lacks the funds for investment, hence it seeks tenders to provide an enhanced service, including the provision of the relevant production facilities. The new assets (the kitchens) are highly specific to this activity and there is no incumbent firm (*Firms*, Chapter 1, defines specific assets).

Question

Suppose you are one of the firms bidding. How will the specific nature of the assets affect your bidding behaviour? (The discussion of the 'hold-up' problem in *Firms*, Chapters 2 and 6 will help you here.)

A firm acquiring this contract for, say, five years, will incur sunk costs in the form of the new kitchens. When the next tendering round occurs, if it then loses the contract, a dispute will arise about pricing the kitchens to hand over to the next contractor. If the contract offers no guarantee of a reasonable price for the kitchens at the end of the contract, you may decide not to bid at all, or offer only minor refurbishment of the kitchen. You fear being 'held up' when the contract ends.

An authority may try to overcome this problem by specifying the terms of the handover of assets. But if the authority sets the figure too low, the winning firm may still under-invest, or run down the assets towards the end of the contract. If the figure is set too high, however, there will be a deterrent effect on competition in subsequent rounds. Alternatively, the authority could retain ownership of the assets and lease them to the winning firm. This helps with the competition problem – but not with the renovation of the run-down assets which was one of the authority's objectives in holding the auction in the first place.

The authority letting the contract faces the further problem that once an incumbent firm has established itself, that firm will have better information than its competitors next time around. Other firms may then be reluctant to bid, fearing both the winner's curse and the hold-up problem. So the incumbent may bet successfully on being able, as sole bidder, to put in a higher bid and raise profits next time round. A public authority is particularly likely to be held hostage in this way and will be vulnerable to price collusion among contractors when it cannot, itself, put up an alternative bid.

Quality and monitoring

Finally, if quality is hard to measure, auctions for local services also face the danger of 'quality shaving' by the competitors (discussed in Section 2.4) either to reduce the bid price or increase the profit margins of the winning firm. So franchising tends to work best for areas of public services where output is more easily measured. One local government contracts officer with a private sector background whom I interviewed put it like this:

... cleaning contractors, like building contractors, will cheat, and you know they're going to cheat, and it's a question of how much you let them. The contractors are much easier to monitor because you know if something's been cleaned or not ... with [manual services] contracts you end up with a statement of fact: it wasn't cleaned, it wasn't cooked, it was cold.

The contrast the speaker was drawing was with social care contracts where quality is very much harder to monitor.

Exercise 8.6

Consider the comparison between refuse collection and social care in the light of the discussion of auctions. Which of the two services do you think more suitable for an auction process and why? (*Firms*, Chapter 6, Section 5, will help with this exercise.)

In general, the best candidates for auctions seem to be easily monitored services that use widely available equipment: for example, grounds maintenance, industrial cleaning and refuse collection. Particularly problematic candidates include those involving large specific investments, such as big IT systems and defence contracting, and those where quality is hard to measure. This last category notably includes services with a care element.

Evidence on the working of local public auctions is still fairly thin, in part because we need a long cycle – ten years perhaps – to pick up some of the dynamic effects of the system. One service which has been studied in detail is refuse collection (Symanski and Wilkins, 1993; Symanski, 1996), and this is often cited as *the* example of the benefits of compulsory tendering. While information is poor on quality changes, the service has seen large cost reductions for the same or even improved contract specifications since tendering was introduced.

In labour-intensive services, such as catering and especially cleaning, much of the decline in costs has come from making the pay and conditions of already low-paid staff worse (Walsh, 1995). In catering, where profit margins are narrow, there have been problems of underbidding, and bidders have not been numerous. In the newer auction market for social care, there is evidence of strong competition on price (some of it at the expense of the wages of low-paid staff), some lack of continuity of care and sometimes of refusal by contractors of difficult work (Mackintosh, 1997). The problem of sustaining quality in services which are hard to monitor depends partly on the working culture, and is a problem I return to in Section 4.

4   Making social markets work: social norms in social markets

Given the increasing international tendency to create markets in social goods, how can these social markets be made to function as well as possible? This section explores a number of answers to this question using as the main example the newly expanding market for social care: the long-term physical and domestic care of those unable to care for themselves but not acutely (or curably) ill. This market is expanding internationally as a result of the growing number of people who are living longer into old age. The social organization of the market is deeply influenced by the social policies of individual countries, since affordable access depends on wide risk pooling and on state subsidy for those on low incomes.

There are several reasons why social care provides a good case study of the potential and problems of commodifying social goods. Some issues have already been explored: notably the difficulty in monitoring the quality of care, and the public concern with access. Social care has some shared goods characteristics. In particular, the nature of the relationship between the carer and the person cared for forms an important element of the quality of care. Social care is therefore a good test case of Anderson's proposition (Section 1.1) that shared goods are devalued by market trading. I explore also the counter-proposition that the devaluing effect depends on the form in which commodification develops, rather than on the process of exchange itself. And this in turn leads to a consideration of working cultures in social care.

4.1   Altruism and market trading

Let me start with the concern for access. I argued in Section 2.1 that goods to which access is a matter of social concern have some shared goods qualities: the access others have to those goods influences our attitude to using them and paying for them. Bringing those kinds of concerns for others to market implies that competitive markets cannot be relied upon to produce a welfare optimum even in the limited sense of Pareto efficiency (Chapter 7). Concern for the access of others undermines the welfare properties of general equilibrium.

The reason for this is the nature of the concern felt for others. Some formulations of altruism can be incorporated quite easily into neoclassical theory. The most straightforward is the 'altruism' of someone who cares about the welfare of others as well as themselves. Altruism of this kind between people in the same household is often modelled by economists (*Households,* Chapter 6). Here I will explore the implications of relaxing the assumption that such altruism is confined to the household and consider what happens when those engaged in market trading feel altruistic towards each other.

Altruistic preferences can be incorporated into utility theory by supposing that one person's utility function includes the welfare of others. Suppose that two people, X and Y, get utility V_x and V_y from their own consumption. However X cares not only about her own consumption-related utility, V_x, but also about that of Y, V_y. So her full utility function is of the form:

$$U_x = f(V_x, V_y)$$

If Y has a full utility function of the same type, then the trade between the two individuals can be illustrated on an Edgeworth box diagram of a two person economy. (Edgeworth box diagrams are explained in Chapter 7).

Figure 8.4 is an Edgeworth box on which quantities of good *G* are measured on the horizontal axis and quantities of good *F* are measured on the vertical axis. X's allocation is measured from the bottom left-hand corner and Y's from the top right-hand corner. The indifference curves on Figure 8.4 correspond to V_x and V_y, the utility that each individual gains from their own consumption alone. The contract curve, *CC*, connects the points of tangency between the indifference curves, the equilibria

Good *G*

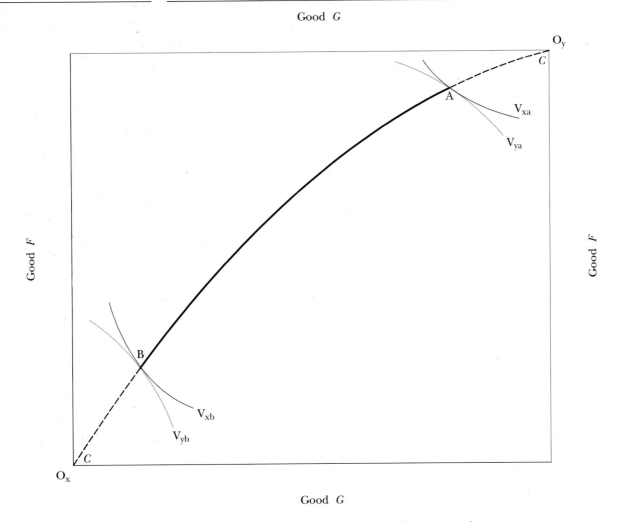

Figure 8.4 **Trade between two people with altruistic but non-meddlesome preferences**

corresponding to different price lines if X and Y were simultaneously to maximize the utility each gets from their own consumption (see Chapter 7, Section 4.2). I can call *CC* the 'private contract curve' since it takes no account of the utility X and Y get from each other's consumption-related utility.

However, once we take into account that X and Y also care about the utility the other gains from consumption, then there are points on the private contract curve that can no longer be considered Pareto efficient. Suppose that X's altruism means that she prefers her allocation of good *F* and good *G* at point A to any allocation between A and O_y that leave Y on a lower utility level from private consumption than V_{ya}. In that case the points along the dotted segment AO_y can no longer be considered Pareto efficient. Similarly, if Y's altruism leads him to prefer his allocation at B to any other allocation between B and O_x that leave X on a lower utility level from her own consumption than V_{xb}, then the points along the dotted segment, O_xB, are no longer Pareto efficient. On Figure 8.4, therefore, X's most preferred point along the contract curve is A and Y's most preferred point is B.

The remaining part of the private contract curve, BA, can be called the 'social contract curve'. It connects the allocations of goods *F* and *G* that are Pareto efficient once we take account of the altruism X and Y feel towards each other. Since X and Y care about each other's consumption-related utility – and not about the particular mix of goods *F* and *G* that the other prefers – we know that the social contract curve does not include points that do not lie on the private contract curve. This sort of altruism does not make new allocations Pareto efficient.

Now consider what happens in general equilibrium. If one person's initial endowment is so small that the general equilibrium outcome would lie outside the social contract curve, then both X and Y would be made better off by moving to a point between A and B. This could be achieved by the richer person voluntarily transferring some of their initial endowment to the other, with trading then occurring as before (Collard, 1978). So altruistic preferences of this limited kind shrink the contract curve, but otherwise leave the welfare properties of general equilibrium untouched, so long as gifts, as well as trades, can be made between X and Y.

The same is not true, however, as soon as X and Y begin to care what particular mix of goods *F* and *G* the other consumes – as they do the moment they take the view that poverty should not constrain people's access to certain social goods. Then X's full utility function will be of the form:

$$U_x = f\,(C_x, C'_y)$$

where C_x, is all of X's consumption, but C'_y is just the consumption of, say education, health and social care by Y.

Such preferences can be described as 'meddlesome' because the weighting that X puts on the components of Y's consumption is different from Y's weighting of those components. From a different political perspective, such preferences can also be described as 'caring'. Goods over which many people hold such preferences for other people's consumption are sometimes called 'merit goods' (*Changing Economies*, Chapter 23). Merit goods have always fitted uneasily into neoclassical discussions of social welfare because they overturn the assumption that individuals are the best judges of their own welfare.

For precisely that reason, this type of altruism undermines the welfare arguments for allowing private contracting. Altruistic preferences can be thought of as one kind of consumption externality: your consumption affects my welfare, and vice versa. Such preferences can operate like other externalities to undermine the welfare properties of general equilibrium (Chapter 7). If people have non-meddlesome preferences then, as just shown, allowing gifts as well as trades is enough to restore the welfare properties of general equilibrium. However, with meddlesome preferences, the social contract curve is skewed compared with the private contract curve because the individuals care about each other's consumption of the social good, *G* say, but not of the other good, *F*. So with meddlesome preferences, the social contract curve does not coincide with the private contract curve, and private trading no longer produces a Pareto-efficient outcome.

In these circumstances, individuals may be willing to make transfers of social goods to others through voluntary redistribution. In the two-person case, it might be possible for the two to reach a Pareto optimum co-operatively, with one person transferring specific goods to the other (which they must, however, be willing to consume!) In the case of contracting among large numbers, some kind of organized redistribution is needed, bringing with it the potential problems of free riding, since each person donating will, presumably, wish to ensure that others in similar circumstances also contribute, so that the redistribution is effective. Once members of an economy decide that all citizens should have access to at least a minimum level of a given service – such as social care – in response to need, we are back with a role for tax financing, or for large scale co-operative action. Markets for social goods then have to operate with such a redistributive framework and be compatible with it.

4.2   Reputation and commitment in social care markets

In social care provision there are complex three-way relationships among those receiving care, those giving care, and those funding the care giving. State-supported social care does not always involve market relationships, but in industrialized countries it has strong, though varying, market elements. In some European countries, such as France and Italy, the state provides funds to those with disabilities to purchase care. In others, such as Sweden, municipalities employ relatives as care givers on market wages (Ungerson, 1995). In still others, such as the situation in Britain after the Community Care reforms, local government pays care-giving 'provider' firms (public, private and non-profit) to provide care for individuals on the basis of means testing and needs assessments. It is the British model, with state 'purchasers' buying on behalf of those requiring care, which is typically described as a 'quasi-market'.

The sociological literature on these markets focuses on the complex networks of kinship, obligation and affection which structure both the care given and the payment systems. European countries all have complex and shifting boundaries between unpaid care, 'formal' paid care, and the 'grey' area in-between of small payments to neighbours, volunteers and kin. Most volunteers and informal carers are women, hence, caring is deeply influenced by changing gender roles. The economic literature, by contrast, tends to focus mainly on 'formal' paid care. This section looks at relations between funding bodies and firms supplying formal carers; the next section returns to user-carer relations.

Social care contracting between local government and providing firms suffers from a number of the problems identified for health care: asymmetric information (the providers have most of the information on the quality of care they are providing); vulnerable clients who may find it hard to judge the care and hard to assert themselves, and who may have low expectations; services which, as a result, are difficult and expensive to monitor; and a danger of 'quality shaving'. If we assume profit-seeking firms and self-interested purchasers, then we can model the problem to be solved as a prisoners' dilemma game. Such games inevitably over-simplify complex issues, but they do allow us to explore the problem of how monitoring costs can be kept under control while providing incentives for high quality, on different assumptions about participants' motivations.

Purchaser \\ Provider	high quality	low quality
low monitoring	15 \\ 15	20 \\ 5
high monitoring	5 \\ 20	10 \\ 10

Figure 8.5 **The monitoring problem as a prisoners' dilemma game**

Figure 8.5 shows a game between a local government purchaser of social care services and a profit-seeking provider. The provider is assumed to have a choice between high quality and low quality care. The pay-offs to the provider reflect the fact that quality shaving pays, but when the authority spends a lot on monitoring it has less to spend on care, reducing the provider's profits (and the total care provided). The purchaser has a choice between high (expensive) and low (cheap) monitoring, and is chiefly concerned to meet the government's targets of avoiding financial waste and public complaints. The purchaser's pay-offs, therefore, reflect these concerns: you do not want to be caught funding shoddy care. The worst case scenario for a purchaser is, therefore, to monitor little and find you have (probably) paid for low quality (but you are not sure): this is likely to lose you your job. Next worst is to find out, through high monitoring, that you have paid for low quality. In this situation you can at least claim to have identified the problems. It would be better to be reasonably sure you have paid for high quality. And best of all to be sure that you have done so.

Exercise 8.7

Show that the game in Figure 8.5 is of the prisoners' dilemma form with a single equilibrium, and explain why.

So what can be done? How can monitoring costs be kept down and quality maintained? Game theory suggests two routes out of the dilemma: reputation and commitment.

Reputation effects can, in theory, rescue contracting parties from a prisoners' dilemma in a competitive market where there are repeated interactions. Even with low monitoring, a purchaser will get an idea that quality is slipping when complaints start to increase. If the parties contract repeatedly with each other in a 'game' of indefinite length, and if they punish each other for apparent departures from – in this case – the high quality/low monitoring equilibrium by retreating to low quality or high monitoring, then each will have an incentive to sustain their reputation by not succumbing to the low quality and high monitoring temptations.

Firms, Chapter 2 analyses a reputation game. In *Firms*, Chapter 4, Vivienne Brown explains how a 'trigger' strategy of co-operation (in this case high quality/low monitoring) while the other party co-operates, and of punishing default by default, can sustain co-operation in a repeated prisoners' dilemma game. The trigger strategy works so long as each party cares sufficiently about their future as well as current pay-offs.

The other way out of the prisoners' dilemma is to change the pay-offs by altering the players' motivations. Suppose that instead of the self-interested assumptions underlying Figure 8.5, we assume that the providers and the purchasers both care about the clients as well as their own self interest. In this case the providers will care about both profits and the quality of care to patients; and the purchasers will care about both watching their backs and the quality of care to patients. This, at least in my experience, is a more realistic reflection of the mixed motives and pressures such quasi-markets generate.

Provider / Purchaser	high quality	low quality
low monitoring	20 / 20	15 / 5
high monitoring	5 / 15	10 / 10

Figure 8.6 **The monitoring problem as an assurance game**

In Figure 8.6, the pay-offs represent the mixed motives of the players. The provider prefers high quality and low monitoring, because it gives a mix of respectable profits and good treatment of clients. After that, the provider prefers to offer low quality (keeping up profits) rather than high quality for fewer users because of high monitoring costs. The purchaser prefers low monitoring and high quality too, balancing risk to themselves against the welfare of users. But after that risk aversion takes over. They prefer high monitoring and their worst outcome is low monitoring and poor quality.

Exercise 8.8

There is more than one equilibrium in this game. Identify them, and explain how they arise.

Whether the players end up in the top left or bottom right quadrant depends on their expectations of each other. This is the key characteristic of an *assurance game*: that the outcome depends on how much assurance each party has about the behaviour of the other (note that this is *not* true of a prisoners' dilemma game).

To see this, suppose that in Figure 8.6, the provider believes that there is a 60 per cent chance that the purchaser will pick low monitoring. Then the expected value of the provider's pay-off from choosing high quality is:

$$(0.6 \times 20) + (0.4 \times 5) = 14$$

while the expected value of the pay-off from choosing low quality is:

$$(0.6 \times 15) + (0.4 \times 10) = 13$$

(*Firms,* Chapter 1, explains expected values.)

So a rational provider strategy, based on those expectations, would be to choose high quality. Exactly the same calculation is true for the purchaser, since the pay-offs are symmetrical. A reasonable expectation of goodwill from the other causes the game to settle at the top left equilibrium which best suits them both – and seems likely to be better for the users too, on the story I told about the game.

Exercise 8.9

What happens if the provider expects that the purchaser will pick low monitoring only 40 per cent of the time, and the purchaser expects high quality only 40 per cent of the time also?

The 'assurance' in this game can be treated as a shared commitment to patients and/or to a collaboration in which each has some confidence. Such assurance can be interpreted as a norm of expected behaviour within the market, which overcomes some of the problems generated by self-interested and mutually destructive behaviour based on poor information and narrow motivation. The question remains, however, how can such norms arise and how can they be sustained?

One partial answer to that question is organizational culture. A firm's culture offers staff a way of deciding what to do in a variety of common working situations without constant and impracticable recourse to first principles. Culture, therefore, has considerable bearing on firms' objectives (*Firms,* Chapter 1; Kreps, 1988). Now suppose that the environment of a firm, in the sense of the incentives it faces, changes sharply. For example, a big non-profit organization which had previously supplied, partly from public grant funding, a range of support to the elderly infirm now finds itself contracted by a public authority to supply more extensive services. In place of an earlier situation where the organization's self perception was that of a 'voluntary' specialist organization, independently complementing statutory provision, and being appreciated for it, it is now a public supplier subject to higher levels of formal monitoring.

Look back at Figure 8.6. If an organization that has previously been settled into a low monitoring/high quality equilibrium suddenly finds itself subjected to much more intrusive monitoring, then, this game was designed to suggest, it may resent the intrusion and back off into more instrumental profit-seeking behaviour. Its response depends, presumably, on the strength of commitment to clients, and on whether the organization thinks the new behaviour of the public authority is an aberration from which it will recover. British evidence suggests that in these circumstances the organization's culture can go in two directions: it can take on a quasi-public sector role, accepting the political visibility, or it can settle down as a more instrumental contracted supplier. Where non-profit firms act as contractors in competition with profit-seeking firms, evidence from US social care shows little difference in behaviour between the two in terms of quality and cost (Clark and Estes, 1992).

4.3   Professionalism and legitimacy in social markets

So far in this discussion, game players have been organizations. But organizations are composed of people, and within social markets the people frequently have a lot of autonomy of action. Many social goods are provided by staff who see themselves as professionals. One important way in which social markets are policed is through the development of market-specific concepts of professionalism which respond to the commodification of service activity by setting constraints on behaviour. Professions, according to Matthews (1991), are characterized by:

- qualification-based rules of entry
- professional codes of various sorts which provide non-business objectives
- rules which prohibit certain practices, such as touting for clients, which are thought to undermine the professional codes.

All of this can allow for self-interested restrictive practices to maintain professional incomes, especially in the better paid professions. But professional codes of practice or ethics which become internalized as social norms – indeed, as expressions of self on the part of professionals – can play a role in sustaining high quality equilibria against material incentives which tend to work in the opposite direction. In fields such as health and social care, the autonomy of public service staff and their control of quality is frequently recognized by salary-based payments systems detached from 'results'. Commodification through quasi-markets brings pressure for results-based payments systems, and for clocking in and out, which can have perverse results. If people who saw themselves as professionals trusted to take responsibility suddenly find themselves treated as if their motivation were wholly mercenary, they may react by 'working to rule' and reducing their effectiveness.

In social care, where the extent of developing professionalism remains at issue, the process is contested for a number of interlocking reasons. Professions exhibit hierarchy. The health and social care hierarchy has doctors at the top and carers at the bottom of the health-related activities. Those higher up tend to contest the 'professional' credentials of lower-paid professionals. Among informal carers, ideas about payment are complex. Relatives often resist payment from kin, although research shows that family members will often accept payment if the funds come from the state for the purpose of acquiring care (Baldock and Ungerson, 1994). Neighbours are more willing to be paid. Once paid care becomes prevalent, wage payments – and conditions of service – become matters to be negotiated more openly. A key difficulty with the social care market in Britain is that low and casualized wage payment is developing at the same time as increasing demands are made of care staff for levels of responsibility, autonomy and risk-acceptance which are much more characteristic of salaried professions.

The messages concerning professional culture are therefore mixed. If, as suggested in Section 2 in relation to health care, good quality services of the social goods type require trust and co-operation between users and staff, then these circumstances do not easily generate such assurance. It is not merely that those needing care are often distressed; it is, as two social policy researchers put it, that users and informal carers dealing with the care market are coping with an 'unscripted' process: they lack information, but are also uncertain what *should* be done. They are thinking through the ethics as they search for solutions (Baldock and Ungerson, 1994).

People, furthermore, are not sure of the legitimacy of paying for certain things at all. There is no feeling that home nursing is devalued by nurses being paid – only a resistance to paying cash for what people feel should be tax financed, or an embarrassment or nervousness at a cash transaction. But cash payment to kin for care is more complicated, through fear of behaving improperly or giving offence. The British social care market is still very unstable in terms of what is sold, to whom, for what, and within what relationships.

5   Conclusion

Social markets involve goods which are important to people: basic needs, services which respond to vulnerabilities, and goods which are tied up with personal relationships and with ideas about the kind of society we live in. As a result, people attach social meanings to the organizations that supply the goods to the staff who work in them and to the terms of access to the goods. Many of these social goods are also problematic commodities for technical reasons, because of natural monopolies and externalities.

This chapter has explored the operation of markets in these social goods and services. Not all social goods are marketed, and all societies set limits to such social markets by 'blocking' some exchanges (the phrase is from Walzer, 1983). Blockage may be statutory: the chapter began with a current debate on one such legal prohibition, on brothels and soliciting. Or the blocking may be built into our understanding of social relationships, as with the sense of contradiction surrounding the buying of love and friendship. Over time, our willingness to treat or recreate social goods as commodities changes, and recent years have seen a new wave of market creation in social goods. This chapter has analysed different ways of organizing social markets: as 'clubs' and through auction mechanisms. The final section drew on the analysis of Sections 2 and 3 to argue that motivations and incentives matter greatly to the operation of social markets (as in other markets); and that the recognition of ethical as well as material motivations of staff may be key to the tolerable operation of social markets.

Further Reading

The article by Elizabeth Anderson (1990) 'The ethical limitations of the market', *Economics and Philosophy*, vol.6, referred to at the start of the chapter, is readable and stimulating.

Keiron Walsh (1995) *Public Services and Market Mechanisms* is a non-technical survey of the UK quasi-market reforms.

An accessible book on the economics of health care is Donaldson, C. and Gerard, K. (1993) *Economics of Health Care Finance: The Visible Hand.*

CHAPTER 9

ETHICS, ECONOMICS AND THE ENVIRONMENT

by Graham Dawson

1 The ethics of contracting

This chapter discusses some ethical issues about contracting in the context of a case study concerning international negotiations about a major environmental problem, global warming. Ethical issues were discussed in *Markets*, Chapter 2 and in *Households*, Chapter 5, while contracting was analysed in *Firms*, Chapter 1 and *Markets*, Chapter 7. I am not going to try to sum up such a wide-ranging set of analyses but I hope you will find that this chapter rounds off these earlier discussions and leaves you with ideas for further reflection.

1.1 The 1995 Berlin climate change negotiations

The fact that the six hottest years on record occurred in the 1980s did much to put the issue of climate change, especially global warming, on the international political agenda. In March and April 1995, the First Conference of the Parties to the Framework Convention on Climate Change ('the Framework Convention') took place in Berlin. The purpose of the conference was to consider how to promote the implementation of the Framework Convention, agreed at the 1992 Earth Summit in Rio de Janeiro.

The Framework Convention is a response to the belief, widely held in the scientific community, that global warming is caused, at least in part, by the increase in the emission of 'greenhouse gases', most notably carbon dioxide (CO_2), associated with industrialization. This account of the conference, which draws on Rowlands (1995) and Paterson (1996), will focus on two provisions of the Framework Convention. First, the industrialized countries (or 'the North') are committed to ensure that their emissions of greenhouse gases will be no greater in 2000 than they were in 1990. In fact, only six OECD countries (Denmark, Germany, Luxembourg, the Netherlands, Switzerland and the UK) seem to have any chance of meeting this requirement. Second, the industrialized countries undertook to provide new resources, including the transfer of technology, to help the developing countries (or 'the South') meet their commitments under the Framework Convention. These commitments are to draw up inventories of their greenhouse gas emissions and programmes of measures designed to limit them. The Berlin climate change negotiations ('Berlin') revealed a conflict of opinion between Northern and Southern countries concerning both of these provisions.

The emission of 'greenhouse gases', associated with industrialization, is thought to be partly responsible for global warming

The main outcome of Berlin – the Berlin Mandate – stated that the participating countries ('the Parties') recognized that the two commitments were inadequate but deferred a decision about how to strengthen them. A proposal for strengthening the Framework Convention was put forward by the countries which are most vulnerable to the impact of climate change, in that they will be partially, or in some cases completely, submerged by rising sea levels. The Alliance of Small Island States (AOSIS) proposed that by 2005 industrial countries should reduce carbon dioxide emissions by 20 per cent from their 1990 levels. However, most of the Northern countries were reluctant to go beyond their existing commitments, on the grounds that future increases in greenhouse gases will be most marked in the developing world. The North therefore sees an extension of the scope of the commitment to reduce gas emissions to include the developing world as a more urgent priority. In reply, most of the Southern countries, led by India and China, drew attention to the industrial countries' disproportionate share of historical and contemporary emissions. They argued that extending the scope of emission reduction programmes would curtail industrialization by the Southern countries, amounting to a form of 'eco-colonialism'.

Turning to the second provision, technology transfer, the most important outcome of the Berlin conference was the 'Joint Implementation' (JI) agreement. The JI agreement involves Northern and Southern countries 'swapping' emission reduction commitments. JI 'means that a country (the investor country), where the costs of reducing CO_2 are assumed to be high, invests in emission-reducing measures in a country with lower reduction costs (the host country) and is credited, in whole or in part, for emission reductions in its own climate gas account' (Nordic Council of Ministers, 1995, quoted in Rowlands, 1995, p.4). The case for JI is based on the observation that a given quantity of greenhouse gas not emitted in a developing country has the same effect on global climate change as the same quantity not emitted in an industrial country. JI also assumes that the costs of reducing CO_2 emissions are higher in some countries than in others. The proponents of JI argue that the use of energy in developing countries is relatively inefficient and that the opportunity cost of emission reduction – the benefits of energy use foregone – is therefore lower in developing countries than in industrial countries. If this controversial claim is true, economic efficiency requires that the developing countries should be the host countries for JI measures. However, the developing countries regarded JI as a form of neo-colonialism, on the grounds that it entailed 'taking action in the South in exchange for continued affluence in the North' (Rowlands, 1995, p.5). The conflict of interest between developing and industrialized countries limited agreement to the establishment of a 'pilot phase' of JI; projects can go ahead between countries that are willing to collaborate but they will not accrue any credits on the emission reduction accounts. This means that emission reductions from JI schemes cannot be counted as part of an investor country's efforts to reduce its emissions to 1990 levels by 2000.

Reflection

What are your first thoughts about the 'rights and wrongs' of these two outcomes of the Berlin conference?

1.2   Ethics, contracting and Berlin

The purpose of this chapter is to use Berlin as a case study for the discussion of some of the ethical issues raised by contracting. Contracting has been a central principle of liberalism since the Enlightenment and the 'neoliberal revolution' in political and economic thought since 1979 has seen an increased reliance upon it as a method of organizing economic activity. In the previous chapter, Maureen Mackintosh examined the extension of contracting into the provision of social goods, which some people believe are unsuitable for the impersonal and self-seeking world of market exchange. The contemporary context of the discussion is the development of markets, subject to government regulation, in areas which have traditionally been thought of as requiring public provision, such as health care and long-term social care. This redefinition of the boundary between the market and the state is, itself, part of a wider movement towards contracting and market exchange, which encompasses the construction of capitalist economies in Eastern Europe.

You may recall the variety of types of contract and contracting behaviour which were set out in *Firms*, Chapter 1. Such variety makes it difficult to think of a common feature which is shared by all contracts. Perhaps the most useful general way of thinking about contracting is to focus on the contracting parties' motivation: mutual advantage. This is probably as close as we can hope to get to a common feature. Do you remember Friedman's remark that was quoted in Chapter 2: 'under any institutions, there are essentially three ways that I can get another person to help me achieve my ends: love, trade and force'? Well, what differentiates trade – and hence contracting – from both love and force is its reliance on mutual advantage. This underlies the ethical appeal of contracting, in that contracts, offering each contracting party the prospect of promoting his or her own advantage, are essentially voluntary.

In Chapter 2 ethics was defined as the philosophical analysis of the principles governing the moral behaviour of a group of people. By moral behaviour I mean the ways in which people believe they ought to behave rather than the ways in which they actually do behave. We can ask two questions about any general principle which we might consider using to regulate our moral behaviour. First, we can ask whether the decision it yields in a particular case is compatible with or disturbs our moral sentiments, beliefs or intuitions about the right thing to do in that case. Second, we can ask whether the general principle is supported by a coherent line of argument from reasonable assumptions. Try to keep these two questions in mind as the discussion unfolds. My intuitions about the rights and wrongs of particular cases might differ from yours. So do not be surprised if you find yourself wanting to take issue with me. The intention is to encourage ethical reflection rather than to secure a particular verdict.

Reflection

What do you think are the most appealing and the least appealing features of contracting, from an ethical point of view?

The use of Berlin as a case study raises the question of how appropriate it is to analyse negotiations among nation states in terms of ethical principles which are primarily intended to apply to the moral behaviour of individuals. One objection to this procedure could be that there are deep conflicts of interest within states, for example between the rich and the poor members of the population. States are like households in that, while they are presumed to exist for the benefit of their members, conflicts of interest among the members are common (*Households*, Chapter 6). The problem is to find a satisfactory procedure for aggregating and representing members' conflicting interests. A complete analysis of the ethics of Berlin would require a discussion of the adequacy with which different interest groups within a state are represented by its negotiating team. Nevertheless, I think that ethical reflection on the behaviour of the contracting parties at Berlin, which abstracts from the problem of whom they represent to treat them as if they were individuals, is a defensible and potentially illuminating project.

My reason for making this claim is related to the brief discussion in Chapter 1, Section 6, of the Marxist argument that industrial capitalism has split the world into a minority of rich, industrialized and economically independent countries and a majority of poor, non-industrialized and economically dependent countries, and there is increasing polarization between the two groups. Some commentators believe that the consequence of this process is that inequalities between states have become greater than those between different social groups within states. For example, Brown (1992) suggests that although during the eighteenth and nineteenth centuries, inequalities within countries were much greater than those between countries, increasingly from the late nineteenth century onwards that picture has been reversed. Less inequality within nations than between them implies some unity of interest within a nation. This is a controversial thesis but it is not necessary to accept it in full in order to find it exemplified by the positions of the Northern and Southern countries at Berlin. The question at Berlin was essentially that of whether the Southern countries can continue to industrialize, and hence increase their greenhouse gas emissions, in the face of Northern pressure to extend the emission reduction programme to them. In this particular case it seems to me that the conflict of interest between rich Northern and poor Southern countries is greater than most such conflicts within countries.

Two traditions of ethical thought which rely in different ways on the idea of contracting will be used to discuss the ethical issues raised by Berlin. We will see in Sections 2 and 3 that the libertarian and contractarian theories of distributive justice return quite different and incompatible verdicts on the ethical status of the outcomes of Berlin. My conclusion in Section 4 is that the contractarian approach offers the more challenging critique of the Berlin negotiations.

2 Libertarian ethics

There are several ways in which ethical principles impinge upon economic analysis. One of the most important concerns the equity, fairness or justice of the distribution of goods and resources. The Pareto criterion identifies a range of efficient market equilibria but it does not provide any guidance for making ethical judgements about the equity, fairness or justice of the distribution of goods associated with each equilibrium. The economy could settle at any one of a number of Pareto efficient competitive general equilibria, each one reflecting a different initial endowment of resources (see Chapter 7). Is any one of these equilibria more just than the others? The problem is that there is no generally accepted principle of distributive justice to which we can appeal for an authoritative answer to this question.

2.1 A libertarian theory of distributive justice

The idea of contracting has been seen by libertarians as the institutional foundation of a market economy. For the libertarian, the aim is to try to present contracting – the voluntary transfer of goods in a market – as the institutional structure which settles distributional issues. The idea is that, provided economic agents are entitled to hold their initial bundle of goods, any redistribution of those goods which comes about through voluntary exchange will leave agents with goods that they are entitled to hold. Whether a distribution is equal or unequal is of no concern, provided only that it was arrived at by agreeing contracts to transfer legitimately held goods.

The libertarian tradition, which severely limits attempts to redistribute market-generated holdings of goods, finds contemporary expression in the entitlement theory of justice (Nozick, 1974). The central principles of the entitlement theory are (a) that a distribution of holdings is just if everyone is entitled to the holdings they possess under that distribution; and (b) that a person is entitled to a holding if they acquired it in accordance with the principles of justice in acquisition or it was transferred to them in accordance with the principles of justice in transfer.

Let us for the moment assume that agents acquired their goods and resources justly and are entitled to hold them. This 'pre-transfer' distribution of holdings is therefore just in that it has been arrived at in accordance with the principles of justice in acquisition. Nozick argues that any subsequent distribution of holdings (of goods and resources) is also just, provided that it is the end-result of a series of transfers in which no one's entitlements (or rights to hold goods and resources) were violated. This is essentially the principle of justice in transfer. Transfers of holdings which do not violate entitlements preserve justice, in the sense that a distribution of holdings which is the end result of a process of entitlement-respecting transfers (starting, remember, from justly acquired holdings) is itself just.

Question

As an economist, what do you think is the best example of a just transfer of holdings?

The paradigm case of a transfer which does not violate the entitlements of agents is, for Nozick, a contract for the voluntary exchange of goods and services in a competitive market. With regard to any particular market, the initial distribution of resources is exogenously determined, but only by the history of previous contracted transfers (assuming just acquisition). The implication is that any distribution of goods arrived at only through market transactions is just. This historical or process approach to distributive justice therefore validates any distribution of goods, no matter how unequal, providing it was arrived at justly. The policy implications seem to be conservative, prohibiting any redistributive measures (except the 'redistribution' or restoration of stolen and hence unjustly acquired property to its rightful owner).

Nozick's entitlement theory of justice has certainly provided influential arguments for the curtailment of the redistribution of income through highly progressive taxation and public expenditure on welfare benefits in kind. It has been buttressed by his commitment to individual liberty, which he believes to be incompatible with any settled distribution of income. Even an egalitarian distribution of income would not long survive voluntary exchange in a market economy, because there would always be entrepreneurs who would amass fortunes from the freely transferred payments of others. Consequently, a particular favoured distribution of income, such as complete egalitarianism, a minimum poverty line or a ceiling on high incomes, could only be preserved by constant interference in the voluntary transactions of individuals (pp.163–4).

Let me now relax the assumption that holdings have been acquired justly. What exactly does it mean to acquire holdings of goods and resources 'in accordance with the principles of justice in acquisition'? The basis of Nozick's argument is the principle put forward by the seventeenth century English philosopher John Locke, that a person justly acquires land (or, as we would say today, resources) by 'mixing' his or her labour with it. For example, Locke and many of his contemporaries regarded the western frontier of the territories that became the original thirteen states of the USA as unowned land, which anyone was free to acquire by settling on it and cultivating it. So the foundation of the libertarian entitlement theory of distributive justice is a parable about the acquisition, through labour, of land to which no one is acknowledged to have a prior claim. However, Locke added a qualification to his theory of acquisition.

The 'Lockean proviso', as Nozick refers to it, is that acquisition (by mixing labour with resources) is just, providing that 'enough and as good is left in common for others'. In Nozick's view, the Lockean proviso would be violated only in a catastrophic or 'desert island' situation. For example, the requirement to leave 'enough and as good for others' entails that 'a person may not appropriate the only water hole in a desert and charge what he will' (p.180). Outside extreme situations of this kind, Nozick argues that 'the free operation of a market system will not actually run afoul of the Lockean proviso' (p.182) and he concludes that the Lockean proviso 'will not provide a significant opportunity for future state action' (p.182).

2.2 A libertarian perspective on Berlin

There is a close congruence between the distributions of goods and resources which Nozick's entitlement theory of justice would count as just and the distributions associated with the free operation of a market system. To this extent the entitlement account of distributive justice supports the neoclassical economic approach to environmental issues.

A leading neoclassical economist, Professor Frank Hahn, has expressed his confidence in the ability of economics to cope with the problem of environmental degradation: '... we all recognize that from the economic point of view the environment is not a difficult intellectual problem. Yes, there are interesting aspects of the subject on a factual level, but otherwise they are an elementary matter. In general it is an undergraduate exercise' (Ravaioli, 1995, p.23).

The central intuition of the neoclassical approach is summed up in the principle of willingness to pay, which captures the idea of market valuation as a benchmark. If consumers in a competitive market buy a good, it is because they are willing to pay for it and we can, therefore, be sure that it is worth what they (willingly) pay for it. It is as if consumers compare the price of a good against their willingness to pay, and buy it only if their willingness to pay is equal to, or greater than, its price. The main task in the application of neoclassical economic analysis to environmental problems is to devise substitute measures of value for non-marketed environmental goods. 'This is the essence of the process of economic valuation: it involves finding a willingness to pay measure in circumstances where markets fail to reveal that information' (Pearce, 1993, p.4).

The foundation stones of neoclassical economic valuation, underlying the willingness to pay principle, are individual utility maximization, where utility is understood as preference satisfaction, and Pareto efficiency. The Pareto requirement that no one should be made worse off in their own estimation is based on the assumption that the individual is the best judge of his or her own welfare. This is sometimes interpreted as a descriptively true statement but it can also be understood as an ethical principle (Mishan, 1981, p.10). For the libertarian, individual liberty requires that each person ought to be treated *as if* they are the best judge of their own welfare. So the libertarian position is closely related to, although not synonymous with, one of the assumptions underlying neoclassical welfare economics. For example, suppose that a contractual agreement which benefits a number of parties leaves others worse off than they would have been if the agreement had not been reached. In principle, the contract could still be Pareto superior, provided that the people who incurred the utility losses can be compensated so that, on balance, they are no worse off in their own estimation. From a libertarian viewpoint the end-result distribution of goods and resources after this contracting process is just, provided that no one's entitlements are infringed. This condition is met, because the voluntary transactions made in accordance with the contractual agreement, including the compensation arrangement, exchange only justly held or acquired goods. However, environmental issues raise serious questions about the adequacy of the ethical implications of the neoclassical approach and the libertarian account of justice.

A libertarian perspective on greenhouse gas emission reductions

Let us apply this account of distributive justice to Berlin, beginning with the first provision of the Framework Convention concerning the rate of greenhouse gas emission reduction. Suppose that the contracting parties agree upon a rate of gas emission reduction which fails to avert the threat of catastrophic flooding of the islands and low-lying states that comprise the members of AOSIS. Would it be distributively just to allow these populations to trade-off emigration from their island and low-lying home countries before they are submerged, in exchange for citizenship in another country plus financial compensation?

The assumption that well-being is measured by the utility of individuals, in their own estimation, is important here. Given that assumption, the loss of a national territory is a loss of the utility that would have been derived from its continued occupation. If the affected populations are willing to accept compensation in the form of citizenship in another country and a financial award, they are, in their own estimation, receiving an off-setting quantity of the same 'thing' – utility. This leaves them, on balance, no worse off. The contract is voluntarily agreed and no one's entitlements are violated, so the outcome, in libertarian terms, must be just.

Island of Baros, the Maldives: vulnerable small islands will be partially or totally covered by rising sea levels caused by global warming

However, it seems to me that there are good reasons for being unsure of the justice of such an arrangement, the main one being the probability that the potential losers lack the bargaining power to secure adequate compensation. From the neoclassical economic perspective, the compensation would be decided on the basis of willingness to pay. How much are the other Parties, particularly the industrialized countries, willing to pay (in terms of lost GDP through gas emission reductions) and how much are the AOSIS members willing to accept in compensation, in order to reach an agreement on a global rate of gas emission reduction? Most of the AOSIS members are small and impoverished countries that would have little choice but to accept whatever level of compensation was offered. As Jacobs (1991) puts it, 'many of the world's people are very poor, and their monetary valuations are therefore likely to be very low' (p.68).

Neoclassical environmental economists are well aware of this problem. Pearce (1993), for example, makes the point very clearly: '... willingness to pay is weighted by the incomes of those expressing their willingness to pay. The economic votes of the poor count for less in the market place than the economic votes of the rich' (p.9). Clearly, the people of the AOSIS member states want somewhere to live as much as the people of, say, Switzerland, but they cannot afford it. They lack the bargaining power to ensure the continued existence above sea level of their home countries and, since their willingness to pay, constrained by low incomes, is low, the compensation they would be able to secure for the loss of their accustomed location will also be low.

Reflection

Do you agree with this criticism of the libertarian view? Do you think that there are relevant considerations in defence of the libertarian position which I have overlooked? Do you think that I should have expressed the objection to the libertarian position more forcefully?

A libertarian perspective on technology transfer and JI

Turning to the second provision of the Framework Convention, it is possible to interpret technology transfer from North to South under JI projects as a step towards an optimal or economically efficient way of reducing greenhouse gas emissions. The condition for the efficiency of JI as a policy instrument is that 'the marginal cost of emission reduction be equal in all complying countries. Therefore, there are no opportunities for reducing total costs by shifting a unit of emission reduction from one country to another' (Mabey *et al.*, 1997, p.29). The point is that since the marginal cost of emission reduction is not equal in all complying countries, it is possible that JI projects facilitate the shifting of units of emission reduction from one country to another in search of the efficient solution. Supposing that JI projects were to equalize the marginal cost of emission reduction in all complying countries, would such an outcome be ethically acceptable from a libertarian perspective? If a developing country agrees to take part in a JI project which involves only the just transfer of justly acquired holdings, the outcome must itself be just. So JI projects seem to be justified on the grounds of both economic efficiency and distributive justice, understood in libertarian terms.

There are, however, grounds for challenging both the economic and ethical justifications. First, let us consider the economic argument. The economic case for JI assumes that energy production in developing countries is technically inefficient; a given input of fuel produces a relatively small output of energy for use by consumers. There is scope for providing the same output of energy from a more efficient use of fuel, so the output loss from gas emission reductions can be offset, to some degree, by improvements in technical efficiency. 'Consequently, reductions in carbon dioxide emissions can be realised relatively cheaply, not only by fuel substitution, but also by industrial and energy infrastructure rationalisation' (Rowlands, 1995, p.5). This conclusion is not disturbed by the wider considerations of economic or Pareto efficiency. Measured in terms of the loss of utility suffered by individuals in their own estimation, the marginal cost of emission reduction in developing countries is low.

This argument is called into question, however, by the role of behavioural criteria in the application of the concept of utility, which enables us to make interpersonal comparisons of utility (*Households*, Chapter 4, Section 2.3). This makes it clear that an adequate measure of energy efficiency would relate to the utility of the final user, which implies that energy use is subject to diminishing marginal utility. The use of limited supplies of energy in many developing countries for basic cooking needs contrasts with the use of abundant energy supplies in industrialized countries for purposes with a much lower marginal utility pay-off. This criticism of the efficiency argument is consistent with the basic capabilities approach to human flourishing (*Households*, Chapter 4, Section 5.2), in that energy use in developing countries is more closely related to the provision of basic capabilities. Perhaps the use of energy in the developing countries is more efficient, in terms of its contribution to the well-being of final users, than its use in the industrialized countries. If so, the case for JI is not supported by the argument from economic efficiency.

The ethical justification, based on a libertarian interpretation of distributive justice, may be challenged on the basis of an argument about the effects of institutions on the behaviour of individuals, that I have adapted from Paterson (1996, pp.182–3). This argument is based on a recognition of the effects of taking part in negotiations as one among a large number of Parties. The climate change negotiations, from Rio de Janeiro to Berlin and beyond, have established an international institutional framework for the discussion of global warming. As the Parties become more used to dealing with one another, norms are established, a pattern of give and take emerges and in some areas – for example, in the interpretation of the scientific evidence – a consensus begins to be built. As Paterson puts it, 'institutions stabilize expectations about others' actions, so that states know their cooperation will be reciprocated' (p.182). The implication is that the most powerful states find it difficult to use their power advantage to get their own way against the wishes of others in this kind of institutional context; negotiations involving a large number of states tend to exert a pressure towards convergence. By contrast, the JI agreement envisages projects linking a single investor country and a single host country. Moreover, these bilateral transactions usually bring together a rich, industrialized and economically independent investor country and a poor, developing and economically dependent host country. The US has been at the forefront as an investor country and has set up JI projects with Belize, Costa Rica, Russia, Honduras and the Czech Republic as the host countries (Rowlands, 1995, p.10). In this way, JI projects resemble the tradable permits discussed in Chapter 2, Section 5. Paterson (1996) comments that they 'may enable the traditionally powerful countries to regain predominance, which the multilateral processes in the climate negotiations ... have denied them' (p.184). The extensive use of JI projects could leave the developing world bearing much of the cost of emission reduction (in terms of slower growth), while economic growth in the industrial world, which is responsible for most of the gas emissions, continues relatively unhindered by pollution controls.

To sum up, it seems to me that contracting between two parties of very unequal power, while it may lead to just outcomes in the libertarian sense of not violating entitlements, is unlikely to produce outcomes that are compatible with my own 'first thoughts' about justice.

Reflection

Try to clarify what might be unjust about a contract between parties of unequal power, given that contracts are generally voluntary and involve mutual advantage.

---

3   Contractarian ethics

In this section I will discuss the theory of distributive justice put forward by Rawls (1972). The Rawlsian theory of distributive justice belongs to the contractarian tradition. Contractarians or social contract theorists use the metaphor of the 'state of nature' as an imaginary illustration of the intuition that society is the product of rational choices made by individuals. In a state of nature, individuals (or, in practice, nuclear families) are assumed to live either isolated from others or in a condition of war with them. A rational and self-interested individual who has had experience of life in a state of nature and life in society would choose to live in society. The loss of liberty to injure others for the sake of individual gain would be more than compensated for by protection from the marauding behaviour of others. The social contract is a metaphor designed to dramatize this process of reasoning; the fact that society exists is as if rational individuals contracted to relinquish certain liberties in exchange for certain securities.

For the contractarian, the distribution of goods generated by market transactions may be unjust on the basis of the fictional social contract which is regarded as the foundation of society. Rational agents would not agree to a contract to set up a society in which their own place was entirely uncertain. They would require assurances concerning the redistribution of market-generated holdings of goods to ensure that everyone has, at least, the minimum quota needed for an acceptable standard of living. From a contractarian perspective, the purpose of the contract is to inform the design of society's basic institutional arrangements for ensuring justice in the distribution of goods, on those occasions when, according to their understanding of justice, the market has not done so.

3.1   The liberal theory of justice

Rawls (1972) presents his theory of justice as a contribution to the liberal, as well as the contractarian, tradition of political thought. The notion of liberalism is a deeply contested concept but it might be helpful to suggest a way of differentiating it, for the purposes of this chapter, from the related idea of libertarianism. Liberals and libertarians agree in placing a high priority on the liberty or freedom of the individual but disagree on the role of private property. Libertarians believe that the only 'morally significant limitations on freedom are those that result from deliberate attempts of others to prevent people from pursuing their goals' (Hausman and McPherson, 1996, pp.122–3). In practice, according to libertarians, such attempts are almost always made by the state. It follows that, for the libertarian, the unrestrained accumulation of private property by one individual presents no threat to the liberty of other individuals. It is, therefore, ethically acceptable.

Liberals, however, argue that in a world of scarce resources and externalities, the freedom of one private individual can be threatened, even curtailed, by the actions of another, particularly by the actions of an individual with the power that is conferred by the private ownership of large-scale productive resources. For example, John Stuart Mill argued that 'the rich ... in the absence of law and government ... would probably be successful in converting the poor into their slaves' (Mill, 1861; reprinted in Warnock, 1972, p.315). The liberal view is, therefore, that individual liberty itself requires that the state should set limits to the accumulation of private property.

Reflection

Try to recall some of the arguments for redistributing income and wealth, and the methods of doing so, discussed in *Changing Economies*, Chapters 22 and 23. What are some of the difficulties that might arise in using the liberal principle that the unrestrained accumulation of private property threatens the freedom of the individual as the basis for redistributive policies?

The liberal theory of justice put forward by Rawls (1972) justifies economic institutions with a 'tendency to equality' (p.100) by arguing from the assumption that individuals are rational and self-interested. Rawls aims to provide a foundation for the principles of justice, which would 'define the appropriate distribution of the benefits and burdens of social co-operation' (p.4). And he wants to do this without departing from the liberal interpretation of human nature as rational and fundamentally self-interested, which has dominated much of modern western thought and neoclassical economics in particular. Rawls' aim is to show that there is a coherence between 'our considered moral judgements' and 'the principles that would be chosen by rational beings' (p.50).

As a contractarian, Rawls sees the basic institutional arrangements governing the distribution of goods and resources as the product of negotiation among rational self-interested individuals. You might recall from Chapter 2, Section 4, that game theory can be used to show how individuals, following their own best interests, can set up particular institutional forms. The structure of Rawls's argument is broadly similar. However, although individuals are assumed to be self-interested, they are also assumed to have very little information about where their interests lie. Rawls dramatizes this assumption by describing 'the original position' (pp.118–92). This is a hypothetical situation in which a number of individuals negotiate the rules that will regulate their subsequent economic and social life together. In order to minimize any bias that they might impart to the principles they draw up, the contracting individuals are placed behind a 'veil of ignorance' (pp.136–42). It is generally agreed that any theory of justice must acknowledge its close connection with impartiality. The veil of ignorance is a device for thinking about what impartiality might require. Self-interest is clearly incompatible with impartiality, so self-interested agents must be denied the information they would need to pursue their own interests. This is why Rawls places the negotiating individuals behind a veil of ignorance. They are not allowed to know what their positions in the future society will be, nor their skills, talents or tastes. The set of economic and social rules which emerges from this original position has a good claim, Rawls suggests, to be considered as the principles of justice.

There are two principles of justice. First, the *principle of equal liberty* states that 'each person is to have an equal right to the most extensive basic liberty compatible with a similar liberty for others' (p.60). The interpretation of this principle depends on the meaning of the term 'basic liberty'. Rawls defines basic liberties as '(the right to vote and to be eligible for public office) together with freedom of speech and assembly; liberty of conscience and freedom of thought; freedom of the person along with the right to hold (personal) property; and freedom from arbitrary arrest' (p.61).

Second, the *difference principle* or the 'maximin' principle, as it is sometimes known, states that 'Social and economic inequalities are to be arranged so that they are ... to the greatest benefit of the least advantaged' (p.83). Rawls argues that rational individuals would agree on this principle because they do not know whether they will be among the most or the least advantaged members of the future society. If Rawls is right in thinking that rational individuals are risk averse – and it is a controversial proposition – then, from behind the veil of ignorance, they will be anxious to ensure that the worst position in which they might find themselves is as good as it possibly can be. What counts as a good position, in Rawls's view? The answer is that well-being is understood in terms of having access to 'primary social goods' as described in Chapter 2, Section 5. These are the things that a rational person wants whatever else he or she might want, and which it lies within the scope of social life to provide, the most important being 'rights and liberties, opportunities and powers, income and wealth' (p.92).

How strong is the difference principle's tendency to equality? On the face of it, the difference principle is a strongly egalitarian one. It rules out inequalities in the distribution of primary social goods unless they can be shown to improve the condition of the worst off members of society. However, it has been disputed that the difference principle has strongly egalitarian implications. For example, the incentive effect of an unequal distribution of income might cause such a surge of entrepeneurial and innovative activity that the least advantaged are better off than they would have been in a more egalitarian but less dynamic economy. Nevertheless, the difference principle places the burden of proof on the shoulders of those who favour inequality.

The egalitarian tendency of the difference principle becomes clearer if we recall that the distribution of initial endowments that agents bring to the market exerts a powerful influence on the incomes that they take away from it. Rawls argues that in a well-ordered society there would exist 'institutions which narrow the range of inequalities so that excusable envy does not arise' (p.545). In saying this, Rawls seeks to do more than justify the deployment of the instruments of income redistribution, such as progressive taxation and public expenditure on programmes that benefit disadvantaged groups, to redress inequalities in the end results of market processes. The aim of redistributive measures should also be to redress inequalities arising at an earlier stage – in the distribution of natural abilities and talents, and the circumstances of birth. Rawls argues that 'the difference principle represents, in effect, an agreement to regard the distribution of natural talents as a common asset and to share in the benefits of this distribution' (p.101). One way of acting upon this agreement is to design a social system so that 'no one gains or loses from his arbitrary place in the distribution of natural assets or his initial position in society without giving or receiving compensating advantages in return' (p.102). For the Rawlsian theory of justice, the initial endowment of resources is not taken as given in determining the distribution of goods. Rawls points not only towards 'after the fact' redistribution but also in the direction of 'efforts to equalize the starting points of successive generations' such as 'policies to discourage the accumulation of hereditary fortunes' (Hausman and McPherson, 1996, p.157).

Perhaps what is really worth taking away from the Rawlsian theory of justice is the principle of regarding the distribution of natural talents as a common asset. If we take seriously the aim of 'equalizing the starting points of successive generations', we might be able to construct a framework for thinking about the environment and our responsibilities towards future generations.

Reflection

Which account of distributive justice do you find more convincing – libertarian or contractarian? You might want to consider whether this choice depends ultimately on whether you prefer individual freedom to equality. Perhaps the liberal, as distinct from libertarian, background of the contractarian approach suggests otherwise.

3.2   A contractarian perspective on climate change

The application of a Rawlsian or contractarian perspective to Berlin reveals, it seems to me, its superiority over the libertarian or entitlement theory as an account of distributive justice. I will suggest that the main strength of the Rawlsian theory of justice is the way in which it interprets distributive justice in terms of impartiality. While it is beyond the scope of this chapter to survey the sizeable literature on Rawls, I do want to discuss briefly the difficulty the Rawlsian approach has in specifying exactly what it means to maximize the well-being of the worst off social group.

A contractarian perspective on greenhouse gas emission reductions

In Chapter 2, Section 5, it was suggested that transferring polluting industries to less developed countries (LDCs) would be Pareto efficient but would deny the populations of the recipient LDCs the right to certain primary social goods including unpolluted air and good health. Suppose that we now express this latter point by saying that the transfer of polluting industries to LDCs would be unjust because, by entailing their loss of primary social goods to which people are believed to have an intrinsic right, it would not be maximizing the position of the worst off members of the world population.

This answer does, I think, capture the spirit of the Rawlsian approach. The question which Rawls seems to pose is: 'Would the transfer of polluting industries to LDCs be permitted if the world economy, including its arrangements for locating dirty industries, had been devised by rational agents in the original position, that is, behind the veil of ignorance?' The answer seems to be a clear no. The Rawlsian metaphor of the veil of ignorance provides a standard against which we can judge actual negotiations, such as those that took place in Berlin in 1995 concerning climate change. A chasm divides the hypothetical procedure of the original position and the actual negotiations at Berlin.

The formation of alliances and the limited nature of the agreements are predictable on the assumptions that, within the institutional framework of the climate change negotiations, (a) states behave strategically in pursuit of their own interests and (b) there are differences in the relative bargaining power of states. Starting with the oil-exporting countries, and going through the USA and on to the members of the EU, who occupy the middle ground, to the majority of Southern states and finally the members of AOSIS, the contracting parties line up in order of self-interest, from those with most to gain from blocking progress on the emission reduction programme in industrial countries, to those with most to lose from the associated displacement of further emission reductions to the developing world. This is not to condemn the contracting parties; each negotiating bloc has important interests to defend. The point is simply that self-interest is a powerful motive. Paterson (1996) acknowledges that, after the start of formal climate change negotiations in 1991, the influence of international organizations, such as subsidiary bodies of the UN, declined and 'state (perceived) self-interest ... became more important in determining outcomes' (p.123).

The strength of self-interest is further exemplified by the emergence of a new set of alliances in the climate change debate. As Rowlands (1995, pp.13–14) argues, business agents such as producers of fossil fuels and fossil fuel users have traditionally favoured a 'go slow' approach. But recently three new business groups have appeared: the insurance industry, shaken by the natural disasters which are predicted to become more frequent as climate change accelerates; the renewable energy technologies sector; and the natural gas industry, whose carbon dioxide emissions are only 60 per cent those of coal. These industrial groupings have aligned themselves with those states that are exerting pressure for increasing the severity of emission reduction programmes in the industrial world.

The influence of the relative bargaining power of each bloc on the outcome of the negotiations also seems to be clear. In the 'Berlin Mandate', the contracting parties acknowledged the inadequacy of the Framework Convention commitments, but only in very general terms. Indeed, 'the final legal instrument could embody any of a whole range of possibilities and still be faithful to the Berlin Mandate' (Rowlands, 1995, p.4). This looks like a fudge. It seems reasonable to interpret it as reflecting a balance of power in favour of blocking progress on the emission reduction programme. So much for the reality of the Berlin climate change negotiations.

Question

What kind of outcomes would you expect if the contracting parties at Berlin were located behind a veil of ignorance about their place in a future world society?

The alliances that were formed at the Berlin climate change negotiations reflected the various ways in which the interests of the different groups of the Parties converged; they were based on knowledge (or at least beliefs) about the Parties' own interests. If they were placed behind a veil of ignorance, the Parties would become a group of (self-interested) individuals undifferentiated by any knowledge of national allegiances or interests. In that situation, would they have been impartial in their deliberations and arrived at the emission reduction programme which maximized the well-being of the least advantaged group?

The answer, it seems to me, is that the contracting parties would have impartiality thrust upon them but they would not necessarily arrive at the maximin principle. The veil of ignorance deprives agents of the knowledge they need in order to identify and pursue their own self-interest. In highlighting the significance of impartiality, or freedom from bias or favour grounded in self-interest, Rawls's imaginary device succeeds in giving expression to a central principle of liberalism. However, while impartiality may be a necessary condition of negotiating an outcome that most favours the least advantaged group, it is not a sufficient one. I think that it is easy enough to identify the worst off members of society, or in this case, the global community. The members of AOSIS seem to me to have an unchallengeable claim to occupy that position, because climate change threatens their very existence. However, it is not altogether clear that 'Rawlsian contracting' (negotiations among rational agents behind a veil of ignorance) would produce an agreement to make the well-being of AOSIS members as high as it possibly could be. The JI agreement at Berlin provides a focus for discussing this question.

A contractarian perspective on technology transfer and JI

In Section 2.2, I suggested that negotiations involving a large number of states, such as those at Berlin, tend to exert a pressure towards convergence, with the result that the most powerful states find it difficult to exercise their powers to get their own way against the interests of other states. By contrast, the bilateral transactions envisaged under the JI agreement allow greater scope for powerful countries to promote their own interests. It seems to me that the Rawlsian goal of maximizing the well-being of the worst off group cannot be systematically pursued through a series of JI projects, which, as we saw in Section 2.2, have so far been arranged on the initiative of the most powerful country. The institutional pressure for convergence provided by the climate change negotiations is a step in the direction of the impartiality required for the implementation of the Rawlsian maximin principle.

However, supposing that the populations of the AOSIS states are agreed to be the worst off group. There is more than one way in which rational agents negotiating behind a veil of ignorance might take their well-being into consideration. Let us describe the maximin principle of seeking institutional arrangements which make the worst off members of society as well off as they can possibly can be as 'maximizing the floor'. Then there are at least three other principles which it seems to be possible that rational agents negotiating behind a veil of ignorance could choose. According to Mueller (1989, p.421) these are:

- maximizing the average level of well-being
- maximizing the average, subject to a floor constraint
- maximizing the average, subject to a range constraint.

So the impartiality which is afforded by the Rawlsian original position is not enough to guarantee that rational agents would adopt the maximin principle. While the well-being of the worst off group will be taken into consideration in some way under all of the alternative principles (in that it will at least be on the agenda) the aim of the contracting parties will not necessarily be to maximize it.

Question

Suppose that the contracting parties were to agree on the Rawlsian maximin principle. What do you think might be involved in trying to maximize the well-being of the worst off group?

You might recall from *Households*, Chapter 4, that redistributive measures require us to be able to define and measure well-being, or at least compare it across different situations. Even if the decision is made to maximize the well-being of the worst off members of society, rather than choosing one of the three alternative principles, it might be difficult to specify what is to count as satisfying this requirement. Compare the following two descriptions of the greatest possible advantage to the populations of the AOSIS group.

1   The other contracting parties acknowledge the right of the populations of the AOSIS group to continued residence in the country of their birth, albeit at a low material standard of living, and accelerate the emission reduction programme with the intention of preserving the land mass of AOSIS members.

2   The AOSIS populations are offered citizenship in affluent countries (safely above sea level) plus financial compensation.

The question is whether it would be distributively just to permit the submergence of AOSIS countries so that the industrial countries responsible for most of the greenhouse gas emissions would not have to make a proportionate reduction.

There seem to be two possible answers to this question, reflecting two different verdicts on the descriptions that individuals behind a veil of ignorance might give. First, they might take the view that the right to continued occupation of national territory is intrinsic or inalienable. It takes priority over all other primary social goods and so cannot be the subject of trade-offs or compensation of any kind. There is, therefore, an absolute prohibition on the second situation. Second, they might, instead, believe that the right to indefinite or unconditional occupation of national territory is just one primary social good among others and is one that can legitimately be traded-off against access to or availability of other social goods. The second situation, involving compensation for the loss of national territory, cannot be ruled out in principle. But there is still a presumption against it, because, as we have seen, contracting between parties of unequal power is unlikely to lead to outcomes that favour the least advantaged.

4   Conclusion

In this chapter I have tried to compare the ethical appeal of libertarian and contractarian approaches to the ethical issues raised by climate change negotiations. The libertarian account of distributive justice sees the voluntary transfer of goods through market transactions as the exemplary case of justice in the transfer of holdings. The market itself settles issues of distributive justice, in that any distribution which comes about through market-based contracting is just. From the contractarian perspective, the market left to itself is unlikely to yield a just distribution of goods and resources. Justice requires impartiality, while market contracting permits the pursuit of self-interest by the powerful. Society's basic institutional arrangements for ensuring justice in the distribution of goods and resources are just to the extent that they coincide with those that would be chosen by impartial agents.

Reflection

Let me leave you with a final reflection about the ways in which market contracting and the contractarian approach might be complementary. For example, thinking of the alternative principles for taking the well-being of the worst off group into account, we – as hypothetical rational agents behind a veil of ignorance – might consider maximizing the average subject to a floor constraint. Provided the floor, or the well-being of the worst off group, is safeguarded at an acceptable minimum level, contracting and the play of self-interest in competitive markets can be left to maximize the total level of well-being, regardless of its distribution. You might want to reflect upon the other principles which rational agents might choose, and how they might allow scope both for the social contract approach and for contracting in markets.

Further Reading

Hausman, D.M. and McPherson, M.S. (1996) *Economic Analysis and Moral Philosophy*, Cambridge, Cambridge University Press: an authoritative and comprehensive survey of ethical theories and their significance for economic analysis.

Jacobs, M. (1991) *The Green Economy: Environment, Sustainable Development and the Politics of the Future*, London, Pluto: an accessible discussion of the main issues in environmental economics.

ANSWERS TO EXERCISES

Chapter 1

Exercise 1.1

Here are two possible reasons.

1   Economic growth has many determinants other than investment, for example, the quality of management or workforce, educational levels and the existence, or otherwise, of institutions like banks or wholesalers (you might well have thought of other examples).

2   Investment includes both net investment (new capital goods) and gross investment, which includes replacement of existing capital stock. Net investment is thought to be more significant for growth since new capital goods may incorporate innovations which bring about faster growth.

Exercise 1.2

1   There is not a marked pattern, but a rough trend is for total fertility to fall after income reaches 5000 per head. A falling curved line would approximate the trend for the data set.

2   Some possible reasons for this are:

- as income rises in poor countries, there is less need for people to have children to support the family by their work; there may also be fewer opportunities for children to work and/or restrictions on their employment

- the costs of raising children increase as standards of living rise and their education takes longer.

- as more women go out to work, the opportunity cost of bringing up children increases

- people may be less interested in having children if they have well paid and interesting jobs

3   If GNP per head continues to rise, all things being equal, I would expect fertility rates to remain low, or even decline further.

Exercise 1.3

1   Figure 1.7 shows an uneven rise in the percentage of GDP taken up by state spending between 1880 and 1992, with falls occurring between 1938 and 1950 only in the UK and Japan.

2   Figure 1.8 shows no clear relation between GNP per head and government spending as a percentage of GNP. This suggests that it is not income per head that determines how much of that income is spent by the state.

Chapter 2

Exercise 2.1

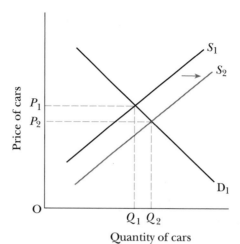

Figure 2.9 **The effects of a fall in the price of steel on the market for cars**

Figure 2.9 shows the initial equilibrium price and quantity traded of P_1 and Q_1. The fall in the price of steel results in a rightwards shift of the supply curve of cars from S_1 to S_2 as car production costs also fall. There is no shift of the demand curve but there is a movement along it as consumers respond to the fall in price by demanding more cars. In a partial equilibrium setting, the equilibrium price falls from P_1 to P_2 and the equilibrium quantity traded increases from Q_1 to Q_2.

In a general equilibrium setting, it is possible that other markets would now be out of equilibrium as a result of the fall in the (partial) equilibrium price of steel and cars. For example, the fall in the price of cars is likely to result in an increase in the demand for a complementary good such as petrol, and an increase in its price. This increase in the price of petrol may then react back on the car market by reducing the demand for cars. On the supply side, the reduction in the price of steel may lead car producers to switch to a more steel-intensive method of production in order to reduce costs still further. This would lead to a further rightwards shift in the supply curve of cars. It would also lead to an increase in the demand for steel as producers find new uses for it. This in turn would tend to raise the price of steel which would then have a new series of repercussions on the market for cars, and so on. The new general equilibrium outcome would depend on the overall quantitative effect of all these changes taken together.

Exercise 2.2

All firms and households have to be price takers, that is, they have to consider themselves to be unable to influence prices in any market.

Exercise 2.3

Firm A \ Firm B	high price	low price
high price	5 / 5	−2 / 10
low price	10 / −2	2 / 2

Figure 2.10 **New pay-off matrix after introduction of penalty clause**

The new pay-off matrix is given by Figure 2.10. The transfer of 10 units, if the agreement is broken by one firm but not the other, results in a drop to −2 units for the offender, and a payoff of 10 units for the recipient. Of course, if both firms break the agreement, the transfers balance each other out. Note that for both firms the dominant strategy is now to charge a high price.

Chapter 3

Exercise 3.1

For professional workers, the estimated coefficient for the return on schooling in Table 3.7 is 0.047, compared to the coefficient of only 0.007 for semi-skilled manual workers. Similarly, the return on experience is 0.077 for professional workers compared to only 0.034 for semi-skilled manual workers. Note that these coefficients are significant to the 1 per cent level, apart from the return to for schooling for semi-skilled workers. While this latter finding limits our statistical confidence in this particular coefficient, overall, we can state that, according to the data presented in Table 3.7, professional workers enjoy a higher return to their human capital than semi-skilled manual workers.

Chapter 5

Exercise 5.1

If the rate of interest is 11 per cent, the safe project, A, no longer pays as the cost of funds, 11 per cent, is greater than the expected return, 10 per cent, and so the expected return will be negative (10–11= –1).

However, it is still profitable to borrow to fund project B, the risky project, despite the expected return of only 4 per cent. In the good state of the world (if things go well) there is a net return to investors/borrowers of 9 per cent and in the bad state 0. If 50 per cent of the borrowers default, the expected return to the borrower is 4.5 per cent:

$$((20 - 11) \times 0.5) + (0 \times 0.5) = (9 \times 0.5) = 4.5$$

The bank receives either 11 per cent (the interest paid in the good state) or 0 in the bad state. If 50 per cent of the borrowers default, the expected return is 5.5:

$$(11 \times 0.5) + (0 \times 0.5) = (11 \times 0.5) = 5.5$$

Table 5.2 **Returns with interest at 11 per cent**

	Project A	**Project B**		
	Return (certain)	**Good state of the world**	**Bad state of the world**	**Return (expected)**
Return	10	20	0	
Bank	11	11	0	5.5
Borrower	– 1	9	0	4.5

When the interest rate is 11 per cent, no one will borrow to finance project A. All the bank's customers will invest in project B. Therefore the total expected return to the bank coincides with the bank's expected return to project B (because this is the only one chosen by investors/borrowers). Hence, an increase in interest rate from 8 per cent to 11 per cent leads to a decline in the bank's expected return from 6 per cent, as shown in Table 5.1, to 5.5 per cent, as shown in Table 5.2.

Chapter 7

Exercise 7.1

After the first price of 120, excess demand is negative so the price is reduced to 70. However, a price of 70 leads to positive excess demand, so the price is raised, though not as high as before, to 100. This still leads to negative excess demand, so the price is reduced to 90. This still leads to negative excess demand, so the price is cut again to 80. Now excess demand is positive, so the price needs to rise to 85 (say). From the information given so far we can plot some points on an excess demand function, as in Figure 7.18.

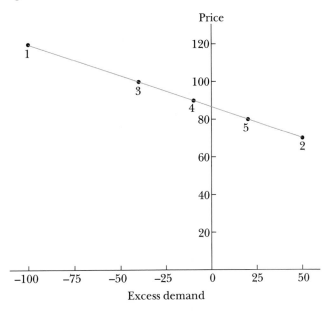

Figure 7.18 **Excess demand as revealed by a Walrasian process of price adjustment**

From Figure 7.18 it can be seen that the equilibrium price should lie between 80 and 90.

Exercise 7.2

Figure 7.19 shows the excess demand curve for this good. There are three equilibrium prices: P_E^1 and P_E^3 are stable and P_E^2 is unstable.

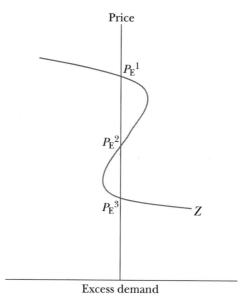

Figure 7.19 **The excess demand curve for a Giffen good**

Exercise 7.3

The initial allocation is shown at point A.

1. Colin's equilibrium consumption bundle is 25 kilos of figs and 25 kilos of grapes.
2. Brenda trades 5 kilos of figs for 15 kilos of grapes and Colin trades 15 kilos of grapes for 5 kilos of figs.
3. The price ratio $\dfrac{P_G'}{P_F} = \dfrac{1}{3}$
4. The Edgeworth box diagram is shown in Figure 7.20.

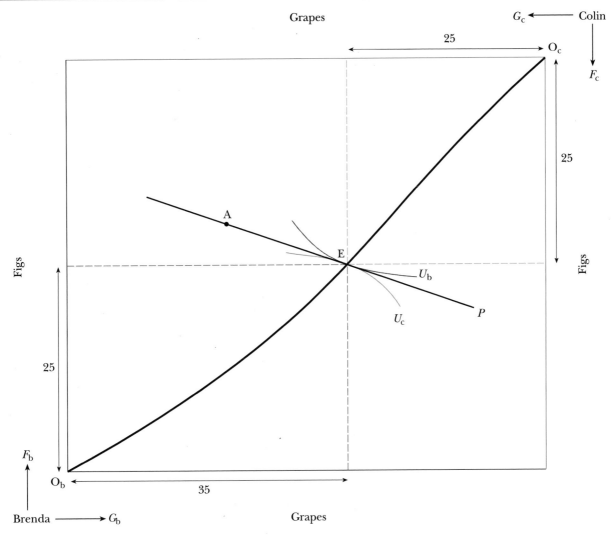

Figure 7.20 **A different competitive equilibrium**

Exercise 7.4

If the price of grapes rises relative to that of figs, more figs are traded for each kilo of grapes and the price line pivots in a clockwise direction.

Exercise 7.5

At E_3 more figs are traded for each kilo of grapes than at E_1. This means that the price of grapes relative to figs is higher at E_3 than at E_1, so $MRS_{G,F}$ is greater at E_3 than E_1.

Exercise 7.6

If the equilibrium price of grapes in terms of figs is higher than shown in Figure 7.16, this implies that the equilibrium output mix is at a point on the PPF which is further to the right since the price line is tangent to a steeper portion of the PPF. This output mix contains fewer figs and more grapes. In this situation, grapes are a more highly valued commodity in relation to figs, and so the consumers' MRS of grapes for figs is also higher.

Chapter 8

Exercise 8.1

1 Preventative care has considerable externalities, that is, effects not experienced by the immediate user of the service. Vaccinations and learned improvements in hygiene and maternal and child nutrition, for example, can greatly reduce the spread of disease to others. Primary care includes a mix of such prevention and information, inextricably associated with minor curative care and diagnosis.

2 See Figure 8.7 which shows a competitive market for primary care. The marginal social benefits (*MSB*) of a given number of visits exceed the marginal private benefits (*MPB*). But it is the marginal private benefits which users compare to the price charged for the visit (*MPB = D*). The marginal cost curve, *MC*, is the supply curve for primary care. Hence primary care will tend to be under-supplied in competitive equilibrium: Q_1 will be supplied at price P_1 rather than Q_2 which would be the optimum output at price P_2

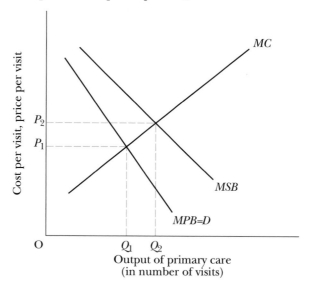

Figure 8.7 **Externalities and market equilibrium in primary care**

3 The World Bank argues that there are no externalities in curative care, hence the *MPB* and *MSB* curves will coincide so the competitive market equilibrium will be a fully efficient one, that is, in equilibrium:

$$MSB = MPB = MC$$

In discussing this issue, it is relevant that a high proportion of curative health care in low income countries deals with infectious diseases such as tuberculosis; curing these may have an external effect in preventing disease spreading, thus casting doubt on the statement that curative care is a wholly private good.

Exercise 8.2

A doctor makes a decision about treatment, faced with an anxious patient. Since the insurer (a 'third party') is paying, the private cost at the moment of decision is zero to the patient (much less than the social cost) so the patient has no financial incentive to resist treatment. The more treatment given, the more the doctor will gain, hence the doctor has a positive incentive to increase treatment. Furthermore, in an imperfect market, the doctor may be able to influence the fee per treatment, and faces no incentive not to attempt this. Collusion among doctors would reinforce both effects.

Exercise 8.3

Suppose clients of insurance companies range between good and bad risks. Clients know more than the insurance companies about their own health and, therefore, have a better idea where they are likely to fall on the spectrum of good to bad risks. Suppose further that a proportion of bad risks succeed in representing themselves as good risks. The insurance company will then find that premiums do not cover the full costs of treatment, because some bad risks are underpaying. They will therefore put up premiums. As premiums rise, some good risks will find the insurance not worth the price, so they will drop out of the market. This just leaves the worse risks, so premiums have to rise again. A vicious circle of rising premiums and declining coverage will set in, the result of which will be that many people who would have been willing to pay an appropriate premium for the risk category into which they fall may fail to find insurance at a premium they are willing to pay.

Exercise 8.4

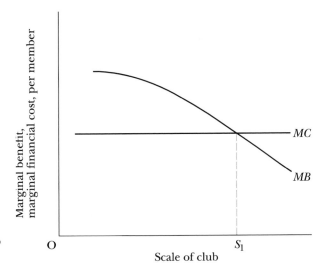

Figure 8.8 **Optimal scale of club for a given membership**

Figure 8.8 illustrates the idea. I have drawn the *MC* curve as horizontal. The marginal benefit curve, MB, is the same shape as it would be for a private good: marginal utility falls as more of the club good is consumed. The optimal scale is S_1. Note that these are not the same marginal benefit and marginal cost curves as in Figure 8.1. On Figure 8.8, the marginal costs are financial costs, while the marginal benefits are enjoyment of the club good.

Exercise 8.5

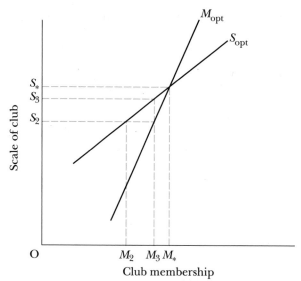

Figure 8.9 **Comparing a non-optimal and an optimal club**

At scale S_2, the optimum membership – shown by the line M_{opt} – is M_3. However a group of size M_3 would prefer a larger scale club, at S_3. However, at scale S_3. the optimum membership is higher than M_3. Only at M_* and S_* is there no incentive to change. This is an equilibrium at the optimum club scale and membership.

Exercise 8.6

Auctions are most likely to reduce costs without a decline in quality where:

* there are a lot of potential bidders who find it hard to collude
* there are well-established markets with widely available technologies and rather low levels of uncertainty about future conditions, so that the private information of the incumbent firm does not imply too large an advantage
* there is X-inefficiency to be addressed
* assets are not highly specific and sunk costs are low
* cost of inputs can be reduced
* quality of output is easy and cheap to monitor.

Refuse collection seems to fit more of these criteria than social care. In Britain, tendering for refuse collection was introduced at a time when there was scope for innovation and changing working methods; monitoring of quality is relatively easy; assets are not highly specific (there is quite a wide market for refuse trucks) and technology is not complex. *But* collusion among contractors is not difficult. In social care, there are large numbers of providers at present, though some areas are dominated by a few; the service is highly labour intensive, and some innovations can reduce quality (for example, cook-chill meals). There seem to be few ways to reduce costs except for paying already low-paid staff less, which may also reduce quality of care; and most serious, quality is very hard to specify and monitor, since the relationship with the carer is key to service quality. Refuse collection looks a better bet.

Exercise 8.7

The purchaser will choose high monitoring over low monitoring whether they believe the company will produce high or low quality: high monitoring is the dominant strategy. Similarly, the provider has a dominant strategy, choosing low quality for each possible decision of the purchaser on monitoring (and therefore also on the level of provision). So the single equilibrium is in the lower right-hand quadrant. However, both would have preferred the upper left to the lower right-hand quadrant, since it produces higher profits for the provider and a better outcome for the purchaser.

Exercise 8.8

There are two equilibria, top left and bottom right. They are both Nash equilibria in that once the game settles on that quadrant, players have no incentive to move. So if the purchaser is engaging in low monitoring, the provider will prefer high quality, and vice versa. But if the purchaser is doing high monitoring, the provider will prefer low quality, and vice versa. The outcome of the game depends on the *expectations* each player holds of the other's behaviour.

Exercise 8.9

The expected value for the provider of choosing high quality is:

$(0.4 \times 20) + (0.6 \times 5) = 11$

and from choosing low quality is:

$(0.4 \times 15) + (0.6 \times 10) = 12$

So the provider will choose low quality. The purchaser on the same calculation will choose high monitoring. The game will settle at the lower-right equilibrium.

REFERENCES

Addison, J.T. (1983) 'The evolving debate on unions and productivity,' *Journal of Industrial Relations*, no.25, pp.286–300.

Addison, J.T. and Siebert, W.S. (1993) 'Recent developments in social policy in the new European Union', *Industrial and Labor Relations Review*, no.48, pp.5–27.

Adelman, M.A. (1951) 'The measurement of industrial concentration', *Review of Economics and Statistics*, vol.33, November.

Aglietta, M. (1976) *A Theory of Capitalist Regulation: the US Experience*, London, New Left Books.

Amsden, A. (1989) *Asia's Next Giant*, Oxford, Oxford University Press.

Anderson, E. (1990) 'The ethical limitations of the market', *Economics and Philosophy*, vol.6, pp.179–205.

Aoki, M. (1990) 'Towards an economic model of the Japanese firm', *Journal of Economic Literature*, vol.28, March, pp.1–27.

Armstrong, P., Glyn, A. and Harrison, J. (1991) *Capitalism Since 1945*, Oxford and Cambridge, Mass., Basil Blackwell.

Auerbach, P. (1988) *Competition: the Economics of Industrial Change*, Oxford and Cambridge, Mass., Basil Blackwell.

Authers, J. (1996) 'The industry in the US: alarm call for the American dream', *Financial Times Survey of Venture and Development Capital*, 20 September, p.6.

Baldock, J. and Ungerson, C. (1994) *Becoming Consumers of Community Care*, York, Joseph Rowntree Foundation.

Bank of England (1996) *The Financing of Technology-based Small Firms*, October, London, Bank of England.

Baran, P. and Hobsbawm, E. (1961) 'The stages of economic growth: a review', *Kyklos*, vol.14, pp.234–42.

Baumol, W.J. (1958) 'On the theory of oligopoly', *Economica*, vol.25, pp.187–98.

Baumol, W.J. (1967) *Business Behaviour, Value and Growth*, revised edition, New York, Harcourt, Brace and Company.

Baxter, C., Poonia, K., Ward, L. and Nadirshaw, Z. (1990) *Double Discrimination: Issues and Services for People with Learning Difficulties from Black and Ethnic Minority Communities*, London, Kings Fund Centre.

Bazen, S. (1990) 'On the employment effects of introducing a national minimum wage in the UK', *British Journal of Industrial Relations*, no.28, pp.215–66.

Bell, D. (1973) *The Coming of the Post-industrial Society: a Venture in Social Forecasting*, New York, Basic Books.

Bentham, J. (1789) *Introduction to the Principles of Morals and Legislation* (Chapters 1–5), in Warnock, M. (ed.) (1962) *Utilitarianism: Selections from the Writings of Jeremy Bentham and John Austin*, London, Collins.

Berglof, E. (1990) 'Capital structure as a mechanism of control: A comparison of financial systems', Chapter 11, pp.237–62, in Aoki, M., Gustaffson B. and Williamson, O.E. (eds) *The Firm as a Nexus of Treaties*, London, Sage.

Berle, A. and Means, G. (1932) *The Modern Corporations and Private Property*, New York, Commerce Clearing House (republished in 1993 by Legal Classic Library).

Besley, T. and Gouveia, M. (1994) 'Alternative systems of health care provision', *Economic Policy*, no.19, October, pp.200–58.

Blackaby, D., Clark, K., Leslie, D. and Murphy, P. (1994) 'Black–white earnings and employment prospects in the 1970s and 1980s: evidence for Britain', *Economic Letters*, no.46, pp.273–9.

Blackaby, D., Leslie, D. and Murphy, P. (1995) 'Unemployment among Britain's ethnic minorities', Discussion Paper 95–103, Department of Economics, University of Wales, Swansea.

Borzaga, C. (1996) 'Stakeholder co-operatives in European welfare', *Soundings*, no.4, pp.203–12.

Braverman, H. (1974) *Labor and Monopoly Capital*, New York, Monthly Review Press.

Brown, C. (1992) *International Political Theory: New Normative Approaches*, Hemel Hempstead, Harvester Wheatsheaf.

Brown, V. (1994) *Adam Smith's Discourse: Canonicity, Commerce and Conscience*, London, Routledge.

Brown, W. and Wadhwani, S. (1990) 'The economic effects of industrial relations legislation since 1979', *National Institute Economic Review*, no.131, London.

Buchanan, J.M. (1965) 'An economic theory of clubs', *Economica*, vol.32, pp.1–14.

Buchanan, J.M. and Vanberg, V.J. (1991) 'The market as a creative process', *Economics and Philosophy*, vol.7, no.2, October, pp.167–86.

Campaign for Racial Equality (1994) *Labour Force Survey*, EUROSTAT, Brussels.

Chernichovsky, D. (1995) 'Health systems reform in industrialised democracies', *Millbank Quarterly*, vol.73, no.3, pp.339–72.

Clark, L. and Estes, C. (1992) 'Sociological and economic theories of markets and non-profits: evidence from home health organizations', *American Journal of Sociology*, vol.97, no.4, pp.945–69.

Coghlan, A. (1996) 'Pennies from heaven', *New Scientist*, 24 August, pp.14–5.

Collard, D. (1978) *Altruism and Economy*, Oxford, Martin Robertson.

Corbett, J. and Jenkinson, T. (1994) 'The financing of industry, 1970–89: an international comparison', *CEPR Discussion Papers*, no.948, May.

Corbett, J. and Mayer, C. (1991) 'Financial reform in eastern Europe: progress with the wrong model, *Oxford Review of Economic Policy*, vol.7, no.4, pp.57–75.

Cornes, R. and Sandler, T. (1996) *The Theory of Externalities, Public Goods and Club Goods*, 2nd edition, Cambridge, Cambridge University Press.

Craig, C., Rubery, J., Tarling, R. and Wilkinson, F. (1982) *Labour Market Structure, Industrial Organization and Low Pay*, Cambridge, Cambridge University Press.

Crossman, A. (1995) 'The reform and abolition of the licensed residential establishments Wages Council: the impact on pay and conditions in four London hotels', *Review of Employment Topics*, no.3, pp.43–73.

Department for Education and Employment (1995) *New Earning Survey*, London, HMSO.

Dickens, R., Machin, S. and Manning, A. (1994) 'Minimum wages and employment: a theoretical framework with an application to the UK Wages Councils', *International Journal of Manpower*, vol.15, no.2/3, pp.26–48.

Dickens, R., Machin, S., Manning, A.,and Wilkinson, D. (1995) 'What happened to wages and employment after the abolition of minimum wages in Britain?', mimeo, Centre for Economic Performance, London School of Economics.

Donaldson, C. and Gerard, K. (1993) *Economics of Health Care Finance: The Visible Hand,*, Basingstoke, Macmillan.

East Anglian Regional Health Authority (1990) *Contracting for Health Outcomes*, Cambridge, Office of Public Management.

Economist, February 1996.

Elster, J. (1992) *Local Justice*, Cambridge, Cambridge University Press.

Equal Opportunities Review (1995) 'Junior barristers face sex discrimination', March/April.

Fazey, I. H. (1996) 'Funds enjoy vintage years', *Financial Times Survey of Venture and Development Capital*, 20 September, p.1.

Fernie, S. and Metcalf, D. (1996) 'Low wages and minimum wages: the British evidence', Special Report, Centre for Economic Performance, London School of Economics.

Finegold, D. and Soskice, D. (1988) 'The failure of training in Britain: analysis and prescription', *Oxford Review of Economic Policy*, no.4, pp.21–53.

Frank, A.G. (1966) 'The development of underdevelopment', *Monthly Review*.

Freeman, R.B. and Medoff, J.L. (1984) *What Do Unions Do?*, New York, Basic Books.

Friedman, D. (1978) *The Machinery of Freedom*, New York, Arlington House.

Fröbel, F., Heinrichs J. and Kreye, O. (1980) *The New International Division of Labour*, Cambridge, Cambridge University Press.

Fukuyama, F. (1992) *The End of History and the Last Man,* London, Hamish Hamilton.

Garrard, A. and Martin, W. (1996) 'Annex: minimum pay', in Martin, W., *Labour's Economics,* UBS Global Research.

Gerschenkron, A. (1962) *Economic Backwardness in Historical Perspective,* Cambridge, Mass., Harvard University Press.

Glyn A. and Sutcliffe, B. (1992) 'Global but leaderless? The new capitalist order', in Miliband, R. and Panitch, L. (eds) *Socialist Register 1992,* London, The Merlin Press.

Gordon, D. (1988) 'The global economy: new edifice or crumbling foundations?', *New Left Review,* no.168, March/April.

Gough, I. (1979) *The Political Economy of the Welfare State,* London and Basingstoke, Macmillan.

Greenwald, B. and Stiglitz, J.E. (1992) 'Information, finance, and markets: the architecture of allocative mechanisms', *Industrial and Corporate Change,* vol.1, no.1, pp.37–63.

Hahn, F. (1987) 'Auctioneer' pp.136–8 in Eatwell, J., Milgate, M. and Newman, P. (eds) *The New Palgrave: A Dictionary of Economics,* London, Macmillan.

Hahn, F. (1973) *On the Notion of Equilibrium in Economics,* Cambridge, Cambridge University Press.

Ham, C., Robinson, R. and Benzeval, M. (1990) *Health Check: Health Care Reforms in an International Context,* London, Kings Fund Institute.

Hargreaves-Heap, S. (1988) *Rationality in Economics,* Oxford, Blackwell.

Harris, O. (1987) 'Extended Family', pp. 251–3 in Eatwell, J., Milgate, M. and Newman, P. (eds) *The New Palgrave: A Dictionary of Economics,* London, Macmillan.

Hausman, D.M. and McPherson, M.S. (1996) *Economic Analysis and Moral Philosophy,* Cambridge, Cambridge University Press.

Hayek, F. (1945) 'The use of knowledge in society', *American Economic Review,* vol. 35, no.4, September, pp.519–30.

Hayek, F. (1982) *Law, Legislation and Liberty: A New Statement of the Liberal Principles of Justice and Political Economy,* London, Routledge and Kegan Paul.

Heilbroner, R. (1989) 'Reflections: the triumph of capitalism', *The New Yorker.*

Helm, D. (1995) 'British utility regulation: theory, practice and reform' *Oxford Review of Economic Policy,* vol.10, no.3, pp.17–39.

Henderson, D. (1986) *Innocence and Design: The Influence of Economic Ideas on Policy,* Oxford and New York, Basil Blackwell.

Henderson, R. (1993) *European Finance,* London, McGraw-Hill.

Hey, J.D. (1991) *Experiments in Economics,* Oxford, Blackwell.

Hicks, J. (1935) 'Annual survey of economic theory: the theory of monopoly', *Economica,* vol.3, no.8.

Hirschman, A.O. (1970) *Exit, Voice and Loyalty: Responses to Decline in Firms, Organizations and States,* Cambridge, Mass., Harvard University Press.

Hirst, P. (1994) *Associative Democracy,* Cambridge, Polity Press.

Hodgson, G.M. (1988) *Economics and Institutions,* Cambridge, Polity Press.

Hutton, W. (1995) *The State We're In,* London, Jonathan Cape.

ISTAT (1988) 'Indagine statistica sull'innovazione technologica nell'industria italiana', *Notiziario,* vol.4, no.41, Issue 13, December.

Jacobs, M. (1991) *The Green Economy: Environment, Sustainable Development and the Politics of the Future,* London, Pluto.

Joshi, H., Layard, R. and Owen, S. (1985) 'Why are more women working in Britain?', *Journal of Labor Economics,* no.3, Supplement, S147–S176.

Kaplinsky, R (1991) 'Direct foreign investment in Third World manufacturing: is the future an extension of the past?', *Institute of Development Studies Bulletin,* vol.22, no.2.

Kaufman, R. (1989) 'The effects of statutory minimum rates of pay on employment in Great Britain', *Economic Journal,* no.99, pp.1040–53.

Kester, W.C. (1992) 'Industrial groups as systems of contractual governance', *Oxford Review of Economic Policy,* vol.8, no.3, pp.25–44.

Keynes, J.M. (1936) *The General Theory of Employment, Interest and Money,* London, Macmillan.

Kregel, J. (1994) 'Capital flows: globalization of production and financing development', *UNCTAD Review,* pp.23–38.

Kreps, D.M. (1988) 'Corporate Culture and Economic Theory' in Alt, J. and Shepsle, K. (eds), *Positive Perspectives on Political Economy,* Cambridge, Cambridge University Press.

Kreps, D.M. (1990) *Game Theory and Economic Modelling,* Oxford, Clarendon Press.

Kuznets, S. (1966) *Modern Economic Growth: Rate, Structure, Spread,* New Haven, Yale University Press.

Landes, D. (1969) *Prometheus Unbound,* Cambridge, Cambridge University Press.

Langwell, K.M. (1990) 'Structure and performance of HMOs: a review', *Health Care Financing Review,* vol.12, no.1, pp.71–9.

Machin, S. and Manning, A. (1994) 'The effects of minimum wages on wage dispersion and employment: evidence from the UK Wages Councils', *Industrial and Labor Relations Review,* no.47, pp.319–29.

Machin, S. and Stewart, M. (1990) 'Unions and the financial performance of British private sector establishments', *Journal of Applied Econometrics,* vol.5, pp.327–50.

Mackintosh, M. (1997) 'Economic culture and quasi-markets in local government: the case of contracting for social care', *Local Government Studies,* vol.23, no.2, pp.80–102.

Maddison, A. (1995) *Monitoring the World Economy 1820–1992,* Paris, OECD.

Mandel, E. (1980) *Long Waves of Capitalist Development*, Cambridge, Cambridge University Press.

Manne, H.G. (1965) 'Mergers and the market for corporate control', *Journal of Political Economy*, no.73, pp.110–20.

Marris, R. (1964) *The Economic Theory of Managerial Capitalism*, London, Macmillan.

Marx, K. and Engels, F. (1973) 'Manifesto of the Communist Party' in Marx's *The Revolutions of 1848*, London, Allen Lane (first published London, 1848).

Matthews, R.C.O. (1991) 'The economics of professional ethics: should the professions be more business-like?', *The Economic Journal*, 10 July.

Mayhew, K. and Rosewell, B. (1979) 'Labour market segmentation in Britain', *Oxford Bulletin of Economics and Statistics*, vol.41, no.2, pp.81–116.

McNabb, R. (1987) 'Testing for labour market segmentation in Britain', *Manchester School*, no.3, pp.257–273.

McNabb, R. and Psacharopoulos, G. (1981) 'Further evidence on the relevance of the dual labour market theory for the UK', *Journal of Human Resources*, vol.16, no.3, pp.442–8.

McNabb, R. and Ryan, P. (1990) 'Segmented labour markets', in Sapsford, D. and Tzannatos, Z. (eds) *Current Issues in Labour Economics*, London, Macmillan.

McNabb, R. and Wass, V. (1996) 'Gender discrimination in salary levels and promotion probabilities', Cardiff Business School Discussion Paper in Economics, 95–021.

McNabb, R. and Wass, V. (1997) 'Male–female salary differential in British universities', *Oxford Economic Papers*.

McNabb, R. and Whitfield, K. (1996) 'Labour market segmentation in Britain: evidence from the Third Workplace Industrial Relations Survey', Cardiff Business School Discussion Paper in Economics, 95–022.

Metcalf, D. (1988a) 'Water notes dry up', Discussion Paper 314, Centre for Labour Economics, London School of Economics.

Metcalf, D. (1988b) 'Trade unions and economic performance: the British evidence', Discussion Paper 320, Centre for Labour Economics, London School of Economics.

Metcalf, D. (1990) 'Union presence and labour productivity in British manufacturing industry. A reply to Nolan and Marginson', *British Journal of Industrial Relations*, no.29, pp.349–66.

Mill, J.S. (1861) *Utilitarianism*, in Warnock, M. (ed.) (1962) *Utilitarianism: John Stuart Mill*, London, Fontana.

Mincer, J. (1985) 'Intercountry comparisons of labor force trends and of related developments', *Journal of Labor Economics*, no.3, Supplement, S1–S32.

Mishan, E.J. (1981) *Introduction to Normative Economics*, Oxford, Oxford University Press.

Mitchell, B.R. and Deane, P. (1962) *Abstract of British Historical Statistics*, Cambridge, Cambridge University Press.

Morishima, M. (1982) *Why Has Japan 'Succeeded'? Western Technology and the Japanese Ethos*, Cambridge, Cambridge University Press.

Mueller, D.C. (1989) *Public Choice II*, Cambridge, Cambridge University Press.

Neave, E.H. (1989) *The Economic Organization of a Financial System*, London and New York, Routledge.

Newman, P. (1978) 'Francis Ysidro Edgeworth', pp.84–98 in Eatwell J., Milgate M. and Newman P. (eds) *The New Palgrave: A Dictionary of Economics*, London, Macmillan.

Nolan, P. and Marginson, P. (1990) 'Skating on thin ice? David Metcalf on trade unions and productivity', *British Journal of Industrial Relations,* no.28, pp.227–47.

Nozick, R. (1974) *Anarchy, State and Utopia*, Oxford, Basil Blackwell.

OECD (1992) *Technology and the Economy: the Key Relationships*, Paris, OECD.

Office of Population Census and Surveys, Social Survey Division (1976) *General Household Survey 1975*, London, HMSO.

Office of Population Census and Surveys, Social Survey Division (1992) *1991 Census*, London, HMSO.

Okun, A. (1981) *Prices and Quantities: A Macroeconomic Analysis*, Oxford, Basil Blackwell.

Pareto, V. (1971) *Manual of Political Economy*, London, Macmillan (first published 1909, revised edition 1927).

Paterson, M. (1996) *Global Warming and Global Politics*, London, Routledge.

Peacock, T.L. (1831) *Crotchet Castle*, London, T.Hookham (Chapter 2 quotation from the Harmondsworth, Penguin edition, 1969).

Pearce, D. (1993) *Economic Values and the Natural World*, London, Earthscan.

Penrose, E.T. (1959) *The Theory of Growth of the Firm*, Oxford, Blackwell.

Pentelow, M. (1996) 'Docks: the payback', *The Record*, Transport and General Workers Union Publications.

People Management, 6 February 1997, p.16

Personnel Management, December 1992

Personnel Management, May 1993

Porter, M. (1992) 'Capital disadvantage: America's failing capital investment system', *Harvard Business Review*, September/October, pp.65–82.

Prais, S.J. (1995) *Productivity, Education and Training: An International Perspective*, Cambridge, Cambridge University Press.

Prowse, S. (1994) 'Corporate governance in an international perspective: a survey of corporate control mechanisms among large firms in the United States, the United Kingdom, Japan and Germany', Bank of International Settlements, *Economic Papers*, no.41, July.

References

Ravaioli, C. (1995) *Economists and the Environment*, London, Zed Books.

Rawls, J. (1971) *A Theory of Justice*, Cambridge, Mass., Harvard University Press.

Rebitzer, J. (1993) 'Radical political economy and the economics of the labour market', *Journal of Economic Literature*, no.31, pp.1394–1434.

Ricketts, M. (1994) *The Economics of Business Enterprise,* 2nd edition, Hemel Hempstead, Harvester Wheatsheaf.

Robbins, L. (1935) *An Essay on the Nature and Significance of Economic Science*, 2nd edition, London, Macmillan (first published 1932).

Robinson, J.C. and Casalino, L.P. (1996) 'Vertical integration and organizational networks in health care', *Health Affairs,* vol.15, no.1, pp.7–22.

Roe, M.J. (1994) *Strong Managers, Weak Owners: The Political Roots of American Corporate Finance*, Princeton, NJ, Princeton University Press.

Rostow, W.W. (1960) *The Stages of Economic Growth: a Non-communist Manifesto*, Cambridge, Cambridge University Press.

Rothschild & Sons, *The London Gold Fixing*, information pamphlet, London, N.M. Rothschild & Sons Limited.

Rowlands, I.H. (1995) *The Climate Change Negotiations: Berlin and Beyond,* Discussion Paper 17, The Centre for the Study of Global Governance, London School of Economics.

Rowthorn, R.E. and Wells, J.R. (1987) *De-industrialization and Foreign Trade,* Cambridge, Cambridge University Press.

Ruigrok, W. and van Tulder, R. (1995) *The Logic of International Restructuring*, London, Routledge.

Samuels, W.J. (1987) 'Institutional Economics' in Eatwell J., Milgate M. and Newman P. (eds) *The New Palgrave: A Dictionary of Economics*, London, Macmillan.

Scherer, F.M. and Ross, D. (1990) *Industrial Market Structure and Economic Performance*, 3rd edition, Boston, Houghton Mifflin.

Schneider-Lenne, E. R.(1992), 'Corporate control in Germany', *Oxford Review of Economic Policy,* vol.8, no.3, pp.11–23.

Schumpeter, J. (1939) *Business Cycles: a Theoretical, Historical and Statistical Analysis of the Capitalist Process* , New York and London, McGraw-Hill.

Shackle, G.S. (1972) *Epistemics and Economics*, Cambridge, Cambridge University Press.

Smith, A. (1776) *An Inquiry into the Nature and Causes of the Wealth of Nations,* London (Chapter 2 quotation from the 1976 edition, eds Campbell, R.H. and Skinner, A.S., Oxford, Clarendon Press).

Snell, M., Glucklich, P. and Povall, M. (1981) *Equal Pay and Opportunity,* Department of Employment, Research Paper no.20.

Stewart, M. (1991) 'Union wage differentials in the face of changes in the economic and legal environment', *Economica,* vol.58, pp.155–72.

Sutcliffe, B. (forthcoming) *Imperialism After Imperialism*, London, I.B. Tauris.

Symanski, S. (1996) 'The impact of compulsory competitive tendering on refuse collection services', *Fiscal Studies,* vol.17, no.3, August.

Symanski, S. and Wilkins, S. (1993) 'Cheap rubbish? Competitive tendering and contracting out in refuse collection, 1981–88', *Fiscal Studies,* vol.14, no.3, August.

Tawney, R.H. (1942) *Religion and the Rise of Capitalism,* Harmondsworth, Penguin.

Tiebout, C. (1956) 'A pure theory of local expenditures', *Journal of Political Economy,* vol.65, pp.416–24.

Titmuss, R.M. (1970) *The Gift Relationship,* London, George Allen & Unwin.

Touraine, A. (1973) *The Post-industrial Society,* New York, Random House.

Tylecote, A. (1987) 'Time horizons of management decisions: causes and effects', *Journal of Economic Studies,* vol.14, no.4, pp.51–64.

Tylecote, A. and Demirag, I. (1992) 'Short-termism: culture and structures as factors in technological innovation', pp.201–25 in Coombs, R., Walsh, V. and Saviotti, P. (eds) *Technological Change and Company Strategies,* London, Academic Press.

Ungerson, C. (1995) 'Gender, cash and informal care: European perspectives and dilemmas', *Journal of Social Policy,* vol.24–1, pp.31–52.

United Nations (1994) *Handbook of International Trade and Development Statistics,* New York, UN.

United Nations (1995) *World Investment Report 1995: Transnational Corporations and Competitiveness,* United Nations Conference on Trade and Development, Transnational Corporations and Investment Division, Geneva, UNCTAD.

United Nations Development Programme (1995) *Human Development Report 1995,* Oxford, Oxford University Press.

Vaughn, K.I. (1980.) 'Economic calculation under socialism: the Austrian contribution', *Economic Inquiry,* vol.18, pp.535–54.

Verdier, E. (1994) 'Training and Enterprise in France', pp.301–34 in McNabb, R. and Whitfield, K. (eds) *The Market for Training,* Aldershot, Avebury.

Vietorisz, T. and Harrison, B. (1973) 'Labor market segmentation: positive feedback and divergent development', *American Economic Review,* no.63, pp.366–76.

Walker, D.A. (1987) 'Léon Walras', pp.852–63 in Eatwell J., Milgate M. and Newman P. (eds) *The New Palgrave: A Dictionary of Economics,* London, Macmillan.

Waller, D. (1994) 'German groups reluctant to list', *Financial Times* 21 February, p.21.

Walras, L. (1954) *Elements of Pure Economics,* George Allen & Unwin, London. (first published 1874).

Walsh, K. (1995) *Public Services and Market Mechanisms: Competition, Contracting and the New Public Management,* London, Macmillan.

Walzer, M. (1983) *Spheres of Justice: a Defence of Pluralism and Equality*, Oxford, Blackwell.

Warnock, M. (ed.) (1962) *Utilitarianism: John Stuart Mill*, London, Fontana.

Warnock, M. (ed.) (1962) *Utilitarianism: Selections from the writings of Jeremy Bentham and John Austin*, London, Collins.

Weber, M. (1930) *The Protestant Ethic and the Spirit of Capitalism*, London, George Allen & Unwin (first published 1902).

Wholey, D., Feldman, R. and Christianson, J. (1995) 'The effect of market structure on HMO premiums', *Journal of Health Economics*, vol.14, no.1, pp.81–105.

Williams, B. (1973) 'The idea of equality' in *Problems of the Self*, Cambridge, Cambridge University Press.

Williamson, O.E. (1964) *The Economics of Discretionary Behaviour: Management Objectives in a Theory of the Firm*, Englewood Cliffs, NJ, Prentice Hall.

Williamson, O.E. (1988) 'Corporate finance and corporate governance', *Journal of Finance*, no.43, pp.567–91.

World Bank (1995a) *World Data on CD-ROM*, Washington, World Bank.

World Bank (1995b) *World Development Report 1995*, Oxford, Oxford University Press for the World Bank.

World Bank (1996) *Health Policy in Eastern Africa: A Structural Approach to Resource Allocation, Volume I, Main Report*, Eastern Africa Department, Africa Region, Nairobi, April.

Wright, E. and Ermisch, J. F. (1990) 'Male–female wage differentials in Great Britain', Department of Economics, Birkbeck College, Discussion Paper.

Wright, E. and Ermisch, J. F. (1991) 'Gender discrimination in the British labour market: a reassessment', *Economic Journal*, no.101, pp.508–22.

ACKNOWLEDGEMENTS

Grateful acknowledgement is made to the following sources for permission to reproduce material in this book

Chapter 2

Figures

Figure 2.7: adapted from Hodgson, G. M. (1988) *Economics and Institutions*, Polity Press/Blackwell Publishers, copyright © Geoffrey M. Hodgson, 1988. Also by permission of the University of Pennsylvania Press.

Photograph

p. 56: Courtesy of Fiat UK

Chapter 3

Photograph

p. 76: Crispin Hughes/Photofusion

Chapter 4

Figures

Figure 4.1: Adapted from Vietorisz, T. and Harrison, B. (1973) 'Labor market segmentation: Positive feedback and divergent development', *American Economic Review*, **63**, (2), May 1973, American Economic Association;

Tables

Tables 4.1 & 4.2: Adapted from Fernie, S. and Metcalf, D. (1996) *Low Pay and Minimum Wages The British Evidence*, © The Centre for Economic Performance; *Table 4.3:* Adapted from Prais, S. J. (1995) *Productivity, Education and Training An International Perspective*, Cambridge University Press, © The National Institute of Economic and Social Research, 1995.

Chapter 6

Tables

Table 6.1: Adapted from Corbett, J. and Meyer, C. (1991) 'Financial reform in eastern Europe: Progress with the wrong model', *Oxford Review of Economic Policy*, **7**, (4), by permission of Oxford University Press.

Table 6.2: Berglöf, E. (1988) *Ägarna Och Kontrollen Över Företaget - En Järnförande Studie Av Finansiella System*, Statens Offentliga Utredningar.

Photograph

p. 166: Ashley Ashwood/Financial Times Photographs

Chapter 7

Text

'The London Gold Fixing', reproduced by courtesy of N.M. Rothschild & Sons Ltd, London.

Chapter 9

Photographs

p. 242: Mark Edwards/Still Pictures; p. 249: J.Allan Cash Ltd

Cover

Detail from *Contrathemis 3240* © Dwinell Grant *Contrathemis 3240* . Courtesy of Michael Rosenfeld Gallery, New York.

INDEX

access
    to health care 210, 211, 213-14
    to social goods 68–9, 226, 227, 232
adverse selection 135, 140, 216, 218
advertising 52
Africa 3–4, 19, 20
age
    age-earnings profiles 82–3
    at marriage and unemployment 15
    and labour market disadvantage 76
agents, economic 14, 52, 53
    principal-agent theory 142–3
agricultural sector 10–12
Alliance of Small Island States (AOSIS) 242, 248–9, 256–7, 258
allocation of resources 41–52, 53–4, 64–6, 207–8
    and central planning 42, 47, 64–5
    other than by price mechanism 42
    role of price mechanism 41–52, 53–4, 134, 140, 207–8
altruism 214, 232–5
Anderson, E. 209, 210–11, 232
anti-discrimination policy 101–2, 103
appropriability, of innovation 151, 160–1, 164, 167
arithmetic scales 30, 31–2
Asia 19, 20
assets
    knowledge as intangible 151, 166
    liquidity and marketability 143–4, 146
assurance games 237
asymmetric information
    in bank-based financial systems 152, 155–6
    in capital markets 134, 135–6, 139–40, 145, 146, 166–7
    managers and shareholders 141–2, 145
    principal-agent theory 142

    screening and rationing to offset 135, 140–1, 148, 155
    in social markets 215, 216, 235
    in stock market-based financial systems 152
auctioneer, Walrasian 176–80, 205
auctions 135, 140, 182–3, 227–31
    auction markets 135, 140
    Chadwick-Demsetz 228
    oral double 182–3
    in social markets 227–31
Australia 72, 130–1
Austrian economics 39–40, 52–7, 205

Bank of England 159
Bank of Scotland 144
bank-based financial systems 152–9, 160–1, 163–4, 166–7
    and innovation 160–1, 163–4, 166
    stakeholders and corporate control 152, 154, 155–7, 158
banks and banking
    central 158–9
    German 34, 145, 148, 152–7, 158–9
    Japan 145, 149, 152–7, 158
    relational or transactional 152, 155–6
    risk management 138–41, 155
    securitized mortgages 144, 146
    universal 148
bargaining, trade union 122
Becker, G. 79–81, 103
behaviour
    consumer 59–60
    ethical 244–5
    moral 244
    norms 62, 93, 101, 231–9
    strategic 205
benefit, private or social 51, 202, 204–5
Bentham, J. 63
Berlin climate change negotiations 241–5, 247–51, 255–7
bonding costs 142
Bosman, Jean-Marc 117–18
bourgeoisie 5
brokers and broker markets 136, 145–6, 150

budget constraint 42, 184
building societies 144

Canada 215–16
capital accumulation 133, 150, 151, 166–7
capital gains 141
capital markets 133–50
    and asymmetric/imperfect information 134, 135–6, 139–40, 141–2, 145, 146
    brokers and broker markets 136, 145–6, 150
    formal 136
    forms of 145–9
    informal 136, 137
    institutional structure 133–4, 145–9, 150
    intermediary markets 146–8, 150
    internal 148–9, 150
    liquidity and marketability 143–5, 146, 147, 148
    neoclassical approach 134–6, 141
    organized financial 136, 142–5
    and uncertainty 134, 135–6, 140, 145
capital stock 5
capitalism 3–36, 133
    classes 5
    determinants of 16–18
    forms of production 4–6
    industrial 4–13
    institutions 5, 14–18
    Japanese 17
    and Protestant work ethic 16–17
    regulation theory 17–18
    time and space differences 25–31
    as winner over socialism 35
capitation charges 218
carbon dioxide *see* greenhouse gas emissions
central banks 158–9
central planning 4, 42, 47, 55, 64–5, 169
    tâtonnement as form of 182
Chadwick-Demsetz auctions 228
change 19
    climate *see* Berlin climate change negotiations; Framework Convention on Climate Change
    technological 5, 58, 94, 110–11